CARIBBEAN CULTURE AND BRITISH FICTION IN THE ATLANTIC WORLD, 1780–1870

Tim Watson challenges the idea that Caribbean colonies in the nineteenth century were outposts of empire easily relegated to the realm of tropical romance while the real story took place in Britain. Analysing pamphlets, newspapers, estate papers, trial transcripts, and missionary correspondence, this book recovers stories of ordinary West Indians, enslaved and free, as they made places for themselves in the empire and the Atlantic world, from the time of sugar tycoon Simon Taylor to the perspective of Samuel Ringgold Ward, African-American eyewitness to the 1865 Morant Bay rebellion. With readings of Maria Edgeworth and George Eliot, the book argues that the Caribbean occupied a prominent place in the development of English realism. However, Watson shows too that we must sometimes turn to imperial romance – which made protagonists of rebels and religious leaders, as in *Hamel, the Obeah Man* (1827) – to understand the realities of Caribbean cultural life.

TIM WATSON is Assistant Professor of English at the University of Miami.

CAMBRIDGE STUDIES IN NINETEENTH-CENTURY
LITERATURE AND CULTURE

Nineteenth-century British literature and culture have been rich fields for interdisciplinary studies. Since the turn of the twentieth century, scholars and critics have tracked the intersections and tensions between Victorian literature and the visual arts, politics, social organization, economic life, technical innovations, scientific thought – in short, culture in its broadest sense. In recent years, theoretical challenges and historiographical shifts have unsettled the assumptions of previous scholarly synthesis and called into question the terms of older debates. Whereas the tendency in much past literary critical interpretation was to use the metaphor of culture as 'background', feminist, Foucauldian, and other analyses have employed more dynamic models that raise questions of power and of circulation. Such developments have reanimated the field. This series aims to accommodate and promote the most interesting work being undertaken on the frontiers of the field of nineteenth-century literary studies: work which intersects fruitfully with other fields of study such as history, or literary theory, or the history of science.Comparative as well as interdisciplinary approaches are welcomed.

A complete list of titles published will be found at the end of the book.

Frontispiece 'Family Worship in a Plantation in South Carolina', engraved by
Mason Jackson, *Illustrated London News*, vol. 43, 5 December 1863

CARIBBEAN CULTURE AND BRITISH FICTION IN THE ATLANTIC WORLD, 1780–1870

TIM WATSON

CAMBRIDGE UNIVERSITY PRESS

CAMBRIDGE UNIVERSITY PRESS
Cambridge, New York, Melbourne, Madrid, Cape Town, Singapore, São Paulo, Delhi

Cambridge University Press
The Edinburgh Building, Cambridge, CB2 8RU, UK

Published in the United States of America by Cambridge University Press, New York

www.cambridge.org
Information on this title: www.cambridge.org/9780521876261

First published 2008

Printed in the United Kingdom at the University Press, Cambridge

A catalogue record for this publication is available from the British Library

ISBN 978-0-521-87626-1 hardback

For my parents, Pat and Roger Watson

Contents

ix

Illustrations

Acknowledgements

This book has been long in the making, and I have incurred many debts, material and intellectual, during its research and writing. Although I did not know it then, this project began while I was still in graduate school, with the research for the chapter on Jamaica and George Eliot that now comes at the end of this book. My teachers at Columbia challenged, encouraged, and sustained me, and I continue to be inspired by their examples and their lessons: I am forever grateful to John Archer, Winston James, Rob Nixon, the late Edward Said, and, most of all, Gauri Viswanathan. I was lucky to be at Columbia in the 1990s, among a fabulous group of graduate students, many of whom, then and since, have helped me as I wrote this book: Sunil Agnani, Siraj Ahmed, Moustafa Bayoumi, Patrick Deer, Ana Dopico, Brent Edwards, Gayatri Gopinath, Neville Hoad, Qadri Ismail, Sanjay Krishnan, Tim Lawrence, Sanda Lwin, Colleen Lye, Fenella Macfarlane, Amy Martin, Mark Sanders, Milind Wakankar, and Alys Weinbaum. In San Francisco and New York, Emma Bianchi and David Kazanjian were brilliant interlocutors and good friends too.

Colleagues and friends at Montclair State, Princeton, Miami, and elsewhere have read chapters, discussed ideas, and otherwise helped to make this book happen in ways large and small: I want to thank Daphne Brooks, Laura Chrisman, Jeff Dolven, Diana Fuss, Catherine Gallagher, Jennifer Greeson, Michele Grossman, Catherine Hall, Emily Isaacs, Claudia Johnson, Donna Jones, Neil Lazarus, David Luis-Brown, Sally McWilliams, Jeff Nunokawa, Frank Palmeri, Sandra Paquet, Jeffrey Shoulson, Richard Stein, Mihoko Suzuki, Candace Ward, Ashli White, Benj Widiss, Susan Wolfson, and Michael Wood. Terry Roberts was extremely generous and helpful in answering my queries about his ancestor, Charles White Williams. Four graduate students with whom I worked at Princeton taught me a great deal about teaching, advising, and writing, and I want to thank them here too for their impact on my thinking: Abby Bender, Kerry Bystrom, Danielle Elliott, and Nadia Ellis.

I have been fortunate over the years I have been working on this book to receive financial support in the form of fellowships, teaching release time, sabbatical leaves, summer stipends, and travel grants, for which I have to thank the Mellon Foundation, for postdoctoral fellowships at Columbia and the John Carter Brown Library; the Center for the Study of Religion at Princeton for a faculty fellowship; the office of the Dean of the Faculty at Princeton for sabbatical leaves and salary top-up funds; the University Committee for Research in the Humanities and Social Sciences at Princeton for research and travel funds; and the office of the Dean of the College of Arts and Sciences at Miami for summer funding in 2006.

I have spent countless hours, almost all of them happy ones, reading in research libraries in the course of writing this book. I want to thank the staff of these institutions for their invaluable help tracking down and retrieving the microfilms, papers, books, and articles that are the raw material of the pages that follow: the Institute of Commonwealth Studies, London; the John Carter Brown Library, Providence; the National Archives (formerly the Public Record Office), Kew; the New York Public Library; Cambridge University Library, especially its Munby Rare Books and Manuscripts Division and its Royal Commonwealth Society collection; Butler Library at Columbia; Firestone Library at Princeton; Rockefeller Library at Brown; and Richter Library at Miami, especially the Special Collections division of the last, and the interlibrary loan offices of the last four. In addition, I want to thank Nadia Ellis (again) for carrying out additional research for me at the Institute of Commonwealth Studies when I was unable to travel there.

Portions of this book were first presented in conferences and seminars over the years, and I am grateful for the opportunity to share my work, and for the feedback I received on those occasions at North Carolina State University (thanks particularly to Michael Malouf and Deborah Wyrick), Brown University (thanks to Nancy Armstrong, Stuart Burrows, and Madhu Dubey), the John Carter Brown Library (thanks to Norman Fiering, Hal Langfur, and Matt Pursell), the CUNY Graduate Center (thanks to Gerhard Joseph), the Society for Caribbean Studies (thanks to Diana Paton), and the Atlantic Studies group at the University of Miami (thanks to Carmen Ruiz-Castañeda and Elena Sabogal). An earlier version of chapter 4 appeared in the first issue of the online journal *Jouvert: A Journal of Postcolonial Studies* in 1997; thanks to North Carolina State University and Deborah Wyrick for permission to reprint it here.

It has been a pleasure to work with everybody at Cambridge University Press on this book, and in particular I want to thank Gillian Beer, the series editor (also long ago but so memorably my undergraduate teacher at Cambridge), Linda Bree, as meticulous and insightful an editor as one could hope for, and Maartje Scheltens, Elizabeth Noden, and Joanna Breeze. Linda Randall's creative and painstaking copyediting improved the book in its final stages. Two anonymous readers for Cambridge University Press provided crucial advice and criticism at two different stages of the project, and the second reader in particular made suggestions that led me to make major changes in the structure of the book and, I hope, significantly improved it as a direct result. Truly, peer review is a precious thing, even if it is often a thankless task.

I think it is important to acknowledge those people who cared for and taught my son Leo Ramsey-Watson between the ages of one and five, and who therefore in the most fundamental way made this book possible. Many thanks go to Cynthia Applegate, Christiana Augustine, Lori Cardona, and Darlene Michael, and to the teachers and staff at U-League Nursery School in Princeton (especially Linda Rockoff and Joy Scharfstein) and the Early Childhood Center in Coral Gables (especially Lourdes Arteaga, Shellee Ballestas, Lizette Halley, Oremia Ramirez, and Anita Seage).

My family helped me, and helped this book along, in every way imaginable. My parents, Pat and Roger Watson, are my first and best teachers, and continue to offer sage advice about publishing, research, and the challenge of balancing work and family life now that I am a parent myself. I could not have done any of this without them; this book is dedicated to them. My parents-in-law, Dorothy and Jerry Ramsey, have been unfailingly generous and supportive with their time and wise counsel, and I think myself lucky to have found a welcome home in the high desert of central Oregon. A thousand thanks also to my brother Richard and sister-in-law Nicky Watson, and my nieces Cara and Gemma; my brother Joe; and my brother Mark and sister-in-law Sarah Watson, and my nieces Rosie, Ella, and Georgia. Regular summer gatherings of the Watson clan in Bishops Stortford have been things of beauty and sources of pleasure for years now, and they just keep getting bigger and better.

My son Leo has lived with this book his whole life, and many pages here evoke for me the ambiguous pleasure of codeswitching between fatherhood and academia. Sometimes when I hear Leo announcing, with his insatiable curiosity, 'We could look it up on the internet!', I'm not sure where the scholar ends and 'Papa' begins. Leo says he wants to be a teacher when he grows up; he is perhaps still just a bit too young to realise that he already is. Finally, I have to thank the person who contributed the most to this book, Kate Ramsey. From the bars of Brooklyn to the playgrounds of Miami,

Kate has been with me every step of the way. Her fine critical eye, her incredible knowledge of the Caribbean, and her insistence that things be done right: these have been my inspirations these last twelve years. She has lived and worked interdisciplinarity (she has had institutional homes in four different disciplines), when most of us just speak of it as a goal. She is always my implied reader because so often she has been my first, best actual reader. Kate, thanks.

Introduction: realism and romance in the nineteenth-century Caribbean

In the 5 December 1863 number of the *Illustrated London News*, the paper's book reviewer hailed the appearance of two new volumes of James Anthony Froude's multivolume *History of England*. Greeting with 'delight' Froude's writings on the reign of Elizabeth I, the reviewer intuited the feelings of the newspaper's readers: 'Of novels, sensational and unsensational, they must have had enough, and more than enough; and they will find it refreshing to turn for a while from fiction to fact, from fancy to history.'[1] Turning from the fanciful world of novels to the sturdier rewards of 'fact', the reviewer encouraged his readers to participate in a progressive narrative of history as an unfolding of British civilisation, an historicism that understands the present as the inevitable and verifiable outcome of past events that refuse to be consigned to the past:

[In the second volume] will be read an account of the first slaving voyage of John Hawkins, to which may be traced back through three centuries of spreading Christianity, of advancing civilisation, and of African slavery, during which the negro has not ceased to be deprived of that personal liberty which is his birthright, the rending asunder, at any rate for a time, of a mighty Republic.[2]

The contemporary civil war in the United States is imagined as a kind of bloody romance – 'the rending asunder . . . of a mighty Republic' – while Britain, by contrast, is the subject of history in its realist mode, in which the abolition of slavery in the British Caribbean, the affirmation of the right to 'personal liberty' for all, becomes the hallmark of British enlightenment and world leadership, the cornerstone of an imperial edifice built on 300 years of 'spreading Christianity' and 'advancing civilisation'. Here is a typical British post-emancipation position: to understand and write the Caribbean under the signs of realism, historicism, and humanitarianism, and to see the abolition of slavery as an index of the righteousness of British imperial policy even as other, presumably less civilised nations continue to deprive 'the negro' of liberty. One of the goals of *Caribbean Culture*

I

and British Fiction in the Atlantic World is to trace the way in which the British colonies in the West Indies came to occupy such a powerful place in the British historical imagination by the 1860s even as they moved to the periphery of geopolitical and economic circuits in the Atlantic and imperial worlds of the nineteenth century.

Of course, nineteenth-century understandings of Caribbean culture, of slavery, and of history were anything but monolithic, and it is the tensions and switchbacks between these different accounts of the nineteenth-century Caribbean that form the subject matter of this book. If, on the one hand, the ending of slavery could function as a mark of British moral uprightness, this coexisted with a view of slave societies as places of romantic simplicity that allowed many in Britain to support the Confederate forces against the army of the North during the US Civil War. The front cover of the same issue of the *Illustrated London News* depicts a heroic Confederate soldier waving his hat to encourage his comrades attacking a Union supply line; his romantic heroism is answered by the sublime grandeur of the cliffs and rocks that dwarf the northern forces.[3] And on the page facing the review of Froude's history of England, the newspaper's editors explain the origin and significance of a striking image elsewhere in that issue,

in which the owner of a cotton plantation, South Carolina, is, with his wife and children, engaged in Divine worship, surrounded by his slaves, in a state of almost patriarchal simplicity. In the character of the negro as developed in the Slave States of America the two most marked features are his capacity for strong attachment and fidelity to his master when kindly treated and his susceptibility to religious influences.[4]

The illustration is entitled 'Family Worship in a Plantation in South Carolina'; it is also the cover illustration for this book.[5]

Caribbean Culture and British Fiction in the Atlantic World tracks and analyses the shift from realism to romance and back again in writing about the West Indies in the nineteenth century. Caribbean societies and economies that had been dominated by plantation slavery were transformed into cultures where, by the mid-1860s, the smallholders and minor merchants who were the descendants of the enslaved had become forces to be reckoned with, sufficient to challenge the British assumption that plantation slaves would become plantation wage labourers and to make some wax nostalgic for the days before emancipation. Such nostalgia lies behind the appeal of 'Family Worship in a Plantation in South Carolina', in which the white patriarch and his white 'family' are 'surrounded by his slaves', a contemporary American scene that functions as a kind of counterfactual Caribbean history. What if emancipation had not happened in the British empire? Would 'patriarchal simplicity' have reigned in the Caribbean too, just as it apparently did in the cotton fields of South Carolina, the southern territory most closely linked to the British West Indian colonies?[6]

However, the documentary appeal of the illustration is actually an illusion, as we can glean from the editorial note that accompanies it. 'The Illustration bearing the above title is from a sketch made in a rude chapel erected for the slaves on a cotton plantation near Port Royal (South Carolina), now in the possession of the Federal forces.'[7] Port Royal island was in fact the very first bridgehead for Union forces in South Carolina; it fell in 1861. Starting in late 1862, the Emancipation Proclamation was read throughout the small territory controlled by the army of the North; earnest and well-meaning New England humanitarians had already settled in the area to carry out the so-called 'Port Royal Experiment', with plans to turn the freedpeople into industrious workers and self-sufficient farmers; British missionaries and philanthropists who had been doing similar work in the Caribbean for almost seventy years would have recognised and applauded their project.[8] The South Carolina plantation in the illustration was the home of newly freed African Americans, not slaves at all. The fact is that 'Family Worship in a Plantation in South Carolina', far from being an objective record of life in the 'Slave States of America' in a time of war, imaginatively re-enslaves free African Americans in the interests of a paternalistic vision of black culture. 'Strong attachment and fidelity' to the 'master' was precisely the kind of locution used by proslavery advocates to describe Caribbean slaves in the period before 1833. The book reviewer's progressive narrative of 'advancing civilisation', in which the end of slavery is seen as an undoubted good deed and an historical inevitability, is turned into the romance of a lost world of rustic simplicity about to be overrun by the symbolic arrival of modern, northern capitalism in the shape of a Federal supply train that neither sublime, looming cliffs nor gallant Confederate fighters can hope to turn back.

The history of the Caribbean – which from the point of view of Britain is the history of vast wealth, success, and imperial centrality turning into impoverishment and marginality – is continually transforming itself into romance. By the turn of the twentieth century, in a popular imperial history series aimed at British schoolchildren, the West Indies did not even merit a complete volume, as India, Canada, and New Zealand did, but were bundled with Gibraltar and Malta in the volume *Outposts of Empire*. The author, John Lang, introduced the volume thus:

No attempt has been made in this volume to write a history of any of the places touched upon; the endeavour rather has been to extract from their history a portion of the Romance with which each is saturated. But to deal adequately with such a subject is impossible; there is in the history of the British West Indian Islands alone sufficient Romance to fill space many times larger than this book.[9]

As the place almost exclusively of piracy and slavery, the Caribbean became the very opposite of an outpost of progress. It is a short step forward from Lang's schoolboy romance to the notorious pronouncement of V. S. Naipaul: 'The history of the islands can never be satisfactorily told. Brutality is not the only difficulty. History is built around achievement and creation; and nothing was created in the West Indies.'[10] And it is likewise a short step back from Lang's account of the outposts of empire to James Anthony Froude's notorious pronouncement in *The English in the West Indies*:

There are no people there in the true sense of the word, with a character and a purpose of their own, unless to some extent in Cuba, and therefore when the wind has changed and the wealth for which the islands were alone valued is no longer to be made among them, and slavery is no longer possible and would not pay if it were, there is nothing to fall back upon. The palaces of the English planters and merchants fall to decay; their wines and their furniture, their books and their pictures, are sold or dispersed. Their existence is a struggle to keep afloat, and one by one they go under in the waves.[11]

Writing twenty years earlier in response to Froude's history of England, the book reviewer of the *Illustrated London News* might have been forecasting these very lines while assuring the paper's readers that the turn from fiction to history would nevertheless have its literary rewards: 'They need not fear a dearth of romance, for many are the romantic features of history, and the expressiveness of those features suffers no detriment from so powerful a limner as Mr. Froude.'[12] For Froude, the disappearing world of the planters makes the West Indies a place of loss and, therefore, fundamentally a place of romance.[13]

My book works against the idea that the Caribbean was a nineteenth-century 'outpost' easily relegated to the mode of historical romance while the real story took place at the imagined centre, with the history of England. Instead, I try to recover some of the stories and, however imperfectly, the experiences of specific people in a specific place and time. In this book there are moments of history in its realist mode, my modest contribution to the proliferating and impressive body of work on the history of the nineteenth-century Caribbean.[14] At the centre of my story, the setting for at least a portion of each of my chapters is southeastern Jamaica, consisting of the parishes of St David and St Thomas-in-the-East (combined they became the parish of St Thomas after the administrative reorganisation of the island in the later 1860s). This area could be seen as typical of the anglophone Caribbean in the nineteenth century. Dominated economically, culturally, and politically by large sugar plantations, it was also a place of smallholdings, medium-sized coffee plantations, and regional ports like Morant Bay. While connected to the commercial capital Kingston and the political capital Spanish Town to the west, and therefore to the wider world of the Caribbean region and the imperial centre in London, eastern Jamaica was dominated topographically by the immense mass of the Blue Mountains, home to the free Maroon communities, and a place symbolically and legally that the apparatus of British rule could barely reach. Without overlooking the significant differences between this area of Jamaica and other parts of the island, and indeed of the Caribbean region as a whole – and with the cautionary point in mind, made well by David Lambert in his recent book on creole culture in Barbados, that Jamaica has often been made to stand in uncritically for the Caribbean as a whole – I focus on this one part of the island as a typical, rather than central, part of the empire, and I hope that by returning to it in each chapter, I can give some sense of subaltern Caribbean life and culture in the nineteenth century.[15]

Alongside, and sometimes against, an emphasis on how the Caribbean is described and understood from the point of view of Britain, therefore, I spend significant time in the pages that follow analysing colonial documents, missionary archives, and Jamaican newspapers and pamphlets in order to recover some of the contours of everyday life in a world being transformed by religious revolutions and political developments. To do so, of course, is to read the archives against their own grain, dominated as they are by the point of view of the British and creole authorities that created and maintained them. Two related problems emerge in my study at this point. On the one hand, I confront the issue that this kind of history from below always involves what Dipesh Chakrabarty calls a 'scandalous' translation of the fundamentally religious worldview of the subaltern classes into the necessarily secular language of the disenchanted historian.[16] On the other hand, I show how the very archives from which we can begin to reconstruct the history of an event like the Demerara rebellion, for example, which I address in chapter 2 – missionary letters and records, trial transcripts and depositions, British Parliamentary Papers, and so forth – tend themselves to follow the mode of romance when it comes to Caribbean materials, rather than the administrative realism they display on the surface, thus blurring again the distinctions between history and fiction, and between romance and realism.

In the end, then, *Caribbean Culture and British Fiction in the Atlantic World* shows that realism and romance in the Caribbean context cannot be easily disentangled, just as in the nineteenth century Britain and the West Indies were mutually constitutive rather than discrete entities. Again and again, the attempt to narrate the Caribbean from the point of view of plausibility, verifiability, and reason – realism, in other words – turns into the very forms it seeks to avoid: romantic narrative and its cognates, the gothic, the sentimental, and the melodrama. For example, Benjamin Moseley's *Treatise on Tropical Diseases* (1803) interrupts its scientific apparatus to provide an excursus on the power of the moon, something that had been recognised by classical authorities and by peasants everywhere but that has been lost by modern civilisation, according to the army doctor in Jamaica (see chapter 1); likewise, Moseley's resolutely statistical account of the preeminent tropical commodity in his *Treatise on Sugar* (1800) is also the principal source for the tale of the Jamaican outlaw Three-Fingered Jack.[17] The reverse is also true: it is sometimes in the distortions, exaggerations, and assumptions of superiority in Caribbean romance that the latterday historian and cultural critic can discern the reality of everyday life in the nineteenth-century West Indies. The implausible gothic romance of *Hamel, the Obeah Man* (1827), set in eastern Jamaica, whose likely author I identify in chapter 2 as the creole Blue Mountain coffee planter Charles White Williams, may give us more valuable information than the more humane accounts of missionaries and colonial administrators about Caribbean slave revolts, conversions to Christianity, and the attempts by the enslaved to create relatively autonomous zones of cultural life. Romance and realism are never far apart in the transatlantic circuits that joined Britain and the Caribbean in the nineteenth century.

Catherine Hall, in her magisterial *Civilising Subjects*, has painstakingly demonstrated the wealth of personal, religious, and commercial links that bound Britain – and the regional centre of Birmingham, in particular – to Jamaica in the nineteenth century both before and after emancipation in the 1830s.[18] (Here I might add a quirky footnote to Hall's book. The copy of John Lang's romantic history of the Caribbean, *Outposts of Empire*, that I consulted had somehow made its way across the Atlantic to the stacks of Richter Library in Miami: inside was a tram ticket, issued by Birmingham Corporation Tramways, 'Ordinary / Fare $2\frac{1}{2}$d', suggesting that Caribbean romance found a place in the mundane daily life of the English Midlands commuter in the early twentieth century.)[19] I take Hall's timeline and cross-cultural methodology as my models here, and seek likewise to disrupt the conventional sense that the Caribbean colonies during this period were peripheral and becoming more so. But since my focus is more on cultural production than Hall's, I hope also to challenge the marginal status of the Caribbean in the critical discourse of nineteenth-century literary history. In relation to British fiction, and to realist fiction in particular, postcolonial criticism has been pushing the Caribbean from margin to centre. Gayatri Chakravorty Spivak's influential essay 'Three Women's Texts and a Critique of Imperialism' insisted on the importance of the Jamaican creole Bertha and of the problem of slavery in reading *Jane Eyre*; a few years later, Edward Said announced the project that would become *Culture and Imperialism* with his provocative and transformative analysis of *Mansfield Park*, showing the ways in which the resolutely English and domestic worlds of Jane Austen could only be understood in terms of their dependence on Antiguan culture and commodities.[20] Spivak's and Said's work has been extended and amplified in eighteenth- and nineteenth-century literary studies of the Caribbean by critics such as Srinivas Aravamudan, Moira Ferguson, Thomas Krise, Keith Sandiford, and Jenny Sharpe, among many others; moreover, Sean Goudie has recently made a compelling case for the central role of the Caribbean in the literature and culture of the early years of the United States republic.[21] Increasingly, histories of literature in English, and of the novel in particular, have to treat the Caribbean not as the 'other setting', as Said characterised Austen's use of Antigua in *Mansfield Park*, but as a central aspect of literary history. I hope that this book takes its place within that critical trajectory.

It is perhaps useful to remind ourselves, then, that the novel traditionally assigned the status of founding text of the English realist novel, Daniel Defoe's *Robinson Crusoe*, is a Caribbean story. By this I mean not simply that the bulk of the novel is set in the Caribbean: its 'setting' has often been the first aspect of Defoe's novel to disappear in critical accounts that emphasise the development of character or the relationship among realist plausibility, manipulable objects, and the rise of capitalism. It is rather that the Caribbean is the source of realism and imperial capitalism themselves, the place where the proper use of tropical things comes to define the individual liberal subject of modernity embodied in Crusoe. The objects Crusoe rescues from the wreck are in fact doubly creolised: they are mostly European items from Brazil – whence Crusoe and his doomed shipmates set out for West Africa on a slaving voyage – now recovered to form the basis for a new European culture on the Caribbean island. As Crusoe learns the proper use value of everything on the island, his cultivation of the land and control over the labour power of, in turn, Friday, Friday's father, and the Spanish and English sailors make the Caribbean the preeminent site for the establishment of a series of general statements about the development of colonial ownership from small-scale settlement to the sovereignty over whole regions of the earth. Crusoe speaks in a cumulative and accumulative sequence of 'my house' (49), 'my enclosure' (50), 'my habitation' (51), 'my country-house, and my sea-coast house' (82), 'my side of the island' (88), 'my arable land' (93), 'my man Friday' (164), and, logically and finally, 'my island, as I now call it' (176).²² The relationship between personhood and thinghood, and between the individual and the social contract, are from the beginning and at the same time the key problems of British realist fiction and of Caribbean culture, as *Robinson Crusoe* demonstrates.

Friday embodies the tension between slavery and the imagined primacy of the liberal subject. This contradiction is there in the incoherent gap between the 'my' and the 'man' of 'my man Friday', and in the fluid series of roles – servant, companion, assistant, and creature – that Friday fills in Crusoe's imagination as he sees the former fleeing from his would-be butchers on the beach: 'It came now very warmly upon my thoughts, and indeed irresistibly, that now was my time to get me a servant, and perhaps a companion or assistant; and that I was call'd plainly by Providence to save this poor creature's life.'²³ But if we see the beginnings of the discourse of humanitarian imperialism here that would come to dominate British colonial ideology by the end of slavery days in the 1830s – the legitimation of the domination of one people by another under the banner of saving poor creatures' lives – we also see that in literature the coloniser could acknowledge, albeit surreptitiously and haphazardly, the culture of the colonised. Friday is named for the day he is saved, but the practice of day names is actually something Defoe borrows from West African culture.²⁴ Although Defoe is careful to make Friday an indigenous Central American, rather than a 'Negro' – 'His hair was long and black, not curl'd like wool . . . his nose small, not flat like the Negroes, a very good mouth, thin lips'²⁵ – he is aligned here with the countless enslaved Africans named Cuffee (Friday), Quamina (Saturday), and Quashie (Sunday) in the Americas.

And if Friday's naming suggests the importance of a creolised slave culture with which the Caribbean authorities had forever to contend, it also suggests a problem in the structure of the realist mode of fiction itself, based as it is on calculability, reason, and verifiable facts. Although Crusoe imagines that the providential arrival of a future slave or companion means that the Englishman comes to possess time itself – 'now was my time to get me a servant' – the fact is that Crusoe cannot properly keep track of the days in the Caribbean, that the calculations on which the commerce of sugar and slavery depended were liable to failure, and that therefore 'Friday' has the wrong name:

I fell into a sound sleep, and wak'd no more, till by the sun it must necessarily be near three a-clock in the afternoon the next day; nay, to this hour I'm partly of the opinion, that I slept all the next day and night, and till almost three that day after; for otherwise I knew not how I should lose a day out of my reckoning in the days of the week, as it appear'd some years after I had done.[26]

Crusoe is able to cure himself of his tropical fever through his immersion in the Bible and his personal conversion experience, but this moment of rescue is also the moment of the failure of accounting practices: 'I found at the end of my account I had lost a day or two in my reckoning.'[27] Friday, then, might more accurately be named Saturday (in which case he would share his name with Quamina, the leader of the Demerara slave rebellion I discuss in chapter 2).

The Atlantic world in general, and the slave trade in particular, are the prime sites for what Ian Baucom has called 'actuarial historicism' – the production of objectified 'types' based on the protocols of insurance and accounting, and associated by Baucom with the typical characters of realist fiction.[28] Nevertheless, *Caribbean Culture and British Fiction in the Atlantic World* suggests that bookkeeping practices were never fully capable of transforming the humanity of the enslaved into numbers. Realist fiction, associated with metonymy, contiguity, and the attempt to represent an expanding web of social relations from the eighteenth century onwards, became an important venue for the creation of imaginative relationships that link England, and its expansionist commercial classes in particular, to the Caribbean and other corners of the empire. These imaginative relationships are governed by the logic of sensibility, in which the newly mobile bourgeois (for example, Crusoe, the third son of a German-born merchant) show 'their ethical superiority to their aristocratic rivals by demonstrating their capacity to share in (or, at least, remonstrate against) the sufferings of their unequal, lower-rank, fellows', like the poor creature, Friday.[29] If realist fiction functions on one level as part of the imperial, capitalist project of the 'contractual management of inequality',[30] however, it also contains the potential for the representation of human relations as fellowship, in which Friday is a 'companion' and a sovereign subject, rather than a 'servant' or an 'assistant'. Ironically, though, this potential fellowship tends to flash up in moments of romance, rather than the ostensibly more egalitarian realm of realism. Friday is a fellow on the basis of a loss we can associate with romance – in this case, the loss of a day in Crusoe's account, which throws realism out of joint. And while *Hamel, the Obeah Man*, for example, presents Jamaica as the exotic, other setting of romance, and even though it presumes the inequality of planter and slave, white and black, it is also the novel with the fullest depiction of slave insurgency, with the strongest representation of Caribbean humanity in its eponymous hero, and with the most intimate sense of the relationships that bound Britain and Jamaica together in the nineteenth century. If in history writing the Caribbean has suffered from a surfeit of romance, as John Lang's and James Anthony Froude's works suggest, in fiction we could almost say that the problem has been that there has been too much realism and not enough romance.

Caribbean Culture and British Fiction in the Atlantic World is divided broadly into two parts. Chapters 1 and 2 deal with the period between the late eighteenth century and the moment just before emancipation in the 1830s; chapters 3 and 4 focus on the 1860s, with the Morant Bay rebellion of 1865 as the catalysing event of the period. Like Diana Paton, in her fine study of the Jamaican legal system *No Bond but the Law* – a book that, in a happy convergence, covers precisely the same period as this one – I am trying here to challenge the 'assumption of a complete break between slavery and "freedom"', and to join with those 'scholars of slavery and emancipation [who] look across the great divide of the 1830s'.[31] The first half of the book focuses on syncretic African-Caribbean versions of Christianity as the lens through which to analyse respectability and insurgency amongst the enslaved population of the Caribbean. Although British representations tended to divide Caribbean religion into the typical figures of the dangerous obeah man or woman, on the one hand, and the respectable, subservient churchgoer on the other, the reality on the ground was that these figures were often one and the same. If George Liele, the Georgia-born former slave who was the first to bring Baptism to Jamaica in the eighteenth century, complained to the Baptist Missionary Society in London that his work was hampered by 'superstition' among the Jamaican slaves, it is also true that Liele and his followers like Moses Baker laid the foundations for the syncretic, Afro-Christian 'Native Baptist' churches that so often troubled the official Baptist churches after the British missionaries began to arrive at the end of the eighteenth century (and eastern Jamaica in particular was fertile ground for these independent Baptist churches).[32] Recognising the centrality of subaltern religious life in Caribbean nineteenth-century culture, I focus in the first two chapters on such figures as Mary Lindsay (chapter 1), an enslaved woman who became a contributor to a society for converting fellow slaves in St Thomas-in-the-East in the 1820s; on Hamel, the title character of the anonymously published 1827 novel (chapter 2), who explodes the stereotype of the obeah man from the inside by practising and defending what he does not hesitate to call his 'religion' against the incursions of a Methodist missionary and the colonial military and political authorities; and (again in chapter 2) on the rebel slaves of Demerara in 1823, such as Quamina and his son Jack Gladstone, with their heterodox religious beliefs and insurgent tactics mixing African and British influences.

Also in this first part of the book, I develop an analysis of what I call 'creole realism' (chapter 1), focusing on the figure of bookkeeper, planter, and colonial politician Simon Taylor (1740–1813), the wealthiest man in Jamaica in the period leading up to the 1807 abolition of the slave trade. Taylor left a trove of letters, journals, and accounts from which to extract a rich picture of elite Jamaican life in the eighteenth and early nineteenth centuries. I analyse these documents for their detailed account of slave purchases, transatlantic trading patterns, and the private life of a powerful figure in Jamaica. But I also trace the affiliations between the tone and method of Taylor's personal papers – which, unsurprisingly, begin and end with bookkeeping and the facts of commerce – and the embattled attempt of white Jamaicans like historian Bryan Edwards, and lesser known people like Thomas Higson (a merchant and botanist) and Edward Bancroft (a physician), to represent Jamaican life according to the protocols of narrative realism, just as the abolitionist movement gathered strength by representing the West Indies as a place of excess governed by the genres of gothic melodrama and tropical romance. Taylor embodies simultaneously the cruelty of someone who took for granted the justness of slavery and an early creole nationalism that rejected the oppression of British rule. Yet while Taylor threatened a thousand times to take himself and his wealth out of Jamaica and settle in the United States, in order to escape the tyranny and tax levies of London and its representatives in the island, in fact he stayed in the colony to the end of his life, in a long-term relationship with Grace Donne, a mixed-race woman with whom he had a daughter, and to whom he bequeathed money, a house and its contents in Kingston, and several enslaved Africans.

This illegitimate, creole version of the marriage plot of eighteenth- and nineteenth-century British fiction is counterpointed in chapter 1 to the metropolitan realism of Maria Edgeworth's novel *Belinda*. The analogue for Simon Taylor in the novel, the wealthy creole suitor Vincent, is considered but found wanting as a potential mate for the eponymous heroine in London, and he must be banished from the borders of England at the end. Nevertheless, England is saturated with Caribbean objects of all kinds in Edgeworth's novel – birds, herbal remedies, obeah fetishes – and the plot turns on the possible incorporation into English life of Vincent's black 'servant', Juba, who in the first edition of the novel marries a rural

Englishwoman, Lucy, and settles into industrious English freedom. I argue that the effective annulment of Juba's marriage in later editions of the novel speaks to an instability at the heart of English realism, unable to follow through on its promise of inclusiveness. In chapter 2, I show how the image of the white creole as venal and corrupt, perpetuated in *Belinda*, eventually rendered creole realism impossible. While Thomas Higson could present an 'Account of an Ascent to the Summit of the Blue Mountains of Jamaica' in an early number of *Blackwood's Magazine* as a catalogue of plants and a kind of land survey, deliberately eschewing the romantic and the sublime in favour of the solidity of facts with Latin names, by the mid-1820s one of his mountain-climbing companions, Charles White Williams, had turned to imperial romance to memorialise the impending loss of the world of the plantocracy in his semi-fictional *Tour through the Island of Jamaica* (published under the pseudonym Cynric Williams) and his novel *Hamel, the Obeah Man*, published anonymously in 1827. Ironically, I argue, it is these proslavery romances, freed from the necessity of presenting the facts of the West Indies, that – for all their racial demagoguery and sentimental claptrap – allow the cultural historian greater access to the hidden worlds of the enslaved Jamaicans themselves, the real creoles of the late eighteenth and nineteenth centuries and the world to come after emancipation in the 1830s.

In the second half of the book, I focus on the civic and political endeav-ours of an emergent black internationalism, and what we might call a proto-pan-Africanism, centred on Jamaica in the 1860s. In chapter 3, I analyse the Jamaican Morant Bay rebellion of 1865 via an examination of the transatlantic life of Samuel Ringgold Ward, the African-American minister who was born into slavery in Maryland in 1817 and who, via a cir-cuitous route, ended up an independent Baptist pastor in eastern Jamaica in the 1850s and 1860s, preaching to a poor black congregation while at the same time currying favour with the white establishment on the island. I analyse Ward's *Autobiography of a Fugitive Negro* (1855) and his 1866 pam-phlet in support of Governor Edward Eyre's suppression of the uprising in St Thomas-in-the-East, *Thoughts upon the Gordon Rebellion*, which have tended to put Ward on the wrong side of history. For all his deference to imperial authority, however, Ward also championed the interests of the smallholders and peasant farmers in Jamaica, hoping grandiosely for a kind of intra-imperial cooperative association of black farmers and labourers. As part of my study of 1860s Jamaica in chapter 3, then, I recover the history of the Jamaica Commercial Agency, a cooperative venture along the lines that Ward advocated, and as it turns out, another victim of the backlash on the part of the colonial authorities after Morant Bay. I argue that Ward's attempt throughout his public life to create an international language for the group he called 'our Africo-American brethren' helped to bring into being the new languages of the modern, humanitarian British empire of citizen-subjects after Morant Bay.

The example of Ward serves to introduce another element of my argument in the pages that follow. Precisely the kinds of invaluable recuperative and revisionist histories of the last thirty years that have established the everyday life of the black subaltern classes in the Americas as a legitimate, even necessary, part of historical realism have a tendency also to turn themselves into romance, raising up forgotten heroes from the past and finding resistance everywhere the historian turns.[33] Because he seemed to turn himself from abolitionist militant to imperial collaborator (but also because he moved so much that he tends to fall out of histories adopting the boundary of the nation as the horizon of analysis), Ward has not been well served by histories of the nineteenth century. I think a realistic appraisal of his complex life and thought in the circuits of the nineteenth-century imperial and Atlantic worlds is long overdue. I also think it might function as a corrective to the romantic impulse in some contemporary history writing, including my own, that can end up sounding some of the same notes as the planter class in the nineteenth-century Caribbean who saw plots, conspiracies, and revolt everywhere they looked.

In chapter 4, I continue the discussion of the 1865 Jamaica rebellion, but focus on its impact in Britain. George Eliot's novel *Felix Holt*, published in 1866 exactly at the height of the controversy over Morant Bay, tracks and represents an English ambivalence over questions of citizenship, inheritance, and race that were all made central by the events in Jamaica. I argue that the slavery subtext in Eliot's novel – Harry, the ultimate heir to the Transome estate, is the son of an enslaved Greek woman – is a displaced version of the problems roiling Britain in the wake of Morant Bay. On the one hand, *Felix Holt* is another turn in the cycle of realism and romance, with Esther and Felix representing a rejection of the imperial romance of the East brought into England by Harold Transome and of the romance of hidden bloodlines that would have made Esther a kind of noblewoman in disguise. Instead, they suggest that enlightened, modern England is better represented by a widening lateral web of relations in which citizenship is based on civic education rather than on descent and inheritance: only realism can hope to capture this version of a new, culturally and politically reformed England. On the other hand, Darwin's new theory of the origin of species proposed that a widening web of lateral relations could in fact only be explained by descent and inheritance, and for some thinkers, like the new anthropologists of race such as James Hunt, this presented the opportunity for yet another return to romance. In flagrant contradiction of Darwin's concept of inheritance with variation, Hunt and others in the Anthropological Society of London cheered on Governor Eyre's suppression of the Jamaica rebellion to the extent that they saw his beliefs about 'the negro character' confirming their own theories of unchanging types based on blood descent and inheritance of physical and behavioural traits. While George Eliot obviously had little time for such nonsense – instead exchanging correspondence with Frederic Harrison, one of the more prominent of Eyre's opponents in Britain – a kernel of Caribbean romance remains at the centre of *Felix Holt* in the eventual descent of the country estate to the child Harry, consistently represented as both playful and savage. Even as a new, more centralised British empire emerged after Morant Bay, based on a humanitarian imperialism borrowed from earlier abolition campaigns and the new 'civilising mission', and emphasising ideas of imperial citizenship and equality before the law, it is haunted and tailed by a romance that, on the one hand, figured the modern apparatus of empire as the loss of the simple world of the landed classes, but also, on the other hand, allowed for the possible eruption into English and imperial space of wayward, eccentric, savage figures from the margins imbued with romantic interest.

Moreover, by the 1860s, from the point of view of Britain, the Caribbean really could be said to be lost. In my epilogue, I signal the shift already well underway by the time of the Civil War that brought the Caribbean firmly within the sphere of influence of the United States, rather than Britain and the other European colonial powers. I return to Samuel Ringgold Ward, and a quixotic scheme of his to encourage African-American settlement in Jamaica, set against his actual rivalry on the ground with John Willis Menard, a fellow African American who had founded a literary society in the Jamaican parish of St David where he and Ward lived, and who was deported to New Orleans by Governor Eyre for sedition in the events of the Morant Bay rebellion, before going on to become the first African American elected to the US Congress in 1868. I end the epilogue, and the book, by turning briefly to the figure of Frederick Douglass, who stopped off in Jamaica in 1871 as part of his trip through the northern Caribbean to muster support for the proposed annexation of the Dominican Republic to the United States. I read each of these three peripatetic black men as examples of what David Scott calls 'conscripts of modernity',[34] but I also suggest that their versions of black internationalism, instead of simply being complicit with imperial and great power interests, developed structures of communication and a language of international community that were borrowed and transformed in their turn by the late nineteenth-century discourses of imperialism as a civilising mission or a white man's burden.

If we return finally to the cover image of this book once more, such an emphasis on a relatively autonomous zone of black culture in the Caribbean and the Atlantic world would lead us to look again at the figure of the black preacher who is simultaneously central and marginal to the illustration. On the one hand, the viewer sees mostly his back and his respectable dress, in contrast to the full face view of the plantation owner, who occupies the geometrical centre of the drawing. On the other hand, apart from the white patriarch, all the other figures, black and white, are looking intently at the speaker himself, just as the latterday historian and cultural critic must now clearly look beyond the stories of the plantation owners to capture cultural life in the Americas. The description of the image elsewhere in the newspaper tells us a little about the man, although it does not give his name:

The 'incumbent' was an intelligent old house servant, a slave. He could read, but not write; and his extempore sermons, although sometimes marred by his predilection for high-sounding phrases and long words (not always appropriate), were characterised by strong good sense and a certain rude native eloquence, often rising to the dignity of pathos, and admirably adapted to the comprehension and temperament of his audience.[35]

Looking past the condescension here, we can see that the pastor is that crucial figure common throughout the Americas, the largely self-taught black religious leader who navigated and mediated between the official, orthodox buckra world and the subaltern world of popular religious life. He is something like 'Old Peter', a freedman on the Pine Grove plantation in St Helena Island, next to Port Royal, who was observed by a sympathetic northern white witness, 'H. W.' (Harriet Ware), in 1862:

I sat down on the women's side [of the plantation chapel, the 'praise house'] next a window, and one of the men soon struck up a hymn in which the others joined and which seemed to answer the purpose of a bell, for the congregation immediately began to assemble, and after one or two hymns, Old Peter offered a prayer, using very good language, ending every sentence with 'For Jesus' sake'. He prayed for us, Massa and Missus, that we might be 'boun' up in de bellyband of faith'.[36]

Of course, after the white folks left, the chapel became the site of 'the Shout', which woke Ware up at three o'clock one morning but remained more or less a closed book even to northern white abolitionists, just as 'obeah' functioned throughout the nineteenth century primarily as a sign of white failure to understand African-Caribbean religious life, both before and after slavery.[37]

Old Peter is the romantic hero of my book, appearing – as romantic heroes do – in several different guises: he is Graman Quacy, the Surinamese herbalist and diviner (chapter 1); he is Hamel, the obeah man and revolutionary (chapter 2); he is Samuel Ringgold Ward, the minister and orator (chapters 3 and 4); and he is John Willis Menard (epilogue), the teacher, politician, and poet. But if the black preacher is a composite figure through whom we can celebrate Caribbean, and black Atlantic, culture, there remains the problem that romantic heroes tend to be lost heroes, consigned to a non-modern world of far away and long ago. In the end, it is only in a realist mode that we can write the cultural histories of the Caribbean, Britain, and the United States together, paying as close attention to the differences that separate them as to the relations of similarity that join them. Quacy and Hamel, Ward and Menard, Mary Lindsay and Simon Taylor, Belinda and Juba, Frederick Douglass and Felix Holt: they all jostle for space in the pages that follow, and I hope to show that they might all be joined together in some kind of plausible narrative, one that simultaneously joins and unsettles the disciplines of history and literary criticism in an account of a nineteenth-century Atlantic world that we have not yet lost.

CHAPTER I

Creole realism and metropolitan humanitarianism

On 15 June 1751, Anglican minister John Venn wrote from Spanish Town, Jamaica, to Bishop Thomas Sherlock in London, having heard that the bishop was 'desirous to know the State of the Church in this Island'; Venn wished to pass on the insights gained by an eleven-year residence in the Caribbean. In the middle of the eighteenth century, the Church of England in Jamaica ministered almost exclusively to the resident white population of the island, and Venn's letter expressed a desire to expand the reach of the church while at the same time giving a frank acknowledgement of the 'insuperable Difficulties' of the task lying ahead.[1] For Venn, the problem was not just the well-known resistance of the 'masters' to allowing their enslaved workers to hear the potentially egalitarian message of the church, but equally the resistance of the enslaved themselves based on the survival of their African religious, social, and cultural practices. Venn wrote that the enslaved were allowed little time away from the plantation fields,

which is (by Law) Saturday Afternoon & Sunday, being taken up in cultivating their own little Plantations, and in their Plays and Sports. And that is another grand Hindrance to their becoming Christians. I myself offer'd to baptize a sensible well-inclin'd Negro, but he declin'd it, saying that after that he must go to no more Dances, nor have any of their antic Ceremonies about his Grave, of which these poor ignorant Creatures are fond to a surprizing degree.[2]

Despite Venn's surprise, however, what is striking here is the matter-of-fact tone the clergyman employed to discuss the religious and cultural practices of African Jamaicans, in contrast to the many gruesome and romantic tales of heathen superstition and African violence that abounded later in the eighteenth century and into the nineteenth century. In this chapter I trace the development of what I call 'creole realism': the attempt to narrate the story of the British colonies from the point of view of a planter class defined by their qualities of reasonableness and enterprise.

We can trace this genre at least as far back as Richard Ligon's *A True and Exact History of the Island of Barbados*, which appeared in 1657; we should also note, however, that Ligon's history was the source for the legend of Inkle and Yarico, the cruel English merchant and the virtuous 'Indian' lover he sold into slavery.[3] The documentary record of the Caribbean told from the white creole point of view is forever turning into the literary genres that it eschews, sentimental fiction, gothic melodrama, and imperial romance. Creole realism was always defensive and embattled – just as the planter class felt themselves to be – at the same time as it proudly asserted its affiliation with the dominant generic norms of the metropole: scientific, empirical, and commercial. It was part and parcel of what David Lambert identifies as the principal mode of white culture in Barbados, and by extension in the Caribbean colonies more generally: 'a vacillation between *loyalty* and *opposition*'.[4] At the end of the chapter, I will suggest that as the creole planter class slowly lost influence in the 1820s and 1830s, it turned more explicitly to the genre of romance to express its opposition to the colonial authorities and their ideological underwriters, the humanitarians and philanthropists of the abolitionist movement in Britain. The discourse of creole realism, under the sign of loyalty to London, did not disappear, however, but was taken up by new creoles, the respectable black and brown converts to Christianity who were the imaginary descendants of Venn's 'sensible, well-inclin'd' African Jamaican.

Venn, the eleven-year resident of Jamaica, is also dispassionate about his failure to convert his own slaves: 'Many [white] People...have their Slaves christen'd when they desire it, but some are not only careless about it, but even averse to it, nor would be made Christians but by Compulsion; as I myself can testify of two or three of my own; who therefore are not christen'd to this Day.'[5] Venn's letter speaks to the necessity of the white Jamaican ruling class accommodating, tolerating, and understanding the 'antic ceremonies' of African-Jamaican culture and religion in the eighteenth century, with their elaborate funeral rites, 'plays', 'dances', and 'sports', in sharp contrast to the later eighteenth-century British obsession with 'obeah', African-Caribbean 'superstition' and magic.[6] This realism, however, aids and abets the inhumanity of chattel slavery in the Caribbean: the creolised white rector musters little affective response to the brutality of the slave regime in Jamaica, the everyday toll of violence, cruelty, and death: 'To deprive them [African Jamaicans] of their funeral Rites by burning their dead Bodies, seems to Negroes a greater Punishment than Death itself. This is done to Self-murderers.'[7] In a place where even the dead had to be punished, where escape through suicide had to be made impossible by interfering with the proper burial of the deceased, creole whites – even the sensible, well-inclined ones like John Venn – spoke in the distancing language of 'actuarial historicism', to use one of the terms of Ian Baucom's *Specters of the Atlantic*.[8] Such a system of thought, based on the protocols of insurance, itemised and reduced the enslaved populations of the Caribbean to objects of bookkeeping, defined, as Baucom puts it, by 'the typical structures of mortality, exchange, or history that circumscribe these things and operate as their historically peculiar circumstances'.[9] If for Baucom insurance practices – and the tragedy of the *Zong* episode in particular – are the model for the production of these types, their genre is the realist novel: we know these figures from the archive 'primarily as the typicalizing mind of insurance knows the world... [which] is also of course to know them as characters in a novel'.[10] Avoiding the potential for a romantic historicism that might work by 'soliciting our readerly sympathy, by inviting us not merely to encounter the dead but to identify with them, to put ourselves in their place', as Baucom suggests Walter Scott's novels will do early in the next century, Venn opts instead for the dead language of the self-explanatory type: 'Self-murderers', 'sensible, well-inclin'd Negro', 'poor ignorant Creatures'.[11]

Prime examples of this 'creole realism' would be the sprawling volumes of Edward Long and Bryan Edwards, whose natural, economic, and political histories of Jamaica and the West Indies respectively helped to establish the legitimacy of white West Indian culture, albeit at the very moment it came under sustained attack both from the enslaved people of the colonies and from metropolitan outsiders.[12] Other critics, however, have devoted considerable space to analyses of both Long and Edwards.[13] Instead, I focus in this chapter on the private papers and letters of one of the foremost practitioners of this genre, the wealthy Jamaican creole Simon Taylor, and on lesser known Jamaican whites, such as Edward Bancroft and Thomas Higson. I suggest that, despite the relatively low status of white West Indians in British society at this time and the widespread circulation of gothic, sentimental, and romantic discourses of the Caribbean, people like Taylor, Bancroft, and Higson laboured hard to establish realism as the dominant discourse of the West Indies.

This was never a complete success, of course. Jamaican society was riven by both external and internal tensions. Its creole society was characterised, as Kamau Brathwaite puts it, by 'a complex situation where a colonial polity reacts, as a whole, to metropolitan pressures, and at the same time to internal adjustments made necessary by the juxtaposition of master and slave, élite and labourer, in a culturally heterogenous relationship'.[14] So in this chapter I also tell the story of twin challenges to this realist mode of discourse and to the hegemony of the planter elite at the beginning of the nineteenth century. Firstly, the primacy and legitimacy of the white West Indian resident who has the presumed benefit of local knowledge are consistently undermined by the recurring figure of the black doctor, who combines creolised folk wisdom and the superior handling of local objects. Tropical medicine had to acknowledge the indigenous and creole remedies that it 'discovered' in the contact zone, with their obvious ties to 'superstition' and folk healing, and their challenge to a white Jamaican elite that obviously depended on the medical knowledge of black doctors and nurses.[15] Secondly, as David Lambert puts it in his impressive book on white Barbadians during this same period, 'metropolitan, especially evangelical, notions of morality, political organisation and economic activity triumphed over those articulated by the West Indian planters'.[16] The bookkeeping discourse of the white creoles was itself annexed and deployed by the London-based abolitionists, whose registers of slaves and accounts of souls saved became the raw materials of a winning campaign to join commerce, imperialism, and humanitarianism, and who thereby undermined the advantage of the insider status of the creoles.

We can see the first challenge to creole realism in John Venn's letter itself. Venn was rector of St Catherine's parish, which included the then capital Spanish Town, from 1748 until his death in Jamaica in 1764; in his letter to the bishop of London he was at pains to argue from his position as local eyewitness that Jamaica 'in general is not that savage Place' that many 'Travellers, thro Folly [and] Malice' have claimed it to be.[17] It is precisely in travellers' tales of the Caribbean in the eighteenth and early nineteenth centuries that the ubiquitous figure of the African folk healer appears, linked to the 'antic ceremonies' of African religious survivals that Venn observes, and a powerful challenge to the eyewitness insiderism of the creole whites. In reality, these black medico-religious leaders were male and female, young and old, but in the travelogues of the West Indies, they tend to devolve into two complementary generic figures: the obeah man and the mulatto nurse. Both appear in perhaps their most embellished forms in the most interesting – because most contradictory – traveller's tale of the late eighteenth-century Caribbean, John Gabriel Stedman's *Narrative of a Five Years' Expedition against the Revolted Negroes of Surinam*, first published in 1796.

Stedman's narrative paints the definitive picture of the Caribbean as savage tropical space; the savagery, moreover, is distributed across all classes and groups of Surinamese society, though concentrated at the top amongst the venal, pompous, and cruel creole whites. As a counterpoint, Stedman describes his romantic relationship with Joanna, a mixed-race enslaved

Figure 1.1 'The Celebrated Graman Quacy', engraved by
William Blake, from J. G. Stedman, *Narrative, of a Five Years'
Expedition, against the Revolted Negroes of Surinam* (1796)

woman, whose conventional feminine beauty and virtue combine with her
medical skills to allow for a sharp critique of the institution of slavery within
a text that nevertheless cannot follow through on its abolitionist tendencies
(not least because its author was a mercenary hired by the authorities in
Surinam to fight the Maroons who threatened the survival of plantation
slavery there). In the 1820s, Joanna was even excerpted from Stedman's
narrative and given a book of her own, in the flourishing of sentimental
antislavery literature.[18] The role of the obeah man is taken in Stedman's
narrative by Graman Quacy, 'one of the most extraordinary black men in
Surinam, or perhaps in the world', and the subject of a drawing by Stedman
interpreted and engraved by William Blake (see figure 1.1).[19]

What is interesting about Stedman's account is the way in which it turns the meaning of Quacy's medico-religious practice into an acquisitive, commercial one. By a narrative sleight of hand, Quacy's 'sorcery' becomes a kind of industry, an extension of his ability to free himself, and made legitimate by the fact that it is employed in the service of the slave regime itself:

In the first place, by his insinuating temper and industry, this Negro not only obtained his freedom from a state of slavery time out of mind, but by his wonderful artifice and ingenuity has found the means of acquiring a very competent subsistence. For instance, having got the name of a *looco-man*, or sorcerer, among the vulgar slaves, no crime of any consequence is committed at the plantations but Graman Quacy (which signifies Greatman Quacy) is sent for to discover the perpetrator, and which he so very seldom misses, because of their faith in his conjurations, and his looking them steadily in the face, that he has not only often prevented further mischief to their masters, but come home with very capital rewards to himself.[20]

Thus 'superstition' is made palatable – because it is made calculable, a source of monetary gain – for administrative realism. However, if African medical practice was important when it was deployed in the service of the colonial authorities – Quacy gave the black soldiers fighting the Surinamese Maroons '*obias*, or amulets, to make them invulnerable' – it raised difficult problems when it intersected with European scientific and medical practice, as it inevitably did in the contact zone of the Americas.[21] Black herbalism could not in the end be allowed to challenge the supremacy of European medical methods, even though European writers were forced sometimes to acknowledge the African or indigenous American roots of much tropical medicine. Quacy's chief claim to fame, in fact, is that 'he had the good fortune to find out the valuable root known under the name of *Quacy Bitter*, of which this man was absolutely the first discoverer in 1730, and which . . . is highly esteemed in many other parts of the world for its efficacy in strengthening the stomach, restoring the appetite, &c.'.[22] This 'discovery', however, marks the limits of Quacy's powers, as far as Stedman is concerned: he could have made a great deal of money from this medicinal root, 'were he not in other respects an indolent dissipating blockhead, whereby which he at last fell into a complication of loathsome disorders of which the leprosy is one'.[23] Instead, 'quacy bitter' was 'made known to Linnaeus by Mr. Dahlberg', a creole Swedish plantation owner in Surinam.[24] The black healer is sidelined and left to struggle with diseases that are beyond his power to treat.

I spend some time on Graman Quacy because he represents the meeting point of several different figures and narratives that I discuss in this chapter and the ones that follow. On the one hand, he is a version of the 'sensible, well-inclin'd negro' mentioned by John Venn: as yet unconverted in religion, but well on the way to being a tractable and industrious subject of the empire. Crusoe's Friday is his forebear; realism is his genre. British culture will continue to reward and promote this figure throughout the nineteenth century and into the twentieth, the successful 'native' who validates the civilising mission. On the other hand, he is a comic, debased figure, grown fat and 'indolent' in his toadyism (Blake's engraving pairs Quacy's excessive belly with his overelaborate European costume). His descendant is the overeducated Hurree Babu in Kipling's *Kim* (a novel that repeats more than a century later the conflict between the realism of bureaucratic rationality and the romance of the imperial contact zone).[25] Moreover, he returns in the figure I analyse in chapter 3, the African-American minister, orator, and writer Samuel Ringgold Ward, likewise feared and ridiculed for his size and blackness and celebrated for his embrace of the protocols of the British empire, before and after he emigrated to Jamaica in 1855. Quacy is also one of the ancestors of the literary figure Hamel the obeah man I discuss in chapter 2, a rebel and African religious leader who manages at the same time to remain loyal to the colonial authorities; romance is the dominant genre here, but the romance of the periphery made possible by Scott's celebration of the lost culture of the Scottish Highlands. All these strains meet in Quacy, and make him a powerful and generative figure.

Quacy also marks the meeting point of the two counternarratives to the white creole eyewitness that I mentioned above, the humanitarian appropriation of creole realism and the story of the black doctor as the real creole. In Maria Edgeworth's 1801 novel *Belinda*, which I discuss in more detail towards the end of this chapter, and which is in part a metropolitan catalogue of tropical objects, we find several references to 'anima of quassia', touted as an infallible cure for every conceivable ailment by Lady Boucher. She tells her friend Lady Delacour of the

sundry wonderful cures that had been performed to her certain knowledge, by her favourite concentrated extract or anima of quassia. She entered into the history of the Negro slave named Quassi, who discovered this medical wood, which he kept a close secret till Mr Daghlberg, a magistrate of Surinam, wormed it out of him, brought a branch of the tree to Europe, and communicated it to the great Linnaeus.[26]

Edgeworth's novel began as a sketch entitled 'Abroad and at Home', and, as I argue below, it is simultaneously repelled and fascinated by the importation of tropical objects and people into the realm of London society. Of course, tropical objects are hardly incompatible with English realism, which

after all conventionally begins with Defoe's *Robinson Crusoe* and its catalogue of Caribbean island things (plus salvaged – we might say, creolised –
European objects from the shipwreck) for which Crusoe must learn the
proper use value, as I discussed in the introduction above. Quacy's remedy
is derided by Lady Delacour as a 'quack balsam', but, as I show below,
it worms its way into London medical practice all the same, just at the
moment that the white creole figure in the novel, Vincent, is expelled from
England as unworthy of our rational eponymous heroine. Humanitarian
realism allows for the conjunction of antislavery sympathy, an economic
rationality that now excludes slavery as atavistic, and a sentimental attachment to the figure of noble black wisdom (achieved, it must be said, in
the case of *Belinda* partly through the denigration of the 'obeah woman'
and the metropolitan feminist). In this new dispensation, the white creole
apparently has nowhere to go. Some, like Simon Taylor, developed a kind
of incipient Jamaican nationalism, as I show below. Others, as we shall see
in chapter 2, tried to cobble together a new genre of Caribbean romance
from elements of the same travellers' tales John Venn deplored and from
the historical romance of the periphery of the British Isles made popular
by Walter Scott.

CREOLE REALISTS I: SIMON TAYLOR

Simon Taylor, wealthy creole planter, estate manager, and merchant, dominated the Jamaican economic and political scene for much of the last
quarter of the eighteenth century and well into the early years of the nineteenth. Unlike his peers Bryan Edwards and Edward Long, he did not
write for public consumption, but many of his letters and estate papers
have survived, and they paint a compelling and disturbing picture of elite
white attitudes and practices in pre-emancipation Jamaica. Simon Taylor
did not just deploy the tropes of bookkeeping and accounting in order
to describe the world around him; he actually was a bookkeeper and an
accountant, as well as a highly successful businessman and politician. He
was also irascible, and zealously protected what he perceived to be his
economic interests, against rival planters, against the hundreds of enslaved
Africans and African Jamaicans on his estates, against the commercial and
taxation regimes of the British government in London and its representatives in the island, and against the missionaries and antislavery activists
who threatened the destruction of his world of sugar money.[27]

To begin with, we can note that Taylor's letters contain innumerable
references to slave purchases, and voyages by his slaving ships – one of

which was called the *Simon Taylor* – before the abolition of the slave trade in 1807, and in none of them do 'negroes' appear as anything other than calculable objects. In fact, in none of them do black Jamaicans appear as named individuals at all: they are always described as a mass, always simply 'the negroes'. For example, in 1774, Taylor wrote to Chaloner Arcedeckne in England, for whom he managed the Golden Grove estate in St Thomas-in-the-East, reporting the purchase of 102 'negroes' from a Mr Kelly:

I do also assure you I think them a prodigious acquisition to your Estate & that you will not feel the purchase as you will by this means be enabled to enlarge your Crop and save your Capital and there will be no occasion of pushing so hard as we were formerly Obliged to on the Estate. Let me recommend it also to you to give Orders for the Purchase of 20 Young Negroes Annually to be bought for the use of the Estate and by that means they will become as good as any Creoles and very little risque in the seasoning of them and the yaws which is the most destructive thing in a wett Country does not make half the impression on them as it does on grown people & make no doubt but that you will find your income yearly increasing more than sufficient to pay for them.[28]

In 1801, Taylor wrote to a David Reid, whose son 'hired out negroes', with a description of the 'new negroes' he had bought recently who would counter 'all the Chimeras that is reported of the Sense and Capacity of the Negroes on the Coast of Guinea; nine tenths that come here are as helpless and have as few Ideas as sucking Piggs'. (He goes on, however, to say that those who 'have been Merchants and Traders . . . are knowing enough but People are not fond of buying them or Warriors taken in battle they being considered dangerous'.)[29] A few years later, as the date of the end of the slave trade approached, Taylor reported to his cousin Robert Taylor (his principal agent in London) that there were twenty slave ships lying in Kingston harbour, but 'there absolutely is not Money on the Island to pay for Negroes from the Number that have arrived', given the depressed state of the local economy. The result is that 'many [Africans] must die of Course and this mortality totally and solely owing to the Abolition which has made such a glutt'. Nevertheless, Taylor himself has purchased many more people, 'for if I had not done so my Estates would be wearing away to nothing . . . They [the British government and abolitionists] are ruining themselves their own Manufactures and fellow subjects under the pretence of Humanity to Africa with whose people they have no concern on Earth.'[30]

The creole realism of the Jamaican-born Taylor has nothing but scorn for the self-serving 'pretence of humanity' of Wilberforce and his ilk in England. 'Humanity' is simply a weapon to use against the planters who have built the prosperity of the empire, and indeed of Britain itself – 'We who have implored their [the British government's] Humanity who have been toiling labouring, and Shedding our Blood to raise them a revenue'[31] – and who are now being betrayed by the turn against sugar and slavery in the metropole. Despite, or perhaps because of, the ability of someone like Taylor to turn black Jamaican life into an account of bills of exchange, it is the planters who really have 'concern' for the Africans, who treat them for the yaws, who promise, for example, to hire a good overseer for Golden Grove, to 'putt none but a good Man there to take Care of the Negroes and Stock, which [sic] is [sic] the life and Soul of a property'.[32] Once again, the realm of medicine – 'tak[ing] care of the negroes and stock' – is the zone where black and white Jamaicans are joined, where a local, creolised knowledge developed on the ground in the island – 'the yaws... is the most destructive thing in a wett Country' – comes into conflict with the misplaced 'humanity' of English outsiders. Writing from Kingston, sending the accounts of several large estates in eastern Jamaica that helped fuel the growth of the empire, the bitterness and defensiveness of the representative of the peripheral elite are scathing:

The Press, the Pulpit, and House of Commons for these ten years have been Sounding and Resounding these Malignant Lies respecting us, and their own Humanity, and compassion for the wretched inhabitants on the Coast of Africa, who by the by they have nothing to do with, and who have never signified the least wish or desire of their Humanity Pity or Compassion to be partakers of, but as words cost nothing they have had them in great abundance as well as the tears of Mr. Wilberforce, if we are to believe him, receive the medall.[33]

Here the aggrieved correspondent from eastern Jamaica must acknowledge, albeit negatively, the wishes and desires of Africans themselves, who reject the compassion (at a distance) of the antislavery faction in Britain, led by William Wilberforce, the humanitarian MP routinely referred to by Taylor in his letters as the 'Imp of Hell'.[34]

The accounts of Golden Grove estate can give us some figures to assess the extent to which the institution of plantation slavery could conceivably be reimagined as a project of humane whites building a viable society in Jamaica by having something 'to do with' the enslaved population of the island. In 1799, seven 'mason negroes' were hired at salaries ranging from £20 to £35 a year; seven 'carpenter negroes' were hired for £10, £20, and £30 a year; on 18 February, 16s 8d was paid to 'Negroes in Town for bills' (suggesting that black Jamaicans were handling bills of exchange as well as being the objects bought and sold on them)[35]; and 'the Midwife' was paid £6 for 'delivering 18 women this year at 6/8' each. The bookkeepers, overseers, white masons, and carpenters are all named in the accounts, with salaries ranging from £50 to £280; Robert Bolton, a white doctor, was paid £210 'for medical attendance on said Plantation', and after Simon Taylor had paid himself the 6 per cent annual commission as estate manager (amounting to £1070 5s 0d), he remitted to the absent Arcedeckne a profit of £11,484 18s 4½d on total sales of produce shipped out of Jamaica that year of £17,837 12s 10d: a profit margin of almost 65 per cent.[36] The differences between black and white Jamaicans – between those numbered and those named – appear therefore to overwhelm the connections between them. Nevertheless, it is notable that black wage labour coexists here with slave labour, albeit on a small scale; at the end of this chapter I will return to the figure of the entrepreneurial African Jamaican who emerged from the ruins of white creole culture as the standard bearer of a new form of Caribbean culture.

Another document in the Vanneck-Arcedeckne Papers tells us the name of 'the Midwife' at Golden Grove, who was called Judy, but our latterday attempt to infuse her with humanity must struggle against the fact that the first thing we learn about her is her number, 72, on the list of 181 'original' slaves on the estate in 1792, a list that comes before the separate account of the 210 'slaves bought by Chaloner Arcedeckne'.[37] These lists of creole and African slaves do allow us to confirm the fact, however, that the most common way in which white Jamaican planters, overseers, attorneys, and doctors had something 'to do with' black Jamaicans was through sexual relationships. The 'increase' of the enslaved at Golden Grove and Bachelor's Hall that kept Judy busy in the last years of the eighteenth century had a lot to do with enslaved women giving birth to white men's children. From the list of 'original' slave children born between 1775 and 1792, we learn of Mul[atto] Mary (number 143), daughter of B[lack] Nancy, and Mul[atto] Nancy (number 146), daughter of Lucia; one of the two 'House-Wenches' at Golden Grove, Mulatto Sally (the other was Mulatto Jenny), was the mother of five 'quadroon' children by 1792: John, Nelly, Robert, Patrick, and 'Ansh.y'.[38] Here is striking evidence of the hierarchy on plantations that elevated creole slaves over African ones: of the 210 people bought by Taylor for Golden Grove, 153 of them were field workers, and none of them were house servants, while of the 'original' slaves, only 42 worked in the fields, and all the drivers, headmen, and house servants, and most of the nurses, masons, and carpenters, were drawn from their ranks. The closer black Jamaicans came to the house itself, the more they were in a position to negotiate a place in Jamaican life for themselves.

It is important not to idealise or romanticise these forms of negotiation, however, as Jenny Sharpe argues convincingly, especially in the cases of enslaved women: 'Because of the structures of slavery that sanctioned their sexual appropriation by white men, slave women had extremely limited options. They could be raped, paid a small sum for their outward "cooperation", or enter into more formal and long-term arrangements, but there was no position from which they could refuse.'[39] Pro-planter advocates in Britain cited Taylor's alleged tough stance on whites in Jamaica entering into 'concubinage' relationships: 'Twenty years ago I heard the late Mr. Simon Taylor . . . say, that he would discharge from his employ any man . . . who should be guilty of this act.' However, while staying at Golden Grove in 1802, Maria Nugent, wife of Governor George Nugent, met a 'little mulatto girl . . . a sickly delicate child', and she commented in her diary: 'Mr. T. appeared very anxious for me to dismiss her, and in the evening, the housekeeper told me she was his own daughter, and that he had a numerous family, some almost on every one of his estates.'[40] As Taylor entered the final stages of his life, he wrote to his cousin Robert, explaining that he was not well enough to travel to England:

My Faith gone my Hearing and Eyesight not good and I should be only an Incumbrance anywhere. There is a very decent Woman by whom I had a Daughter about 33 or 34 years ago. Both she and her Daughter and Grand Daughter are in the House with me and take every pains to nurse me and I wish to lay my Bones in my native land.[41]

The 'decent woman' Taylor lives with, like Joanna in Stedman's narrative, shows that the figure of the mulatto nurse-wife is the hinge between mutually incompatible narratives and scenes: the medical touch dispels the aura of immorality associated with interracial sex, and the white man's bedroom becomes the place where the authority of the planter's estate can be seamlessly merged with the healing folk wisdom of the African and creole black Jamaicans. Of course, however, there were limits to the viability of the role of the 'decent woman' of colour: writing to his sister-in-law, Lady Elizabeth Haughton Taylor, the widow of his brother John Taylor and mother of his legal heir (Simon Richard Brissett Taylor), Simon Taylor attested that he had Lady Taylor's children's interests always at heart, 'never having had any Children of my Own'.[42] The 'decent woman' of colour is hidden – even though she must have been an open family secret – from the sensibilities of the civilised white woman in England.

The 'decent woman' and her daughter and granddaughter are the opposite of obeah women to the extent that they come close to the civilised values of white female domesticity; and at the same time, they rely on the herbal and religious authority of the 'wretched inhabitants of the coast of Africa' that was transvaluated as obeah in the Caribbean to the extent that they can never in fact attain the civility of white, English femininity. This family romance confirms the charge made most often back in England about white creoles, that they were too intimately connected to the very black slaves whom they treated inhumanely as objects of their cruelty. The domestic, medical scene marks the difference between England and Jamaica. Crucially, for Taylor at least, this declaration of a kind of family, and one that had lasted for more than three decades, produces an assertion of a specifically Jamaican identity – 'I wish to lay my bones in my native land' – as opposed to an imperial, English one:

It is highly improbable that I shall ever leave this Country. I am persuaded that a Voyage to Europe would hasten my End for I really could not bear the Cold nor the vicissitudes of the British Climate. I am so used to the Customs of this Country that any alteration of them would now (living rather securely) be very uncomfortable to me.[43]

It is not that the link to England has been abolished: in the same letter, Taylor instructs his cousin to be on the lookout for an English estate for him to purchase, and to spend £150,000 or so ('ten or twenty thousand pounds more or less makes little difference to me in the purchase', he says blithely); in this way, Taylor hoped to follow in the footsteps of many other large Caribbean landowners who traded wealth in the West Indies for an estate and social standing in England.[44] But Taylor – who visited England only once during his long adult life in Jamaica, despite his English education at Eton – is defiantly out of touch with the codes and expectations of the English aristocratic life into which his enormous wealth could have easily bought him entry: 'I do not wish to have Castles or Magnificent Houses with large Parks Extensive Plantations Stables for running Horses nor Kennels for Fox or other Hounds. I could wish a tolerable good Family House and that is all and especially an Estate that has large Extent of land and is improvable.'[45] Taylor died in Kingston in 1813 without visiting England, and the bulk of his wealth passed to his profligate English nephew Simon Richard Brissett Taylor, whose death three years later did finalise the transfer of West Indian wealth into English status, with the inheritance of Taylor's Jamaican properties by his niece Anna Susannah Taylor and her husband George Watson, who took the surname Taylor and became the MP for four different constituencies on the south coast of England from 1816 to 1832.

We can deduce, however, from a copy of Taylor's will from 1782, that he made at least some arrangements for the 'decent woman' of his sickbed letter of 1811; we also learn that her name was Grace Donne, 'a Free Quadroon

Woman who now lives with me'.[46] He planned to give her £100 plus an annual payment of £50, his house in Orange Street, Kingston, and

> my Own Bed and Bedstead & the Furniture belonging thereto, also Twelve Chairs, Four Tables, My Beaureau & Book Case with Mahogany Doors, a Case of Silver Handled Knives & Forks & Silver Spoons, Twelve of Sheets, Twelve Table Cloths, all my China & Glass Ware in Town . . . [and] any One of my Draft Horses that she shall choose.

Securing Grace Donne's status in Jamaican society, in addition to these valuable objects, Taylor also bequeathed to her some of the people whom he owned as property: 'I give devise and bequeath to the said Grace Donne the following Negroes, Viz. Sandy & Bessy and Mulatto Becky to hold to the hand of the said Grace Donne her Heirs and Assigns for ever.' Taylor instructed his executors to buy 'six New Negroe Women, the Bill of Parcels for which to be made out by the Guinia Factor in the Name of the said Grace Donne'. Along with the house on Orange Street came 'a wench named Mulatto Sally'; to Taylor's 'natural Quadroon Daughter', Sally Taylor, he gave 'six Negroes to be purchased and delivered to her on her attaining the age of Eighteen Years'; he gave £100 to his son Jack Taylor, 'a Free Quadroon . . . now under the Care of Capt. David Watt . . . & I also direct that my Executors pay the expence of bringing him out to Jamaica'. Obviously, these amounts pale in comparison to the tens of thousands of pounds and hundreds of enslaved people eventually inherited by Taylor's English niece and her husband, but still he felt the need to defend his support for his Jamaican family in the accompanying letter to his brother back in England: 'You will say I have made a great Provision for the Woman who lives with me. I own it, but she has been a Faithful Serv[an]t to me, & I never had occasion to call twice for any thing, or awake her in any of my Severe Fitts of Illness.'[47] Grace Donne becomes the very type of the 'incomparable nurse', as Stedman had described Joanna:

> Colonial eyewitnesses considered the doctoring of mulatto women to be superior even to Western medicine . . . Whereas nursing and doctoring became disassociated from housework in seventeenth-century Europe, it was very much a part of domestic duties in the West Indies. This explains why the 'brown girl' is better even than the white lady at nursing white men through their illnesses.[48]

However, when Taylor's white niece in England and her new husband inherited the Jamaica properties, they were scandalised by the domestic inefficiency of the estates, according to English standards. In the period after emancipation, the Watson Taylors sent a certain John Cooper out to inspect the Jamaican estates they were living off but had never seen.

At Holland estate, one of Taylor's principal properties in St Thomas-in-the-East, Cooper reported that there were twenty-four carpenters, thirteen coopers, twelve masons, and three blacksmiths:

I am entirely at a loss to find out what they are employed about. I see but few monuments of their industry. There is a head carpenter and a head mason employed upon this property who dine at the Overseers table, the former with a salary of £160 and the latter at £120 p. year currency. I will engage that one English carpenter and one Mason would keep the premises in good repair and do any other work besides that would be required. To a practical man, to one who has been brought up in the school of English Economy, this does appear a most shameful abuse of labour and discreditable neglect of the Interest of the Proprietor.

At Lyssons, another of Simon Taylor's former estates in the parish, things were a little better, but 'the head people appear rather too numerous. The tradesmen as at Holland are far more than are required. They are an indolent and stupid race. I would recommend that with a few exceptions they be put into the field and their place supplied with Englishmen.'[49] Again, even in the apprenticeship period that heralded the end of slavery in the Caribbean, what makes this scene 'Jamaican' from the standpoint of 'English economy' and common sense is the shameful intimacy between managers and labourers, two of whom 'dine at the Overseers table', and who are too numerous in general. The latterday cultural historian is more likely to interpret the workings of labour on the estate as the result of incremental, hardwon gains made by the formerly enslaved themselves, increasing the numbers employed while thereby reducing the workload in an industry notorious for its ability to wound, disable, and kill its workers at extraordinarily high rates. Henceforth the 'school of English Economy' would have to reckon with the cultural arrangements of eastern Jamaica that sometimes valued and rewarded labour practices that looked inefficient, 'shameful', and 'discreditable' from the point of view of the metropole. Of course, there is another possible interpretation: probably many of the workers attached to the plantations were in fact keen to leave them and construct monuments of their own industry, but legally during the period of apprenticeship they were bound to provide labour to the estates on which they lived and worked at the time of emancipation in 1833.[50]

Whichever interpretation makes the most historical sense, all scenarios point to a large imaginary, cultural, and economic gap between Britain and Jamaica that was only to widen as the nineteenth century went on, despite the fact that Caribbean wealth had formed the cornerstone of the eighteenth- and early nineteenth-century empire. Almost as common in

Simon Taylor's correspondence as his indifference to the humanity of black people is his vitriolic anger towards abolitionists, towards the British politicians who adopted the perspective of antislavery, and consequently towards Britain itself. We have already seen how Taylor referred to Wilberforce; he was no more charitable to the evangelical missionaries who began to arrive in Jamaica at the very end of the eighteenth century, calling them 'a gang of Wolves in Sheeps cloathing... preach[ing] Sedition Murder and Massacre among our Slaves'.[51] Once British politicians began to align themselves with antislavery, Taylor's invective gathered strength. '[Charles] Fox and his Gang' were 'timid' in the face of the dire threats facing the country: 'Abolition of the Slave Trade, Reform of Parliament or Irish Emancipation are Synonimous and cant Phrases for oversetting the Constitution Murdering the King and Nobility confiscating their Property and bringing universall Anarchy and confusion.'[52] William Pitt (the younger) was no better: his imposition of the first income tax in the late 1790s prompted Taylor to vow never to pay it, claiming that Pitt 'seems to use every means in his Power to destroy the Colonies'.[53] Sometimes, Taylor's outrage at Britain even produces an idea of a Jamaican nation: 'I have given up every Scheme or thought of ever going to Britain, or for investing money or Property in a Country that has been persecuting mine these ten years past. I cannot think of doing it and I would rather throw the Money in the Sea than invest it there.'[54] As we have seen, towards the end of his life, Taylor at least considered reneging on this promise and buying an English country estate, but it is instructive to witness the way in which a colonial British identity vied with other local and regional spheres of influence in the life of one of the richest of all British subjects at the turn of the nineteenth century.

Unsurprisingly, 'America' is the place that emerges most often in Taylor's letters as a rival to Britain, but also a point of reference and a possible haven for Taylor himself in his increasingly embattled sense of white West Indian identity. He saw Pitt's policies driven by a determination to ruin the Caribbean colonies – 'Delenda est Carthago was his Resolution' – and foresaw the result in increasing American influence: 'The Americans will fill the Continent with their Articles and India Goods as well as the French and Spanish Islands and also German goods for they [Americans] are a most adventurous sort of People... No Nation can vie with them.'[55] He had, of course, lived through the rebellion of the American colonies and the emergence of an independent United States, and he railed against the British enforcement of the Navigation Acts after US independence that restricted the previous trade between North America and the Caribbean.[56]

He persisted in seeing the world from the perspective of an idea of 'America' that joined the mid- and north Atlantic colonies to the Caribbean, complaining that restricting Jamaican trade with the USA was 'alienating them [Americans] more and more from the Country they originally came from' by not letting them supply 'the British colonies with what Britain itself nor its dependencies could [not] furnish and which was permitted by every other Power more or less that had settlements in America'.[57]

He threatened constantly, if idly, to leave Jamaica and move to the United States, which this man who was a product of the first British empire imagined as a kind of return:

> To have Doctrines preached us to have our own throats cutt, our Properties destroyed our Women and Children massacred, to be held up as Barbarians and a Horde of Savages, to [be] persecuted and hated because we have putt our faith in Royal Proclamation and British Acts of Parliament is too much, these are the Causes of Discontent and why I mean to return to America, and carry what part of my Property I possibly can there.[58]

This is the fractured position of the creole English in the Caribbean: at once the most loyal of subjects, faithful to the king and acts of parliament, and at the same time regional rebels, ready to throw money into the sea rather than send it to Britain.

'America' becomes a kind of safe haven, but also a counter-metropole to England in a version of the Atlantic world that joins Jamaica and Ireland, and indeed all 'countries dependent on England', in a kind of transperipheral, circumatlantic sphere:

> I am very sorry to find a Rebellion has broke out in Ireland, & the People have had recourse to Arms. It has been long brewing & I doubt not but it will be traced in time to the Opposition in England, which seems to be the Pandora Box of all Evill. But indeed the People that live in all Countries dependant on England are treated so exceeding ill, & have so many oppressions added to oppressions dayly, that I am not surprized to see them rise, for my part, I positively assure you that if I possibly could gett my Property from hence, even to seeing one half of it, I would instantly quit the Country & go & live some where in the Northern States of America, merely to be rid of the Tyrany, Injustice, & Malevolence of the English Nation.[59]

Again and again, despite his massive and ever increasing wealth, Taylor foresaw the destruction of his native land: 'I think a War between England and America inevitable and that will bring on the final Destruction of the Whole of the British Colonies, for they cannot subsist or exist without the Aid of America as usefull Colonies to any state.'[60]

Although British policy might be the final cause of this destruction, its agents will be 'the negroes' themselves. This is the impossible logic of the white creoles. On the one hand, 'the negroes' are well treated and better off than the English, Scottish, and Irish working classes; on the other hand, it is inevitable that 'the negroes' will rebel.

Altho the Intentions of the Negroes were frustrated in breaking out last Christmas, there cannot be the least doubt but that it will be again and again attempted and will at last succeed. My belief is that there was nothing that could have given the late Minister [Pitt] more pleasure than to have heard that the throats of every white Person on the Islands had been cutt and that the Negroes had been in Possession of the Islands.[61]

Taylor was inordinately fond of the idea of the creole whites having their throats cut, and even as his estates prospered through the abolition of the slave trade and beyond, he continued to call for the economic and political prophylactics necessary to avert the massacres. Cast as barbarians and savages by the adherents of 'humanity', Taylor and his peers impute the savagery to 'the negroes' Pitt and Wilberforce and the missionaries are using to destroy the empire.

The agriculture and trade of someone like Simon Taylor created a powerful case for considering the Atlantic world as a regional unit of analysis; his letters enumerate decades full of commodities, people, and ships crossing and recrossing the spaces between Kingston, London, Havana, Freetown, Liverpool, Port-au-Prince, Bristol, and New York City. It is this world that is acutely threatened at the beginning of the nineteenth century, and people like Taylor saw the emergence of a new empire that spoke in the name of 'humanity' that would replace what later historians came to call the 'First British Empire'. George Hibbert, the principal agent for Jamaica in London, and a prominent member of the influential West India Committee of Merchants and Planters, wrote to Taylor in 1803 bemoaning the decline in power in London of 'the West Indian Interest':

We have sometimes gained a trifling or temporary point or two, but the System goes on and it is either openly or secretly undermining us. I have no doubt that, as you say, they are willing first to reduce our Significancy to the empire before they professedly abandon us, but that they have persuaded themselves . . . that, being dependent on Negro Population, we must before many years are over share the fate of St. Domingo and that we are therefore not worth their care and anxiety.[62]

Hibbert saw the centre of the empire moving steadily eastwards – 'the East India Posessions of the Empire are the Toy that is to amuse us and delude us like Children under our Suffering the loss, not very gradual, of all our old Colonies' – and the politicians in London uniting on 'the negro question': 'Differ as much as they please in other respects, the Pitts, Grenvilles, Foxites and Moderates . . . , they are all equally against us. And 'tis the Negro Question that is the Corner Stone of their Agreements against us.'[63]

From the perspective of the planters and their British-based partners, the talk of 'humanity' coming out of London coincided dangerously with the daily resistances of the enslaved. People like Taylor and Hibbert found themselves close to the centres of political and economic power and at the same time sidelined by new schemes to resolve the 'negro question' that would all have had the effect of increasing the authority of non-West Indian outsiders, missionaries, and London MPs alike, and reducing the relative local autonomy of Caribbean whites. Christopher Brown makes this point about the centralisation of state power in his excellent essay on late eighteenth-century antislavery schemes: 'Any plan for emancipation presented the specter of enhanced imperial authority, if not a formal shift of power from the colonial assemblies to Parliament. Even a gradual, voluntary end to slavery would demand institutions empowered to mediate between freedmen and former slaveholders.'[64] Sure enough, the beginning of the end for the Caribbean planter class came when abolitionists in Britain astutely campaigned for a detailed registry of slaves as a necessary statistical tool in the project of 'improvement' for the lives of the enslaved peoples of the British empire.

Turning the creole realism of the slave traders and slave owners against them, the registry's principal advocate, James Stephen, argued forcefully in several pamphlets in the mid-1810s that accurate lists of slaves were the only way to ensure that illegal smuggling of slaves would stop. He had hoped the abolition of the slave trade in 1807 would be followed 'by a benign, though insensible revolution in opinions and manners, by the encouragement of particular manumissions, and the progressive melioration of the condition of the slaves, till it should slide insensibly into general freedom'.[65] That this had not yet happened by 1814 therefore compelled the supporters of 'melioration' to push for another act of the imperial parliament to compensate for the failure of local laws in the colonies themselves to improve the situation on the ground. While slavery 'continue[s] to be the reproach of the freest and happiest empire that ever the sun beheld', the future happiness and freedom of the slaves themselves is to be ensured by the most accurate enumeration and certification of their condition as slaves.[66] The prospect that the slaves will be transformed from objects into subjects is to be opened up by a better list of the slaves as objects:

The general object of this plan is to obtain a public record of the names and descriptions of all persons lawfully held in slavery in each respective island . . . Full and accurate returns should be made of the existing stock of Slaves . . . Such a registry being formed, and perpetually kept in a public office within the colony, is to be hereafter the necessary evidence of the servile condition of persons resident within the island to which it belongs.[67]

By presenting the language of bookkeeping as the creation of an impartial 'public record', Stephen and his supporters turn the bookkeeping practices of a figure like Taylor into secret narratives of concubinage and horror. Jamaica, along with other Caribbean colonies, had passed legislation providing for returns of slave births, deaths, and sales each year in response to abolitionist pressures in the late 1780s and 1790s. Most of the assemblies that passed laws at this time 'admitt[ed] them to be necessary on views of policy and humanity, as checks on private cruelty, and life-wasting abuses';[68] Jamaica, however, did not even go through the motions of following through on its own regulations, thereby joining local assertions of political power to the gothic domestic scene of 'private cruelty and life-wasting abuses'.[69]

Stephen scathingly quotes a letter Simon Taylor wrote to Lord Balcarres, the governor of Jamaica, in 1804, in which Taylor – writing in his capacity as custos (chief magistrate) of St Thomas-in-the-East – told the governor that he could not provide a breakdown of numbers of slaves born in Jamaica and those brought from Africa; moreover, he went on,

It is true . . . that almost every person keeps an account for himself or herself of what slaves they possess, as well as of the increase of them by purchase, inheritances, or births, and also of the decrease by deaths, sales, or otherwise; *but these lists they consider as their private property, and are not obliged by any law to divulge.*[70]

The lists of slaves, as much as the slaves themselves, were the 'private property' of the planters; Stephen's aim was to turn the genre of the itemised list into a public document of 'humanity'. Rereading the private correspondence of Simon Taylor, with its lists of slaves, and of their 'increase and decrease', with its convoluted and contradictory sense of family, of home and abroad, of Jamaica and England, I have tried to show how deft and successful was Stephen's redeployment of the discourse of creole realism. Taylor's death, and the transfer of the bulk of his property – including of course the hundreds of enslaved people on his estates – to the English branch of his family, represents the end of the long eighteenth-century era of Jamaican slavery. He can be said to embody the inhumanity of the West Indian plantocracy, and versions of Taylor are common stock figures in British nineteenth-century fiction, as we will see when I turn to a discussion of Edgeworth's *Belinda* in the following section of this chapter. But we should note that the 'humanity' of organised antislavery borrowed some of the bookkeeping forms of plantation slavery, and that both sides of the debate over slavery shared most assumptions about the relative status of Africans and Europeans in the scale of civilisation. Writing to George Hibbert a couple of weeks before the act to abolish the slave trade came into effect – and thus at the moment of his most frenzied purchases of new African slaves before it became illegal to do so – Taylor dispensed some tropical medical advice, perhaps learned from Grace Donne herself, and almost certainly passed on originally by enslaved Africans and their descendants in eastern Jamaica: 'Pray has Mrs Hibbert ever tried for her Rheumatick Complaints Gum Guaicum dissolved in Brandy this is two ounces of Guaicum in a Pint of Brandy and about two thimblefulls in a Wine Glass with Water to be taken at going to Bed . . . I have felt good Effects from it myself.'[71] The white creole Jamaican ended up transmitting the medical knowledge of black Jamaicans to the metropolitan centre, where there was a willing and growing audience for the charms of tropical medicine and the literature of the tropical periphery. I turn therefore to the Anglo-Irish novelist Maria Edgeworth, whose literary realism likewise imported West Indian people, ideas, and objects and transformed them into a new kind of metropolitan humanitarianism in the period just before and after the abolition of the slave trade in 1807.

HUMANITARIAN REALISM: MARIA EDGEWORTH'S *BELINDA*

Maria Edgeworth's novel *Belinda* was first published in 1801, with subsequent editions in 1802 and (much revised) in 1810, when it was published in Letitia Barbauld's British Novelists series. Edgeworth's early sketch for the novel was entitled 'Abroad and at Home', but contained no non-English characters: home and abroad corresponded roughly to 'private' and 'public' and referred to the struggle of Belinda to help her friend and benefactor Lady Delacour to harmonise her inner, personal life and her outer, social standing as a flirtatious and aggressive participant in the elite culture of London. In the first two editions of the novel, however, 'home' and 'abroad' greatly expanded their range of meanings and associations, and Lady Delacour's conversion to respectable married life is paralleled by, and counterpointed to, Belinda's attraction to, and final repudiation of, the wealthy white West Indian suitor, Mr Vincent. Vincent's expulsion from England at the end of the novel is itself contrasted to the settlement within English society of his black 'servant', Juba, who marries a poor, rural Englishwoman, Lucy. In the third, revised edition of the novel, however, Edgeworth removed all references to Juba's marriage to a white woman, and toned down the seriousness of Belinda and Vincent's courtship – suggesting that after the abolition of the slave trade in 1807, such liaisons had become dangerous representations in British culture. The novel, in its multiple revisions, demonstrates the truth, but also the challenge, of Catherine Hall's astute account of the impossibility of separating England and the West Indies (and its largest colony, Jamaica, in particular) as 'home' and 'abroad': 'Jamaican family connections, Jamaican property in enslaved people, did not stay conveniently over there; they were part of the fabric of England, inside not outside, raising the question as to what was here and what was there, threatening dissolution of the gap on which the distinction between colony and metropole was constructed.'[72] In *Belinda*, part of the blurring of this boundary is carried out specifically by the tropical remedy discovered by and named after Graman Quacy, the 'anima of quassia' I discussed at the start of this chapter. However, in all three editions of *Belinda*, despite the shifting importance of the West Indian characters, the Caribbean is also represented as the place of superstition and malicious magic through the figure of obeah.

Firstly, Juba is tricked by the monstrous feminist figure, Harriet Freke, into believing that he is the victim of obeah, when she conjures a flaming figure in his bedroom that terrifies him, because 'he was sure she was one of the obeah-women of his own country, who had pursued him to Europe to revenge his having once, when he was a child, trampled upon an egg shell that contained some of her poisons' (B 221). In a parallel moment in the novel, Lady Delacour herself, under the malign influence of both laudanum and 'methodistical writings', is also fooled by Freke into believing that she sees a flaming figure in her garden. Here the evangelical Christianity of most West Indian missionaries is aligned with superstition and African religion, echoing official and conventional scepticism about the 'enthusiasm' and mystical nature of Methodism in particular, and evangelical Christianity in general, with its emphasis on the personal conversion experience. This alignment blurs the novel's distinction between home and abroad, just as Juba's marriage and settlement in England does. While Methodist and Baptist missionaries at this moment were the most outspoken proponents of the humanity of the Africans in the West Indies, and of the need for a humanitarian foreign policy to rectify the problems posed by the slave system in Britain's Caribbean colonies, Edgeworth here attempts to give the idea of humanity a decidedly more rational and orthodox cast.

Vincent's initial mirth at the foolishness of his servant's belief in witchcraft is quickly dispelled by his 'humanity' as a master: 'The extreme absurdity of this story made Mr Vincent burst out a laughing: but his humanity the next instant made him serious; for the poor victim of superstitious terror, after having revealed what, according to the belief of his country, it is death to mention, fell senseless to the ground' (B 221). Quickly, Vincent turns to Belinda for help, because 'he had observed, that she had listened with much attention and sympathy to the beginning of the poor fellow's story' (B 222). Belinda's sympathy, and her relentless rationality – which is what ensures her status as the novel's eponymous heroine, but which has tended from the moment of the novel's publication to diminish readers' interest in her part of the story – quickly unmask Freke's trick. Belinda's humanitarian intervention has to be pitched at the appropriate level for the African's primitive mind. Instead of simply explaining the trick (which will later work for Lady Delacour, and even set her on the path back to orthodox Anglicanism), Belinda seems compelled first to repeat it, undoing her role as the rational foil to Harriet Freke's unorthodox views on gender roles and the political organisation of society, and aligning Belinda precariously with the very cruelty of the slave system that the novel works so hard to cast as the epitome of social disorganisation: 'Miss Portman [i.e., Belinda] proposed that a figure should be drawn with phosphorus, as nearly as possible to resemble that which Juba had described, and that it should be shown to him at night, to try whether it would excite his apprehensions' (B 222). Confronted again with the flaming apparition, Juba

exhibited all the signs of extreme terror. Belinda then suggested that one of the children should show him the phosphorus, and should draw some ludicrous figure with it in his presence. This was done, and it had the effect that she expected. Juba, familiarized by degree with the object of his secret horror, and convinced that no obeah-woman was exercising over him her sorceries, recovered his health and spirits. (B 222)

While later Lady Delacour will be cured both of her belief in spirits, and of a festering breast wound, by the hyperrationalism of Belinda and the humane surgeon, Dr X, here there is no attempt to alter Juba's belief in obeah per se, but simply to demonstrate to him that in this case, in England, obeah cannot reach him. With the African, pedagogy proceeds first by 'extreme terror' and only afterwards by recovery, and even Juba's disabusal takes the form of a repetition of the earlier anxiety: his eventual familiarity 'with the object of his secret horror', as the narrator puts it.

Belinda must become, in other words, a kind of obeah woman herself in order to cure Juba of his fear of obeah.

While the education of the Percival children in the novel follows closely the pattern outlined in *Practical Education*, the famous treatise that Maria Edgeworth and her father Richard wrote in 1799, with its emphasis on rationality, on experiment, and on the initiative of the children themselves, Juba's education is dominated by sympathy, by humanity, and (as a corollary of these) by a sense of the limits of his capacity for initiative and self-fashioning and the necessity, therefore, to employ a certain kind of violence and even terror to bring about a humane transformation of consciousness. Juba, in other words, is almost exclusively a vehicle for the demonstration of humanity and sympathy on the part of the novel's principal characters. As Marcus Wood notes in his important book on the culture of British writing about slavery, 'In historical terms Atlantic slavery was consistently narrativised in relation to European and American capacities for empathetic displays.'[73] However, it is not simply the case that Juba is less than human: he is able to marry Lucy precisely because he demonstrates, as Lucy's grandmother puts it, that he is 'a most industrious, ingenious, good natured youth' (B 244), who constructs for Lucy's family a 'pretty cane chair' and a 'necklace of Angolan pease' for his fiancée (B 244), and who makes a 'banjore' (an African stringed instrument) as a gift for Belinda herself (B 258). Thus, in England, Juba proves his humanity by his ownership of his own labour power, fulfilling John Locke's principal criterion for the establishment of property rights, and thus for the distinction between humans and nature, subjects and objects: 'Whatsoever, then, he removes out of the state that nature hath provided and left it in, he hath mixed his labour with, and joined to it something that is his own, and thereby makes it his property.'[74]

It is crucial, therefore, that Juba is never called 'slave' in *Belinda*, but is always described as Vincent's 'servant'. The novel's humanitarian gesture is to go along with the popular understanding of Lord Mansfield's famous 1772 decision that in England a master cannot compel his slave to leave the country, a decision that came to be seen (misleadingly) as establishing the principle that chattel slavery could not exist within the realm of England.[75] But this apparently categorical distinction between 'home' and 'abroad', between England and the West Indies in this case, is undercut elsewhere in the novel by its fascination with the appearance of tropical objects – animate and inanimate – in England itself. Juba takes his place in a series that includes Lady Delacour's servant Marriot's macaw, Helena Delacour's goldfish, a miniature painting of Captain Sunderland, Virginia St Pierre's bullfinch and a handbill advertising its loss, Vincent's dog Juba (named after Juba the man) and a billet-doux contained in its collar, and the money that Vincent loses gambling that leads to the breaking off of his engagement to Belinda. In cataloguing these objects, *Belinda* borrows some of the elements of the Caribbean-based creole realism I discussed earlier in this chapter, but transforms them in the service of a new humanitarian realism.

In this respect, then, the novel functions as a version of the popular eighteenth-century 'it' narrative, or 'novel of circulation', novels and tales told from the perspective of inanimate objects such as hackney coaches, tubs, and black coats – and indeed volume two of *Belinda* opens with a footnote to perhaps the most famous 'it' narrative of all, Charles Johnstone's 1760 *Chrysal, or the Adventures of a Guinea* (B 164). In this context, it appears somewhat less surprising that Edgeworth's heroine takes her name from the poem that took the literary metamorphosis of objects to its mock epic apotheosis, Alexander Pope's *The Rape of the Lock*.[76] But as Jonathan Lamb comments, in his fine essay on metamorphosis and things in eighteenth- and early nineteenth-century narratives, the question of slavery transforms and unsettles the genre of 'it' narratives, since in the writings of former slaves 'the pen and the voice tell of an imperfect double metamorphosis – from human to chattel and chattel to human – that tests a quality belonging neither to a circulating commodity nor to a civil self'.[77] Now clearly *Belinda* is not a slave narrative, but the list of circulating objects in the novel above shows that Juba the 'servant' is part of a series of objects, mostly animals, that are likewise neither commodities nor civil selves. Although on the one hand Juba labours to turn objects in their natural state (Angolan pease, for instance) into circulating commodities or gifts, on the other hand he is all but indistinguishable functionally from, for example, the dog that is named after him (B 345).

As the novel tiptoes around the question of chattel slavery, it converts Juba quite literally into a 'thing'. As Vincent declares that his dog is the 'best creature in the world', Belinda 'smiles' at his vanity: '"No doubt... since he belongs to you; for you know, as Mr Percival tells you, every thing animate or inanimate that is under your protection, you think must be the best of its kind in the universe"' (B 345–6). But of course his 'servant' also belongs to Vincent, and when the master reiterates his belief in Juba's preeminence in the universe, Belinda playfully alludes to the secret horror of slavery by asking, '"Juba, the dog, or Juba, the man?... you know, they cannot be both the best creatures in the universe"' (B 346). Here the dog and man are categorically distinguished at the same moment as they are functionally aligned as pieces of property to be dealt with humanely ('every thing animate or inanimate that is under your protection'), and equally as signs of Vincent's inability to think rationally and logically – in 'the power and habit of reasoning... he was totally deficient' (B 218). This, then, is the flipside of Vincent's 'humanity', of his excess of sentiment. As Jonathan Lamb points out, it is only 'by means of the grossest delusion' that Vincent is able 'to make such sentimental equations between the lives of humans and animals',[78] as he does when he replies to Belinda's question 'Juba, the dog, or Juba, the man?' by replying '"Well! Juba, the man, is the best man – and Juba, the dog, is the best dog, in the universe"' (B 346). Lamb argues that Vincent's shoddy and sentimental thinking is 'meaningless', and indeed worse than that, since 'Mr Vincent is close enough to the hideous events that have fetched humans and animals to a common level of brutality... not to be allowed the refuge of stupidity.'[79] But the equation of humans and animals as 'things' is anything but meaningless in the world of the novel, and in the raging debates over slavery that preoccupied both ordinary folk and those in positions of cultural and political power in Britain and the West Indies at the turn of the nineteenth century. The novel cannot decide where to place Juba: with his canine namesake and the tropical and domestic birds that inhabit its version of London, or with the human residents of its social and moral world? Edgeworth tries to finesse this problem in the third edition by editing out Juba's marriage to Lucy, but thereby removes also the references to his industry and labour that are the foundation of his subjecthood in English society (these attributes are now transferred on to a new character, James Jackson, whose gift of a necklace to Lucy is no longer of Angolan pease).[80] Juba remains a crucial figure in driving the action of the story, however – as Edgeworth's narrator says in regard to the role of servants in the world of the upper classes, 'on these "coquettes of the *second* table", on these underplots in the drama, much of the comedy and some of the tragedy of life depend' (B 294; emphasis in the original). It is precisely 'life' that is reserved for the principal cast here, though.

In this respect, the novel departs little from most of the other British writing about slavery and the West Indies in the period leading up to emancipation. But *Belinda* is instructive in the extent to which it foregrounds the question of its principals' 'humanity' in relation to the animate and inanimate objects under their protection, at the very moment that Simon Taylor was complaining in his letters that the idea of humanity was being used against the planters like a weapon. Almost all of the main characters in the novel are described as exhibiting 'humanity', in the sense of the 'disposition to treat human beings and animals with consideration and compassion, and to relieve their distresses' (*Oxford English Dictionary* (*OED*) entry for 'humanity', 3b), or its correlate, 'humane', either by the anonymous narrator, or by their fellow principals. Thus Belinda (four times), Clarence Hervey (three times), Lord Delacour (three times), Lady Delacour (twice), Vincent (once), and Captain Sunderland (once) are all ascribed – or aspire to – 'humanity' in their dealings with the people and things in their environment. Unsurprisingly, none of the minor or socially inferior characters, such as Juba, Marriott, or Virginia, is described in these terms, since their role is to be the beneficiaries of humanity rather than its exemplars.

Is humanity to be found in the white creole, Mr Vincent? His goodhearted nature endears him to Belinda, but tips over into excessive sentimentality. He is the 'man of feeling' of late eighteenth-century fiction, but the novel makes clear that this version of humanity comes at the price of a loss or lack of 'reason', that essential quality of middle-class English subjectivity. Vincent continues, as an adult, to indulge his childhood passion for gambling, which he had learned in the Caribbean, in too close proximity to the enslaved people: 'His father used to see him [Vincent as a boy], day after day, playing with eagerness, at games of chance, with his negroes, or with the sons of neighbouring planters' (B 422). Proving once again that excessive intimacy between whites and blacks, masters and slaves was the prevailing view of Caribbean society from the other side of the Atlantic, Vincent abdicates his role as a possible match for Belinda: 'Thus persisting in his disdain of reason as a moral guide, Mr Vincent thought, acted, and suffered as a man of feeling' (B 424). Clearly, the inhabitants of the West Indies, both white and black, lack the essential criteria that would allow them to settle properly in England, Juba's marriage to Lucy notwithstanding. We might return, therefore, to the narrator's first description of Vincent's character, and note the striking absence of Juba from the list of things that he is said to love, even as he, like Simon Taylor, expresses a kind of Jamaican patriotism: 'He talked with fluent enthusiasm of the excellent qualities and beauties of whatever he loved, whether it were his dog, his horse, or his country' (B 218). On the one hand, the novel here registers a discomfort over its own discourse on slavery, by omitting any reference to Vincent's status as a slave owner; on the other hand, the novel registers the dubious nature of his humanity by marginalising his devoted 'servant' in this list of love objects and emphasising Vincent's tendency towards 'enthusiasm' over reason.

Is humanity then to be found in Clarence Hervey? Certainly he is introduced to the reader in these terms: he has a 'chameleon character', and 'could be all things to all men – and to all women', but equally, unlike Vincent, 'he was not profligate; he had a strong sense of honour, and quick feelings of humanity' (B 14). However, his humanity is certainly called into question in his most explicitly philanthropic project, his attempt to educate Virginia St Pierre as a Rousseauian 'natural' woman to be his eventual bride, completely outside the influence of the corrupting society in which Hervey himself fits so well. Needless to say, the scheme is a disaster, partly because of Virginia's natural inclination to ruin herself through indiscriminate reading of romance novels, but partly through Hervey's inability to supervise his ward effectively in her seclusion in Twickenham. (The novel borrows this scenario from the life of Thomas Day, the author of *The Dying Negro*, and a friend of the Edgeworths, who concocted a very similar plan in his infatuation with Rousseau, with similarly disastrous results.) And although Hervey is clearly destined from the start for Belinda by his intelligence, good looks, and his substantial wealth, and although, unlike the West Indian Vincent, he is crucially able to learn from his youthful mistakes and thus earn the right to the heroine's hand at the denouement of the novel, it should also be noted that the novel undercuts his English rationality by associating him, if only indirectly, with Harriet Freke's flaming 'obeah' figure. At a masked ball early in the novel, Hervey constructs an elaborate serpent costume for himself, but his role as Lady Delacour and Belinda's quasi-Satanic tempter is destroyed even before he gets to the party:

His grand difficulty had been to manufacture the rays that were to come from his eyes. He had contrived a set of phosphoric rays, which he was certain would charm all the fair daughters of Eve . . . [But] when he was just equipped as a serpent, his rays set fire to part of his *envelope*, and it was with the greatest difficulty that he was extricated. He escaped unhurt, but his serpent's skin was utterly consumed; nothing remained, but the melancholy spectacle of it's skeleton. (B 23)

Hervey's experiments with phosphorus harm only himself, unlike Freke's malign tricks, but the novel aligns the two characters uneasily, and links Hervey's failed performance as a serpent to Harriet Freke's parodic performance of West Indian 'witchcraft', just as they are linked more explicitly when Freke and Lady Delacour take their inspiration for the duel in which Lady Delacour receives her breast wound from a pamphlet of Hervey's on the 'propriety and necessity of female duelling' (B 59).

Although the novel that grew out of a sketch entitled 'Abroad and at Home' obviously plumps for the home-grown Hervey over the West Indian planter to resolve its main romantic drama, question marks remain about the Englishman's fitness for the role. And, intriguingly, in the final chapter, when Lady Delacour directs a spectacle in which she arranges the soon-to-be-married couples in appropriate poses of conjugal felicity, she suggests that before Hervey and Belinda's marriage can take place, the former needs to spend more time abroad, or at least at sea. The mysterious Captain Sunderland, who all but magically arrives on the scene in order to marry Virginia, has recently returned from Jamaica, and is once again, as Lady Delacour explains, "'under sailing orders, and he must be absent for some weeks, so that you [Virginia] will have time to become accustomed to the idea of a new lover, before his return. Clarence, I advise you to accompany captain Sunderland on this cruise; don't you, Belinda?'" (B 476–7). Belinda does not reply, but the novel ends with an odd twist, in which the male suitors' absence abroad, and probably even to the Caribbean, still the preeminent naval bases for English ships, is a necessary precondition for their happy settlement at home. Crucially, therefore, Hervey must travel with, and thereby learn from, Captain Sunderland, who has proved his worth not through the kind of misplaced humanitarian gesture that led Hervey to try to keep Virginia naturally pure, but through a much more muscular and immediate form of aid. As Virginia's father Mr Hartley explains, giving his unqualified consent to the marriage between Sunderland and his daughter, "'This gentleman [Sunderland] was stationed some years ago at Jamaica, and in a rebellion of the negroes on my plantation he saved my life. Fortune has accidentally thrown my benefactor in my way'" (B 476). Although Edgeworth once again resists the temptation to use the word 'slave', it is clear that Hervey, the man who earlier attempts to prove his humanity by providing the most moving recitation of *The Dying Negro*, must prove his fitness for the role of husband by aligning himself with the man about whom almost the only thing we know is that (presumably, given the British record of suppressing slave revolts) he has killed 'negroes' in the re-establishment of the plantation economy in the West Indies. The need to suppress black insurgency, then, turns out to be the flipside, or the condition of possibility, of humanitarian intervention in the world of *Belinda*. Ironically, the English hero must prove his fitness for the marriage plot, and his superiority over the white creole suitor, by becoming a traveller in the West Indies.

So, finally, is 'humanity' to be found in *Belinda*'s eponymous heroine herself, rather than in the military display of British masculinity? At first glance, it appears so. Belinda conjoins rationality and sympathy, leading Lady Delacour kindly and logically towards a reconciliation with her husband and daughter, and away from the foolish delights of flirtation, gossip, and society intrigue. As Kathryn Kirkpatrick argues in her introduction to the novel, Edgeworth thus demonstrates her sympathies with a certain kind of late eighteenth-century feminism, while inoculating herself against feminism's reputed excesses through the character of Harriet Freke: 'Edgeworth's emphasis on Belinda's developing rationality locates her novel in the tradition of Enlightenment feminism, which had long maintained that the education of women in the right use of reason produced the best wives and mothers.'[81] Juba, with the supposed benefits of primitive, pre-rational insight, shows an instant affinity for the kindness of Belinda (hence the gift of the banjore), and an equally immediate distaste for Freke: after meeting the latter for the first time, he 'with much simplicity, expressed [to Vincent] his aversion of the *man-woman* who lived in the house with them' (B 219). And Belinda's rational version of humanity – in marked contrast to Virginia's attachment to the protocols of romance – expresses itself clearly in her 'decidedly Whiggish'[82] choice of reading materials. Like the slightly later Fanny Price in *Mansfield Park*, another overly passive foster child who grows into the heroine's role, Belinda would hardly be caught dead reading novels themselves: when Freke bursts into Belinda's room in a misguided attempt to tempt her away from the rational delights of the Percival household, she discovers Belinda reading Adam Smith's *Theory of Moral Sentiments*, the travel writings of John Moore, and an 'Essay on the Inconsistency of Human Wishes' (B 228).[83] Clearly Belinda is alert to the possible contradictions and inconsistencies of 'humanity' and its wishes and desires, especially as a young, unmarried woman in an age in which female domesticity and rationality were in uneasy tension.

However, unlike Lady Delacour, Clarence Hervey, or even Vincent, and despite her edifying reading materials, Belinda *learns* little or nothing through the course of the novel, since she enters the story with her character all but fully formed. As Beth Kowaleski-Wallace argues, Belinda's 'very immunity to the charms of a social life surrounding her . . . precludes real moral growth or instruction for the heroine'.[84] In fact, as Heather MacFadyen has argued, 'readers have frequently found the eponymous heroine of the novel to be a tiresome distraction from the more appealing and irrepressibly witty woman of fashion, Lady Delacour'.[85] Ironically enough, then, the version of ideal humanity represented by Belinda herself tends to turn her back into a kind of inanimate object, the very opposite of human, bereft of 'life'. As Edgeworth herself worried, in a letter to an aunt in 1809 as she was preparing the third, much revised edition of the novel, 'I really was so provoked with the cold tameness of that stick or stone Belinda that I could have torn the pages to pieces – and really have not the heart or patience to correct her – as the hackney coachman said "Mend you! better make a new one".'[86] In a novel in which, as Andrew McCann argues, the 'characters are constantly assailed by fetishistic fashion and ritual objects that embody the non-modern insofar as they encourage forms of social life based on the suspension of rational individual choice',[87] the character who is supposed more than any other to embody rational individual choice – and thus humanity and subjectivity – is turned herself into a kind of object, denied ultimately even the choice to answer Lady Delacour's question about whether her future husband ought to sail to the Caribbean on the eve of their wedding or not.

In other words, the only characters whose humanity is not in doubt are the ones whose relatively minor role means that they need not exemplify the inconsistency of human wishes: Lord Delacour, who shows his humanity by rescuing Juba after his brawl with Baddely, and Captain Sunderland, who fortuitously is present at the same quarrel, and likewise demonstrates his 'humanity', as Lady Delacour later explains as she wraps up the tale (B 474), by interceding on Juba's behalf, and thus becomes available to resolve the romantic tangles of the novel. This, however, is a complicated moment in *Belinda*. On the one hand, Juba is the loyal servant, daring to fight the English only because he is right to defend his beloved master, and thus eligible for the humane intercession of the other upper-class Englishmen in the vicinity (Lord Delacour and Captain Sunderland). On the other hand, Juba here represents a submerged and displaced figure of black insurgency and slave rebellion transposed to English shores, and as such he must be converted immediately into the pathetic figure of the 'disabled negro' (B 474) and figuratively quashed by the humane Sunderland's later association with the suppression of the slave revolt on Mr Hartley's Jamaica plantation. 'Humanity', in other words, while it appears to offer the potential to resolve colonial, and even domestic, conflict, and to re-establish order on a more ethical plane, must of necessity ground itself in a practice of violence, just as English colonial rule in the West Indies always had since its inception in the seventeenth century.

In this equation, the 'stick or stone' Belinda herself is merely an object to be exchanged, her humanity recoded as a sign of appropriate feminine kindness that will stand her in good stead in her marriage to Clarence Hervey. As she was awaiting the publication of the first edition of *Belinda*, Edgeworth wrote to her sister Harriet in the spring of 1801, 'Pray give her ladyship [i.e., Lady Delacour] a better character than she deserves, and do not despise Belinda even if you should meet with her in a circulating library.'[88] But this conventional suspicion and devaluing of the novel form – conventional even, and perhaps especially, for female novelists of the period – is rendered in a somewhat different form when we notice where the scene of Juba's revolt and Lord Delacour's and Sunderland's humanity plays itself out. It is Lady Delacour who relates the event subsequently to Belinda: "'The baronet [Sir Philip Baddely] swore; the black [Juba] struggled; the baronet knocked him down. The great dog [Juba] . . . flew at your baronet, and would have eaten him up at three mouthfuls, if sir Philip had not made good his retreat to Dangerfield's circulating library'" (B 437). Belinda and Juba are figuratively joined for a moment in the circulating library, a place that – despite Edgeworth's remarks to her aunt – proves itself to be a site of heroic struggle, which Baddely profanes by engaging in inappropriate forms of reading there. When Juba, the man, pursues the baronet, "'Sir Philip was actually reading miss Luttridge's billet-doux aloud, when the black entered the library. He reclaimed his master's property, with great intrepidity; and a gentleman [i.e., Sunderland], who was present, took his part immediately'" (B 437–8). The library is the site where objects – books, amorous notes, and dogs – circulate, but it is also the site in which the 'black' transforms himself from object into subject, from chattel into an insurgent, potentially civil self who cannot quite be reincorporated back into the world of objects by upper-class 'humanity'. This representation of black insurgency is coded as an appropriate struggle, involving as it does the servant's loyalty and the master's 'property' (the dog? the billet-doux?), but the novel plays a dangerous game by putting a positive spin on what is in fact a slave revolt against the English ruling class, notwithstanding the fact that the representative of the latter is an especially disagreeable one.

The novel – *Belinda*, but also the novel in general – is a degraded form of object itself, the kind of thing one might 'despise' by its presence in a circulating library, but at the same time becomes itself the site for radical, even magical metamorphoses, turning circulating objects into subjects who might circulate themselves. A novel that is at pains to explain away in rational terms the magical world of 'obeah' comes itself to represent a version of non-modern metamorphosis, as its emphasis on the circulation and transformative power of non-commodified objects such as birds, dogs, and billets-doux testifies. So it is perhaps not surprising that the novel keeps returning to the 'quack balsam', anima of quassia, in which Graman Quacy's medical and sacred knowledge is both registered and appropriated. In the crucial scene of Juba's revolt against Baddely, when Lord Delacour and Sunderland rescue Juba from the circulating library and take him back to the Delacours' house across the street, it is for the West Indian herbal remedy that Lord Delacour cries out at the moment that he affirms his own humanity by caring for a suitably 'disabled' African. His wife tells Belinda the story:

'Now, lord Delacour, besides being a man of honour, is also a man of humanity... My lord was concerned to see the poor black writhing in pain... [and
carried Juba back to the Delacours' house]. Guess for what: to try upon the
strained ankle an infallible quack balsam recommended to him by the dowager
lady Boucher... "Mrs Marriott", cried my lord, "pray let us have lady Boucher's
infallible balsam – this instant!" Had you but seen the eagerness of face, or heard
the emphasis, with which he said, "*infallible* balsam", you must let me laugh at the
recollection.' (B 438)

But then the tale is left hanging, and we never find out whether Graman
Quacy's herbal remedy actually does cure the African writhing in pain.
The note of comedy, here insisted on by Lady Delacour – 'you must let
me laugh at the recollection' – allows the term 'quack' to go unexamined.
Nevertheless, Edgeworth's novel leaves open the possibility that Quacy's
'medical wood' does indeed cure Juba here, at a moment when the man
of science, Dr X, is unavailable. In the first edition of the novel, this
symbolically allowed African medicine to play a key role in support of
European 'humanity' in the proper placement of Juba as a slave converted to
modernity and potential citizenship in England itself, while the West Indies
nevertheless remains a site of unrest and violence, symbolically dominated
by the degraded figure of the white creole. Later editions, in denying Juba
his place in the English marriage plot, even of the subsidiary variety, seek
to enlarge the imaginary distance between 'home' and 'abroad', between a
humanitarian England and a violent West Indies, while at the same time
Quacy's Surinamese remedy joins Britain and its tropical colonies through
the healing power of African-Caribbean medicine.

WHITE TRAVELLERS AND BLACK DOCTORS IN JAMAICA

Eighteenth-century medical treatises about the Caribbean, written by white
doctors for a European audience, all show (even if they deplore the fact)
that most medical practice on the island was carried out by black men and
women whose medical expertise was inseparable from religious authority.
Thus Hans Sloane's 1707 natural history of Jamaica – the most influential eighteenth-century medical and botanical guide to the island and, by
extension, the Caribbean region as a whole – begins with an account of
black medical practice, which Sloane affects to scorn (it involves cupping
and lancing), but then goes on to use himself in his treatment of a black
woman suffering from some form of derangement: 'I had her Cupt and
Scarified in the Neck, [and] ordered her a very strong Purge... to be forced
down her Throat.'[89] The reliance of both white and black inhabitants on
African healing practices is suggested by the fact that, as Sloane says,

'at first, the Inhabitants would scarce trust me in the management of the least Distemper' until he had successfully shown how what he called the 'European method' – presumably to distinguish it from the African and creole methods of the Caribbean – worked with the family of Governor Albemarle.[90] Eventually, in an unremarked but nevertheless flagrant contradiction of his earlier claim that 'I have heard a great deal of their [blacks'] great Feats in curing several Diseases, but could never find them any way reasonable, nor successful in any', Sloane himself turns to an African medical practitioner – who must therefore also have been a figure of religious authority, despite the fact that Sloane thinks that Africans and Indians in the islands 'have no manner of Religion by what I could observe of them' – to treat his inflamed foot:

I had a *Negro*, famous for her ability in such cases, to look upon it, who told me it was a *Chego*. She (who had been a Queen in her own Country) open'd the Skin with a Pin above the swelling, and carefully separated the Tumour from the Skin, and then pull'd it out, putting into the Cavity whence it came, some Tobacco Ashes which were burnt in a Pipe she was smoking. After a very small smarting it was cured.[91]

A hundred years later, with the European method of medical practice better institutionalised in the West Indies, Matthew Lewis, author of the perennial bestseller *The Monk*, newly arrived in Jamaica to visit and manage the plantations he had inherited from his father, had to negotiate with his enslaved labourers over their medical treatment. A certain Bessie came to see him, suffering from leprosy, asking for a blanket and some medicine, and telling Lewis that although she had been seen by the white physician, Dr Goodwin, he

could do her no good. She wanted to go to a black doctor, named Ormond . . . I told her that if this black doctor understood her particular disease better than others, certainly she should go to him; but that if he pretended to cure her by charms and spells, or any thing but medicine, I should desire his master to cure the black doctor by giving him the punishment proper for such an impostor.

Bessie assures Lewis that Ormond 'was not an Obeah man', and the English planter, keen to demonstrate his benevolent management of the enslaved population of his plantations, agrees to let her pay Ormond a visit.[92] However, well into the nineteenth century the distinction between 'medicine' and 'charms and spells' was not hard and fast in the Caribbean. To some extent, clearly, the 'black doctor' figure by the time of Lewis's journal has lost some of his religious authority, just as herbalists, diviners, and other religio-medical figures in the enslaved populations of the Caribbean had to reinvent their roles in a community torn from its indigenous cosmologies in West and Central Africa. But in shifting towards the medical register, rather than the magical or religious one, he or she tended to infiltrate the presumed European realm of science and medicine itself.

Travelling in the Caribbean troubled the boundaries between scientific medicine and superstitious magic. For instance, the English physician Benjamin Moseley's fourth edition of his *Treatise on Tropical Diseases*, which is largely based on his experiences as a military doctor in Jamaica in the 1770s and 80s, adds a long excursus on the influence of the moon on human illness. For instance,

in 1780, all the soldiers in the military hospitals in Jamaica, under my care, in dysenteries and intermittents, almost constantly relapsed at the lunar syzygies; and at *Up-Park* [the principal barracks in Kingston], in November, several people died suddenly, in convulsions, that were seized at the new and full moon, with the pestilential fever, then making dreadful havoc in the camp. Most of the men attacked at these periods, who escaped death, lost their memory for a considerable time. – They forgot their names, and the regiments to which they belonged.[93]

This imperial forgetting, this temporary suspension of the new order of administrative rationality, is carefully catalogued and described by the modern man of science, but his conclusion is itself a suspension of the empirical language of his treatise and an imaginative return to the wisdom of simple and ancient folk, who are invariably those who live by the cycles of the moon: 'The operations of nature are anterior to books; and the best books, on natural things, are but the maxims of planters, and cultivators of the earth; breeders of cattle; herdsmen, and shepherds; fishermen, and mariners: – with whom the moon has ever been an object of great consideration.'[94] If the best thinking about 'natural things' is that of the 'cultivators of the earth', then the gentleman of science must reverse – albeit temporarily – the social hierarchy of Jamaica and seek to follow the maxims of the slaves themselves, whom he now slyly calls 'planters'. In other words, the travelling English doctor discovers that black doctors are the true creoles in the Caribbean.

By this logic, and despite an earlier dismissive reference to the ignorance of Caribbean slaves on religious matters – 'making a sacred compact was above the capacity of their minds, fettered with the superstitious chains of spells, sorcery, and incantations'[95] – Moseley ends by endorsing the lunar wisdom of the Spartans, Romans, Hebrews, and their contemporary avatars, 'savage African negroes, who have no idea of infringing on the state of nature . . . [and who] have their dances, noises, and religious honours, and invocations to the moon, whole nights in the open fields, at her full'.[96] These are, then, the same 'dances' that John Venn's sensible, well-inclined African chose not to give up. The lessons learned inside the imperial confines of Up-Park Camp are in fact those given by the Africans and African Jamaicans who worship and work in 'open fields' and constitute a contemporary, if oblique, link both to an imagined European past of Greece and Rome and to the 'state of nature'. The Jamaican authorities put a great deal of energy into restricting African movement off the plantations, especially at night, when, as W. Stanford, rector of Westmoreland, observed, slaves were devoting considerable time and energy to 'the rites observed at heathenish funerals, their walking several miles to and from them, their singing, dancing and drinking at them, and all this in the open air, for many hours in the night in an unwholesome tropical climate, and from thence directly proceeding in most instances to the labours of the day in the field'.[97] The power of these gatherings as a threat to the plantation order is clear; Moseley takes that power and turns it into a kind of folk wisdom that both romantically validates it and coopts it for the new science of empire.

CREOLE REALISTS II: EDWARD BANCROFT
AND THOMAS HIGSON

These European medical travellers, who all found creole black doctors at the heart of Jamaican society, were answered in the 1810s and 1820s by a fledgling creole white medical and scientific establishment that had developed in Jamaica in the period before emancipation. For example, one of Benjamin Moseley's successors as army doctor in Kingston was Edward Nathaniel Bancroft, who, unlike Moseley, stayed in the island, becoming president of the Jamaican horticultural and agricultural society and deputy inspector-general of army hospitals; he lived in Kingston until his death in 1842.[98] In 1829, he delivered a paper to the Jamaican Society for the Encouragement of Horticulture and Agriculture, in which he denounced and corrected the errors of all medical and scientific visitors to Jamaica on the subject of the hog-gum tree, and its product, a botanical remedy known in Jamaica as hog-gum, in Haiti as *bois à cochon* (hog-wood), and in South America as *mawna*.[99] Bancroft painstakingly catalogued – in exemplary empiricist fashion – the failure of successive European gentleman scientists to correct the original mistake in identification made by none other than Hans Sloane himself in his natural history of Jamaica: 'That Sir Hans Sloane was entirely misled on the subject is clear from his account of the tree which he believed to yield the gum in question', which is accompanied,

Bancroft argues, by a picture of the wrong tree.[100] He thereby positioned himself and the man who provided much of the research for his paper, Thomas Higson, a white Jamaican merchant and the curator in the 1820s of the botanical gardens in Bath in the parish of St Thomas-in-the-East, as the natural successors to the medical and botanical authorities he cites: creole editors and scientists correcting and augmenting the metropolitan knowledge represented by Hans Sloane and the other English travellers.

However, both metropolitan and internal challenges to creole realism were stronger by the late 1820s than they had been in the time of John Venn and Simon Taylor. When Bancroft's paper was finally published, thirteen years later, after an unexplained editorial delay, in the prestigious *Journal of Botany*, the editors in London reclaimed the British capital as the centre of scientific inquiry by announcing in the headnote to the paper that they had silently corrected an error made by the scientist of the periphery: 'We omit the discussion relative to the genus of the plant, because it is quite clear that it is the *Monobea coccinea* of Aublet, which has been lately so admirably illustrated by Martius, in his *Nov. Gen. et Sp. Pl. Brasil,* or a very nearly allied species. – ED.'[101] Likewise, the internal challenges to creole realism are also strong; like the gentleman travellers before him, Bancroft finds black Jamaican doctors at the heart of tropical medicine:

That such a series of errors concerning one and the same tree should have been committed both here and in St. Domingo, by individuals certainly possessed of superior attainments, may appear very strange; yet the occurrence, as I conceive, admits of easy explanation. As the *Hog-Gum* was always in demand, the Maroon Negroes, by whom alone it was collected, made a mystery of it, that they might keep the monopoly to themselves, and purposely deceived those who asked for information, by pointing out to them some other than the real tree.[102]

By a circuitous route, the white creole scientist has ended up back in the realm of Caribbean romance, with a 'mystery' that cannot be easily solved, even by those whites with detailed local knowledge. As confirmation of his claim about the Maroons, Bancroft cites a conversation with a Dr Arnold of Port Antonio, on the northeast coast of the island, who 'had repeatedly endeavoured by promises and otherwise, to prevail on Maroons to show him the tree, but had always been misled by them, so that up to that time he had never seen it'.[103]

Nevertheless, Bancroft tries to ward off the possibility that Caribbean science will turn into the metropole's favoured genres of Caribbean writing, the adventure tale and imperial romance: he passes blithely over the fact that he has reconstructed Higson's botanical research after many of the papers were damaged by the seawater when Higson 'was shipwrecked in the Bay of Buenaventura'.[104] We see this same attempt to avoid romance in an article entitled 'Account of an Ascent to the Summit of the Blue Mountains of Jamaica', reporting the adventurous climb to the top of the highlands of Jamaica by 'three gentlemen from this city [Kingston]' that appeared in an early number of *Blackwood's Edinburgh Magazine* (which had rapidly established itself as the conservative house journal of a certain kind of transperipheral imperial culture).[105] There the adventure of mountain climbing had to be conveyed only by hints and gentlemanly understatement, just as Edward Bancroft played down Thomas Higson's shipwreck and rescue in the interests of securing an accurate botanical description of the hog-gum tree. On the way to the summit in the *Blackwood's* piece, the legendary Jamaican outlaw bandit and obeah-inspired rebel Three-Fingered Jack puts in a fleeting appearance, only to be defeated not by brave Maroons but by the calculated indifference of geography and botanical science; creole realism once more:

Next morning, accompanied by a fourth person, the necessary means, supplies, &c. proceeded N.E. having Wild Cane-River on the left, and Morgan's on the right, with a view of the spot where Three-Fingered Jack was killed, up a steep and narrow ridge, well wooded with the Santa Maria (*Calophyllum Calaba*), the Beefwood (*Achras Xylobocion*), Rod Wood (*Loetia Guidonia*), Guava Mountain (*Psidium Montanum*), Mammee-Apple (*Mammea Americana*), Naseberry Bully-Tree (*Achras Mamosa*), Red Bully-Tree (*Achras Anona*), White ditto, or Galimeta Wood (*Achras Salicifolia*), varieties of Bastard Figs (*Ficus Americana*), ditto of Cane Peppers (*Piper longum*), and gigantic Juniper Cedars (*Juniperus Bermudiensis*), some dead from age, but from its incorruptible wood, standing in despite of storms, &c. & c.[106]

There is an almost heroic refusal of the genre of the adventure tale in this aptly named 'account', where the logic of the etcetera and the calculations of the thermometer and barometer – 'thermometer here was 60°, barometer 24. 60, elevation 5682 feet' – compete for attention with fleeting glimpses of the mountainous sublime – 'the laborious steep was surmounted, when the grandeur and sublimity of the view amply repaid the toil, though, from the constant passing of the mist, generally the case in Alpine regions, it was partially restricted'.[107] As with Bancroft's account of the hog-gum tree, there is painstaking attention paid to the accounts and names of the white gentlemen who have gone before (and erasure of the Jamaican slaves whose labour as guides, porters, and valets undoubtedly made the trip possible in the first place): 'Sowed several seeds assimilated to a cold clime; placed a journal of proceedings so far in a bottle, with copies of four other journals found there, the originals being too far injured to be intelligible much longer, viz. by Messrs Delprat, Hering, and Campbell, in 1802; E. H. Adams and Charles Macneal, 21ˢᵗ March 1807', and several others named here, 'which bottle was sealed up, and placed conspicuously under an African yew-tree (*Taxus elongata*), on which had been cut several initials, and they added WC and TH'.[108] Later *Blackwood's* tales of the West Indies, most obviously in the extraordinary success of Michael Scott's nautical romance, *Tom Cringle's Log*, played up the Caribbean as a theatre of adventure and comic foibles. Here, however, decorously hidden behind the gentlemanly initials carved schoolboy-fashion in an exotic tree, the Jamaican ruling class preferred to deploy the language of utility and the certainties of numbers and scientific classification, hoping that some readers would be able to enjoy 'the pleasure of more minutely exploring the Alpine forest lands of St George's, Portland, and St Thomas's in the east, of which there appeared some thousands of acres comparatively level and capable of cultivation'.[109] The ascent to the summit offers the prospect of an escape from the lowland world of slavery into the imaginary, higher realm of 'Alpine' travel: 'After about one mile had been passed, not a mark or vestige of human footsteps having ever trod there before could be traced.'[110] However, the messy business of African labour, enslaved and free, cannot be evaded. That is precisely what botanical science is *for* in Jamaica in the early nineteenth century: nowhere is it clearer than in the colonial society that science and commerce go hand in hand, and that is what it means to gaze out from the top of a mountain and see 'evanescent views of shipping, conjectured to be at Falmouth, being in a direction N. W.' and thousands of acres of land 'comparatively level and capable of cultivation'.[111] Likewise, Edward Bancroft and Thomas Higson adduced their botanical knowledge for the Society for the Encouragement of Horticulture and Agriculture, and found the eastern Jamaican Maroons at the root of the mistake over the hog-gum tree.

The connection between these two articles, one in the learned scientific journal and one in the popular but edifying magazine, is more than aleatory, moreover. Almost certainly, the 'TH' (and elsewhere in the piece 'THn') who carved his initials into the Blue Mountain tree is indeed the merchant and island botanist Thomas Higson; judging by the amount of space taken up with botanical descriptions in the *Blackwood's* article, Higson was likely also the author. The opening paragraph of the article describes the three gentlemen of Kingston arriving at a Mr Francis's estate in the foothills of the Blue Mountains 'by way of the Botanic Garden, Hagley Gap, and Duckworth' respectively; later in the 1820s, Higson was the chief botanist and curator of the Jamaican botanic gardens at Bath, one of the oldest in the empire, and the second oldest in the western hemisphere.[112] Higson was not just a scientist and gardens manager, but also a planter and slave owner: the *Jamaica Almanac* of 1816 lists him as the owner of Montpelier estate in the parish of St Andrew, in the hills above Kingston, where fifty enslaved Jamaicans lived and worked.[113] In 1834, towards the end of his life, he was still anxious to stick to the discourse of scientific realism as he wrote in a Jamaican medical journal about an indigenous South American cure for snake bites that he had observed in the 1820s and thought might be useful in Jamaica. Just as he hoped that the accumulation of meteorological and botanical data might overwhelm the romantic sublime – and the figure of Three-Fingered Jack – in the Blue Mountain climb, this time Higson accumulates numerous observations of the efficacy of the guaco plant as an antidote to snake venom, as administered by the local 'snake doctors, or as they are called, curandoes': 'I have been thus particular in hopes it may be the means of dispelling some of the scepticism that is so apt to accompany detail, savouring of the marvellous; but on the continent south of us, thousands can vouch for the virtues of a plant, placed by providence where it is most necessary.'[114] It is a curious moment, as the regional scientist claims the mantle of calculation to be the result of telling marvellous stories about indigenous healers sucking snake venom out of girls' heels.

In 1820–1, as opposition to slavery and to the planters intensified, at least one traveller had sought to rehabilitate the white creoles of Jamaica from their associations with cruelty, depravity, and the tropical marvellous, and Thomas Higson was one of the beneficiaries. The English artist and architectural draughtsman James Hakewill, who had established his reputation with his 1820 collection, *A Picturesque Tour of Italy*, visited Jamaica and returned with many drawings of pleasant estates, with happy slaves tilling the fields: one of the plantations he visited was that of Thomas Higson, called Windsor Farm by Hakewill. The illustration in figure 1.2 almost certainly depicts Higson and his wife, looking down from their bucolic estate on to the commercial and military hub of the British West Indies at the time: the plate is entitled 'Kingston and Port Royal, from Windsor Farm', taken from Hakewill's *Picturesque Tour of the Island of Jamaica*.[115] Hakewill's plates are striking for the ways in which they join European classicism and tropical colour, so that the well-ordered estates of the generous, benevolent planters whose hospitality he enjoyed could be easily associated in the metropolitan viewer's eye with the more familiar estates of England, with the odd palm tree added here and there, and black rustics rather than

Figure 1.2 'Kingston and Port Royal from Windsor Farm', by James Hakewill, from Hakewill, *A Picturesque Tour of the Island of Jamaica* (1825)

white ones.[116] Higson – obviously a minor member of the creole elite in Jamaica – looks down from a position of domestic harmony on to the whole power of the empire in the harbour below: an economic and naval power that was increasingly seen by Jamaican whites as threatening their culture rather than maintaining it, but which here is figured as a harmonious link to the agricultural life of a Jamaican plantation called a 'farm' in defiance of the local terminology that favoured 'estate', 'plantation', and 'pen'. It was, in a way, the last hurrah of a class under threat.

THE ST THOMAS-IN-THE-EAST BRANCH ASSOCIATION OF THE INCORPORATED SOCIETY FOR THE CONVERSION AND RELIGIOUS INSTRUCTION AND EDUCATION OF THE NEGRO SLAVES IN THE BRITISH WEST INDIA ISLANDS

In the preface to his book, Hakewill makes clear that his views of a kind of anglicised Jamaica are the product in part of his opposition to the abolitionist movement gathering strength again at that moment in Britain: to make the planters appear more sympathetic, he makes them and their estates look more English. Nevertheless, the figure of the black doctor appears once more. Travelling in eastern Jamaica at Christmas, Hakewill meets

a negro driving a mule heavily laden; the man was head cattle-man on Batchelor's Hall Penn, belonging to A. Arcedekne, Esq., an appendage to his fine estate of Golden Grove. He had been at Morant Bay for his Christmas stock, and had purchased a cask of wine, a ham, and many other luxuries, which with his poultry of every description, of which he had abundance, and the estate allowance of fresh beef, would enable him to keep open house for three days for all his acquaintance. This man being an expert cattle doctor, had frequently leave of absence; and at his return, after the lapse of a fortnight, would bring home a very considerable sum of money.[117]

This figure of the entrepreneurial slave cropped up with increasing regularity in the dying days of the slave regime in Jamaica, and more often than not he or she was associated with Simon Taylor, the former manager of Bachelor's Hall and Golden Grove, now reimagined as the embodiment of planter benevolence and reasonableness. However, we might read these figures of black self-fashioning as embellished versions of a real group emerging from the ashes of slavery: the Jamaican small settlers and Christian converts who would play an increasingly important role in island life, as I show in more detail in chapter 3 below.

For example, in an influential story, Alexander Barclay, a Jamaican planter and fierce opponent of emancipation, described a group of coconut palm trees that were planted for ornamental purposes by Taylor on Holland estate, but which over time were claimed as a source of food by slaves on the plantation, 'who soon considered, not only the fruit, but the trees as their own property'. Wishing eventually to cut down the trees, Taylor benevolently refused to do so unless compensation was paid to each person who claimed ownership of a tree: 'Thus Mr. Taylor paid to his own labourers £1. 6s. 8d. for each cocoa-nut tree cut in his own garden.' His reasoning in this matter, as reported to his overseer, Mr Hunter, was that, 'They [the African Jamaicans] have long claimed these trees as their own, and that claim I never shall dispute with them.'[118] That benevolence could of course signify that Taylor had no choice but to negotiate with the enslaved workers on his estate who had established their own small-scale economic interests in the coconuts they had tended and harvested for years. In 1829, Benjamin Greene in his exchange of letters with Thomas Clarkson on the subject of slavery, reported the existence of a slave on Simon Taylor's Holland estate who 'has no less than £70 in the hands of his Master, and is himself the Owner of several Slaves', but who would not sell one of his own slaves to his master in order to obtain his own freedom because 'it would ill become him to leave the house and ground, which he held rent-free of his Master, and to lose the Negro who cultivated his land'. This example – along with the claim that the 600 slaves at Holland possessed 'property to the amount of £10,000 in asses, pigs, poultry, and furniture' – demonstrated to Greene's satisfaction that 'the Planters, notwithstanding the malicious insinuations which have been propagated at their expense, are capable of exercising towards their Slaves a high degree of kindness and benevolence.'[119] In the light of what has come before, we might instead read this 'kindness and benevolence' as a sign of the collapse of the planter elite and the beginning of the transfer of its bookkeeping practices and creole realism to the people who were still items on slave registers, but who would not be for much longer.

I began this chapter with John Venn's account of the white Jamaican practice of burning the bodies of enslaved suicide victims, and of the failure of eighteenth-century conversion schemes in the Caribbean in the face of African religious organisation. I end this chapter by moving into the period when widespread conversions of black Jamaicans to Christianity did take place: the period after the death of Simon Taylor, the period when philanthropy and humanity took centre stage in the Caribbean. While missionary work clearly involved its own forms of objectification of the enslaved, I want to argue here that it also opened up a space for the enslaved to assert their own rights and privileges. In the nineteenth century, 'philanthropy' became for the enlightened English the way in which to demonstrate a proper, non-magical relation to objects, including people-as-objects and animals-as-objects. However, as *Belinda* demonstrates, philanthropy – the performance of 'humanity' – carries its own dangers for its practitioners. The supposed beneficiary Virginia fails to become the dutiful wife of Clarence Hervey and indeed threatens the central romance of the novel between Clarence and Belinda. And at one point, the wise Dr X is compelled to rush away to Cambridge to treat an old friend, Mr Horton, 'a gentleman of great talents, and of the most active benevolence, who had just been seized with a violent fever, in consequence of his exertions in saving the poor inhabitants of a village in his neighbourhood from the effects of a dreadful fire, which broke out in the middle of the night' (B 136). Horton is the counterpart, foil, and friend of Virginia's father, Mr Hartley, the Jamaican plantation owner. This English fire, therefore, is the plot double of the insurrection of 'negroes' in Jamaica that Captain Sunderland has to extinguish. Demonstrating the proper, non-magical relationship to objects is a dangerous business, as Harriet Freke, Clarence Hervey, and

Mr Vincent all find as well as Horton, Sunderland, and Hartley. Philanthropy, in other words, can get you burned. If mid-eighteenth-century
Jamaica allowed clergymen to take for granted the propriety of violating
African faith by setting fire to the bodies of the enslaved, early nineteenth-
century Jamaica began to be a place where the enslaved people forced clergymen and others to question their own assumptions and change their own
institutions.[120]

Once objects begin to circulate themselves, whether in metropolitan
circulating libraries or in colonial churches, new transformations of the
imperial field begin to take place. If Simon Taylor worried about uprisings
of 'the negroes' while still treating them as non-individuated objects, in
the 1810s and 1820s these same black Jamaicans began to find a place for
themselves within circumatlantic, imperial institutions, which they thereby
began to transform. In the following chapter, I analyse the relationship
among conversion, insurgency, and romance in the Caribbean in the 1820s;
to conclude this chapter, I want to look briefly at conversion that led
not to insurgency – as most white West Indian commentators, including
Taylor, predicted it would – but to respectability. When I say that this
process involved the very same black Jamaicans whom Taylor described
as an uncivilised mass, I mean this quite literally, and I hope to join the
private correspondence of Taylor to the public documents of 1820s British
philanthropy to show this.

In the list of 'bought slaves' (as opposed to 'original' slaves) in 1792 at
Bachelor's Hall in St Thomas-in-the-East – one of Chalenor Arcedeckne's
estates managed by Simon Taylor – number 13 is Sarah, a field worker. We
cannot tell for sure if she was purchased by Taylor directly from a slave
ship or from another plantation. We know that she had a son, Guy, born
in 1789; needless to say, Guy's father is not named. Guy, aged three, is slave
number 51.[121] We next meet Sarah in the archives in 1820, after she has survived almost thirty years in the fields, and now she has two more surviving
children: Celia, born in 1804, and Eve, born in 1809, twenty years after the
birth of her first son.[122] After the passage of James Stephen's registration
bill, however, and after the abolition of the slave trade and the arrival of
evangelical missionaries in Jamaica and the other Caribbean colonies, the
way slaves are listed has changed by 1820. Now the enslaved are described
first by 'original' name, then by Christian name, where applicable, followed
by occupation and general state of health, as mandated by Stephen's bill.
Bookkeeping and 'humanity' have joined forces here, and even the lists
of the enslaved whose privacy Simon Taylor had fiercely defended against
Governor Balcarres had to follow the public protocols of humanitarianism.

We learn, therefore, that 'Sarah' has taken the name Mary Lindsay, and that she is 'healthy' despite still being a 'field' slave; her son Guy has become Robert Johnson, and he is a healthy carpenter.[123] By 1823, the category 'original name' has disappeared. Number 2 on the 'List of Slaves Belonging to Bachelors Hall Pen, 1st January 1823' is Mary Lindsay; she remains 'healthy', but she has finally, in late middle age, been promoted to a supervisory position, and a relatively unusual one for women on Jamaican plantations, since her occupation is now given as 'driveress'.[124]

I give this schematic account of Sarah/Mary Lindsay's long march up the hierarchy of a Jamaican plantation because I want to raise the possibility that there is another, public document of the 1820s in which she also appears: the list of donors and subscribers to the newly formed St Thomas-in-the-East branch association of the London-based Incorporated Society for the Conversion and Religious Instruction and Education of the Negro Slaves in the British West India Islands. In the 1826 report of this organisation, whose president was the bishop of London, and whose governors included not only William Huskisson (president of the Board of Trade) but also George Hibbert, Simon Taylor's erstwhile correspondent and agent for Jamaica in London, there are two lists of subscribers to the eastern Jamaican branch newly formed in that year. Whites are listed first, followed by 'Persons of Colour'. In this second list, presented in the respectability of alphabetical order by surname, between Rose Ledwick and Helen Lindsay, we find the name: 'Lindsay, Miss Mary'.[125] Instead of a number appearing before her name to mark her enslaved status, a number appears after her name to vouch for her faith, for her industry, and for her commitment to helping others: she gave 13s 4d to the cause of conversion and religious education. At this distance, it is impossible to tell if these Mary Lindsays are in fact the same person. It is perhaps unlikely: field slaves like Sarah/Mary were more likely at this time to have been captured in Africa and transported to Jamaica; 'persons of colour', as the list of subscribers had it, was a term for those of mixed racial descent. However, conversion and respectability could sometimes trump racial designations, and we know that Sarah had converted to Christianity and had risen to the status of 'driveress' at Bachelor's Hall. We know from James Hakewill's story of the prosperous cattle-doctoring slave he met returning from Morant Bay (even taking the visiting artist's probable embellishment of the story into account) that some slaves did earn significant status and money in the community; and in fact the unnamed man Hakewill met on the road was returning to the very estate where Sarah/Mary Lindsay lived and worked, Bachelor's Hall.[126] The distance from Bachelor's Hall to the regional centre of Morant Bay was about ten miles; Sarah/Mary perhaps travelled there to take part in the congregation of Rev. John M. Trew, an Anglican minister who was the driving force behind the creation of the St Thomas-in-the-East branch of the conversion society, and who wrote to the parent organisation in London to announce its formation at a meeting held in the Morant Bay courthouse on 10 January 1826.[127] This was the same building that would later be stormed and burned by the rebels in the uprising of 1865 that I discuss in chapters 3 and 4 below.

Mary Lindsay, perhaps present at this inaugural meeting, shows up in the historical record as little more than a name: she functions here as a type, a character, and a flat one at that. I mobilise her for a sense of the complexity of the cultural politics of slavery in its final stages, and of the British empire as it reconstituted itself as a kind of civilising mission in the nineteenth century. To think about Mary Lindsay is to recognise that this process was not simply unidirectional, the imposition of a veneer of 'humanity' on the continuing oppressions of empire. I want to argue that it was mandated from the margins also, forced on London humanitarians by the actions of ordinary folk in, say, eastern Jamaican estates and chapels. In other words, borrowing both from the metropolitan institution of humanitarian imperialism and from the white Jamaican registers of respectability and realism, Mary Lindsay is the embodiment of creolisation at work in pre-emancipation Jamaica.

This is not the only way to understand her place in history, of course. Someone like Mary Lindsay could be, and indeed was, used by the representatives of the soon-to-be superseded old empire as a sign that all was well in the West Indies. Alexander Barclay deploys the figure of the respectable churchgoing slave in just this way:

In the parish of St. Thomas in the East . . . I affirm from the evidence of my own eyesight, that the congregations in the several places of worship, of which there are six, consisting principally of slaves, would bear comparison, in point of dress and orderly deportment, with the generality of country congregations in Britain . . . In the little village of Bath . . . the number of their horses, which during divine service are tied up under the shade of the trees in the street, never fails to attract the attention of strangers.[128]

And, indeed, a significant portion of the operating expenses of the Caribbean slave conversion society was provided by the organised West India interest in London: the 1826 report lists a donation of £1,000 from the West India Committee of Planters and Merchants, the Liverpool and Glasgow branches gave £100 each, and subscriptions were also received from such prominent Jamaica planters as Sir Simon Houghton Clarke and James MacQueen, both of whom were authors of proslavery pamphlets during this period.[129] Such contributions dwarfed the £5 donation of William Wilberforce, and even the £31 10s of the duke of Gloucester, president of the newly formed Anti-Slavery Society (officially the Society for the Mitigation and Gradual Abolition of Slavery throughout the British Dominions), and suggest that the conversion society was little more than an alibi for the perpetuation of slavery and an antidote by the established church to the missionary zeal of the dissenting evangelicals (about whom more than one Anglican minister and missionary complained bitterly in letters home to London).[130] The widespread support for the St Thomas-in-the-East branch association from local planters, attorneys, and estate managers – such as Thomas M'Cornock, Simon Taylor's replacement as manager of Golden Grove and Bachelor's Hall, who was on the steering committee of the St Thomas conversion association – should be read alongside the declaration of resistance to British meddling in Jamaican affairs made by the freeholders of St Thomas-in-the-East on 29 September 1823, as reported in John R. Grosett's *Remarks on West India Affairs*:

It was unanimously resolved. That at the present alarming crisis, when measures are in progress in the British Parliament, avowedly to despoil us of all we hold dear and valuable, our rights – our liberty – our property – our existence; we feel it our painful but imperious duty to come forward and most solemnly declare to the world, our determination to resist, by every legitimate means in our power, such flagrant injustice.[131]

Given the history of the Jamaican authorities highlighting their ostensibly humanitarian reforms while at the same time perpetuating the slave system, it is perhaps not surprising to see the St Thomas-in-the-East association given a prominent place in the parish civil list in the official island almanac for 1827, just after the list of magistrates, vestry members, and Anglican clergymen.[132]

I would argue, however, that this does not mean that Mary Lindsay, and the other ordinary contributors to the local conversion association, can simply be written off as dupes of the planters or imperialist collaborators. People like Lindsay can be seen as taking advantage of the circumatlantic routes of empire by affiliating themselves with an organisation based in London, potentially bypassing or contesting the hegemony of the planters whose stolid defence of local political privileges was both self-serving and ultimately self-defeating. Here the two challenges to creole realism meet: the humanitarian realism of the metropole can be accessed directly by the black creoles of Jamaica who can see that they, not figures like Simon Taylor and J. R. Grosett, represent the future of the island. Mary Lindsay represents the future eclipse of the white creole establishment whose slow disintegration I have catalogued in this chapter.

What Mary Lindsay and her fellow converts began to do by their affiliation with transatlantic networks is lay the groundwork for a specifically Jamaican set of institutions, the post-emancipation churches. While donations to the St Thomas-in-the-East regional association were surprisingly strong, money was harder to come by in London, despite – or perhaps because of – the donation from the West India Committee. Noting the rise of branches in Jamaica, St Kitts, Antigua, and Grenada, the preamble to the 1826 report of the parent society in London expressed disappointment with the response in Britain: 'The governors would have been happy to state that the increase of Subscriptions at home had corresponded [to the success of the Caribbean societies]. Applications have been generally made, but with very limited success.'[133] In the list of subscribers for 1831, against the name of William Wilberforce is the notation 'refused'.[134] Meanwhile Rev. Trew was reporting from eastern Jamaica that £350 in contributions had been used to employ three catechists, at a salary of £140 a year, to teach enslaved children: '34 Estates are now open to the labours of the association.' Trew went on, 'I am sure the governors will be glad to learn that the Gentlemen of my parish with a liberality truly praiseworthy on those Estates where Instruction has yet been afforded, are perfectly satisfied that respectable persons of colour should be selected for this office.'[135] Braving the condescension of the rump planter class congratulating themselves for their benevolence in allowing the word 'respectable' to qualify the type 'persons of colour', these teachers went about their work. Eugene Kesler was the catechist at Simon Taylor's former estate of Lyssons, where fifty-nine children had been catechised by the end of 1826, within sight of the graves of the brothers John and Simon Taylor, who were buried on the estate; in the Plantain Garden River district of the parish, James Duany reported catechising fifty children at Holland, one hundred at Golden Grove, and twenty-one at Bachelor's Hall, perhaps including Mary Lindsay's own children Celia and Eve.[136]

Times had changed in eastern Jamaica in the decade since Simon Taylor's death. Where his hundreds of letters contain almost nothing about Christianity in general, and nothing but contempt for the idea of converting the enslaved, now Mary Lindsay and her brethren are on the rise in the district, even before their emancipation. William Lloyd, in his *Letters from the West Indies* written during the apprenticeship period, describes a visit to

Golden Grove, the sister estate of Bachelor's Hall, now managed by Thomas M'Cornock, where he found a school house and a chapel under the care of 'a pleasing young man sent out by the Church Missionary Society . . . Such was the interest evinced by the slaves for religion, that they subscribed twenty pounds to buy a communion service cup'; Frank Cundall notes that the chalice was preserved in the Kingston offices of the Church of England and was inscribed, 'Purchased for Golden Grove Chapel by the slaves of the estate, 1830.'[137] The bookkeeping practices of the plantocracy, which had underwritten the horrors of slavery and provided the basis for its justification in the genre of creole realism, had been appropriated and taken over by the descendants of the 'sensible, well-inclin'd' African who had declined John Venn's offer of conversion in the mid-eighteenth century. In the period immediately before emancipation, refusing to see slave registries and mission collection plates as further versions of objectification, African Jamaicans took up church subscriptions and bought their way to respectability. In doing so, they took over the genre of creole realism of white Jamaica, even before the legal end of slavery. The response of the creole whites was sudden and unexpected: they turned increasingly to the gothic and to romance, the former instruments of denigration of Caribbean culture, with the results I will show in the following chapter.

CHAPTER 2

Caribbean romance and
subaltern history

In 1826, the year that the St Thomas-in-the-East conversion society was founded in Morant Bay with Mary Lindsay's support, two travelogues of the Caribbean were published back in London. The first, Henry Nelson Coleridge's *Six Months in the West Indies*, for the most part eschewed the tropes of Caribbean adventure and romance, opting instead for a tone of evenhanded reasonableness, rejecting the extremes of both pro- and antislavery pamphleteers, although making the author's liberal sympathies clear. 'We all profess an intention of ameliorating the condition of the slaves, and a wish to raise them ultimately to an equality with the rest of the citizens of the empire. The dispute is about the means', Coleridge claimed towards the end of the book, before going on to imagine a post-emancipation period in which ex-slaves would need 'some moral stimulus which shall insure habitual industry and correct the profligate propensities of savage nature'. The best stimulus was one that Maria Edgeworth, for instance, would have endorsed: 'Education; – that is to say, by teaching every child to read; by providing Bibles and Prayerbooks at moderate prices; by building or enlarging churches.'[1] These are policy recommendations that align themselves squarely with the interests of the new, respectable converts of the Caribbean, such as Mary Lindsay, as I discussed in the previous chapter, and suggest the increasing success of the humanitarians in having their version of the West Indies seem the reasonable, realist one.

The second travelogue published that year, however, took a very different approach. *A Tour through the Island of Jamaica*, issued under the name Cynric R. Williams, echoing the title of Daniel Defoe's *Tour through the Whole Island of Great Britain*, published exactly a hundred years earlier, depicted a colony full of larger-than-life characters and sublime tropical scenery, everywhere tinged with romance. The English traveller-narrator passes through Jamaica while under the spell and care of a beautiful young mixed-race woman, Diana, guided by two zealous religious slaves, an educated and dignified Muslim called Abdallah and a ludicrous Methodist convert called Ebeneezer, whose butchering of the Bible and endless ideas above his station provide the comic relief in a tale that consistently favours the Jamaican planter class even as it caricatures them. This is a Caribbean history that is not afraid to break out into tales of the marvellous and the ridiculous, and which breaks with the tradition of reasonable gentleman travellers to embrace the literary tropes of gothic melodrama and imperial romance. In this chapter, I argue that as humanitarian realism of the type practised by Maria Edgeworth and Henry Nelson Coleridge expanded its generic hegemony over the subject of the West Indies, proslavery, pro-planter advocates shifted increasingly to romance and the gothic as they felt their world to be endangered.

I think, for instance, that Williams's *Tour* is not at all what it appears to be, the account of an English traveller who – unlike the vast majority of West Indian tourists at this time – just happens to find himself swayed by the evidence on the ground to support the interests of the planters and the continuation of the slave system. Instead, I think that the book is one of the first signs that the white creole class in Jamaica had decided to turn towards imperial romance as they found themselves beleaguered; my research suggests strongly that the author of the *Tour through the Island of Jamaica* was Charles White Williams, who, far from being a disinterested English visitor, had lived in Jamaica for a dozen years until the early 1820s, as the owner of Duckworth estate in the foothills of the Blue Mountains in St Thomas-in-the-East, and the owner of almost 300 slaves. Moreover, the author of Williams's *Tour* was almost certainly also the author of the anonymously published novel *Hamel, the Obeah Man*, a gothic romance set in eastern Jamaica, issued in 1827 by the same press, Hunt and Clarke, as Williams's *Tour*. The identification of Charles White Williams as the author of these two texts would be powerful evidence for my argument that in the waning days of slavery, the white Jamaican creoles turned to the genre of romance to validate a world they believed they would imminently lose. They did so, moreover, in spite of the risk that romance might instead be the appropriate form for representing and validating African-Jamaican culture, folk knowledge, and insurgency, as I hope to show. It is this flourishing of Caribbean romance in the 1820s that is the focus of this chapter. I give my evidence for the attribution of the *Tour through the Island of Jamaica* to Charles White Williams below, and I analyse *Hamel, the Obeah Man* in the final section of this chapter.

The most prominent planter that Williams's traveller protagonist meets in Jamaica is an estate owner called Mathews, who sounds a great deal like Simon Taylor (see chapter 1), as he fulminates against the 'Saints' back in

England (William Wilberforce, James Stephen, and the rest) and boycotts all English objects in his Jamaican home:

According to him, Jamaica is to be wholly free, to be emancipated from the tyranny of England and the humbug of the *Saints*. He acts up this doctrine, by having nothing in his house which is the produce of England, except where he cannot possibly avoid it. His soap, candles, oil, and all his provisions, are transatlantic. He has neither tea, porter, cider, wines, fish sauces, nor hams, from England.

Williams describes Mathews as a 'very original gentleman' who

has suffered his fears to overpower his judgment, and has taken it into his head that the government of England are bent on ruining the colonies before they abandon them either to the negroes or to the Americans; for their destruction, he says, is inevitable, if the system of tampering or trifling with the feelings of the slaves is persevered with.[2]

Ebeneezer, the pompous Christian convert, is presented as unequivocal proof of Mathews's dire predictions, and the Methodist slave is compared unfavourably throughout to Williams's other guide, Abdallah, 'an African, a Papau, a true believer in the faith of Mahomet', who could

read and write what might be Arabic for ought I knew . . . and conducted himself on all occasions with a very dignified air and manner . . . He had as thorough a contempt for the Christian miracles and mysteries he had heard preached, and for the foolish 'fashions', as he called them, of his friend Sneeza [i.e., Ebeneezer], as any of the muftis of Constantinople could have felt or expressed. (T 31)

Williams's tale was unusual for its time in thus paying attention to the presence of African Muslims in Jamaica, although it is clear that Abdallah's principal role is to be foil to, and refutation of, the converted Christian slave; the dangers to the planters of respectable converts were real enough to risk the rhetorical elevation of Muslims and, as we shall see, obeah men to the status of noble heathens. There is no place for Mary Lindsay here; instead, Williams gives us yet another iteration of the beautiful mulatto nurse-companion familiar from John Stedman's narrative and Simon Taylor's letters. Suffering from a tropical fever, Williams is nursed back to health by the mysterious and lovely 'quadroon' Diana; he is not so sick that he cannot share with the reader his account of her delectable figure, and he makes a point of recounting a conversation in which she acknowledges that she is not a Christian convert ('me afraid not') but has natural piety anyway: 'I believe I must do good to every body, and love them like my mother' (T 57). Diana is the kin, therefore, not only of Stedman's Surinamese partner, Joanna, but also of the naturally virtuous Virginia St Pierre in Edgeworth's

Belinda. Even Williams's partisan tale, however, has to acknowledge the new church institutions emerging in Jamaica: while unrelentingly disparaging of the evangelical missionaries, his narrator spares a moment to celebrate the work of John Trew, the founder of the local conversion society: 'I was told here [in Morant Bay] that the clergyman, Mr. T—, a most exemplary minister, has married nearly two thousand couples of negroes and people of colour, according to the rites of the English church' (T 242).

Significant portions of the book, however, are spent far away from the urban and lowland areas of Jamaica where conversions were becoming common, and we track back and forth with our narrator in the highlands of St Thomas-in-the-East and St David parishes, culminating in an attempt on the summit of the Blue Mountains with Mathews, revisiting the territory of Three-Fingered Jack and Thomas Higson's *Blackwood's* Jamaican mountain-climbing article discussed above in chapter 1. This is the area that was hardest for the conversion society and evangelical missionaries to reach. The bishop of Jamaica announced in 1828 the formation of a branch association of the slave conversion society in St David, the parish between St Thomas-in-the-East and Kingston, but noted that

in the Mountain District [of St David], the Negros are from 13 to 20 miles distant from any place of worship, so that hitherto the children have been completely shut out from religious instruction. At present there is no prospect of our being enabled to employ a Catechist in this part of the Parish, from the total want of funds.[3]

The Jamaican highlands, then, become the last refuge of what David Lambert called the 'planter ideal', the romance of benevolent masters and loyal slaves beyond the reach of metropolitan meddling.[4] Unlike Higson's *Blackwood's* article, Williams devotes considerable space to the African Jamaicans who guided and hauled the gentlemen and their gear up the mountain: 'We enlisted a fine, active negro . . . as our guide . . . a fine, picturesque figure, that became the grand scenery around us, and would have served as a study for three-fingered Jack. His bold and intrepid countenance contrasted much to his advantage with the demure Ralpho-look of Ebeneezer' (T 278). (The reference to the servant in Samuel Butler's satirical poem *Hudibras* is interesting, since it suggests a level of self-mockery that is at odds with the overall direction of the book; Ralpho's master, Sir Hudibras, is a pompous fool.) As they prepare for their final attempt on the summit, the group makes a microcosm of happy slave society in a glorious bit of male bonding:

The repast was served with antediluvian simplicity; the masters seated on the upper side of the sloping floor, the servants on that opposite. We feasted, for we had abundance; and we drank the juice sacred to Bacchus, and gave the negroes plenty of *Old Nick*. A more picturesque, or grotesque, group could not be desired; like gypsies, or banditti, we caroused around the fire, and pledged each other in flowing cups. (T 286)

The Highlands of Walter Scott's *Waverley* have apparently been transported to the mountains of the Caribbean, happy bandits and all.

Williams's narrator wanders among the estates in this district and the Blue Mountain district of St Thomas-in-the-East, passing or calling at Petersfield (owned by John Grosett, author of the book *Remarks on West Indian Affairs* mentioned in chapter 1), Monklands, Mount Lebanus, and the Newington estate of Samuel Francis, which serves, as it did in Higson's *Blackwood's* account, as the base camp for the expedition up the Blue Mountains and away from the fertile-but-bloody lowland world of slavery nearer the coast. In fact, almost the only large estate in this region not mentioned in this section of Williams's *Tour* is one named by Higson as the place from which one of his fellow climbers had come: Duckworth, the estate right next to Mount Lebanus and Monklands, and only three miles from Newington, an 1,100-acre plantation populated by 283 enslaved people in 1823, and owned by Charles White Williams.[5] In declining to name this estate, it is almost as if Williams's narrator is drawing attention to it. I think it is highly likely that Charles White Williams is in fact the author of the *Tour through the Island of Jamaica*, and that he was also the mysterious 'WC' who travelled with Higson in 1818 and added his initials to the 'THn' in the yew tree, as I noted in chapter 1. Williams was born Charles White, and it is unclear how he acquired his additional surname. In the Jamaica almanacs of the early 1810s, he is known as 'Charles Williams' or 'Chas. Williams'; in the later almanacs he is listed as Charles White Williams: 'WC' could therefore be the initials of either Charles White or Charles Williams, reversed to maintain some anonymity.[6] There are four sets of initials, 'WC. THn, 1818, RS, 1818, and IWB'; however, Higson's article refers to only 'three gentlemen' who meet at Francis's plantation, arriving from 'the Botanic Garden, Hagley Gap, and Duckworth', and who set off the next morning 'accompanied by a fourth person'. This mysterious fourth person (not a 'gentleman', in other words) is presumably their black guide. The fourth set of initials, I.W.B., possibly indicate 'British West Indies' in reverse. I have been unable thus far to identify 'R.S.'[7]

For Williams to maintain his non-creole persona, he has to distance himself from the 1818 ascent in the *Tour*; nevertheless, he refers to the earlier climb on several occasions, the only references to it I have come across in any writing on Jamaica of this period. Williams talks of 'a party who went up the mountain in 1818' (T 277), of 'the three gentlemen who preceded us in 1818' (T 289), of 'the trees that flourish on these Alps [that] have been partly enumerated by the botanists who visited them in 1818' (T 282), and after reaching the eastern summit of the Blue Mountains, Williams, Mathews, and the others just happen upon a spot to bed down for the night 'that had been cleared some years before by other travellers; it was a little below the [eastern] peak, opened to the south, and consequently sheltered from the north wind' (T 284). It is there that the aforementioned Bacchanalian revelry takes place. Although Williams is more interested in detailing the splendours of the romantic panoramas he sees than Higson was, he does list the trees and plants discovered by the 1818 trip, 'to which I have but little to add, for I regret to say that a very small portion of our time was devoted to botanical research' (T 289–90). The 'little' he adds to the list of plants published in the *Blackwood's* article does suggest some botanical knowledge, however, and seems to show that Williams knew the results of the 1818 ascent very well, and even sought to augment and correct them. Where Higson wrote of 'five species of Myrtle (*Myrtus*), *viz. Buxifolia*, *Monticola*, and *Axillaris*, the other two not known',[8] Williams writes of 'six myrtles, viz. hirsuta, saxifolia, monticola, and axillaris, the other two non detectae' (T 290). Where Higson discovered 'the Felix Arboreus and other Ferns (*Felixes*)',[9] Williams saw 'filix [sic] arborea, this is the adiantum maximum' (T 290). Then Williams adds a curious item that suggests further inside knowledge of the 1818 trip, and a stronger desire to correct the record of that earlier climb. Where Thomas Higson had said he 'sowed several seeds assimilated to a cold clime',[10] Williams follows the list of botanical items with this: 'We looked in vain for the mangoes, the seeds of which a Mr. Thomson had planted some years ago. The climate must be too cold for them, or they could not fail, for the seed will vegetate on the surface of the land below' (T 291). It seems likely that only someone actually present on the 1818 climb would know the identity of the seeds; 'Mr. Thomson' is likely a pseudonym for Thomas Higson, and Williams might almost be sending him a private message in this passage. While this cannot be an absolutely definitive identification, it is strong evidence for Charles White Williams's authorship, when put alongside the author's evident familiarity with eastern Jamaica, where he is continually meeting with old friends. After the party writes their names and 'a short account of our proceedings' and puts it in a bottle under the same yew tree that 'contained the journal of other travellers' (T 291), just as Higson's party had previously done, they descend from the mountain to Mr Francis's estate; from there Williams 'jog[s] on to an estate situated on the banks of Morgan's River' (T 292). Charles White Williams's Duckworth estate was situated on the Negro River less than a mile from Morgans River, albeit over the steep ground of the Kenmure Ridge; the two rivers joined at Mount Lebanus estate, which was about a mile and a half from Duckworth.[11]

Williams acquired Duckworth plantation sometime late in the first decade of the nineteenth century, and by 1811 he was serving on the St Thomas-in-the-East magistrates bench, whose custos (chief magistrate) was Simon Taylor, which could explain how a man who had been dead for ten years could serve as the model for Mathews in Cynric Williams's mid-1820s travelogue. Williams seems to have left Jamaica and returned to England in 1820 or 1821, the latter being the year in which one of his daughters, Emily Williams, was born in Epsom, Surrey.[12] In other words, contemporary reviews of Williams's *Tour* were correct when they highlighted its literary as opposed to its factual qualities: 'It was a sad mistake to mix up fiction with fact, when treating of a country about which so much falsehood had already been published. This same admixture of the story-book with his own experience, likewise exceedingly diminishes the force of much that would otherwise carry conviction along with it', argued the reviewer in the *London Magazine*, which was being published at this time by the same press, Hunt and Clarke, that brought out Williams's travelogue and the novel *Hamel* a year later.[13] Instead of being an outsider visiting Jamaica for the first time to take care of an inheritance from 'a relation', in other words, Williams had been a thirteen-year resident of Jamaica, a large slave owner, and a member of the standing committee of the West India Committee of Planters and Merchants, which in 1823 inaugurated a Literary Subcommittee with the avowed intent of providing subventions and other support for published works that promoted the cause of the Caribbean plantocracy.[14] 'It is necessary to read but a few pages of his book', wrote the *Monthly Review*, 'in order to perceive that it has been much less his object to describe his tour in Jamaica, than to put forth, under that title, a defence of the slave system'. Perhaps with insider knowledge, and certainly not on the basis of the text itself, the *Monthly* reviewer began his or her article with the bald statement: 'Mr. Williams avows himself to be a West India proprietor.'[15] Whether Williams was in Jamaica at all in 1823, the ostensible date of the *Tour*, or whether the whole book is a composite fiction created from his years on the island, cannot be decided at this distance. We do know, however, that he continued to pay attention to affairs in Jamaica, because on the list of contributors to the London parent body of the St Thomas-in-the-East conversion society in 1825 we find one 'C. W. Williams, Esq., Epsom, Surrey'; he subscribed £2 2s.[16]

If we see Williams's *Tour through the Island of Jamaica* as a kind of colonial fiction, it would be a late example of the 'national tale', which flourished at the turn of the nineteenth century as a narrative in which, as Katie Trumpener puts it, 'an English character... travels to a British periphery, expected to be devoid of culture. Instead, under the tutelage of an aristocratic friend, he or she learns to appreciate its cultural plenitude and decides to settle there permanently'.[17] Although the irascible Mathews is no aristocrat, he certainly takes Williams's traveller under his wing, and the book tries to make the strongest case it can for the cultural plenitude of Jamaica, from the witty repartee of the Jewish merchant Nunnez to the warm hospitality of the 'brown' female innkeepers and the exuberant and rich festivity of the black John Canoe (Junkanoo) performers whom Williams meets shortly after his arrival on the island. This last aspect of the culture of the island represents the biggest threat, however, to the genre of the national tale; if it tells the story of the nation of Jamaica as it currently exists in the 1820s, then it must tell the story of the overwhelming importance of black culture. It would tend, therefore, to validate and raise up the likes of Mary Lindsay, whose new role in civil society is indirectly supported by Charles White Williams's private subscription to the West India conversion society and by his public endorsement of John Trew. This is where the genre of the national tale meets its limit for Williams: his story cannot end, as Trumpener describes the finales of Sydney Owenson and Charlotte Smith's novels, 'with the traveler's marriage to his or her native guide, in a wedding that allegorically unites Britain's "national characters"'.[18] Instead, the author of the *Tour through the Island of Jamaica* and *Hamel, the Obeah Man* turns to the genre of fiction that Trumpener argues comes to supplant the national tale: the historical romance of the cultural periphery, of which Walter Scott's *Waverley* is the prime example.

Trumpener shows that the geographical emphasis of the national tale slowly gives way to the historical understanding of cultural change exemplified in Scott's novels: 'The historical novel... finds its focus in the way one developmental stage collapses to make room for the next and cultures are transformed under the pressure of historical events.'[19] This is an account of the nation that emphasises transformation, 'collapse', and loss, and it was perfectly fitted for a white creole understanding of the pre-emancipation Caribbean. Faced with a threatening present, people like Williams turned to the romance of a lost past. Ian Baucom would call narratives of the present such as the report of the West India conversion society 'actuarial historicism', which identifies 'types' – like Mary Lindsay – that 'function as the measurable, abstract, aggregate representatives of what are taken to be contemporaneous, *extant* phenomena'.[20] It is to this narrative that C. W. Williams pledges £2 2s; history, of course, has proven this narrative to be the more accurate one. But Williams's heart is set on another kind of historicism, exemplified by a different type: 'The romantic type, conversely, functions as the representative of something that no longer exists, something that once existed but, by the moment it enters historicist awareness, is now lost: most famously, perhaps, the "Highlanders" who inhabit Scott's texts not as the representative types of a contemporary Scotland but as the typical representatives of a lost time.'[21] Williams's traveller has hardly been in Jamaica a day before he finds himself at a planter's house, 'enjoy[ing] an hour of cheerful conversation ... on family subjects, mixed up with small talk about Walter Scott's novels, Lallah Rookh, and the Loves of the Angels' (T 8). Despite the ease with which Scott crosses the Atlantic, however, there is a crucial difference between the Highlanders of *Waverley* and the black peasantry of the Caribbean: while the resistance of the Highlanders could be plausibly consigned to the past, the history of slave rebellions in the West Indies suggested that there would only be more in the future. If figures like Mathews and the other creole planters were romantic representatives of something that no longer existed in the 1820s, Williams's writing could not exclude the historical forces driving black insurgency from its pages. While his traveller was sipping 'sangree', dallying with Diana, and climbing the Blue Mountains, in the same year in the southern portion of the Caribbean region a wide-ranging, well-organised slave rebellion was taking place in the country that later became Guyana. Williams's *Tour through the Island of Jamaica ... in 1823*, and, even more so, his novel, *Hamel, the Obeah Man*, are troubled by, but at the same time seek to represent in the terms of romance, black insurgency in general, and the 1823 rebellion in Demerara in particular. I turn, in the following section, to a discussion of this rebellion and its lessons for the writing of history and romance.

THE DEMERARA REBELLION OF 1823: 'GOD IS NOT SO SLACK IN HIS PROMISES AS SOME MEN ARE'

According to Dipesh Chakrabarty, any historian must adopt a 'rationally defensible point of view or position from which to tell the story', without which, 'at best', any narrative of the past 'will count as fiction and not history'.[22] Nevertheless, an emphasis on what Chakrabarty calls 'subaltern pasts' – versions of the past structured by the protocols of the peasant's or subaltern's worldview, of the supernatural, of the gods, and of fiction, versions of the past that tend to disrupt the stability of conventional historical accounts and of creole realism – conjures up and foregrounds what he calls the 'scandalous aspects of our [historians'] unavoidable translations' of these materials into the language of the disenchanted social sciences.[23] In the second half of this chapter, I analyse the British romantic novel *Hamel, the Obeah Man* (1827), which builds on and incorporates some of the contemporary pamphlet and other material on the Demerara rebellion in order to justify slavery and to malign the evangelical missionaries who were attempting to convert slaves in the West Indies; I argue that in fact *Hamel* offers us a privileged site in which to read African religious and other cultural practices, and in which to trouble once again these unstable boundaries between secular and religious time, and between history and fiction. But I turn first to Harriet Martineau's tale 'Demerara' (1833) and to an analysis of the primary and secondary documents of the Demerara rebellion itself in order to show that even the most resolutely disenchanted versions of progressive history require a detour through, or perhaps even a foundation in, the mode of romance.

Published in the year that the official act to abolish slavery in the British Caribbean came into effect, Martineau's tale appeared in her popular series 'Illustrations in Political Economy', relatively brief didactic fictions designed to transmit the key arguments of 'Smith, Malthus, Ricardo and Mill' by 'embody[ing] these principles in people and places', as Catherine Hall puts it in her illuminating essay on Martineau.[24] Demerara was the setting for establishing the wasteful nature of chattel slavery and 'the effectiveness of wages as an incentive for work';[25] Demerara is also the site chosen to legitimate the rational narrative of history as a story about the gradual increase of human freedom, in which the supersession of slavery represents the key distinction between the oppressive past and the relatively enlightened present. Alfred Bruce, the son of a Demerara planter who returns to the colony as a twenty-one-year-old man with his sister Mary after fourteen years of education in England, is horrified and spurred to thought and action by the conditions in the West Indies. He lectures his father, adducing historical examples to prove that slavery will eventually end: 'Slavery becomes less extensive with the lapse of centuries.'[26] History moves from 'ancient times', when 'the lords of the race lived in barbarous, comfortless splendour' because 'a great part of the population . . . was the property of the rest', through 'the bondage and villeinage of the Gothic nations', which was 'far more tolerable than the ancient slavery' (D 81). As these bondsmen 'were allowed property . . . their population increased, and the condition of themselves and their masters improved. The experience of this improvement led to further emancipation; and that comparative freedom again to further improvement' (D 81). This ever widening spiral of freedom is the proof that West Indian slavery too is destined for the rubbish bin of history: 'That they ['our bad institutions'] will die out, the slave-history of Europe is our warrant' (D 82).

However, Martineau's version of historical inevitability carries within itself the seeds of romance, in the figure of the dead slaves whose irrevocable loss turns out to be the precondition for the rationality of political economy. 'I fear that our bad institutions will die out only in the persons of those most injured by them', laments Alfred, before the narrator goes on to introduce the key figure of pathos in the story, Hester, an enslaved child who has lost both her parents and is being raised by other slaves not related to her by blood, just as many others are in the cruel world of the West Indies: 'There are many instances where the pupil has been cherished by a mother whose babe had been early taken from her by death or violence; or by a father who had seen his sons carried off to a distance, one by one as they became valuable for their strength or skill' (D 82, 93). Hester, however, is not so fortunate, since she is cared for by the thieving, abusive couple Robert and Sukey after the deaths of her own parents, whose spirits she keeps alive in her romantic dreams:

> Of her father she remembered little. He had been executed for taking part in an insurrection when she was very young . . . She had seen her mother die, and had stood by the grave where she was buried . . . She dreamed almost every night that her arm was round her mother's neck, and that her mother sang to her, or that they were going together to find out the country where her father was waiting for them. (D 94)

The romance of the executed rebel slave lies behind the illustration of political economy, produced via a process of translation that Chakrabarty would call 'scandalous', but which Martineau calls 'natural': 'While endeavouring to preserve the characteristics of Negro minds and manners, I have not attempted to imitate the language of slaves. Their jargon would be intolerable to writers and readers, if carried through a volume. My personages, therefore, speak the English which would be natural to them, if they spoke what can be called English at all' (D 70). The 1823 rebellion in Demerara is mentioned only once in Martineau's tale, but black insurgency is clearly the genealogical origin of the story, the point at which the romance of the authentic but lost other turns into the realism of 'principles' and 'illustration'. In the closing 'Summary of Principles Illustrated in this Volume', the dead insurgent makes a final appearance: 'Where one of the parties under the law is held as property by another party, the law injures the one or the other as often as they are opposed. Moreover, its very protection injures the protected party, – as when a rebellious slave is hanged' (D 140). The bodies pile up, and Martineau announces her project as the transmutation of insurgency itself, 'awakening' and 'firing': 'I have not hesitated to bring calculations and reasonings to bear on a subject [i.e., slavery] which awakens the drowsiest, and fires the coldest', she declares in the preface, recalling the setting alight of many sugar estates in Demerara in the 1823 rebellion (D 70). When it comes to the history of subaltern insurgency – to return to the language of Dipesh Chakrabarty – the 'rationally defensible point of view or position from which to tell the story' that is supposed to distinguish the language of social science from the language of fiction turns out to be founded on the romance of the dead insurgent himself or herself.

The slave rebellion in Demerara (now part of Guyana) in August 1823 was one of the largest and best organised in the Americas, although it was quickly and brutally crushed by the colonial authorities. In April 1823, a group of slaves complained forcefully to the authorities that their owner regularly interfered with their religious practices; as a result, Governor John Murray dusted off and publicised some 1811 instructions from London that had never been fully implemented in the colony, which had the effect of restricting and regulating Africans' customary rights to travel to religious meetings on neighbouring estates, and to hold religious meetings at night on their own estates. Already enraged by these new regulations, therefore, the slaves were ready for further action when subsequently, for several weeks in July and August, they began to hear rumours, and sometimes more concrete information passed on by the servants of powerful whites, including those of the governor himself, that laws had come out from England that meant 'something good' for the slaves. Opinions differed as to whether the new laws offered one or two more days of 'rest', whether they meant an end to the practice of flogging, or whether they meant full freedom for the enslaved men and women of the colony; all, however, agreed that the governor was seeking to delay or prevent the implementation of these laws. Secretly, a group of slaves began organising large-scale resistance to the colonial authorities; many of them were local leaders and other members of the Bethel chapel of the English evangelical missionary John Smith on Le Resouvenir plantation on the East Coast of Demerara, and they gathered after chapel on Sundays to discuss tactics. Some proposed a strike, others an armed uprising. Eventually, on 17 August 1823, when the new laws still had not come into effect, the slaves took matters into their own hands. In all, between 9,000 and 12,000 slaves (and some free blacks) rose up, capturing and firing sixty plantations, putting estate owners, managers, and overseers in the stocks – but not carrying out the mass killings of Europeans that had marked other slave rebellions in the Americas.

If the rebels thought that sparing the lives of their erstwhile masters would save them from the brutal repercussions meted out to previous rebels – most recently, in the anglophone world, in Barbados in 1816 – they were mistaken.[27] As the colonial militia quickly moved to re-establish control over the countryside, summary executions, hasty courts martial, and mass floggings were the order of the day, as they would be again in Jamaica in 1865 (see chapters 3 and 4 below). Rebels, and some slaves simply in the wrong place at the wrong time, were hung and gibbeted, and their decapitated bodies and severed heads displayed as spectacular reminders of colonial power. Martial law lasted for several months, during which time the trials and executions continued, culminating in the prosecution of John Smith on the charge of promoting discontent amongst the Africans, advising them to rebel, and then failing to report the rebellion to the authorities once it had begun. Smith was convicted of most of the charges, on the flimsiest of evidence, and was sentenced to death; instead, he died of tuberculosis in jail in Georgetown on 6 February 1824. The slaves returned to their plantations, and returned to their everyday modes of resistance – perhaps, for instance, poisoning several members of the militia at a gathering in their honour to celebrate the suppression of the uprising.[28] It would take another eight years before formal 'emancipation' was won, and a further six years after that before the dismantling of the hated 'apprenticeship' system finally did away with slavery in Guyana and the rest of the British West Indies.

Until recently, the 1823 Demerara rebellion has been remembered principally as the backdrop to the trial, conviction, and subsequent death in custody of John Smith, the man sent by the London Missionary Society to Demerara to convert and instruct the slave population of the colony. The Smith case became an important controversy in Britain, coming as it did amidst the ongoing debate over the abolition of slavery in the colonies, and importantly prefigured the controversy over Governor Edward Eyre's suppression of the 1865 uprising in Jamaica that is the subject of the following two chapters. It pitted pro-missionary liberals and evangelicals, who were pushing the government further and faster towards the 'amelioration' of slave conditions through religious instruction and reform of colonial slave codes, against a still powerful West Indian planter and merchant lobby, who argued for the local autonomy of colonial legislatures and for their rights over their own private property (i.e., the enslaved populations of the Caribbean). It was into this particular ferment that the Smith case was drawn, with colonists and their allies seeing the 1823 rebellion as proof of the malign influence of the missionaries, cast as 'wolves in sheep's clothing', while abolitionists and evangelicals saw the continuation of a conspiracy against religious freedom, and saw Smith himself as 'the Demerara martyr', as the title of one slightly later account of the case had it.[29]

Gauri Viswanathan's work has convincingly demonstrated that conversions to Christianity under colonialism should not be seen as the obliteration of old identities and practices but as negotiations between unstable positions on a spiritual-political continuum. Conversion can be seen as a response to instability and disruption in 'traditional' religious and cultural arrangements amongst African Caribbeans – always with the proviso that this 'tradition' was itself far from unchanging; but conversions, even to the dominant religion, also destabilised and disrupted colonial societies that trafficked in notions of essential differences between 'whites', 'people of colour', and 'negroes', and between Christians and 'heathens'. As Viswanathan argues, in the context of South Asia, all religious conversions are disruptive to the state because 'by undoing the concept of fixed, unalterable identities, conversion unsettles the boundaries by which selfhood, citizenship, nationhood, and community are defined, exposing these as permeable borders'.[30]

African conversion threatened not only the plantocracy, but even the liberals and evangelicals in Britain who supported and sent missionaries to the Caribbean and who thought they were working in the slaves' best interests. African Caribbeans creolised and converted Christianity itself, and we can see the problem this posed for British antislavery activists in the defensive need of William Wilberforce, for example, to insist in the very structure of the title of his most famous abolitionist tract that 'inhabitants of the British empire' and 'Negro slaves' are fixed, unalterable identities, trying to maintain distinctions that no longer held firm.[31] Wilberforce also sought to demonstrate, contrary to all the evidence that he must have seen as a prominent member of the Anti-Slavery Society and a sometime subscriber to the more conservative Society for the Conversion and Religious Instruction and Education of the Negro Slaves in the British West India Islands that slaves remained trapped in 'pagan darkness': 'It is . . . true, that, low in point of morals as the Africans may have been in their own country, their descendants, who have never seen the continent of Africa, but who are sprung from those who for several successive generations have been resident in the Christian colonies of Great Britain, are still lower.'[32] While Wilberforce's appeal, and the agitation of his fellow abolitionists in Britain, was ostensibly directed against the local colonial authorities and their unwillingness to implement religious and political reforms, his call for the centralisation of imperial power in London must also be seen, I would suggest, as an indirect response to the religious and political self-fashioning of African Caribbeans who were not prepared to wait to 'be gradually prepared for the enjoyment of freedom', or to be subjected to 'the humane and liberal principles by which the slavery of the blacks should be mitigated', as Wilberforce phrased it.[33]

In Demerara, we can uncover this relative autonomy of African-Christian slave religion by analysing the anxious questions asked of chapel-going slaves by the prosecutor during John Smith's trial (who effectively therefore undercut his own case that Smith had indoctrinated the slaves into rising), and by John Smith himself in his defence. The rebel slave Azor was asked by the court, for instance, after describing the workings of Smith's chapel, in which there were several deacons and numerous 'teachers' who were less closely supervised by Smith and who instructed the slaves on their own plantations, 'Did the deacons ever meet separately from the rest?'[34] Azor replied that he did not know. Often the prosecutor's questions are not reproduced in the trial transcript, but can be inferred from the witnesses' statements. Appearing immediately after Azor, Romeo, one of the Bethel deacons, said at first that 'The deacons do not meet by themselves, but in the chapel, along with the members and others', but later in his testimony he claimed that the deacons did sometimes meet independently: 'On my master's estate we meet sometimes; but since I have been lame I have not been accustomed to do so; but I send them all to Mr. Smith, as I had nothing more to do with it.'[35] Smith, in his cross-examinations, was clearly concerned to show that chapel members were not setting up separate organisations. When he asked Azor to explain what happened when the deacons met, and Azor responded, 'To meet to prayer, and teach one another', Smith tried to show in a follow-up question that this did not mean African autonomy within the chapel: 'Could any white people go there at that time or occasion [when the 'teachers' were teaching the catechism to fellow slaves, which, Smith stressed, happened in the chapel itself], if they liked?' He also asked Azor, 'Did you yourself ever see Mr. Smith with the teachers of the catechism, whilst they were teaching?', to which Azor replied in the affirmative.[36]

In pre-trial interrogations, Hanover, of Paradise plantation, provided perhaps the clearest account of the extent to which black organisations, using the structures of white churches and yet beyond the purview of both Smith and the colonial authorities, functioned according to their own rules of inclusion and exclusion, and served both political and religious ends:

> I declare that the meetings at Paradise took place four times in the week; they began at half-past seven o'clock at night; that Barson was the man who read the Bible and explained to us ... It was not every night we confined ourselves to religious matters; sometimes we talked stories; the meetings took place at Ambrose's house for religion; but when they had any thing particular to do, they went to Gilbert's house and talked on it. On these occasions they would not speak when I was present, as they excluded the negroes who were christened by Parson Austin [the Anglican minister in Georgetown] from their consultations, and I am one of those that he christened ... Telemachus formerly came to Paradise to teach the negroes, but now Barson and Hercules are the teachers; they used to teach all the people, but since some of the negroes were christened by Mr. Austin, they have not taught them any thing, and only teach their own party, the chapel people, whom they call Mr. Smith's christians.[37]

Of course, students of the colonial archive have learned to be sceptical of 'verbatim' transcripts, and these interrogations were designed to produce evidence against 'Smith's christians', and thereby Smith himself – Hanover distanced himself from them in order to distance himself from the rebellion (he claims elsewhere that he was forced to carry a gun and take part in the uprising against his will). Nevertheless, Hanover's interrogation, even refracted through these multiple lenses, offers compelling evidence of a complex structure of African religious self-expression under the auspices of the Bethel chapel.

Although the chapelgoers and associated slaves on the neighbouring estates called themselves 'Mr. Smith's christians' (and although they called Smith 'massa', as was common with European missionaries throughout the Caribbean), an analysis of the surviving documents suggests that Smith himself was actually peripheral not only to the uprising (about which there can hardly be a doubt) but to the politico-religious institutions in which that uprising was planned. Romeo, recounting the slaves' discussion after chapel on the Sunday before the uprising began, said that 'The negroes said that Mr. Smith was making them fools: they said this in my presence, and there was a great number of people; but they said he would not deny his own colour for the sake of black people.'[38] Manuel, another of the Bethel deacons, recalls discussing with the head deacon and rebel leader Quamina the new law from England that everyone had heard so much about, and suggesting that Quamina should ask Smith about it; even though Quamina was the chapel member most in Smith's confidence, 'Quamina told me [Manuel], I don't believe that he will tell you. I said, never mind, ask him nonetheless.'[39] It appears that even Smith's most trusted deacons did not believe that he had their interests at heart.

We get a picture, then, of a missionary out of his depth, trying hard to maintain control over a congregation of worshippers he did not understand, and whom he described in his private journals and in his public defence as ignorant, deceitful, and savage. He did understand them well enough, however, to know that their ability to interpret his preaching, and Christian doctrine, to suit their own situation and purposes was highly developed. In his journal (later used as evidence against him at his trial) he describes omitting crucial passages from the Bible that he feared slaves might 'misinterpret': 'Having passed over the latter part of chapter 13 [of Genesis], as containing a promise of deliverance from . . . the land of Canaan, I was apprehensive the negroes might put such a construction upon it as I would not wish . . . It is easier to make a wrong impression upon their minds than a right one.'[40] Smith's trial showed that – as was true throughout the Americas – slaves understandably showed particular affinity for the story of the Israelites, and that Smith's attempts to circumvent this were in vain. Bristol, from the plantation Chateau Margo, another of the Bethel deacons, testified:

I have heard some of the boys who read the bible, speak about the Israelites and the Jews, about the fighting of the Israelites when they go to war; when the prisoner [Smith] read about the fighting of the Israelites, after they went home and read it again, I heard them speak about it; they said the people of Israel used to go warring against the enemies; then I explained the meaning of the enemy, and told them it was the people who would not believe the word of God when Moses used to preach to them; the people applied the story of the Israelites and the Jews, and put it on themselves; when they read it then they begin to discourse about it; they said that this thing in the bible applied to us just as well as to the people of Israel.[41]

Eventually, in a further attempt to distance himself from the slaves, Smith ended up providing some of the clearest evidence of the emergence of an independent black church (if we use this term in a capacious way). He noted in his defence that several of the black witnesses, 'whose memories were so very tenacious on the subject of Moses and Pharaoh, and the children of Israel, though it is two years since I have read to them about these persons, have stated that they never heard me apply the history of the Israelites to the condition of the negroes'. He went on to argue that, 'If they themselves read the Bible, and so applied it, the fault must be charged to their ignorance, and shows the necessity of their having more instruction' – but we must interpret Smith's evidence very differently, as, precisely, 'tenacious' creativity rather than ignorance.[42] Finally, since if he portrayed himself as too closely involved with his congregation and their beliefs, he would align himself more strongly in the eyes of other whites with the rebellion, Smith disclaimed all connection to the religious 'teachers' who clearly had such importance in the black community: 'As to the teachers, they were wholly unconnected with the church. The people themselves chose them on their respective estates, without my interference.'[43] Smith, therefore, in an attempt to exculpate himself, conjures up the autonomous African-Christian community he had elsewhere so carefully sought to erase.

The revolt, then, must be seen as a religious as much as a political struggle, and indeed one in which religion and politics can no longer be easily separated. It appears that the participants swore an oath declaring themselves the 'servants of Christ', before the attacks began, although the evidence here is ambiguous, since one detained rebel, Paris, implicated Smith himself in the oath, which seems extremely unlikely:

Then the Parson brought the Bible, and every body put their hands on it, and the Parson repeated the words of, We are the servants of Jesus Christ, as we begin with Christ so we will end with Christ, dead or alive; then every body bowed their heads, and it was agreed by the Parson to us, that let whatever happen we were to call no names.[44]

However, Tom Gibson, a slave on a neighbouring plantation, also described a similar oath-taking, after returning from the open-air meeting of the slaves after chapel on the Sunday before the revolt:

I found they had all gone to Jimmy's house, and collected there; then I saw Austin of the Cove with a Bible in his hand; he had his hand on it and said, 'I live by Christ, and die by Christ'; all the people there did the same thing; he was reading the Bible before I got there, and I took the oath also; the nature of this oath was, that they were all to stay on the estate.[45]

The swearing of oaths, often sealed in blood, at secret religious gatherings had been a regular feature of slave life in the Americas since the beginning; here the slaves' explicitly Christian pact is a direct descendant of these practices. It should also be seen as a direct attack on the practice throughout the region of denying slave testimony at trials of whites, for the reason that slaves could not understand or be expected to adhere to oaths on the Bible.

Moreover, reinforcing the sense that God and Jesus were in fact significant actors in the Demerara rebellion, at least as far as its participants were concerned, we need to note that the train of events that led to the rebellion in the first place began with the powerful complaint to Rev. Austin in Georgetown by a group of some twenty slaves that they had been prevented by their owners and managers from moving between plantations to attend religious meetings. They asked the Anglican minister 'whether their evening meetings on their estates for religious purposes were improper; whether their reading of the Bible was improper'.[46] They had already taken their complaints to Governor Murray, and to the colony's fiscal (the ombudsman who investigated complaints by slaves of their masters, and vice versa), but nothing had happened. Austin was worried by the force and 'the extraordinary style and tone' of their address to him, and proceeded to tell the governor of the meeting, having 'serious apprehensions' of a rebellion.[47] (It was in response to Austin's information that Governor Murray issued the instructions restricting religious assembly in May.) Asked by Smith at his trial to characterise the 'extraordinary style' of the slaves' complaint, Austin remembered that 'one of the expressions made use of was, there was an attempt made to set down their religion, and that they would sooner die than give it up'.[48] Three months later, after swearing allegiance to each other and to Jesus, and (at least in some accounts) taking the sacrament before the rebellion to link their cause still more concretely with the body and blood of Christ, the converted slaves rose up in a religiously inspired revolt that leaves sympathetic future historians, in our disenchanted world, with a particular set of problems about how to narrate and explain these events.

For example, Dipesh Chakrabarty argues in his chapter 'Minority Histories, Subaltern Pasts' that since historians of subaltern struggles tend to be committed to ideas of social justice and modern citizenship, these historians will, therefore, ignore or translate into secular terms the supernatural agency of the gods that has always been the hallmark of subaltern, and especially peasant, rebellions. Despite this, however, he argues that, in fact, 'we [historians] inhabit their [subalterns'] fragments even when we classify ourselves as modern and secular', because 'the capacity (of the modern person) to historicise actually depends on his or her ability to participate in nonmodern relationships to the past that are made subordinate in the moment of historicization'.[49] Therefore the importance of 'subaltern pasts' is to make visible now the 'plurality of times existing together, a disjuncture of the present with itself', such that 'history writing assumes plural ways of being in the world'.[50] For Chakrabarty, therefore, the historian's task is to narrate the past self-consciously, to foreground the necessary translation of supernatural agency into the rational point of view of the historian; in other words, 'to take history, the code, to its limits in order to make its unworking visible'.[51] To do otherwise – to narrate the past in the language of the gods, or of a 'madman', or of 'fiction'[52] – is to indulge a romantic fantasy of unreason. Discussing Ranajit Guha's work on the 1855 rebellion in India of a tribal, peasant group called the Santal, Chakrabarty shows that the problem faced by Guha (and, by extension, by all subalternist historians) is that 'a narrative strategy that is rationally defensible in the modern understanding of what constitutes public life – and the historians speak in the public sphere – cannot be based on a relationship that allows the divine or the supernatural a direct hand in the affairs of the world. The Santal leaders' own understanding of the rebellion does not directly serve the historical cause of democracy or citizenship or socialism. It needs to be reinterpreted'.[53] It is a compelling argument, and one that the cultural critic in particular needs to take seriously, tempted as he or she is by a certain licensed distance from the protocols of academic historiography to reject any argument that tends, as Chakrabarty's does, to consolidate the distinction between 'fiction' and 'history'. To what extent does Chakrabarty's thesis help us make sense of the archive of the 1823 Demerara rebellion?

The first point to be made is that this archive is itself the result of a series of translations, both literal and figurative. The 'transcripts' of trials, depositions, and interviews with rebels have all been rendered into an English acceptable and understandable to Colonial Office civil servants and to latterday postcolonial historians, into the basis for historical realism. The historian or cultural critic's subsequent interpretation of 'the archive' can only assume 'multiple ways of being in the world', in Chakrabarty's phrase, by acknowledging that our well-meaning but scandalous translation of subaltern insurgency into the secular discourse of the academic/public sphere owes its very existence to the purging of the African and creole languages and worldviews of the participants in the rebellion. Occasionally, the violence of this process of translation appears even in the documents of the archive itself, as when the transcript of the post-rebellion trial of Quamina's son, Jack Gladstone, documents some of the process by which his 'confession' was produced, apparently because of a conflict between two of the white participants in Gladstone's trial. Charles Herbert, the lawyer charged with preparing Gladstone's defence, objected to the final portion of the defendant's confession, in which he 'solemnly avow[ed], that many of the lessons and discourses, and the parts of Scripture selected for us in chapel, tended to make us dissatisfied with our situations as slaves; and had there been no Methodists on the East Coast, there would have been no revolt'.[54] Herbert noted that this portion of the defence had been added without his help, as he had discovered when he had gone to the jail to visit the prisoner and 'enlarge upon an idea of Jack's concerning the cause of the rising', and had found that it had already been 'done by Mr. Edmonstone', an aide-de-camp to Col. Stephen Goodman (presiding judge at many of the rebel trials and commander of the Georgetown militia).[55] Edmonstone testified that he would 'go round the Jail every morning', and that on the morning of Gladstone's trial he had seen on the table 'the defence Mr. Herbert had written for Jack, and found that it did not contain many statements which Jack had told me in repeated conversations I had held with him', and so he had added these suggestions – with Jack's approval, he claimed.[56]

This interpolation of Edmonstone's might appear particularly egregious, since 'Methodists' had nothing whatsoever to do with the rebellion (Smith was an independent missionary sent out by the London Missionary Society, which was a group of Anglican and dissenting evangelicals). Methodism, however, was seen at this moment (just as Baptism would come to be a few years later in Jamaica during the so-called Baptist War of 1832) as the principal threat to the West Indian planters and the proslavery lobby in Britain. This looks like an extreme case of colonial paranoia and stereotyping – the spectre of 'Methodist' missionaries inciting rebellion, where 'Methodism' stands in for all non-Anglican missionaries and for humanitarian meddling in West Indian affairs more generally – in which the accused man, trying to save his own life, agrees to speak aloud the fantasmatic projections of the colonial settlers:

The half-sort of instructions we received, I now see was highly improper; it put those who could read, on examining the Bible, and selecting passages applicable to our situation as slaves . . . and served to make us dissatisfied and irritated against our owners, as we were not always able to make out the real proceeding of these passages.[57]

This is precisely the argument reiterated again and again in the picaresque and gothic romances of Williams's *Tour through the Island of Jamaica* and *Hamel, the Obeah Man*. However, Edmonstone's intervention here was typical rather than extraordinary: he was, in fact, the court-appointed translator for many of the rebels' trials, a reminder that many if not most of the slaves and free blacks who testified would have done so in the African languages or Dutch-based creoles that were the vernacular in Demerara, a colony only recently transferred from Dutch to British rule:

Robert Edmonstone, Esq. . . . was sworn as an Interpreter [in the earlier trial of Natt of Enterprise and Louis of Plaisance], to explain to the Prisoner, in the negro dialect, the nature of the Charge, – the Evidence, – to ask any Questions, by way of cross-examination, – and to assist the Prisoner with his Defence. Mr. Edmonstone also interpreted the testimony given by negroes. Throughout the whole of the trials, an Interpreter was engaged.[58]

Every single word of the voluminous archive of the Demerara rebellion, in other words, represents a failure to accept the 'plural ways of being in the world' to which subsequent historians are trying to be responsible as they reconstruct subaltern pasts.

A further reminder of the scandalous translation involved in the construction of this archival record of the Demerara rebellion comes in Charles Herbert's unselfconscious account of his own role in providing the rest of Jack Gladstone's defence, the part that we might be tempted to read as more 'accurate' than the Edmonstone anti-Methodist supplement:

> I wrote the defence just read [i.e., just presented to the court] from the prisoner's own dictation, as far as the words, '*I throw myself on the mercy of the Court.*' Every thing was suggested to me by Jack, and I was very particular in taking down his meaning, and in one instance used his own words. I have endeavoured to form a connected narrative from the story he told.[59]

We might see Jack Gladstone tactically orchestrating the presentations of his defence team from behind the scenes – and apparently doing so successfully, since unlike the vast majority of those captured and tried as leading conspirators in the rebellion, he was not actually executed, but had his death sentence commuted to life imprisonment by the governor. Perhaps it was Gladstone's clever manipulation of Herbert and Edmonstone that compelled Governor Murray to spare his life and incited Joshua Bryant to include his full defence in an account of the insurrection otherwise resolutely opposed to the rebels themselves. Bryant claimed that Gladstone's testimony 'is very remarkable, not only for its ingenuity, but as carrying with it an air of truth and candour'.[60] However, even this reconstruction of Jack Gladstone as agent in his own trial falls prey to the historian's desire to understand the events of the past in the language of the public sphere, here represented by the whole juridical apparatus of truth-telling, an apparatus that lies behind the conventional construction of 'history', with its rules of evidence, argument, cause and effect, and so on.

In fact, slave revolts present a particular challenge to the cultural historian who wants to be alive to the non-secular aspects of subaltern history, since the documents of these rebellions that have survived (which are of course, in the British context at least, almost all produced from the 'rationally defensible' point of view of the colonial authorities) tend to be rather easy to reinterpret in secular, modern terms: slaves fought for (and claimed at the time they were fighting for) 'freedom' and 'rights'. When Governor John Murray rode out of Georgetown on the first day of the revolt and encountered a group of armed rebels, he tried to 'ascertain their views' (as he put it suavely in his subsequent dispatch to Lord Bathurst, the colonial secretary): they told him that they demanded 'unconditional emancipation'.[61] The account of Joshua Bryant, a fifteen-year resident of the colony, is just as succinct: 'His Excellency and suite... reached the side-line between Le Resouvenir and Felicity, when a large body of armed negroes came down upon them, shouting, "We have them, we have them." His Excellency immediately stopped, and demanded what they wanted. They replied, "Our right."'[62] John Smith wrote to a friend and fellow missionary two days into the revolt, recalling a confrontation with the rebels whom he was later accused of instigating and leading, in the plantation house at Le Resouvenir where the rebellion began: 'I entered and asked what they wanted? They answered me by brandishing their cutlasses. I repeated the question. They replied, "We want the guns and our rights." The former they soon obtained... They told us not to be alarmed, for they were not going to hurt any one, but they would have their rights.'[63]

Statements such as these have led even the best historian of the Demerara rebellion, Emilia Viotti da Costa, to characterise it as an apparently inevitable movement towards modernity and Enlightenment values:

> For a short time slaves turned the world upside down. Slaves became masters and masters became slaves. Just as masters had uprooted them from their traditional environment and culture, appropriated their labor, given them new names, forced them to learn a new language, and imposed on them new roles, slaves appropriated their masters' language and their symbols of power and property. Slaves spoke of laws coming out from England. They spoke of 'rights'. They spoke of the King, of Wilberforce, and of 'the powerful men in England'. They used their masters' whips and put their masters in the stocks... And when whites fired at them, they shot back. By the middle of the [first] night [of the rebellion], the old African shells and drums were silent. Only the sound of European guns was heard.[64]

However, the rebels also spoke of God (although, at least to their European interrogators and interlocutors, they no longer spoke of gods), they spoke of religion, and they forged a religiously inspired African movement within the protective shell of European institutions, both secular and sectarian. As Romeo, deacon of Smith's Bethel chapel and religious teacher and leader of the slaves on Success and Le Resouvenir plantations, put it, recalling his interpretation to the congregation of Revelations 3:3, 'God is not so slack in his promises as some men are... My explanation was, that if you deceive

God, God will set a curse upon you and your children.'⁶⁵ Eventually, the
historian comes up against the limits of the very code of history writing –
the place where the gods have a direct role in everyday life – and wonders

> whether behind the seeming transparency of the documentation assembled by
> the whites, from whom the reality of slave experience was always hidden, there
> was a deeper and elusive 'African' reality difficult to grasp... When Cato [a
> prominent rebel] referred to Quamina as 'Daddy Quamina', did this mean that
> Quamina had a special role in the community, something like a 'fetishman',
> or a 'conjurer'?... Could it be that when Quamina was chosen by the Bethel
> congregation in 1817 to be a deacon, the congregation was only redefining and
> confirming a traditional [African] role?⁶⁶

The modern historian who is tempted to translate rebel statements about
'rights' and 'emancipation' into the terms of Western common sense ought
instead perhaps to find himself or herself in the same confusion as John
Smith, when he wrote in the letter cited above, 'What they mean by their
rights, I know not.'⁶⁷

I realise that there is a risk in my argument here of consolidating a distinction between 'African' and 'European' practices in which Africans are
associated exclusively with the spiritual and the non-modern (a fundamentally 'European' view, if ever there was one). Moreover, I am certainly not
arguing that the Demerara rebels did not appropriate *any* of the secular,
modern cultural practices and beliefs of those in power in the colony. For
example, there is a certain echo of the British obsession with recording
and preserving written documents that runs through the accounts of the
Demerara rebellion. Jack Gladstone, Quamina's son and perhaps the principal figure in the revolt, is described by almost every witness as 'reading
a paper' to the slaves as they gathered at Success after chapel on Sunday
17 August that announced the 'fact' that the British king had freed the
slaves but the local authorities in Demerara were refusing to implement
this new law; later he carried papers to whites who were put in the stocks by
the rebels and asked them to sign them to prove they had been well treated
as prisoners; and the crucial communication held against John Smith at
his trial was a written note from the slave Jackey Reed disclaiming his
involvement in the planned uprising, enclosing a note to Jackey from Jack
Gladstone. Some of the political rituals of the humane, modern imperial
power, down to and including the practice of passing along information
in 'enclosures' so familiar now to readers of British government correspondence, are here copied and translated into new forms by the slaves.⁶⁸
The white authorities themselves rejected their own humanitarian

practices – the suppression of the rebellion began with the militia firing indiscriminately into a crowd of unarmed people, killing 200. Later, the colonial authorities attempted to reincorporate the slaves' narrative back into their own: Jack was made to declare at the end of his 'confession' that, 'from the hour I was made prisoner by Captain M'Turk up to this time, I have received the most humane treatment from all the whites', a mocking echo of the slaves' attempt to influence white opinion by the treatment of their prisoners;[69] and in a bitter historical irony, the transcripts of rebel testimony, depositions, and interrogations all come down to us as 'enclosures' themselves, documents attached to dispatches from Governor Murray to Lord Bathurst and reproduced, as expressions both of humane concern and of imperial power, in the sessional papers of the British legislature.

Nevertheless, despite these echoes of 'modern', secular political logic, it is clear that for the rebels themselves – as opposed to both the contemporary colonial authorities and to future postcolonial historians – 'rights' fundamentally signified religious rights. For example, the 'right' to more leisure time (a key complaint of the slaves) was connected to their religious responsibilities and commitments: Bristol said at Smith's trial, 'What created the discontent in the mind of the negroes was, because they had no other time to wash their clothes, or do any thing for themselves, but the Sabbath day, they could not wash their clothes or do any thing for themselves on a Sunday, because they had to go to the chapel.'[70] When Governor Murray encountered the rebels on the road outside Georgetown, he told them that the laws coming out from England would mean an end to the flogging of women and to overseers carrying whips in the field (this, in fact, was the sum total of the 'something good' the slaves had been hearing about); the rebels replied that 'these things . . . were no comfort to them; God had made them of the same flesh and blood as the whites; they were tired of being slaves . . . and they would work no more'.[71] Eugene Genovese has famously argued that African-American conversions to Christianity represented 'a political weakness, which dictated, however necessarily and realistically, acceptance of the hegemony of the oppressor'.[72] (Analogously, and equally notoriously, E. P. Thompson argued in *The Making of the English Working Class* that Methodism deflected the workers from their revolutionary goals.) The evidence from Demerara challenges Genovese's position, and confounds the modern distinction between religion and politics. If religious conversions could produce new respectable churchgoing groups in the Caribbean such as that attended by Mary Lindsay in Morant Bay, the Demerara rebellion suggests that conversion could just as well produce a kind of revolutionary dissent.

One of the most striking aspects of the Demerara events was the way in which African-Caribbean testimony became the basis for the subsequent debate in the House of Commons in 1824, in which MPs on both sides of the case invoked the words of individual slaves in order to back one version of the story or another. We could read this as evidence that the rebel slaves directly influenced the political process; that they compelled a political response in the forms of imperial lawmaking, the workings of pro- and antislavery groups in British civil society, the uneven but inevitable development of the political conditions necessary for slave emancipation in the 1830s. But in order to tell the narrative in this way, we need to confront more explicitly the problematic status of the evidence in the case of Demer-ara, and to foreground what Chakrabarty calls the 'scandalous aspects of our . . . translations' of that evidence,[73] if we are to recover African-Caribbean agency from the colonial archive. That scandal, I want to argue, is inseparable from a certain 'romantic' impulse towards the subaltern past.

James Stephen, prominent abolitionist and opponent of Simon Taylor in the battle over the slave registry act of the 1810s, who was an important civil servant in the Colonial Office with a major hand in writing West Indian policy during this period, made explicit at the annual meeting of the Anti-Slavery Society in 1824 the romantic scandal involved in invoking slave testimony in the Demerara case:

The evidence of Slaves, Sir, is sufficient, it seems, to convict a preacher of the Gospel! [i.e., John Smith]. It is sufficient to condemn him to death; although the Slaves who give the evidence are swearing for their own lives! – It is sufficient to give currency and judicial credit to the most palpable, and monstrous, and inconsistent fables that ever were invented in romance – It is sufficient to prove that a pious self-devoted minister of the Gospel of Peace, is an instigator of sedition, rebellion, and bloodshed – It is sufficient to prove that a man who is sinking into his grave . . . is desirous of being the leader in a bloody and desperate contest of bands of insurgent Slaves, in order that he may be made their Emperor, and reign over them in the swamps and woods of the Guiana continent!![74]

Of course, the sympathetic postcolonial historian may believe he or she is coming at the question from the opposite end of the spectrum from the benevolent paternalism of the outraged abolitionist who here points out the inconsistency of accepting slave testimony in this case while denying it in most others, but only points out that inconsistency in order to defend the reputation of a turbulent, English priest. Trained to read for what the text leaves unsaid, or for the moment at which the text betrays itself in paradox and demonstrates the opposite of what it appears to be saying, the postcolonial historian seeks to uncover and recuperate a hidden truth from the contradictory scraps of the colonial archive. And yet, how is this historian to recover black agency, and black religious practice, from an archive that itself often appears to be structured, as Stephen seems to be arguing, according to the protocols of imperial romance? When slaves testify that 'Quamina insisted on being the king, Jack the governor; Parson Smith was to have been our emperor, and to have ruled every thing', on what grounds does the future historian bracket this off as 'romance', or fantasy, and consign it, as James Stephen did, to the realm of absurdity beyond the pale of responsible historiography?[75]

The uncomfortable truth for the historian and cultural critic committed both to the goals of social justice (with their link to the secular public sphere) and to a certain fidelity to the subaltern past (with its scandalous agency of the gods) is that sometimes her or his work will be virtually indistinguishable from the paranoid fantasies of the colonial authorities. Seeing secret religious organisations and 'primitive' African beliefs hidden behind the façade of chapels was a staple of planter life. Seeing plots and conspiracies and potential uprisings at every turn was part of the structure of elite culture in the West Indies, as I showed in my analysis of Simon Taylor's letters in chapter 1. As the 1824 Anti-Slavery Society report put it disdainfully, mocking their planter foes' tactics, 'No political manoeuvre . . . is more easy or safe than pretences of plots in societies like those of the West Indies.'[76]

Recently, historians have begun to re-examine the documentary evidence about other slave uprisings, including the Haitian Revolution and the Denmark Vesey case in South Carolina, asking whether in fact the famous religious ceremony at Bois Cayman that inaugurated the revolution in St Domingue was nothing other than the fantasy of a French torturer projected on to and repeated by his victims, and whether the slave rebellion planned by Vesey existed anywhere except in the heads of white magistrates in Charleston.[77] How are we to deal today with the possibility of our complicity with the colonial authorities – inventing the same plots the planters invented 200 years ago – arising from our attempts to avoid simply assimilating the subaltern past to our secular, realist historiography? In other words, simply because the archive is structured like a romance, this does not mean that it does not contain the 'facts' about the past. The historian's challenge is to be faithful to the past, and to its archive, even at the risk of writing a kind of historical romance, without thereby reproducing the plantocracy's paranoid fantasies of black people's propensity for 'primitive' forms of violence.

It seems to me that there are two possible responses to this challenge. Firstly, we can make the case that imperial romance is itself a response to subaltern practices and beliefs, rather than a simple exercise in misrepresentation or stereotyping. The metropolitan need to understand the West Indies in terms of obeah, or witchcraft, for instance, which persisted and mutated in the first thirty years of the nineteenth century, might be read as a response to the fact that during this same period African religious practices increasingly began to merge with Christianity, blurring and threatening the boundaries between the two. The second possible response is to foreground the rules of genre that mark certain discourses as 'romantic', and others as 'historical', in order to show that the self-conscious literariness of the former is in fact a necessary component of any responsible historical narrative, an acknowledgement of the limits of the code of history writing that make possible the production of history itself. Walter Scott, who knew a thing or two about the relationship between romance and history, famously declared at the end of *Waverley*, 'Indeed, the most romantic parts of this narrative are precisely those which have a foundation in fact.'[78] In effect, I am arguing for a reversal of this formula: the most historical parts of this narrative are precisely those which have a foundation in romance. In order to investigate these two possible approaches, I want to turn to an analysis of the novel *Hamel, the Obeah Man*.

This novel was published anonymously in 1827, shortly before the bankruptcy of its publishers, Hunt and Clarke; it has been largely forgotten until very recently, except for an article praising it as the best pre-emancipation novel about the West Indies, by the Barbadian poet and historian Kamau Brathwaite.[79] In this moment of resurgent interest in literature of empire in general, and in the nineteenth-century Caribbean in particular, *Hamel* has begun to attract a little more attention recently. Two new editions of the novel are in preparation, and several critics have produced impressive and useful analyses of the novel in recent years.[80] As I mentioned at the beginning of this chapter, internal stylistic evidence, and remarks in two contemporary reviews, suggest that the novel was written by the same author as *A Tour through the Island of Jamaica*, discussed above, which was published under the name Cynric R. Williams by the same publisher, Hunt and Clarke, the year before *Hamel* appeared, in 1826.[81] As I have argued, there is a strong case for identifying the author of *Hamel* and Williams's *Tour* as the Jamaican planter Charles White Williams.

Hamel represents the apotheosis of anti-missionary planter defensiveness couched in the terms of imperial romance. A villainous evangelical missionary, Roland, incites rebellion amongst the slaves in Jamaica in order to gain power for himself in the post-revolution island and capture Joanna, the beautiful daughter of a local planter. Roland is opposed by Fairfax, the heroic white Jamaican heir to a set of sugar estates, who has been unfairly slandered as an arsonist by Roland and so must travel the island with a group of rebel slaves, disguised as a mulatto, seeking to restore order so that he may declare himself openly to his lover, Joanna. For the most part, the slaves are depicted only as loyal (if ignorant) servants or disloyal (and therefore ignorant) rebels, and proslavery rhetoric is placed in the mouths of slaves such as Hamel, a noble African-born religious leader, in order to persuade the novel's readers of the plantocracy's longstanding claim that African slaves in the West Indies were happy, well cared for, and certainly better off than the poor, free, white 'lower orders' of Britain and Ireland. *Hamel* is a romance of the British periphery, explicitly in the mould of Walter Scott's fiction, a celebration and a valediction of a people whose way of life is about to be consigned to the past, the white planter class of the Caribbean.

Hamel in many respects echoes the paranoid fantasies of the Jamaican catastrophe predicted by many planters and their supporters in the region and in Britain to be the result of abolitionist agitation and missionary interference. For example, George Bridges, the most prominent Anglican minister in Jamaica during this period, penned a rebuttal to Wilberforce's *Appeal* in which he berated those 'who labour under the popular mask of philanthropy, to bring down destruction and ruin on our West Indian Colonies, and complete the dreadful tragedy which has been unhappily acted in a neighbouring island [i.e., Haiti]'.[82] Indeed, *Hamel* uncannily prefigures the white response to the 1832 slave rebellion in Jamaica, the largest in the island's history, which was misleadingly attributed to missionary influence and dubbed the 'Baptist War', and which led to the formation, by Rev. Bridges and others, of the Colonial Church Union in the island, a white vigilante group that destroyed mission chapels and physically and verbally assaulted missionaries themselves.[83] At first glance, *Hamel* would appear to be an unlikely venue to find either black agency, or to work out the interpenetration of the generic boundaries between romance and history. But, I want to argue, this proslavery literary text is actually an important site for an analysis of both of these questions.

Black agency can be found in the novel by examining the trope – common both to *Hamel* and to *Waverley* – of the Englishman more or less unwillingly taking part in a colonial rebellion. (The narrative of John Smith in the Demerara rebellion tellingly also follows almost precisely this pattern, especially in its pro-missionary versions – no doubt the all but universal appeal of Scott to the literate classes of Hanoverian Britain contributed to the popularity of the Smith-as-martyr version of the Demerara events.) The figures of Waverley and Fairfax, symbolic captives of subaltern revolts, allow the reader to maintain interest and reading pleasure in the possible overthrow of legitimate order, one of the hallmarks of the romantic novel, while at the same time keeping a proper distance. The Jacobite rebellion of 1745, and the imaginary Jamaican uprising of *Hamel*, are represented but also recontained within the worlds of the novel; nevertheless, this containment can never be complete. Fairfax, for example, appears in the novel most frequently disguised either as a mulatto, Sebastian – in which guise he takes part in a reconnaissance mission with rebel slaves in the very house of his lover, Joanna, and her father, Mr Guthrie – or as a Maroon, caught up in the massive slave insurrection that dominates the second half of the novel. Although the rules of the genre insure that he somehow retains his heroic status despite these disguises, the fact remains that the slave uprising, and the autonomous actions of the slaves themselves, ultimately drive the plot. Indeed, early on in this anti-missionary tract, Fairfax, in the company of the rebels, commits precisely the crime of failing to report a rebellion to the authorities that John Smith was accused and convicted of in Demerara: because this group of rebels freed Fairfax from the Cuban pirates who had earlier captured him, "'I owed to them my safety, perhaps my life, at any rate my liberty and the means of returning to my native land; else I had delivered them up to the magistrates, the instant they set foot in Jamaica.'"[84] Instead, despite Fairfax's best efforts to thwart their revolutionary plans, some of the rebels escape and report back to their leader, Combah – and, at the very end of the novel, they flee to Haiti to recoup and, presumably, fight again another day.

In the world of romance in *Hamel*, amid pirates and wizards and multiple disguises, the reader is led unwittingly – just as Fairfax and Waverley are led, in a sense – to conclusions that are the very opposite of the novel's ostensible message. On one hand, Hamel ventriloquises one element of the conventional attack on John Smith and all the other evangelical missionaries of the time, as he tells Roland that even though he is guilty of monstrous crimes,

'None dare prosecute you; or if they did, and proved you guilty, they dare not punish you. They would condemn you, and send to England for advice, or let you escape; and if they sent to England, are there not thousands like yourself to vindicate you, to prove you innocent, to swear your crimes are imputations, lies, inventions; and that you are, were, and must be, a holy, virtuous, man – a martyr, at the worst?' (H 1:152)

On the other hand, the blurring of the boundaries between Fairfax and Roland, and between Fairfax and the rebel slaves, undercuts and undermines this rhetorical and logical excess, which lays the blame for all Jamaica's ills at the door of the missionaries. As the novel proceeds, its interest in Roland appears to wane – he spends much of volume two offstage, either locked up in jail or hiding in Hamel's cave and lagoon complex – as if in tacit recognition of the illogicality of the novel's own vitriol. The result of this fading from view of the missionary-as-rebel leader is that the rebels themselves come to occupy centre stage. In this respect as well, the fulminations of George Bridges offer a useful parallel text to *Hamel*. In Bridges's thinking, despite the retention of stereotypical views of African Jamaicans as savage, there is an explicit movement towards seeing them as, precisely, agents: he claims that the loose talk of people like Wilberforce will lead to the deaths of 'thousands' of white Jamaicans under 'the scalping knife of men now harmless, contented, and quiet; but whose almost obliterated African passions such language is calculated to inflame, and thus to transform our very servants into agents devoted to our destruction'.[85] In the prose of counterinsurgency of these most unrepentant proslavery advocates, the potential for insurrection is always in excess of its apparent cause, the words and actions of the 'saints', who thereby cease to be the real problem. Instead, the nameless black slaves, and their 'almost obliterated African passions', become the engines of social and historical change, even as they are characterised repeatedly as foolish, drunken, lazy, and irresponsible. These are the figures for whom Srinivas Aravamudan has coined the term 'tropicopolitan', which he says is 'a name for the colonized subject who exists both as fictive construct of colonial tropology *and* actual resident of tropical space, object of representation *and* agent of resistance'.[86]

In *Hamel*, an expansive and inconsistent set of fictive constructs and generic patterns clashes with a narrow pedagogical agenda. The antimissionary invective of the novel allows the missionary's fictional foil, Hamel, to be a complex and contradictory figure, at once a wizard in the 'Oriental' style, like the Travelling Magician in the *Arabian Nights*; a noble African, a natural leader of men (like Graman Quacy), unfairly torn from his native soil and enslaved (like Oroonoko); the loyal servant to the wise Fairfax family (like Juba in *Belinda*); and a dangerous but clever revolutionary strategist (like Toussaint Louverture, whose leadership of the only successful slave revolt in history inspired horror and homage in roughly equal parts in contemporary Britain).[87]

There are frequent Shakespearean epigraphs scattered throughout the novel. On the title page are Brabantio's lines falsely accusing Othello of

sorcery in the wooing of Desdemona: 'I apprehend and do attach thee /
For an abuser of the world, a practiser / Of arts inhibited and out of warrant' – suggesting even before the novel opens that the eponymous hero
is a noble warrior who should not be judged by the prevailing stereotypes
about blacks and witchcraft, a warning that echoes through a tale that falls
back frequently on these very ideas. Chapter headings are followed by lines
from, among others, *King Lear*, *Measure for Measure*, *Macbeth*, and, on several occasions, *The Tempest*. The Shakespearean allusions entail necessary
ambiguities in the reader's response to Hamel, an ambiguity that no other
character in the novel incites: Hamel is Prospero, carefully orchestrating
the movement of people in and out of his magical and mysterious cave
and lagoon complex; Hamel is Caliban, plotting revenge against those who
have enslaved him; Hamel is Othello, a brave warrior who does some service to the state but who ultimately cannot be accommodated by it; Hamel
is even Edgar, the noble son disguised as the subaltern figure of Poor
Tom, leading the blind Gloucester (or, in this case, the blind rebel leader,
Combah) to the seashore (H ii:58). The cultural authority of Shakespeare
and the need to elevate the black religious leader over the English one
combine to make Hamel a rare figure in pre-twentieth-century literature
in English: a black character with complex and legitimate motivations for
his actions. He will do anything he can to save his master, Fairfax, and his
master's beloved, Joanna, from the clutches of the rebel slaves; however, he
himself has organised the slaves in revolt, and he champions their cause and
declares it to be just. '"There is justice upon the earth, though it seems to
sleep; and the black men shall, first or last, shed your blood, and toss your
bodies into the sea!"' (H ii:197), he says to the principal white figures in the
novel, during what Kamau Brathwaite has called 'probably the first Black
Power speech in our literature'.[88] As Barbara Lalla puts it, more prosaically
but perhaps more realistically, 'This novel marks a major development in
the foundation of a Caribbean perspective in that its ultimate protagonist
is black.'[89] The interest of the novel lies in these complications, embodied
in the figure of Hamel, which belie the simple invective of the implied
author and the clunkiness of the novel's narrative style.

   Thus Roland, the ostensible villain of the piece, is undercut almost as
soon as he appears: stumbling by chance during a hurricane into Hamel's
cave, Roland picks up the obeah man's clay lamp, which is covered with
magical inscriptions, in order to light his way. The dependence of the
lost evangelical missionary on the Caribbean 'wizard' is proposed from the
beginning, and reinforced when Hamel lends Roland some of his clothes
to wear. At the narrative level, too, Roland's point of view often gives way

to Hamel's, as during a large nighttime gathering of rebels at an abandoned plantation, where the free indirect discourse of the narration shifts suddenly and without explanation or even a new paragraph, from 'he [Roland] felt that Hamel was his rival' to 'Hamel... contrived to impress his enemy with even a superior notion of his own capability... This was a triumph too dear to the Obeah man, to be renounced or trifled with' (H 1:128–9). While Roland decides to 'mould... the conjuror to his purposes' (H 1:36), the reader soon discovers that moulding and manipulation are actually the prerogative of Hamel himself.

Of course, romance allows the reader to indulge the fantasy of disguise and of revolt; visions of bandits and wizards are so self-consciously fictional that they can hardly trouble the terms of the debate about the future of slavery and the West Indian colonies. Moreover, Hamel is clearly a descendant of other African heroes in English literature, an heir to the legacies of Othello, Oroonoko, and Graman Quacy. And yet, I want to argue here, the loose, contradictory expansiveness of the novel – a looseness born perhaps of a self-righteous assurance of the merits of its anti-missionary argument – does in fact change the terms of the debate over slavery, or at least reveals the presuppositions and hesitancies of that debate, on both sides. Hamel – doubly unthreatening, as a familiar Oroonoko figure, and as the novel's vehicle for proslavery ideology – speaks sometimes in a way that suggests that both proslavery ideology and the myth of the noble-but-enslaved African are in fact *responses* to the threat of slave uprising. It is in this respect that he is a 'tropicopolitan', at once an 'object of representation and agent of resistance', as Aravamudan puts it. Hamel implausibly begs Fairfax to ensure that slavery endures, and mocks the idea of freedom for African Jamaicans: '"Freedom! I am free enough, except the white man quit the island"' (H 1:179). Moreover, if freedom comes, blacks will only squander it, he says: '"The ignorant, nasty, drunken Negroes... Some will make the others work: there will be slaves for ever, unless the white man stay with soldiers and cannons to keep the strong ones from beating the weak ones, and making the women do all the work"' (H 1:179). These are – line for line – the arguments of the planters and their supporters, such as Rev. George Bridges and the white Jamaicans 'Cynric' Williams meets during his tour through the island. But it is as if such ventriloquising licenses Hamel's other statements, which are in themselves contradictory and complicated, not simply the flipside of proslavery rhetoric that ends up reinforcing it. Instead, Hamel plots revenge, in the name of justice, against the whites who stole him from his native land and struggles to retain his flock under pressure from Christian conversions. As Barbara Lalla has argued, 'This explosion of emotion, credible in a Jamaican setting that is socially as well as physically realistic, cuts through the more contrived discourse that relays doctrine.'⁹⁰

Thus the reader listens to Hamel deliver the following speeches, or gains access to his thoughts through the use of free indirect discourse:

> On . . . revolution his own soul was bent: his arts, his influence, his every energy, were devoted to the extermination of the Whites, or to their expulsion from the island. It is not enough to say he detested them: his hatred was charged with the recollection of the outrages he had himself endured. (H 1:130–1)

> 'I was at the bottom of this plan of insurrection – yes – never start or stare. I am determined to yield up myself – my life – everything. I would have revenged myself on the buckras for bringing me away from my own country, and selling me to a Negro. I would have made Combah king of the island . . . to teach the buckras that black men have as much courage, and power, and knowledge, and strength, and right, as white ones. They will repay one day on all your heads. There is justice upon the earth, though it seems to sleep; and the black men shall, first or last, shed your blood, and toss your bodies into the sea!' (H 11:196–7)

> By holding him [Roland] up to the Negroes in a ridiculous light, he exposed the pretensions of the zealot, and prevented his own persuasion from falling altogether into contempt among the black population. (H 11:84–5)

Even when he tells Roland that he can stop the rebellion – a declaration that in fact turns out to be premature – Hamel reserves the right to future resistance, and gestures to a different worldview offstage, as it were: '"There shall be no rebellion; master Roland, you have gone too far! I hate the white men – I abhor them! I wish – But that is no matter"' (H 11:80). So a novel that begins by describing the setting of the tropical sun as something that 'relieved from his scorching rays those Europeans who toil on the northern shores of Jamaica' (H 1:1), without even mentioning the toiling black majority, ends with white and black Jamaicans alike in thrall to the receding figure of Hamel as he sails back to Africa, alone in a canoe:

> They [Guthrie, Fairfax, and 'the Duppie', a loyal slave] rode to the top of the rocks which overhung the sea, whence they could, by the help of a spy-glass, for a long time distinguish the Obeah man sitting in his canoe, in a pensive posture, gazing on the deep blue waves that heaved around him . . . They watched him without regarding the time they so misapplied, until his little boat had diminished to a speck . . . The Duppie gazed till he was almost blind . . . and Mr Guthrie gazed in two or three directions at once with no better success; indeed none of them could assign any reason for gazing at all. Hamel was never heard of more! (H 11:327)

Hamel, the figure, and *Hamel*, the novel, therefore, help us to understand some of the ways in which the genre of romance can actually be useful in revealing historical truths unavailable to history itself, and in laying bare the codes and limits whereby that history gets constructed in the first place. It is perhaps only in anti-liberal, and therefore in a sense anti-secular, rhetoric, and within the protocols of romance, that the agency of the African-Caribbean slaves can be read most clearly, in genres in which the colonial Other is invested with a certain individualistic, eccentric, anti- or non-modern grandeur whose very excess undoes the codes of the humanitarian modernity that underwrote the new imperialism of the nineteenth century. Crucially, even a stereotypical and sometimes poorly constructed romance like *Hamel* expects readers actively to reconstruct its meaning. The novel even foregrounds this particular problem: 'Much must be left to the imagination of the spectator; not because it spares the pains of the painter, but because it is the business of the artist to set the spectator's imagination at work' (H II:60). Thus the apparent paradox that the excessive and patently inaccurate ethnography of a novel like *Hamel*, and by extension of the genre of the romantic novel in general, allows the reader to interpret a certain truth missed by the repressive tolerance of abolitionist writers:

What this novel does, despite its quite natural assumptions about white superiority, is recognize the fact that African slaves, in the New World, despite their transportation, would have continued to be cultured beings, and that obeah men, as the religious leaders of these beings, would have been the main depositories of this culture. And that such slaves were not Nature's playthings, but moral sentient beings neither Toms nor Noble Savages.[91]

In this respect, *Hamel* takes its place next to *Waverley*, to which it is substantially indebted, as a novel that fails to recontain the uprising that it represents. In *Waverley*, the rebel Highlanders have their spokesperson in the figure of Flora Mac-Ivor, who, because she is merely a disempowered woman, can safely articulate genuine historical grievances.[92] As Ina Ferris has argued:

The Waverley Novels both cooperate with and disorient the official discourse of history. At their most general level of implication . . . they leave in place the established reading of historical events . . . The official, inscribed plot of history, in fact, serves as their enabling assumption: the story of the progress of civil society and of the British state (virtual synonyms) that culminates in the 'Glorious Revolution' of 1688. But the oblique and specific approach of his fiction to this plot – most obvious in Scott's concentration on obscure communities and minor events – inevitably novelizes . . . the historical genre. It does so by placing in question the adequacy of a paradigmatic understanding and by uncovering the 'singular' stories inevitably lost in the generalizing sweep of standard narrative history.[93]

In *Hamel*, the eponymous 'wizard' is much more mobile, if more ambiguous in his political pronouncements, than Flora. As the loyal slave of Fairfax, he has a licence to travel throughout the narrative, and the island, always appearing as if from nowhere. As the mouthpiece for proslavery ideology, Hamel also has a licence to speak of rebellion, and even to plan it – although of course it must ultimately be deferred until some unspecified point after the end of the novel, just as the Jacobite rebellion can be portrayed sympathetically in *Waverley* because its historical defeat can be taken for granted outside the frame of the novel. When the slightly bumbling, if good-hearted, planter Guthrie (a copy of Scott's Baron Bradwardine) complains to his slaves after a hurricane that they failed to look after him during the storm, the narrator's (and the reader's) ironic detachment in the face of Guthrie's 'harangue' becomes indistinguishable from Hamel's revolutionary engagement in the face of white paternalism:

> Mr. Guthrie, heated, exhausted, indignant, and enraged, gave vent to his passion in thus stigmatizing the feelings of his slaves for attending to their own affairs in the late emergency, instead of sacrificing them to their concern for his. If his figure and appearance were ludicrous by the lamp light of the preceding night, they were scarcely less than diverting even to his Negroes by day. (H 1:70)

The narrator's strategic 'even', in this last sentence, can do no more than foreground the extent to which the novel consistently finds itself unwittingly adopting the slaves' and rebels' point of view, and thereby undoing its own goals. Ultimately, the proslavery loyalty of Hamel becomes an afterthought, in a reversal of the novel's paternalistic starting point. Trying to rescue Roland from the jail where he is being held on suspicion of fomenting rebellion, Hamel imagines a partnership between the two religious leaders,

> where their mutual services tended to bring about the same end, the object which the wizard had long entertained – the subversion of the power and authority of the whites throughout the island. It is true this feeling of his had been somewhat neutralized by his sense of obligation to Mr. Fairfax, but still a time might come. He would not willingly part with so efficient an agent as Roland, who was exactly the character which Hamel would have sought or desired, to create a confusion in the island, and revenge him and his countrymen on their oppressors. (H 11:140–1)

At the end of the novel, as we have seen, Hamel sails away alone to Africa, "'the land of my birth, my mother's country'" (H 11:326), still a rebel figure, unsettling the traditional marriage settlement between Fairfax and Joanna that ostensibly restores order in the world of romance.

And yet, we could say, rereading the rebel slave as hero (Jack Gladstone or Hamel) is itself a romantic gesture, made legitimate by the rules of a genre that immunises itself from political instability by locating its action once upon a time, or in a land far, far away. Perhaps even more unsettling for the historian reading *Hamel* is the way in which it brings to the forefront and makes explicit – in its literariness – the generic choices and discursive strategies involved in narrating the events in Demerara, for example, from a particular perspective. In order for that narrative to count as 'history', Chakrabarty says, this perspective must be 'rational' and 'defensible'. And yet, it is in the gothic melodrama of *Hamel*'s slave conspiracy that we might uncover the truth about the relationship between John Smith, the Bethel chapel community, and the Demerara rebels. Roland addresses the rebels in an incendiary prayer meeting in the ruins of an abandoned plantation house, but literally underneath his feet the real conspiracy is taking place, an African religious ceremony into which Roland tumbles unwittingly, realising too late that the rebels have used him and his religion for their own ends. It is not rational or defensible to begin an account of the Demerara rebellion with a scene of fictional witchcraft, replete with grave dirt, blood, and human skulls – and yet, I am suggesting, this may be a necessary first step in the writing of a history that recognises its own limits and resists the discipline's own romance with 'facts'. (Later in the novel, the ruins of the rebel meeting place become the camp of the white militia, suggesting the blurring of identities that Viswanathan sees as the hallmark of religious conversion, and which further undermines our ability to narrate a rebellion from a coherent point of view.) An analysis of this novel offers a way of 'tak[ing] history, the code, to its limits in order to make its unworking visible', as Dipesh Chakrabarty suggests responsible historiography should do.[94] When Roland encounters Hamel in the depths of the obeah man's cave at the outset of the tale, he asks in horror, 'Who or what art thou?', and Hamel's first words to both the missionary and the reader make explicit the romantic projection that is the precondition for entry into the world of the subaltern: '"Master"', he says, '"what you will"' (H 1:24).

Finally, then, I conclude that a responsible history of a subaltern revolt has to pass through the irresponsible fiction of the peripheral elite in order to 'unwork' the secular language of historiography. Romance and the gods are not simply the elements that must be excluded in order for 'history' to constitute itself as rational and defensible; they are at once the limits and the condition of possibility for a history that cannot disentangle itself from fiction. Chakrabarty argues that, paradoxically, it is only to the extent that we *refuse* to historicise figures from the past and instead see them as our contemporaries – 'illuminating a life possibility for the present' – that we are able to write them into history at all, because their imaginary contemporaneity to us is 'the condition under which we can even begin to treat them as intelligible to us'.[95] This perhaps is the way out of the dilemma of the postcolonial historian or cultural critic caught between what Ian Baucom calls actuarial and romantic historicisms. Chakrabarty points the way towards a type, the subaltern who is simultaneously past and present, that is neither romantic – the historicism of the lost object – nor actuarial – the type reduced to thinghood and calculability. Instead, he offers a kind of cosmopolitan historicism that is prepared to run the risk of romance in order to establish the legitimacy of its objects as subjects. The abiding irony here is that we have arrived at this figure via an analysis of the fiction of the disgruntled planters determined to maintain their grip on the slave system to the very end.

CHAPTER 3

'This fruitful matrix of curses':
the interesting narrative of the life
of Samuel Ringgold Ward

In this chapter, I analyse the remarkable and strange career of Samuel Ringgold Ward. This black Congregationalist/Baptist minister, activist, and writer was born into slavery in Maryland in 1817, then became a prominent abolitionist in New York State in the 1840s, editing a well-regarded newspaper, the *Impartial Citizen*, before fleeing to Canada in 1851 after helping to rescue an imprisoned runaway ex-slave in Syracuse, in defiance of the Fugitive Slave Act. After working among the black community of Ontario, and lending his name and influence to Mary Ann Shadd Carey's important newspaper, the *Provincial Freeman*, he then journeyed across the Atlantic to Britain in 1853, where he was a huge success on the antislavery, temperance, Sunday School, and missionary circuits, and where he published his *Autobiography of a Fugitive Negro* in 1855 (where figure 3.1 originally appeared as the frontispiece). Just as the book rolled off the presses, however, Ward set off across the Atlantic again, settling first in Kingston and then in St David parish in eastern Jamaica, where he found himself caught up in the events of the Morant Bay rebellion of 1865.

The uprising has garnered increasing attention in recent years, to the point where its prominence in accounts of nineteenth-century British imperialism comes close to matching its importance in histories of Jamaica and the anglophone Caribbean, where it is firmly established as one of the most significant events in the period between emancipation in the 1830s and the rise of the nationalist and labour movements in the 1930s such as Norman Manley's People's National Party. In October 1865, a group of African Jamaicans in St Thomas-in-the-East, led by Paul Bogle, rescued one of their friends from punishment before the hated magistrates in the nearby town of Morant Bay; then they overwhelmed the police sent to arrest them the following day; finally, several hundred of them marched on the town to demand justice. The local worthies, expecting trouble, had called out the local volunteer militia; shots were fired, and several of the rebels were killed; then the rebels laid siege to the courthouse and took over the town,

Figure 3.1 Samuel Ringgold Ward

killing eighteen and wounding dozens, predominantly whites. The insurgents subsequently attacked, occupied, and plundered many plantations in St Thomas-in-the-East, including Simon Taylor's former estate of Golden Grove. Demonstrating its continued importance in the district, however, the main house at Golden Grove was spared the destruction meted out to much planter property in the area, since apparently it was to have become the new residence of Paul Bogle once the insurrection succeeded. The insurgents, however, were never well organised, and they were no match for the might of the colonial military machine once it rolled into action. The governor, Edward Eyre, declared martial law in the district, and in the month-long suppression of the abortive uprising that followed, upwards of 400 people were killed, most without trial, hundreds were flogged, and a thousand houses were burned. Bogle, along with the other leaders of the rebellion, was quickly captured and executed.[1] Despite his background as a militant abolitionist and fervent critic of white paternalism, however, Ward wholeheartedly opposed the rebellion, made several public statements in support of Governor Eyre, and thereby found himself on the wrong side of history.

There has been no full-length biography of Ward, and he is referred to most often in footnotes or passing references in works about his now more illustrious comrades and rivals, Frederick Douglass, Alexander Crummell, and Martin Delany.[2] Ward is hard to place, and not only because his peripatetic life means that its full range obviously cannot be understood within the context of histories that use national frameworks – American, Canadian, British, or Jamaican – or even of those that call themselves imperial, which tend to leave out the United States or relegate it to a sidebar. Ward's confounding politics, especially at the end of his life in Jamaica, have worked against his historical recuperation, even in this moment of accelerating interest in transatlantic histories in general, and black Atlantic stories in particular. I read Ward's autobiography and his Morant Bay pamphlet, *Thoughts upon the Gordon Rebellion*, not only as expressions of black conservatism, but also as complex texts in which Ward continually tried to free himself from potential capture by forces that threatened to engulf him: the syncretic Afro-Christian revival sweeping through Jamaica before the rebellion; the emergence of a 'coloured' elite in Jamaica who tended to look down on blacks; and the colonial authorities who lumped independent ministers like Ward into the category of rabble-rousers and demagogues. Ward fought his whole life for a kind of black internationalism that, paradoxically, he could articulate only within the framework of the British empire and Victorian respectability.

In 1855, as he was coming up to the end of his British sojourn, Ward penned a series of articles for his old comrade and rival's publication, *Frederick Douglass' Paper*, announcing a curious compound figure, the 'modern negro'.[3] Unsurprisingly, at this moment in mid-Victorian life when new forms of modern anti-black racism were emerging (see chapter 4 below), Ward's pieces are couched in what David Scott, in his recent book on C. L. R. James and the writing of postcolonial history, calls the mode of 'vindicationism': 'The demand to confront and repudiate the affront of racism's slander and to defend the integrity and equality of his [James's] race'.[4] Thus Ward begins his third article by declaring ruefully that 'We are compelled, just because the issue is forced upon us by our enemies, in defending our claim to equality, to compare the Negro with the

Anglo-Saxon race.'[5] In the first article, he annuls the differences between himself (black, in Britain) and Douglass ('mulatto', in the United States): 'You, from your stand point, we from ours, are alike enabled to vindicate our race, and to repel the vile, foul slanders by which that race has been – by the baser half of the Anglo-Saxon race – aspersed.'[6] It is precisely because of these 'slanders', in their specifically modern articulation, that an idea of modern diasporic black subjectivity is possible. The 'variety' of Ward's and Douglass's positions and racial classifications, 'negro' and 'mulatto', 'for which neither of us is responsible, praiseworthy, or blameworthy', allows them, Ward claims, '*united* opportunities of illustrating and defending the manhood and the equality of our African ancestry, and our Africo-American brethren'.[7]

Equality and fraternity are quite explicitly produced for Ward out of a starting point of difference rather than similarity: his version of black internationalism will be alive to the difficulty of creating links. In *The Practice of Diaspora*, Brent Edwards has argued convincingly that black internationalism 'necessarily involves a process of linking or connecting across gaps – a practice we might term *articulation*'.[8] Invoking Stuart Hall's work on articulation as a description of society organised by difference rather than similarity, Edwards employs the term 'diaspora' in what he calls an 'anti-abstractionist' rather than an essentialist or abstract mode.[9] Edwards' anti-abstractionist use of diaspora is clearly also an anti-romantic mode, since it refuses the romantic quest for origins and blood connections across time and space, the restoration of a lost essence. However, crucially, such a use must remain vigilant about its possible complicity with romance: 'It is continually necessary to attend to the ways the term [diaspora] always can be re-articulated and abstracted into evocations of untroubled essentialism or inviolate roots.' Edwards's version of diaspora is close to my own here: 'It forces us to articulate discourses of cultural and political linkage only through and across difference in full view of the risks of that endeavor.'[10] Ward, who lived and worked in the United States, Canada, Britain, and Jamaica, who made and broke innumerable personal and political alliances, including this one with Frederick Douglass, and whose black internationalism ended up looking like an endorsement of some of the worst excesses of British imperialism, can serve as an outstanding example of Edwards's thesis.

Given his interest in articulation rather than essentialism, Ward's 'vindicationist' mode does not necessarily lead him in the direction David Scott sees most often associated with this form of writing, 'to the wider formal features of the mythos of Romance and, in particular, to the figuration of the hero'.[11] It is true that Ward finds a few heroes in the ancient past – 'I was delighted to find that the founder of Assyris, whose capital, Nineveh, has recently been exhumed...was a son of Ham', he writes.[12] But Ward's 'modern negro' is a figure who passes through the genre of romance and emerges on the other side into a new, post-emancipation version of historicism. The type of the modern negro is the contemporary product of historical forces, rather than a lost figure of the romantic past; not an idiosyncratic hero, but the result of averaging the historical traces operating in a large group of people across different societies: 'We have 14 millions of our people who have survived the bad oppression, the worse example, and worst of all, *the amalgamation of the unspeakably bad Anglo-Saxon blood*, and are, in all respects, in spite of this treble curse – this fruitful matrix of curses – *somebody*.'[13] Here tropical romance – the kind that brought us Hamel the obeah man, with his wizardry and curses, but also the hidden history of Simon Taylor and Grace Donne – is given a new framework from the language of biology and mathematics. According to the *OED*, the word 'matrix' in the mid-nineteenth century was completing its own journey from its Latin roots in the idea of maternity to its modern scientific cast: from meaning 1.1., 'the womb; the uterus of an animal', to meanings 1.3.b., 'An amorphous or fibrillar material that surrounds cells', and 1.7.a., 'A rectangular array of symbols or mathematical expressions arranged in rows and columns, treated as a single entity.' When the Atlantic world becomes a matrix, the unspeakable history of slavery can be recast as an ironic kind of fruition: the result is a specifically modern type, a 'somebody' who is neither romantic rebel nor commodified chattel. After the pre-emancipation world of creole realism and Caribbean romance discussed in my first two chapters, the complex life and writings of Samuel Ringgold Ward beg to be understood from the perspective of a disinterested, disenchanted historiography that can sift information from the archive in the service of a story not dictated in advance by the protocols of anticolonial longing or black vindicationism. In this chapter, then, I come closest to adopting the perspective of the traditional historian. I analyse the records of missionary and antislavery organisations, of colonial and US governments, and the vibrant newspapers of the mid-nineteenth-century Atlantic world in search of the elusive Samuel Ringgold Ward. The problem quickly arises, however, that this disinterested, disenchanted historical inquiry in the case of Ward can itself look for all the world like an endorsement of the civilising mission of the British empire that he came to see as the last best hope for his 'Africo-American brethren' in the Atlantic world.

MILITANT ANTISLAVERY ACTIVIST OR APOLOGIST
FOR EMPIRE?

Ward might be said to have lived his life in defiant reverse of the Victorian ideal of progress and development: from prominent abolitionist speaker and writer in upstate New York and Boston in the 1840s and in Canada and Britain in the 1850s to obscure, impoverished independent minister and small farmer in one of the two smallest parishes in Jamaica in the 1860s. His Atlantic travels, coupled with his presence on the spot when the Morant Bay uprising in 1865 propelled Jamaica once again into the centre of British imperial affairs, mean that Ward is a figure through whom we can evaluate the various strands of imperial and anti-imperial thinking running across the Atlantic during this crucial period. Ward had been a figure of celebrity and notoriety in Britain and the United States, and his physical stature – 'a man, six feet high, and, we presume, sixteen stone weight'[14] – and hyperbolic blackness – 'being perfectly black and of unmixed African descent, the splendors of his intellect went directly to the glory of his race', commented Frederick Douglass[15] – were routinely indexed as signs of his larger-than-life status. In this respect, he is in a direct line of descent from Graman Quacy, the Surinamese herbalist and imperial collaborator celebrated by Stedman and immortalised by Blake in the late eighteenth century, as discussed in chapter 1. But Ward was also a representative of a new kind of black migrancy in the nineteenth century that cannot simply be reduced to complicity with imperialism, although his attempts at self-fashioning and his support for the self-organisation of black people in the imperial Atlantic world were often constrained by social and political conditions that were beyond his control.

When Ward first arrived in London in 1853, at the same moment as the British publication of Harriet Beecher Stowe's *Uncle Tom's Cabin*, the press could not resist the comparison. Commenting on Ward's appearance at a public breakfast meeting of the Sunday School Union, the *British Banner* reported that 'The friends of the Slave in the New World could not have selected and sent a more meet human Sequel to "Uncle Tom"... There is the book! There is the man! Never was conjunction happier than the publication of "Uncle Tom" and the advent of S. R. Ward.'[16] The visiting black minister was not averse to taking advantage of such a conjunction: he commented later in his autobiography that 'I had arrived in England at a fortunate time... because of the twofold fact that "Uncle Tom's Cabin" was in every body's hands and heart, and its gifted authoress was the English people's guest.'[17] Nevertheless, the association of Ward with Stowe's stoic hero suggests that 'the man' would be expected to adhere to the script of 'the book', even if he had momentarily stepped out of its pages on to the public stages and platforms of British philanthropy and antislavery. In the formulation of David Scott, Samuel Ringgold Ward was a 'conscript of modernity', in which 'modernity was not a choice New World slaves could exercise but was itself one of the fundamental *conditions* of choice'.[18] Ward made many choices in his long public career, in the United States, in Canada, in Britain, and in Jamaica, many of which might now appear dubious or even reactionary when viewed from the standpoint of a postcolonial historiography that, in Scott's words, 'has continued to be concerned with exposing the *negative* structure of colonialism's power and with demonstrating the colonized's agency in resisting or overcoming these conditions'. For Scott, this means clinging to the narrative mode of romance, 'tell[ing] stories of salvation and redemption' from 'an attitude of anticolonial longing, a longing for anticolonial revolution'.[19] Scott enjoins us to give up this attitude, which he sees as a holdover from a project of anticolonial nationalism that in all other ways postcolonial critique has sought to undo or supplement. Ward's story fits neither the genre of romance nor that of tragedy, which Scott argues is the more appropriate genre for responsible histories of the colonial period. As such, the narrative of the life and travels of Samuel Ringgold Ward represents a singular challenge to the writing of postcolonial history, of the history of Africans in the Americas, and of Caribbean history, in all of which he could and perhaps ought to figure, but in none of which he actually does.

My argument here builds on my discussion in the previous chapter about the risks of the postcolonial historian and cultural critic's romantic investment in black resistance and insurgency. The figure of Ward ought indeed to serve as a powerful prophylactic against such a tendency. In his pamphlet *Thoughts upon the Gordon Rebellion*, completed in February 1866, the same month that he testified before the Jamaica Royal Commission (JRC) sent by the British government to investigate the uprising and its suppression, Ward declared that all the measures used by the colonial authorities to put down the outbreak at Morant Bay had been amply justified. Echoing Edmund Burke's attack on the excesses of the French Revolution not only in his grandiose title, but also in the brief pamphlet's hyperbolic content, and retelling the most elaborate rumours (later shown to be baseless) of rebel violence circulating in the planter-dominated Jamaican press, Ward declared:

The lives of the very best of the population had been most savagely destroyed [by the rebels]. Scenes more horrible than the sacrifices of Dahomy had been exhibited.

The very foundations of civilized society had been uprooted and overturned . . . At such a moment *undue severity would have been impossible*. To my own mind justice, *protection and restoration*, and not *vengeance* directed and limited all the aims, and all the acts of the Government.[20]

If in the previous chapter I was concerned to address the circuitous way in which the conscientious postcolonial critic can end up reproducing the paranoid fantasies of insurgency promulgated by the planter class in the pre-emancipation West Indies, here we are faced with an equal but opposite dilemma: what to do when faced with an historical black voice that straightforwardly reproduces those same ruling-class languages of black primitivism and savagery and attempts an affiliation with 'the very best of the population'?

There can be little of the romantic rebel in the Ward who writes to Governor Eyre on 2 January 1866, in response to the governor's circular letter requesting information on the origins and nature of the rebellion and the means used to suppress it, and introduces his letter by begging that,

Your Excellency will allow me to express my deep regret that your measures for the suppression of the late rebellion should have brought so much of censure and actual persecution upon *you* who, under God, saved the Island to the Crown, and saved our lives and properties from threatened imminent certain destruction. May God graciously sustain you in all your trials and lead you to as brilliant a conquest over your assailants as he has given you over the disturbers of Jamaica's peace![21]

With alacrity, Ward aligns himself with those members of the Jamaican ruling class who so quickly concluded that Eyre's suppression of the rebellion had saved the colony from 'imminent certain destruction', and his letter to Eyre hyperbolically mimics the very language that the rattled governor had himself used in his address to the soon-to-be abolished Jamaican House of Assembly on 7 November 1865:

To this prompt and decisive action, I firmly believe we owe it under God's providence that we are able to meet here this day. One moment's hesitation, one single reverse might have lit the torch which would have blazed in rebellion from one end of the island to the other; and who can say how many of us would have lived to see it extinguished? . . . Satisfactory as it is to know that the rebellion in the Eastern districts has been crushed out, the entire colony has long been, still is, on the brink of a volcano which may at any moment burst into fury.[22]

However, I will argue below that Ward's complicity with the colonial authorities – a hallmark of his public career at least since his arrival in Britain in 1853 – does not mean that his positions were never opposed to those of the government. Without for a moment trying to cast Ward as a clandestine revolutionary, I want to argue that his beliefs, statements, and practices were often untenable within the colonial, religious, and political scripts in which he was forced to play his part. Eyre went on in his address to the Jamaican legislature to blame directly the 'misdirected efforts and misguided counsel of certain Ministers of Religion, sadly so miscalled' in producing the violence in the east of the island; Ward needed to be sure he was not included in their number, since he too was a Baptist, like many of those vilified for their alleged sedition and rabble-rousing. From the other side of the political and social spectrum, Ward's religious orthodoxy put him at odds with so-called Native Baptist adherents, and led him back into the discourse of the ruling class. As a foreigner in the island, his position was also fragile, as the deportations of 'aliens' such as fellow African American John Willis Menard and several prominent Haitian exiles after the uprising made clear.[23] In both citizenship and religion, therefore, Ward's place was insecure.

It is clear that anybody with a connection to any figure associated with the rebellion had good reason to be scared in Jamaica in late 1865. During the period of martial law in St Thomas-in-the-East, which lasted for a month, more than 400 rebels and many simply suspected of connections to the rebels had been killed. Several prominent Jamaicans had been arrested and tried for conspiracy and sedition, including two whom Ward had personally known quite well, George William Gordon and Samuel Clarke, who were both hanged after drumhead courts martial. Ward had met Gordon in England back in 1854; he and Clarke were 'intimate', and Clarke actually stopped to pray and consult at Ward's house at Vickersfield on the main road to Kingston as the news of the rebellion spread.[24] Given all these circumstances in the island in late 1865 and early 1866, it is possible that Ward simply overstated his allegiance to the governor and gratefulness to the authorities in order to save his own life, in defiance of the rebels' quickly notorious slogan, 'colour for colour, skin for skin'.

Nevertheless, we should acknowledge that, despite his connections to Gordon and Clarke, Ward had been publicly opposed to the pre-rebellion political movement, led by Gordon (whom I discuss in more detail in chapter 4 below), which had drawn attention to the miserable circumstances of the bulk of the Jamaican population. For example, by Ward's own account he met with several local worthies in the eastern districts of the island in mid-1865 in order to arrange a counter-meeting to the public 'Underhill meetings' being organised by Gordon and his supporters to express the grievances of the Jamaican peasantry and middle class: 'We concluded that the only way to counteract an evil influence engendered in that way [by Gordon's speeches and writings] was to go and hold counter-meetings, teaching the people loyalty and good order, and those gentlemen did me the honour to signify that they thought I might do good in that direction.'[25] (Two months earlier, in June 1865, however, Ward had addressed a supportive letter to the St David Underhill meeting, organised by Samuel Clarke, as I discuss in more detail below, although he did not in fact attend the meeting.) While Gordon and his supporters were denied the use of the courthouse in Morant Bay for their public meeting, and instead met under the shade of a tree outside (on 12 August 1865), Ward was immediately granted the use of the building that was later to be the site of the opening salvos in the rebellion, and which had previously served as the meeting place for Simon Taylor and Charles White Williams when they were magistrates in St Thomas-in-the-East in the late eighteenth and early nineteenth centuries, and for the inaugural meeting of the parish branch association of the slaves' conversion society supported by Mary Lindsay discussed in chapter 1. Accordingly, on 9 September 1865, Ward spoke to 'the magistracy and the people together' and was 'well received', especially by 'the gentry'.[26] (Quickly backtracking on his bland statement that the meeting had gone very well, a little later in his testimony Ward revealed that George McIntosh, later to be hung as one of the leaders of the October rebellion, 'did his utmost to raise a riot against me at the meeting . . . a noisy opposition, and he tried to marshal men to injure me'.[27]) Given his public opposition to the protest movement in Jamaica, and his personal disagreements with Gordon, Ward's support for the governor's methods of suppression, which caused an outcry in Britain and the United States when details began to emerge in late 1865, ought to come as no surprise. In this respect, he is so far from being the romantic figure of black resistance and insurgency that he threatens to become simply a cipher for elite opinion in the island, a black conservative spokesman, and thus alibi, for imperial suppression. Such figures were important in Jamaica in the mid-1860s, where many of the white and 'coloured' elite feared the inevitable moment of black rule, given the overwhelming demographic disparity among blacks, browns, and whites, and the rise of a black political class and middle class. Ward, therefore, is a little like the otherwise anonymous men from Clarendon parish, James Kiffin, Edward Burrell, and William Pinnock, who contributed small sums to the 'Eyre Testimonial Fund' set up in the island to support the legal and other costs of Governor Eyre after his ignominious recall to England in 1866, and whose names are followed on the subscription list published in the Jamaican newspaper *The Gleaner* by the notation 'black man'.[28]

From the point of view of an itinerant black preacher in Jamaica, the empire as an imaginative confederation might have seemed attractive, even if its appeal could only be articulated in the registers of loyalty and counterinsurgency. In this respect, Ward stands in a line of descent from Mary Lindsay and the other 'persons of colour' who supported the St Thomas-in-the-East branch association of the imperial conversion society that I discussed in chapter 1. We can find Ward's name on an imperial list too, just like Lindsay's: he was one of 2,500 Jamaican signatories of an address of support to Governor Eyre in 1866 that adopted an imperial and global perspective, contrasting the English detractors of Eyre with

the vast majority not only of Englishmen in Her Most Gracious Majesty's wide spread Dominions, but also of the rest of the civilized world, [who] will heartily join with us, the Colonists of Jamaica, in . . . utter detestation and abhorrence of the recent atrocities and massacres committed by the lower orders, at the instigation of demagogues and fanatics, while in the full enjoyment of all the blessing and freedom of the British rule.[29]

(It also seems certain that the 'Emily E. Ward' who signed a separate address to the governor from the 'Ladies of Jamaica', almost 3,000 of them, for 'sav[ing] us, our families and our homes from outrage, desolation, and ruin' was Samuel Ringgold Ward's wife.[30]) However, Ward's cooptation into this righteous language of empire and global 'civilisation' is even here marked by his singular, anomalous status. He is the only one of the 2,500 men whose residency status on the island is included: 'Samuel Ringgold Ward, Baptist Minister ten years resident in Jamaica.'[31] Whether the language is Ward's or that of the organisers of the petition is unclear, but in either case the annotation suggests some of the limits of 'the full enjoyment of all the blessing and freedom of British rule'.

Moreover, if Ward's attempts to ingratiate himself with the Jamaican ruling class, and with the governor in particular, seem straightforward and consistent, we need to ask why they were not more successful. In Governor Eyre's cover letter to the colonial secretary, Edward Cardwell, summarising the correspondence he had received in response to his circular letter requesting corroborating evidence for his contention that the rebellion had been widespread and needed firm action, he does mention one or two points from Ward's letter to him (cited above), but only after summarising the key points of seventy others.[32] Ward obviously worked quickly to produce his pro-Eyre pamphlet, *Thoughts upon the Gordon Rebellion*, which carries the date 'February 1866' at the end, in order to present his view of the uprising to the Jamaican reading public: but the pamphlet met with almost complete silence when it appeared. The editor of the *Falmouth Post*, John Castello, mentions receiving Ward's pamphlet in March 1866, but despite Castello's promise to 'refer to it at a future time', the newspaper never carried an account of the pamphlet, despite the fact that Ward's piece for the most part buttressed elite views of the uprising.[33] If Ward sent his *Reflections* to this paper in the northwestern portion of the island, then presumably he sent it to all the major Jamaican papers.[34] I have been unable to review all of the newspapers from early 1866 (several of them have not survived), but as far as I can tell, apart from the reference to Ward in the *Falmouth Post*, his pamphlet was roundly ignored.

This omission is most striking in *The Gleaner*, which carried regular advertisements and acknowledgements of other pamphlets, lectures, and books on the rebellion, but never mentioned Ward's writing even though he was used as a corroborating witness in the paper's attack on John Gorrie, one of the two attorneys sent by the anti-Eyre Jamaica Committee in London to assist the JRC (see chapter 4), who was sending articles back from Jamaica to the London *Morning Star*. The Jamaican press routinely attacked liberal Englishmen who claimed to understand Jamaica after only a brief visit, and *The Gleaner* mocked Gorrie's attempted rehabilitation of James McLaren, one of the rebel leaders, as a 'quiet industrious man': 'He was such a quiet man that, on one occasion he threatened to or did put a minister of the Gospel from the pulpit in which he was preaching. He told Mr. Samuel Ringold [sic] Ward, that unless he got certain lands he wanted, "blood would flow" or language to that effect.'[35] Here was a holdover from the genre of creole realism, which never tired of asserting the superiority of the perspective of the creole white on the spot over that of the metropolitan visitor. Nevertheless, despite this exactly contemporary use of Ward's name in a quarrel with British antislavery, Ward's pamphlet is conspicuously absent from the many advertisements of other Jamaican works on Morant Bay and its aftermath available in DeCordova and McDougall's bookshop and printers' office at 62 Harbour Street, Kingston. Interested Jamaicans could purchase the anonymous *History and Progress of the Jamaica Rebellion MDCCCLXV, with Upwards of Fifty Pictorial Illustrations*,[36] Rev. David B. Panton's *The Present Crisis and How to Meet It*,[37] and *Who's to Blame, by a Thirty Years Resident* (published anonymously, but actually written by the Baptist minister Samuel Oughton, whom I discuss below).[38]

The Gleaner even advertised works by Jamaican residents whose views of the country, and of Eyre's handling of the rebellion, were much closer to those of British antislavery than they were to Ward's and Oughton's: Richard Hill's *The Lights and Shadows of Jamaica History*, Rev. J. M.

Phillippo's *Jamaica: Its Past and Present State*, and Revs. John Clark, Walter Dendy, J. M. Phillippo, and David East's *The Voice of Jubilee: A Narrative of the Baptist Mission in Jamaica*, which were all announced along with 'Cartes de Visite' for sale of Edward Cardwell, the colonial secretary, Edward Underhill, whose letter to Cardwell bemoaning the state of the poor in the island in early 1865 had precipitated the political crisis that led to the uprising, and even Louis Chamerovzow, the secretary of the British and Foreign Anti-Slavery Society (BFASS) and public enemy number one amongst the Jamaican elite.[39] Clearly there was a widespread market among the small educated segment of the Jamaican population for information, images, and accounts of the rebellion. While martial law was still in effect, DeCordova and McDougall's was displaying the hymn book used by Paul Bogle, the principal leader of the rebellion, for the curious to see; a few days later, in response to 'several' requests, *The Gleaner* printed the numbers of the psalms and hymns 'selected and marked' by Bogle from this book, which turned out to be 'The Psalms of David, with the supplementary Hymns, by the Revd. Isaac Watts, D.D.'.[40] In March 1866, the paper was advertising, under the boldface headline 'REBELLION', *cartes de visite* 'from Life, of the two Murderers of Messrs. Walton & Hire, Robt. Nicholas & Alex Taylor, taken at the Jail Yard. Also Views of the Morant Bay Rebels'.[41] It is surprising, to say the least, that Ward's pamphlet, and his justification of the measures to suppress the rebellion, did not find a share of this diverse market in Jamaica at this moment.

Perhaps, however, a provisional answer to this puzzle can be found in the final pages of Ward's pamphlet. After summarising the rebellion, Ward reproduces the three questions that Governor Eyre asked of the prominent Jamaicans (including Ward) in the letter that he sent in December 1865 in order to collect exculpatory evidence for his actions to present to the Colonial Office: 'Three questions are asked by those who think about these affairs in this island and in England. 1. What was the origin of this rebellion? 2. Was it merely local or general? 3. Was undue severity exercised in suppressing it?'[42] Ward answers these questions with a ringing endorsement of Eyre and the military's response to the uprising, as we have seen, reproducing much of the letter he sent to Eyre in January 1866 cited above.[43] However, he then adds a fourth point, not included in Eyre's circular, in an attempt to change the framework of the debate about the rebellion, and it is this attempted reframing that provides some clues as to Ward's continuing marginalisation at this moment, since it is clear that his primary concern is with 'the character of negroes', rather than with the Jamaican ruling class with whom he was apparently in solidarity:

4. The consideration of how this rebellion will affect the character of negroes, as to their loyalty, is to me, and some few who think with me, of some moment. Every body knows that the negro is not judged of by the same rule that is applied to other men. Nobody stigmatises all Irishmen because of the Fenian scheme. Nobody blames all Americans because of the Southern rebellion . . . But the whole mass of negroes are too commonly classed and generalised, with any portion who do wrong.[44]

Operating once more within the language of 'loyalty', Ward tries to find a space for respectable blackness that could not be accommodated after Morant Bay. Crucially, this space is a cosmopolitan, worldly space – the space of the Atlantic world invoked by Simon Taylor, encompassing Ireland, the United States, and the Caribbean as well as Britain.

Claiming that 'the most respectable and best educated negroes' were 'not only loyal, but unsuspected' and that 'the majority of the peasantry and the yeomanry . . . remained true', Ward tries to pin the blame for the rebellion on the rising, politicised 'coloured' class:

The rebellion was evidently planned by a Mulatto [i.e., George William Gordon], and a few whites were accessories, while by their too great ductility too many negroes were led into it as subordinates and made cat's paws . . . Upon a mulatto and his confreres, therefore, and not upon a few such semi-savage negroes as Paul Bogle, rests the guilt and the responsibility of plotting and planning this diabolical affair.[45]

Ward shows his own ductility here, in both senses of the word, gullibility and flexibility: on the one hand, he is easily led himself to adopt the language of paternalism, positioning 'the whole mass of negroes' as 'cat's paws' in the schemes of clever leaders; while on the other hand, he tries flexibly to extend the available languages to rescue black people, educated and uneducated, from the imperial frames of race and civilisation that seek to punish them for their inherent 'savagery' and 'diabolism'. Ward's 'whole mass of negroes' are a diasporic group: he seeks to reposition blackness here in an international frame, via the comparison with 'Americans' and 'Irishmen'. This frame – as I discuss in more detail below – is at once imperial and transatlantic.

In this respect, Ward's pamphlet, as an occasional and unstable intervention into the realm of print culture, acts in a way analogous to the little magazines and short-lived publications of the transatlantic black world of the 1920s and 1930s that Brent Edwards recovers and analyses in his groundbreaking book, *The Practice of Diaspora*. Noting the multiple attempts by francophone black writers to reframe and redefine the French term *nègre*, Edwards argues,

It is not coincidental that the interventions I have outlined so far take place in a particular limited range of sites within print culture, sites that imply a certain transitionality or instability if not rupture. Framing gestures work the edges, in other words: in the manifesto, in the impassioned response or open letter, in the broadside, in the editorial or position paper that stakes out ground in the inaugural issue of a newspaper.[46]

In his Syracuse newspaper, the *Impartial Citizen*, Ward had tried between 1849 and 1850 to reframe antislavery debates in the United States, splicing missionary poetry, temperance stories, and political manifestoes together, before financial troubles engulfed his publication. In the mid-1860s, without the access to the public sphere that a newspaper provided, Ward's attempt to reframe the debate after Morant Bay was even less successful. Can we salvage the figure of Ward who 'work[s] the edges', as Edwards puts it, from the imperial toady? This will be a tricky rescue mission, given Ward's frank praise of Eyre's counterinsurgency tactics.

As we have seen, however, there was something about Ward's position that was not easily assimilable by Edward Eyre and his supporters. And from the other side, from the emerging British consensus on the virtues of an empire that looked like a system of humanitarian citizenship, Ward was equally unwelcome – and it is his ability to disrupt both sides of this debate about imperial administration that makes him a valuable and thought-provoking figure. Questions had been raised about Ward's financial affairs in his final months in Britain in the mid-1850s, and by 1864 the BFASS was listing 'S. R. Ward' among the group of 'Coloured Impostors' about whom 'it has been our unpleasant duty occasionally to warn the British anti-slavery public' for 'practising upon its too ready benevolence, not to say credulity'.[47] Consequently, he was attacked by the liberal English lawyer John Horne Payne during the public hearings of the JRC into the rebellion, who drew attention to accusations of 'immorality' made against Ward several years earlier by one of his former congregants in Kingston.[48] Those present in Spanish Town, the Jamaican capital, on 27 February 1866, the twenty-ninth day of the commission's hearings, would therefore have witnessed the minor courtroom drama of a British lawyer acting for a group of British liberals and antislavery intellectuals attempting to undermine the testimony of a once-prominent African-American antislavery activist.

Payne had been sent from England to question witnesses on behalf of an ad hoc liberal British group, the Jamaica Committee, headed by John Stuart Mill and now well established as a key institution on the right side of the liberal course of history (for more on the Jamaica Committee in Britain, see chapter 4 below). The English lawyer suggested to Ward that he identify himself as a fallen, perhaps even a tragic, hero, and to recall his finest hours in Britain when hundreds flocked to hear his powerful anti-slavery performances: 'You are the celebrated gentleman who escaped from American slavery, are you not, and visited England?', asked Payne. Ward, however, sidestepped the invitation and recast himself as a representative type of modern black history: 'No', he replied, 'I am not the celebrated gentleman. I am not the man who escaped from slavery; I was one of many others.'[49] Ward claimed to be a type rather than an individual, 'somebody' rather than a celebrity. His self-deprecating reply to the lawyer's question was partly a sly attempt to head off an attack that he knew was coming from the well-briefed representatives of the antislavery movement that had once supported him so munificently but had turned against him shortly after his departure from Britain in November 1855. But it was also a sign that Ward's story cannot be accommodated in the end by either the liberal or conservative discourses of empire, but instead articulates them to other histories, of black internationalism and emigration, of African America, and of the 'modern negro'.

'GLORIOUS MOB!': RESCUE MISSIONS IN THE BLACK ATLANTIC WORLD

Glorious mob! . . . they felt for the poor slave, and they wished his freedom. Accordingly, at nine o'clock that evening, while the court was in session trying Jerry for more than his life, for his liberty, the mob without threw stones into the window, one of which came so near to the judge that, in undignified haste, he suddenly rose and adjourned the courts. In an hour from that time, the mob, through certain stalwart fellows whom the Government have never had the pleasure of catching, broke open the door and the side of the building where Jerry was, put out the lights, took him out in triumph, and bore him away where the slave-catchers never after saw him.

 –Samuel Ringgold Ward, *Autobiography of a Fugitive Negro* (1855)[50]

A correspondent at Savanna-la-Mar, writing to the 'County Union', gives a lengthy account of the arrival of a vessel from America having a slave on board and the subsequent release of the man . . . By some means the report got wind and the inhabitants became terribly excited calling upon the Magistracy to interfere and obtain the man's release. The Magistrates were in doubt . . . The people not being intimidated, seeing that the authorities would not interfere, took the matter into their own hands, manned their canoes, and made for the brigantine. Five stalwart negroes first boarded her by main force, and seizing the slave bore him off in triumph. When the man reached the shore the people cheered vociferously.

 –'Liberation of a Slave at Savanna-la-Mar', *Colonial Standard and Jamaica Despatch*, –2 June 1855[51]

On Saturday 7th of October [1865], a Court of Special Sessions was held at Morant Bay Court House, Justice Walton presiding. Before the Court a party was brought accused of trespass. He was convicted. Paul Bogle led a band of law-defying persons to his rescue, with but too perfect success.
    —Ward, *Reflections upon the Gordon Rebellion* (1866)[52]

It is by now well established that the immediate catalyst of the Morant Bay rebellion of October 1865 was the rescue by a crowd of one James Geoghegan from the police outside the Morant Bay courthouse: all contemporary and more recent accounts of the events in Jamaica stress this moment of popular resistance to the magistrates courts in St Thomas-in-the-East, beginning with the third epigraph to this section, Samuel Ringgold Ward's terse and scathing account of the 'band' who defied the law and set the events of the insurrection in train.[53] From the official report of the JRC down to the present day, the failure of the legal system in the island to deliver justice to the poorer segments of Jamaican society has been seen as one of the major symptoms of the broader ills of mid-nineteenth-century Jamaica. The magistrates courts of St Thomas-in-the-East, the local power base of Simon Taylor and Charles White Williams in the pre-emancipation period, were still flagrantly operating in the interests of the tiny creole elite thirty years later.[54] The commission's summary conclusions were that one of the three causes of the outbreak was 'the want of confidence generally felt by the labouring class in the tribunals before which most of the disputes affecting their interests were carried for adjudication'.[55] For Thomas Harvey and William Brewin, who visited Jamaica in the aftermath of the rebellion to report for the British Quakers, the 'most active' causes of the rebellion were 'the entire loss of confidence in the administration of justice as between employers and employed and between the higher and lower classes; and the generally arbitrary, irritating and excessively indiscreet conduct and bearing of the magistracy and other persons of authority'.[56] In a lengthy appendix, the JRC enumerated the problems with the justice system in St Thomas-in-the-East between 1863 and 1865: of 661 cases heard by the court of petty sessions in Morant Bay, only seven were dismissed, and of those convicted, mostly for trespass and crop stealing, 640 were listed as 'labourers'; moreover, 179 of the cases were brought before the court by a member of the magistrates' bench themselves, in their capacity as estate owners or managers.[57] In the commission's long list of individual cases heard in Morant Bay in the three years before the rebellion, it can be seen that almost all those convicted were imprisoned in the notorious Morant Bay lockup, for periods ranging from five days to six months, most often for being 'in default' of the fine and costs imposed by the planter-dominated courts.[58]

Thus it is perhaps not surprising that when things began to come to a head, Paul Bogle and his followers petitioned Governor Eyre, a few days before the rebellion began, for 'protection' from the forces of law and order:

On Saturday, 7ᵗʰ of this month [October], an outrageous assault was committed upon us by the policemen of this parish, by order of the justices . . . We therefore call upon your Excellency for protection, seeing we are Her Majesty's loyal subjects, which protection, if refused, we will be compelled to put our shoulders to the wheels, as we have been imposed upon for a period of '27' years, with due obeisance to the laws of our Queen and country, and as we can no longer endure the same, therefore is our object of calling upon your Excellency, as Governor-in-Chief and Captain of our Island.[59]

The people, in other words, had remained loyal to the law, to the true spirit of the law in an island of post-1838 freedom, but the legal apparatus had failed the people, assaulted them even, and left them with little option but to take matters into their own hands. The petition was no doubt written hurriedly, since it was composed in the aftermath of another moment of popular resistance: a police raid on Bogle's home in Stony Gut in the hills above Morant Bay, in which a crowd of 300 prevented Bogle's arrest and instead seized several policemen and made them swear oaths to 'cleave from the whites and cleave to the blacks', as one of those captured testified later to the JRC.[60] But it is impossible, at this distance, to know whether hasty composition or deliberate ambiguity lies behind the undecidable status of the phrase 'we can no longer endure the same' in the petition to Eyre. Is it, as seems most likely on a first reading, the fact of being 'imposed upon' that cannot be endured? Or is it possible that the people, who had set up their own rudimentary alternative court and justice system in eastern Jamaica, were making a claim for their own ability to *make* the law themselves, not simply to obey an already existing law, and that it is in fact the 'laws of our Queen and country' that can no longer be endured?[61]

Whichever version of Bogle's petition we prefer, in this counter-history of subaltern struggles the rescue of James Geoghegan and the defence of Paul Bogle against the local police take their place within a longer history of popular resistance to unjust laws, and in particular within a pan-American history of black rescue missions. In this section I discuss the relationship between these rescue missions 'from below' and the discourses and practice of British antislavery and liberal philanthropy, which imagined themselves as large-scale humanitarian rescue missions creating model subjects and workers for an enlightened empire. I suggest, in an analysis of the US and post-US writings of Samuel Ringgold Ward, that the two models of rescue are articulated together rather more than we might suppose.

As the epigraphs to this section demonstrate, from the famous 'Jerry' rescue in Syracuse, New York in 1851, which precipitated Samuel Ringgold Ward's flight to Canada, to the 1855 rescue of Joseph Anderson, a Maryland slave who had managed to pass himself off as a free black sailor on the US merchant ship *Young America* in order to secure passage to the British West Indies and legal freedom, to the rescue of Geoghegan from the Morant Bay courthouse, a powerful history of popular struggle can be recovered. In this version of history, the 'mob' is 'glorious', in Ward's words, in its adherence to higher versions of 'liberty' than those enshrined in faulty legislation like the Fugitive Slave Law of 1850. The 'stalwart fellows' of Ward's account of the Jerry rescue, and the 'stalwart negroes' of the newspaper account of the freeing of Joseph Anderson at Savanna-la-Mar in the west of Jamaica, embody the strength of the people who 'take matters into their own hands', forcing at least one magistrate, for instance, to follow their lead and pronounce Anderson free as he stepped on to British soil. The magistrate, Robert Thomas, told the court investigating the Anderson affair that,

I was about returning home when I heard someone say they were bringing him [Anderson] on shore . . . I asked him who are you – before that someone said there's a magistrate – the man then came towards me. I put my hand on his shoulder or on his hand and asked him who are you – he said I am a slave Sir – I said then you are no longer a slave for you are on British soil – the people cheered and the crowd and man went up the street to Mr. Deleon's office. I followed slowly after.[62]

At each stage of the process, 'someone', a member of the crowd, moves the action on, calling the magistrate to perform his duty in liberating the poor slave. Eventually the people move off, leading the way while the magistrate trails behind, in spite of his catalytic role as legal baptiser of freedom.

Of course, the fact that these glorious histories are told in the register of romance does not alter their power to persuade, nor their transmission of an important submerged truth from the history of slavery and its aftermath in the Americas. As I have argued in the first two chapters of this book, 'romance' and 'history' are far from being mutually exclusive terms, and the former is often constitutive of the latter. According to the *OED*, for instance, 'stalwart', used in the accounts both of the Jerry Rescue and the liberation of Joseph Anderson to describe the crowd, is a Scots word brought into English by Walter Scott that finds its way into these mid-century accounts from its use in the romantic poem *The Lady of the Lake*; soon after, it would take its place in the lexicon of US politics as the term used to describe elements of the Republican Party who opposed reconciliation with the South after the Civil War.[63] These stalwart crowds who affirm the true meaning of liberty by defying unjust laws can be seen as the later nineteenth-century inheritors of the emancipatory, mobile, and protean 'motley crew' of sailors, slaves, and revolutionaries who populated the eighteenth-century Atlantic world in the inspirational history told by Peter Linebaugh and Marcus Rediker in their book *The Many-Headed Hydra.*[64] As Samuel Ringgold Ward tells it, Jerry's speech from his cell in Syracuse to his would-be rescuers can stand in for all the heroic calls to action on behalf of freedom for those imposed upon in the name of the law:

'Give me, O give me, gentlemen, that freedom which you say belongs to all men, and it is all I ask. Will you who are fathers, and brothers, see a man dragged in chains to the slavery of Tennessee, which I know is worse than death itself? In the name of our common nature – in the name of the Declaration of Independence – in the name of that law in the Bible which says, "do as you would be done by" – in the name of God, our common Father – do break these chains, and give me the freedom which is mine because I am a man, and an American.'[65]

It is a compelling cry for freedom. So compelling, in fact, that we may be hard pressed to understand the apparent incongruity of Ward's wholehearted support for the rescue of William 'Jerry' Henry in Syracuse in 1851 and his wholehearted endorsement of Governor Edward Eyre's suppression of the rebellion in Jamaica initiated by the rescue of James Geoghegan less than fifteen years later. How can we explain the apparent contradiction between Ward's invocation of freedom in defiance of the law in 1851 and his invocation of the law of Jamaica in opposition to the 'band of law-defying persons' led by Paul Bogle outside the Morant Bay courthouse in 1865?[66] Can anything other than a deep-seated political and moral conversion explain the difference between these two versions of Ward? He had arrived in Jamaica in late 1855, a scant six months after Joseph Anderson's rescue and emancipation in the island; both Ward and Anderson were thus former American slaves who had found their own ways to a form of freedom in Jamaica. How, therefore, could Ward end up vilifying precisely the kind of 'stalwart' folks who intervened to save Anderson's skin?

Clearly, part of the difference for Ward between the Jerry rescue and the Morant Bay uprising is embodied in his movement from the United States, where slavery was part of the legal system until the Civil War, to British territories, where slavery had been abolished in the 1830s. Explaining, in his autobiography, his rapid transformation into a kind of pro-British patriot on his arrival in Canada in 1851, Ward recalls,

Before I knew it, I was preferring the right hand – the British – side of the St. Lawrence, and concluding that on *that* side things were most inviting, and trying to reason myself into the belief of this with a sort of patriotic feeling to which all my life before I had been a stranger, and concerning which I had been a sceptic. Why had I interest in the British side of the noble St. Lawrence? What gave me a fellow feeling with those inhabitants? Simply the fact, that that country had become to me, in a sense in which no country ever was before, my own, and those people my fellow citizens.[67]

Although Ward had begun a speech outside Jerry's cell with the words 'fellow citizens!',[68] and although Jerry's claim to be both a man and 'an American' is central to Ward's support of his liberation in the name of true loyalty to the principles of the Declaration of Independence, black struggles over citizenship in the US are replaced almost immediately, and all but miraculously ('before I knew it', as Ward says), by the sense of possible citizenship in 'free' British territories. Crossing the border into lands governed by British law appeared to change Ward's political aspirations.

In retrospect, such a shift might well look politically naïve, or even self-serving, but it is hard to dismiss the appeal of places where chattel slavery had been outlawed within recent memory: after all, the British act of emancipation had been regularly celebrated in black and antislavery communities throughout the United States every 1 August, and Ward had come of age in that political and religious environment.[69] Within a few years, then, Ward appeared to change his position radically, from seeing Britain as a 'tyrannical nation' to seeing it as the fount of all civilisation. Ward had shot back at the anti-American prejudices of Thomas Carlyle in 1850, citing the personal philanthropy and de facto anti-imperialism of a young Massachusetts woman, Laura Bridgman, who had been made famous by Charles Dickens in his *American Notes*: 'Carlyle asks, "What thing to admire has America ever produced?" She has produced a girl, *deaf, dumb* and *blind*, who with her own hands did sewing enough to buy a barrel of flour to send to Ireland's starving people – the poor victims of a tyrannical nation you so much admire.'[70] (Ward's attack on Carlyle was all the more pointed because the latter had written to Samuel Howe, Bridgman's teacher, most effusively about her almost miraculous achievement in learning to read and write: 'Few things that I ever read have interested me more than this of your dear little Laura Bridgman; – probably one of the most beautiful phenomena at present visible under our sun... The good little

Girl: one loves her to the very heart.'[71]) However, by the mid-1860s, after ten difficult years in Jamaica, Ward's position on the Morant Bay rebellion was all but indistinguishable from that of Carlyle's, who wrote, in agreeing to support the newly formed Eyre Testimonial and Defence Fund, that the governor of Jamaica was 'a just, humane, and valiant man' and 'that . . . by wise effort and persistence, a blind and disgraceful act of public injustice may be prevented', referring to the campaign to prosecute Eyre for murder for his role in the suppression of the rebellion.[72] In other words, Carlyle agreed with Ward that 'public injustice' – the people taking the law into their own hands – was a major problem, not just in Jamaica, but perhaps also 'a vital detriment throughout the British empire, in such an example set to all the colonies and governors the British Empire has'.[73]

Whereas, in the United States 'liberty' appeared to exist for Ward only in the spiritual or unworldly sphere – the motto of the *Impartial Citizen* was 'the Wisdom which is from above is without Partiality' – in the British empire freedom and the law were anything but antithetical, in Ward's view, as in Carlyle's: when black voters in Essex County, Ontario, were disenfranchised by 'a low set of Gosfield Canadians', Ward noted happily that 'The injured parties had recourse to law – British law, thank Heaven! – and triumphed.'[74] Little wonder, then, if heaven itself seems to endorse imperial law, that some latterday commentators have seen Ward as a starry-eyed proponent of 'black anglophilia', blinded by an 'ecstatic identification' with England, by 'too fine an investment in the British drill', taking decidedly too much pleasure in the high rank of his supporters during his British tour.[75]

But is the matter so simple? It is certainly the case that Ward seems enamoured of his quick access to the upper levels of British society after his arrival in Britain in 1853. The dedication of his autobiography to the duchess of Sutherland is fulsome: 'A kind Providence placed me for a season within the circle of your influence, and made me largely share its beneficent action, in the occasional intercourse of Nobles and Ladies of high rank, who sympathize in your sentiments.'[76] On the other hand, he never loses sight of the object of his fraternisation with the British nobility, and never loses an opportunity to assert a version of black kinship that – as I will turn now to discuss – is not always compatible with the discourse of citizenship in the benevolent empire that Ward persistently employs. The dedication continues: 'I am devoutly thankful to God, the Creator of the Negro, for this gleam of his sunshine [i.e., the duchess's support] . . . and desire that my oppressed kindred may yet show themselves not unworthy of their cause being advocated by the noblest of all lands, and sustained

and promoted by the wise and virtuous of every region.'[77] Here the shift
to the universal register – the sunshine of a god who created both black
and white – is also a shift to a global register: 'all lands' and 'every region'.
Ward's 'kindred' are poised between subjection and agency: they may
act by 'show[ing] themselves', but this act is also a reaction to the advocacy
of an international nobility. Nevertheless, it is clear that Ward's move
beyond the borders of the United States involves not simply an embrace of
British civilisation and British law, but also an embrace of a certain black
internationalism, a diasporic view of his 'kindred' that will sometimes be at
odds with the dictates of British law. His dedication concludes by thanking
the duchess for giving the opportunity to Ward of 'representing the claims
of my oppressed race', and arguing that all ranks of society respond 'to
the appeals of my suffering people'.[78] 'Kindred', 'race', 'people': Ward's
shifting terminology is confusing, but clearly driven by a desire to think
transnationally rather than parochially. Ward wrote his book shortly before
he left England for Jamaica – 'before your Grace can see these lines, I shall
be again traversing the great Atlantic', he says – and for all his gratitude
for the benevolence of many Britons during his three years in Europe, his
real dedication is to a diasporic, racial group, no longer simply the poor
slaves of the south of the United States or those travelling north on the
Underground Railroad, but a more expansive idea of black collectivity: 'the
Negro people in all lands'.[79]

Elisa Tamarkin reads Ward's version of England as a kind of 'fantasized
realm within which a cosmopolitan universalism gets realized', but a cos-
mopolitanism that remains centred on the United States: 'Anglophilia in
Ward is not finally about Britain; it is about how American affectations of
Britishness speak to issues of class internal to America.'[80] Certainly Ward
remained invested in US questions, even after his migration to Jamaica:
receiving a letter in 1859 from George Reynolds, the editor of the *Franklin
Visitor*, he responded, 'My Dear Sir: – You can scarcely conceive how
delighted I was to receive two copies of your V I S I T O R. You are the first
and only American editor who has thus exhibited a kind remembrance of
me since I came to this Island in November, 1855.'[81] I think that Tamarkin
is right to think about the continuities between Ward's positions in the
US and after his flight to Canada. However, if we are to think of the ways
in which Ward's positions are consistent across time, rather than having
undergone radical transformation, I would argue that it makes more sense
to trace the incipient, and sometimes explicit, internationalism in Ward's
earlier, American writings than it does to find a US-centric cosmopoli-
tanism in Ward's 'British' writings. Without attempting to harmonise all

of Ward's arguments and positions from the 1840s to the 1860s, we can see that his emergent internationalism during his New York days gets connected from the Jamaican vantage point to a pro-temperance, self-help position that he had held strongly from the very beginning of his public career. In the end, I argue, Ward's statements about his allegiance to the British empire, and the British law that was defied at Morant Bay, are subservient to a particular version of black internationalism, one that Ward had outlined, at least embryonically, in the 1840s in the United States.

For example, Ward's emphasis on the dignity of labour often elicited an international dimension to his US writings. In an early number of his Syracuse newspaper, the *Impartial Citizen*, he inveighed against the rich who despised the poor, an analysis that very quickly became international:

We see around us, in almost every direction, the toiling sons of want, battling against fearful odds. Poverty seems to be their inheritance, and, in some countries, (our own included, *almost*) it seems to pass from generation to generation, by a sort of entail . . . In latter days, in the British empire especially, the estate of the coming generation threatens to be still poorer than that of the past generation. Now, while the factory operatives of England and Scotland, and a very large proportion of the would-be industrial classes of Ireland are famishing, the rich roll and riot in luxury.[82]

This is hardly the language of a future flatterer of English earls and dukes, and the *Impartial Citizen* contained regular correspondence from a certain A. C. Luther, of whom Ward commented,

Brother Luther is a working man . . . He is one of that large class of our fellow citizens who must work hard for a living, and receive but one third of his earnings in cash, and the rest in 'store pay' or 'orders' . . . The bosses who pay in that way are doing much to reduce the poor laboring men in Syracuse, to the condition of like classes in London, Birmingham, Dublin, and New Orleans . . . Speak out, Brother Luther. You and other Workers shall be heard.[83]

In a later column, Luther denounced the US government for its aggression in the US-Mexico War.[84] And some of Ward's most pointed vitriol was reserved for fellow African Americans who 'neglect[ed] black men who are public laborers' by 'fawning upon white men'.[85]

On the other hand, this workerist, internationalist perspective (buttressed by regular doses of international news in a paper that was also resolutely local in its coverage of Syracuse affairs) met its limit in relation to extra-legal violence. While Ward too denounced the US-Mexico War, his solution was peaceful political change: 'We wish that the workers, generally, talked and acted as friend Luther does about the responsibility of voters.'[86]

His faith in the ballot box at this point in his career was strong: Ward was a leading member of the militantly antislavery Liberty Party, remaining with it even after the bulk of the party split off to join Martin Van Buren's Free Soil Party in the presidential election of 1848.[87] And in October 1849, his paper carried an account of a 'Trinidad riot' that was reprinted from the *Colonial Standard and Jamaica Despatch*, with all that pro-planter newspaper's disdain for the 'mob' who put 'law and order... in abeyance' as the colonial police were 'stoned, cruelly beaten, and overpowered'.[88] Perhaps Ward's defence of Eyre's counterinsurgency tactics was not such a sea-change, after all? (However, when the New York State Liberty Party met in 1849, with Ward as party secretary, it unanimously passed a resolution declaring 'That Law is for the *protection*, not for the *destruction* of rights; and that slavery, therefore, in asmuch as it is the preeminent destroyer of right is (constitutions, statutes, and judical decisions to the contrary notwithstanding) utterly incapable of legalization.' Ward wrote an enthusiastic account of this 'radical meeting' of 800 people that 'took high and thorough ground in respect to Free Trade, Repudiation, War, Slavery, [and] Temperance'.)[89]

A firm supporter of the temperance movement, Ward reserved some of his strongest words for African Americans who failed to control themselves (perhaps like the Trinidad rioters) or to attempt to lift themselves up. In one of the earliest numbers of the *Impartial Citizen*, Ward declaimed on the subject of 'self-elevation'. Even if slavery were abolished tomorrow, if schools and colleges were opened up to blacks,

if with such advantages as we have named, we chose not to respect ourselves, to abstain from the dram shop, the gambling hall, the house of ill-fame; if we wouldn't learn to read, and acquaint ourselves with the intelligence of the day; if we would not cultivate polished manners, and refined sensibilities; if we would not fit ourselves for the society of the upright and the elevated; why, we should be just what we now are; i.e., our present position would remain, morally, what it now is. In a word, self-elevation is the *only possible* elevation.[90]

Ward's embrace of 'refined sensibilities' was not a sudden discovery made when he set foot on British soil, in other words, and the reasons for his popularity with British antislavery, missionary, and dissenting church groups after his arrival in the country are not hard to fathom, given their insistent and longstanding stress on respectability and self-help. And in the very last issue of the *Impartial Citizen*, Ward complained bitterly of some of the African Americans he came across in his travels as a speaker on the Fugitive Slave Law:

The negroes of Canajoharie [in New York state] are just the hardest, most God-forsaken looking customers we ever *did* see, except those in Moyamensing [Pennsylvania]. Such persons either must not know, or not care, how much they injure our cause, or they must covet a residence in the Poor House, a burial in Potter's Field, and the disrespect of all mankind. In the name of our crushed and imbruted slave-brothers, we protest against negro-loaferism.[91]

Such statements were tailor-made for quick and easy acceptance into the upper reaches of the British antislavery community, which despised 'idleness' almost as much as it despised those who defended slavery.

The question becomes, then, less one of tracing Ward's 'anglophilia' or of his conversion to the delights of British 'civilisation', than of inquiring why, at a certain point, Ward could no longer be accommodated to the dissenting and antislavery discourses for which he seemed so perfectly fitted. When he arrived in London, he spoke to the Colonial Missionary Society in London and declared that 'in Canada we are as British and as loyal as any subjects Her Majesty has... While you have loyalists in Canada – old, united, Imperial loyalists – the blacks are ultra-loyalists.'[92] How could such a loyal subject turn out to be a troubling presence? Before his final break with the movement in Britain, and just before his move to Jamaica, Ward acknowledged his pleasure and surprise at being 'associated with that band who have no equals in this world and no superiors in any age, the leaders of the benevolent schemes of England'.[93] But the surprise ought not to be that within a month of his arrival in Britain he had been 'upon the platforms of the Bible, Tract, Sunday School, Missionary, Temperance, and Peace, as well as the Anti-Slavery, Societies'.[94] The surprise is that he fell from favour with these same groups, always eager as they were to enlist black speakers and proselytisers for their causes.

Part of the rupture was clearly personal. Ward had a habit of falling out with allies, from the days of his intra-movement battles in the US with Frederick Douglass and Martin Delany. In the letter introducing Ward as a representative of the Canadian Anti-Slavery Society to BFASS in London, John Scoble, the British organisation's secretary, wrote that, despite Ward's being 'most eloquent and powerful as a public speaker', 'a pure negro, of noble personal appearance, [and] cultivated in mind', nevertheless Scoble was concerned about Ward's 'tendency towards a belligerent spirit'.[95] Ward's militancy and his fieriness were clearly worrying to his white patrons. Another part of the reason for Ward's disgrace in the eyes of his benefactors was financial: letters between the Canadian Anti-Slavery Society and BFASS exchanged after Ward left for Jamaica suggest that he borrowed £140 from a certain Mr Baynham and repaid only £24 of it, and that he represented himself as 'worth £5000 – property in Toronto', and 'it was at Ward's instance [sic] that [Baynham] was induced to leave England for Canada and the poor man, on his arrival here, found himself without a penny in a strange land and no Ward or any other to offer him a helping hand'.[96] If Baynham's story turned out to be true – and the group in Canada feared that it must – 'we and you and the anti-slavery cause generally are most deeply affected by such actions, which are certainly . . . in every sense the acts of a swindler'.[97] It is unclear how serious the financial impropriety was, but what is clear is that the (white) officials of the transatlantic antislavery movement closed ranks against Ward at this time, not even telling Ward himself about their internal communications, and in effect leaving him to fend for himself in Jamaica. Chamerovzow's reply to the Canadian group has not survived, but its dismissal of Ward is clear from the response to it:

Many thanks for your communication of 28th ult. It only confirmed what I had suspected to be the case. I must regret the painful circumstances in which Ward has placed himself but it is difficult to see how matters can be remedied. You need be under no apprehension that your statements will be made known to Ward. At present we have the evidence to produce to the same effect.[98]

BFASS removed Ward's name from its list of 'corresponding members' early in 1856.[99]

But this closing of ranks suggests that part of the reason for Ward's newfound disfavour was simply his continued, primary commitment to helping his 'people' and insisting on their agency as subjects of their own histories, rather than as mere objects of philanthropy. From the very beginning, Ward attacked white antislavery supporters for the racism lying behind their professions of concern and humanity: he had written a letter to the Garrisonian *Anti-Slavery Standard* as far back as 1840 protesting against fellow abolitionists who 'best love the colored man at a distance'.[100] After his move to Canada, we might ask whether we see Ward's 'belligerent spirit' or a principled opposition to the objectification inherent in humanitarian intervention in his strong disagreement with the organisers of the Refugee Home Society (RHS) in Canada for its unnecessary mediation role for fugitive ex-slaves north of the border in helping them to find land to settle on, and in particular for its solicitation of funds in the US for the fugitives' resettlement? Ward wrote in December 1852 to Frederick Douglass's newspaper bitterly condemning this as a form of charity that denied the humanity and resourcefulness of those who were supposed to be its beneficiaries. To collect money in the United States for the RHS

is of itself a representation that they [black fugitives] cannot acquire such money for themselves. While the truth is, that so soon as Fugitives come here, they can get work at fair wages, and so can lay by enough to buy land for themselves . . . To represent such a people, as having to have Rev. C. C. Foote [one of the white leaders of the RHS] beg money to buy lands for them, is sheer falsity . . . I object to the Refugee's [sic] Home Society, because of its injustice and tyranny, and land jobbing, under the sacred name of benevolence towards negroes.[101]

There is a certain irony in this accusation of financial mismanagement here, since, as we have seen, Ward was pursued across the Atlantic later on by questions about his own financial transactions. (He claimed his original plan was to spend 'a portion of every year in Jamaica',[102] but there is no evidence that he ever left the island after his arrival there in November 1855.) And we know that Ward was encouraged to go to Jamaica to settle 50 acres of land in the parish of St George donated as a charitable gesture by John Candler, a longstanding Quaker advocate of the antislavery cause, and a Jamaican landowner.[103] But my argument here is that he fell out of favour not simply because of financial shady dealings, but because structurally within the philanthropic movement, black activists were always at risk of sliding very easily from the category of 'gentlemen' to the category of 'charlatans', since they always remained within the category 'Negro'. We can see a hint of this in the glowing introduction the *British Banner* gave its readers about Ward shortly after his arrival in London – 'a man of colour, and noble specimen of the high capabilities of the negro character' – which had to be vindicated against any possible imputation of Ward's charlatanry, even before his mission really got underway: 'It may be proper to say, that Mr. Ward comes thoroughly accredited by men well known in this country to represent the case of his injured people.'[104] The 'specimen' of the evolved 'negro' must still be properly 'accredited', and can only represent 'his injured people' after others, 'men well known in this country', have vouched for him first. The extraordinary speaker and cultivated thinker is always just a step away from being on the list of 'coloured impostors', as Ward of course eventually was.

In his *Autobiography*, Ward wrote of his firm belief that 'the British colonies are both the agency by which, and the medium through which, the gospel can, ought, *must*, be given to the heathen world'.[105] With such an endorsement of the British empire and British evangelisation, it is hard to imagine how Ward could fall afoul of the liberal imperialists of the antislavery movement in Britain, when he was speaking precisely the language that they themselves were, and perhaps even more explicitly. But I think that his pro-empire discourse in fact ran counter to his intra-imperial travels, which were also movements within a black Atlantic world. Ward told his British audience that he loved the empire. He told a meeting of the Colonial Missionary Society in 1854 that 'God had given to England these great provinces for the purpose of sending the Gospel to the distant parts of the earth, and to tell all the nations that this was her glorious privilege',[106] but, in the words of his defence of the 'colonies' in his autobiography, he treated the empire as 'medium', rather than 'agency', for the spreading of the gospel – and Ward's gospel was his vision of black diaspora that was incompatible with the conventional language of the 'negro' (although of course Ward often used the term 'negro' himself). Ward's move to Jamaica was expressed in simple terms: 'It may be, that our Heavenly Father will permit me to be of some service to my people in that island.'[107] Ward's 'people' both were and were not the 'loyal subjects' of the British colonies: their peoplehood clearly came before their subjection to imperial rule, however useful the latter might be in turning black 'heathens' into black Christians and black slaves into black freedpeople: 'I belong to a degraded race. Of the one hundred and sixty-four millions of my unfortunate race, one hundred and fifty millions are heathens, eight millions are slaves!'[108] The fortuitous intersection of Ward's black uplift and temperance message with the language of dissenting antislavery in Britain was in the end a temporary one. There was, from the metropolitan point of view, a troubling lack of fit after Ward's move to Jamaica, and he disappeared largely from view (as, indeed, he has to latterday historians).

Ward's last address to the BFASS was at their 1854 convention. There, in what he foresaw would be his valedictory speech at the legendary Exeter Hall, he proposed a new kind of rescue mission, one that pointed out the discrepancy between the egalitarian language of British subjecthood in the empire and the discriminatory practices operating throughout the Americas, whether governed from London or independent states, increasingly based on questions of race. Ward argued for intervention to stop the practice of capture and enslavement of free black British subjects who set foot on the soil of the southern states of the USA. He claimed that 'thirty or forty persons were detained in this manner every year; and the thing had been going on . . . for the last thirty years, without any decisive attempt being made to stop it'.[109] Referring repeatedly to these black sailors as 'British-born subjects', 'freeborn Englishmen', 'British people', and 'British negroes', Ward called on his British listeners to 'stand up for the liberty of their fellow-citizens', just as he had invoked the rights of US citizenship in his speech outside Jerry's cell in Syracuse four years earlier: 'The words of the old song were common enough in the mouths of the people, – "Britons never will be slaves"; [–]but that seemed to depend very much upon where you catch them. It depended upon their colour.'[110] In the *British Banner's* report of Ward's speech, these statements were followed by 'laughter and cheers' and 'hear, hear', and Ward ended his speech to 'loud cheers'.[111] Ward was able to elicit support in this way from his listeners by joining imperial citizenship to black internationalism, but it is clear from his speech that the former is subsumed to the latter – or that, at the very least, the relationship between the two is ambiguous and strategically open. Once again, Ward did not ask for charity: 'He did not ask the people of England nor the Government to pity these poor negroes . . . There were many people much more disposed to pity and weep than to do their duty; but what he did ask was justice – common justice, simple justice, even-handed justice, and that was all.'[112] Twelve years later, Ward's language returned to the centre of metropolitan life in England, as I discuss in chapter 4 below, even if Ward himself had all but disappeared from view, as the leading lights of the rapidly formed Jamaica Committee clamoured for exactly this same 'even-handed justice' for the 'British subjects' in Jamaica. In an abiding historical irony, it was the Jamaica Committee's own lawyer, John Horne Payne, who sought to discredit Ward's testimony before the JRC, as I noted at the start of this chapter, while Ward himself came to support the maintenance of law and order over the claims of justice, denouncing Paul Bogle and his 'band of law-defying persons' in his spasm of post-rebellion anger.

THE JAMAICA COMMERCIAL AGENCY

This irony is compounded because Ward and British liberals had even more in common than their mutual veneration of the figure of the respectable citizen-subject as the foundation of a just society. Throughout his international career, and despite the presence of 'Brother Luther's' columns in the *Impartial Citizen*, Samuel Ringgold Ward expounded a pro-trade, capitalist vision of black emancipation that appeared, on its surface, to be entirely compatible with the kind of entrepreneurial capitalism in which almost all the leading British liberal abolitionists and missionaries believed. For the thirty years between the abolition of slavery and the rebellion at Morant Bay, for instance, the Baptist Missionary Society (BMS) in London, and the quasi-autonomous Jamaica Baptist Union (JBU) that was formed in the island in 1845, heralded the emergence of an emancipated, industrious peasantry in the West Indies, and in Jamaica in particular. In 1852, the Baptist missionary John Clark wrote a pamphlet outlining the establishment of many 'free villages' in Jamaica.[113] Clark was effusive in his account of the success of the freedpeople:

The settlement of the emancipated negroes in these free villages has been productive of great good: they have become more industrious, thoughtful, and frugal, and generally are desirous of occupying respectable stations in society . . . Were a comparison to be instituted between their former and present condition, it would probably be found that no people on the face of the earth ever made greater progress in the same space of time.[114]

Clark's rhetoric may have been overblown, but the spread of what came to be called the 'small settlers' in Jamaica did indeed transform the economic and political landscape of the island: Paul Bogle and his followers came largely from this class.[115]

The key political question in the island became how to manage the inevitable conflicts between this emerging group, who made increasing inroads into the domestic market for foodstuffs, and the planter class, who continued to have a stranglehold on large-scale international and intra-imperial trade.[116] John Clark's pamphlet suggests the way in which the dissenting missionary groups, and the Baptists in particular (as the most successful and most integrated into the fabric of Jamaican society), tried to mediate between these two elements of the economy:

Yams, cocoas, and plantains are extensively grown [in the free villages] for family use, and to supply the island markets. A considerable quantity of sugar is made for the same purposes, and it is greatly to be desired that central manufactories were established by enterprising capitalists where, by the appliances of modern science, the peasantry could have their cane converted into sugar, and thus be enabled to become exporters on a large scale. In this way it is believed the exports might be largely increased, to their advantage, and to the promotion of the exclusion of the slave-grown sugars of Cuba and the Brazils from the home market.

Clark also hoped that advances in cotton production would lead the peasantry 'to compete in this article with the slave-holders of the southern states of America'.[117]

Compare such a vision of 'enterprising' and modern capitalism to the plan of black emancipation-through-trade outlined by Samuel Ringgold Ward in a letter sent from England in 1854 to the *Provincial Freeman* in Canada:

What we need now to learn, is how to use our liberty, and to make it serviceable to the crushed millions of our native land. My own mind is, that the happiest way in which we can do both of these, is to *seize every means and opportunity for our individual advancement in all things* ... Let every man among us buy land. And let it be bought and tilled, with the distinct understanding, that there is a most abundant two-fold market for everything, almost, that we can raise in Canada. Wheat, flax, pork, &c., will always command a good price in England, and in the British West Indies. Besides, in the latter we can find for what we send, an abundance of tropical productions to exchange ... Thus the free in Canada can trade with the free of the West Indies, both being profited, and both contributing to the elevation of our British American colonies, into successful competition with the North and South of the United States.[118]

Ward's grand plan – never matched, of course, at the level of practice – meshed self-help rhetoric with intra-imperial black entrepreneurship, and connected Canada, Britain, and the Caribbean in a vision of free black trade ('the free in Canada can trade with the free of the West Indies'). Also in 1854, in a lecture in England, around the time he was making the decision to join the 'free of the West Indies' himself, Ward extolled the virtues of the small settlers of Jamaica. After slavery ended, they had been offered abysmally low wages by the plantation owners, he said, but nevertheless,

they went to work at these low wages and by great economy saved enough to enable them to purchase land; and there were now 100,000 of them who owned on the average about three acres each. The consequence was they soon found out that by working for themselves they could earn £50 per acre ... they therefore preferred to be their own masters, while the old proprietors talked of the laziness of the negroes and said the country was being ruined.[119]

Ward sounds here just like John Clark and the other British evangelical missionaries, who preached economic independence as a form of spiritual development. For the Baptists at least, the founding of the autonomous JBU in 1845 was part and parcel of this message, since it functioned as a sign that the churches and chapels in Jamaica were able to support themselves and their pastors without taking money or direction from Britain (although in practice the BMS in London remained closely involved in Jamaican affairs). Soon after Ward arrived in Jamaica in late 1855, to become one of the small settlers he had praised in his speeches in Britain before he left, he left the fold of the Congregational Church and joined the Baptists in the island. At the moment of his disgrace within one arm of the antislavery movement (after the financial questions that dogged his last months in London), Ward completed his conversion to another branch of the movement, by joining the community of Baptists in Jamaica who traced their beginnings back to another African-American preacher, George Liele, who had founded the Baptist church in the island in the late eighteenth century, and which had consistently positioned itself on the side of the slaves and the freedpeople, against the planters and the ruling class of Jamaica.[120]

Conventionally, the Baptist movement in Jamaica in the nineteenth century has been divided into two distinct groups: firstly, the 'official' Baptist movement, led by white missionaries, with the support of the BMS in London and of the JBU, and secondly, the 'Native' Baptists, who operated more or less autonomously, without institutional coordination between their churches, and often preaching a more heterodox version of Christianity that was viewed with suspicion by the more respectable elements of the church communities in Jamaica. Typically, however, Ward does not fit neatly into either of these categories. Instead of moving on to John Candler's donated land in St George, Ward settled in Kingston, and although the evidence for his five years in the Jamaican capital (1855–60) is sketchy, he was chosen as pastor by a group of Baptists who had split off from the main JBU church in Kingston, in East Queen Street, taking advantage perhaps of the absence in Britain of the white minister, Samuel Oughton, who was widely disliked, and whom the East Queen Street congregation had been trying to oust for several years. Ronald Burke says that, 'In Kingston, Jamaica [Ward] accepted the pastorate of a group of dissidents from Kingston's Baptist Church.'[121]

Protracted legal and political battles over the East Queen Street property had spilled over into street disturbances in 1854 and 1855 shortly before Ward arrived from London. Oughton, who had been in Jamaica as a missionary since the 1830s, had moved steadily towards a pro-establishment position, to the dismay of his mostly poor, mostly black congregants, so that at the height of the conflict over the East Queen Street property, the bulk of the congregation, numbering over a thousand, occupied the main chapel, while Oughton's rump contingent held out in the smaller mission building attached to the church, after the former group had 'cut off all communication with that part of the Premises in which their former Pastor still resided, by erecting a strong barricade'.[122] In early 1855 the Jamaican Court of Chancery, in a complicated case, ruled invalid a new trust deed for the church property that would have passed control of the building into the hands of the anti-Oughton faction. Thousands protested the decision in the streets, and other properties in the city associated with Oughton and his supporters were attacked and burned. Twelve hundred members of the congregation moved to a chapel nearby on Church Street, leaving Oughton to minister to 'less than a hundred, out of which I numbered some thirty boys and girls' in the main chapel, under military protection.[123] Although the unrest subsided and Oughton remained official pastor of the church, he soon left Kingston to travel to Britain for an extended tour with his wife. The *Baptist Magazine* reported regularly in its 'Missionary Herald' section on Oughton's travels in Britain throughout 1856 and 1857, and the couple only returned to Kingston in June 1858, two and a half years after Ward's arrival in Jamaica.[124] Although we do not know exactly what Ward's relationship was to East Queen Street and its congregation during this time, his association with the church in Oughton's absence was powerful enough that *The Gleaner* could mockingly refer to it as 'Ward's chapel' almost ten years later (as I discuss in more detail below).[125]

East Queen Street Baptist church, which had once had a congregation of 3,000 and, according to Horace Russell, had been the 'largest Baptist church in the world',[126] did not recover its full strength after Oughton's return, and in 1859, it still had only 250 members in a building that accommodated 2,000.[127] Little wonder, then, that shortly before his final resignation from the pastorship in 1866, Oughton would try to consolidate the stark difference between official and 'Native' Baptists by claiming that his American rival had himself been converted by a 'Native' Baptist:

The so-called Native Baptist churches, which are so numerous, are chiefly presided over by any [sic] ignorant men, and in many cases by persons of openly and grossly immoral character. Several of these Native ministers are men who have been expelled from the mission churches for immorality or dishonesty. The notorious Mr. Ward, who some years ago so grossly deceived the people of England, was baptized by one of them and became their minister.[128]

The situation on the ground, however, was always more complicated than Oughton's clear-cut distinctions might suggest. Oughton railed against Ward: he aired in his book *Jamaica: Who Is to Blame?* the accusations of 'immorality' against Ward that were later used by John Horne Payne to attack Ward during the JRC hearings.[129] But, as Catherine Hall argues, the idea that 'Native Baptists hated them [official Baptists] and kept themselves quite separate' in fact

tell[s] us about the missionary anxiety to draw firm boundaries where no such boundaries existed, to mark those who were within from those without, those who believed the right things from those who were deluded, those who were really Christians from those who were really heathens. The problem with these constructed binaries was that they tried to make distinct what was not, for the missionary regime of truth did not always hold.[130]

While, on the one hand, Oughton had accused Ward and other black Baptists of immorality, presumably of a sexual nature, on the other hand,

Oughton's own handpicked favourite to succeed him as pastor at East Queen Street, a Mr Wood, was forced to withdraw his name from consideration when there surfaced in London 'a report prejudicial to his [Wood's] moral character which existed prior to his leaving Jamaica [where he had been a Baptist missionary] in 1848'.[131] Apparently, accusations of 'immorality' were common currency in nineteenth-century Jamaica, and not restricted to the 'native ministry'.

As 'native' pastors – i.e., black and 'coloured' ministers – gained prominence in the official Baptist churches in Jamaica, the dividing lines between JBU and 'Native Baptist' congregations became less easy to draw. After the Morant Bay rebellion, the white missionary John Clarke's history of Jamaican Baptists even includes a brief section on 'native preachers unconnected with the Baptist Missionary Society', and allows that 'some of these Native Pastors appear to have been sincere Christian men': 'Self-constituted ministers, no doubt, some were. Others, it is likely, were called to the office by those churches who recognized their fitness for it.'[132] Any faith organised according to congregationalist principles, such as Baptism, would have to be open to such thinking, despite the tendency to shun non-official Baptist churches on the part of the Baptist leadership. Although white Baptists in Jamaica worried that the syncretic forms of Christianity that emerged in some Baptist chapels meant that 'congregational principles do not appear suited to this region',[133] other Baptists quietly continued to work across and between the division between Union and Native churches. John Clarke names several of the 'sincere Christian men' who led unofficial Baptist churches, and notes that 'the little Native Churches' were numerous in the area around Morant Bay (failing to mention, however, that Paul Bogle himself was a Baptist preacher there). Clarke's book ends, then, with a redemptive narrative of post-uprising reconciliation within Jamaican Baptism, beginning in St Thomas, where, he claims, implausibly, 'surviving members of the little Native Churches are glad to come under the care of those they had previously shunned, from loving their old ways too much':

As an educated Native ministry is brought to occupy the field in connection with all the societies labouring there, we may expect that eventually, the class of preachers we have been noticing [i.e., Native Baptists] will disappear, and yet it may be claimed for them that while they existed the island needed them, and was benefited by their labours.[134]

Samuel Ringgold Ward, however, despite his ten-year ministry in the island, does not show up in this narrative of Jamaican Baptism, unless he is the preacher referred to in the following anecdote that disrupts John Clarke's smooth account of the Native Baptists who benefited Jamaica with their labours:

It was narrated of one, however, that once, when he had been rather liberally supported by his people [i.e., his congregation], he gave his horse a name which led them to think how full and comfortable he was becoming through their contributions. From the date of that discovery his prosperity began to decline, until he sank into great destitution, and was glad to have a few children in a village-school to teach. If such was the cause of his descent into poverty, it was certainly a warning to his brethren, 'that when they fared well, to hold their tongue'.[135]

If Clarke describes Ward here, there is some circumstantial evidence to support this reading. For instance, we can infer Ward's poverty in the mid-1860s by the fact that his name does not appear in the public lists of Jamaican subscribers to the Eyre Testimonial Fund (despite his signature in the addresses of loyalty to Governor Eyre mentioned above), which were published regularly in *The Gleaner* and other Jamaican newspapers.[136] We also know that Ward and his daughter did indeed keep a small school in their house in St David, with 'very few' students.[137] We also know that his bitterness in the mid-1860s was aimed, as always, at the people who would not 'elevate' themselves: he claimed there was 'an entire absence' of 'moral training and domestic influence' in the homes of the peasantry, and that only 'one out of a thousand' parents had any interest in educating their children.[138] But perhaps some of this bitterness was indeed a result of a fall into poverty and ridicule at the hands of the very same people whose self-elevation he had always championed. The cosmopolitan Samuel Ward, given his chance to speak to a global audience through the medium of the JRC, when asked whether the lack of respect and 'insolence' that he saw in Jamaica 'is prevalent pretty well all over the world', replied, confoundingly, 'I have not been much over the world.'[139]

But if the much-travelled Ward was feeling his isolation in impoverished St David, his teaching was being taken up by a fellow black Baptist minister, Samuel Holt, from the Black River area in the southwest of the island, who in late June 1866 set sail for England to raise funds for a recently established cooperative trading venture, the Jamaica Commercial Agency (JCA), which was founded in order to allow the small settlers in Jamaica to bypass the big merchants and large landowners on the island, and to trade directly with the metropole.[140] Ward's hope that 'the free . . . can trade with the free' was apparently about to be fulfilled. In a letter Ward had written that was read at a public meeting in St David in June 1865 – one of the 'Underhill meetings' held in many places in Jamaica in the months before the October rebellion – Ward called for 'the smaller yeomanry' who would be attending the meeting to organise themselves: 'You are the men who do their own work. Every country situated as Jamaica is must depend chiefly upon the class of self-helping tillers of the soil.' Dismissing the planter class as 'useless' and whining – 'put[ting] up the piteous wail of ruin thrice in every decade' – Ward urged his listeners to 'increase your productions rather than diminish them. Enlarge your fields, rather than contract them', and to educate their children so that they 'will have the advantage of cultivated minds and skilled hands, and Jamaica will have what she never had before: a free educated, industrious, and moral class of self-helping young yeomen'.[141] At the end of his letter, he called for

the appointment of a central corresponding committee, whose business shall be to counsel with the small planters all over the Island, and by interchange of views, and the reciprocal expression of brotherly feeling, unite them as one man for the maintenance of their interests, rights, and position. Thirty thousand independent farmers are not to be despised in any part of the British empire . . . Thirty thousand sturdy yeomen, who have raised themselves, under God, from nothing to your present position in thirty years, ought not to be discouraged by the lowering of a few clouds of adversity in this good year of grace.[142]

Ward later tried to distance himself from the St David meeting, which had been organised by his sometime friend and rival in the district, Samuel Clarke, who was later hanged for sedition in the aftermath of the October rising. Ward claimed that he did not attend the meeting 'because I did not believe in the object for which the meeting was called . . . to express belief in the starvation of the people'.[143] Nevertheless, the St David Underhill meeting adopted two resolutions that closely followed the text of Ward's letter, calling for 'the establishment of an Island agricultural loan bank or joint stock company for the small settlers and the commercial trading interest of this Island', and appointing a '"Central Communicating Committee", whose business shall be to correspond with the yeomen throughout the Island on subjects of agriculture and other branches of native industry'. Ward, in his absence, was appointed to this committee, and to the deputation that would present these resolutions to the governor.[144] The group from St David, then, constituted a follow-up to an address presented to Eyre by Samuel Clarke, 'on behalf of the Small Settlers' of that parish, on the occasion of Eyre's fact-finding tour through the island in the middle of 1864. The address, signed by 'upwards of 300 of the small proprietors of the parish', was couched in the familiar terms of loyalty to the government and the queen ('Long may She live to reign over us'), but warned of some people, 'too lazy to work for themselves', who 'lurk in secret places to plunder' the small settlers' fields, and complained that 'we are lacking a continuous and remunerating labour . . . looking for better days when our clothing and food will be reduced, as the present prices are intolerable'.[145] It seems highly likely that Ward would have signed this address, which – in a foretaste of Eyre's aggressive response to the Underhill meetings of the following year – the governor answered by noting the settlers' concerns, but telling them that they must 'improve in civilization' and 'exert themselves to train up their children properly'.[146]

Despite the impetus given to peasant and smallholder autonomy by the events of 1865, Ward's vision of an islandwide cooperative association of small farmers, which for the diasporic African-American minister was a vision of intra-imperial black independence – 'not to be despised in any part of the British empire' – was in fact never to be realised. But a little further west, at Black River in the parish of St Elizabeth, Samuel Holt, Charles Plummer, and William Brydson were already by this time laying the foundations for the JCA. They were also already meeting the firm opposition of the ruling class of the island, which would eventually doom the project before it had begun to pay dividends (either literally or metaphorically). Their scheme for the small settlers to bypass the big planters and the wealthy merchants and ship their produce directly to Britain ran directly counter to the notorious 'Queen's Advice', written by longtime Colonial Office civil servant Henry Taylor in London in response to Underhill's complaints about the conditions in Jamaica, which claimed, in part, that

the prosperity of the Labouring Classes as well as of all other classes depends in Jamaica, and in other Countries, upon their working for Wages, not uncertainly or capriciously, but steadily and continuously, at the times when their labour is wanted, and for so long as it is wanted . . . and they may be assured that it is from their own industry and prudence, in availing themselves of the means of prospering that are before them, *and not from any such schemes as have been suggested to them*, that they must look for an improvement in their condition.[147]

As I hope to show in the remainder of this chapter, the 'Queen's Advice' was not simply a general statement of laissez-faire economics, but a specific response not only to the peasant organising of the Baptists, but even more so to the cooperative economic organisation of the small settlers and their allies in new institutions like the JCA. Edward Eyre ordered that Taylor's uncompromising reassertion of the central place of the sugar plantation in the economic and social life of Jamaica should be posted publicly throughout the island, and the 50,000 copies that were published and distributed in July 1865 contributed in no small measure to the events that followed towards the end of that same year in St Thomas-in-the-East.

The fullest and most fulsome account of the activities of the JCA was carried in the London magazine *The Freed-Man*, which was the organ of the London Freedmen's Aid Society, established in the mid-1860s to support slaves and free blacks during the US Civil War.[148] When news of the Jamaica uprising reached England, some advocates for the US freedpeople argued that the remit of the group should be expanded to include blacks in the West Indies too, and although this precipitated a split within the freedmen's aid movement in Britain, *The Freed-Man* carried regular items about Jamaica for the next year, pushing the merits of the JCA in particular.[149] Holt, Plummer (a coloured schoolteacher from St Elizabeth), and Brydson (a coloured St Elizabeth magistrate) visited England in the summer of 1866 to carry the message that 'The negroes of Jamaica wish . . . to say to us [the British], we [Jamaicans] are willing to work and to send to your markets what our Island can produce if you in England will establish an agency that will deal directly and fairly with us.' Black people are not lazy, they said: 'The black man is the man that clears the land for cultivation, he is the man that plants, he is the man that manufactures the produce . . . in short, he is the man that does most of all which is done to produce money' in Jamaica.[150]

In the following issue of the magazine, Charles Plummer wrote an article surveying the island, informing his British readers that the Jamaican people wanted to repay the 'interest in their welfare' on the part of the metropolitan audience by 'prov[ing] that they can and will labour, that they are ready to apply themselves to increased industry, to help themselves and their children and not to depend on the government to help them'. Sounding a great deal like Samuel Ward, Plummer emphasised the loyalty of Jamaica's black majority, and noted that while the authorities in St Elizabeth had feared unrest in that district too in 1865, in fact, 'the people, instead of planning a wicked rebellion, were busily engaging in their usual quiet avocations, and were organizing a more sensible and legal affair in the shape of a co-operative association'.[151] In a private letter to the custos of St Elizabeth, John Salmon (who was a staunch opponent of such schemes), Plummer complained that 'this horrible rebellion [has] knocked it [the cooperative association] to pieces'. He worried that 'the English people' would cease to be interested in the company: 'Will they have any thing more to do with such a cut-throated set of barbarians as the negroes have turned out to be?' Declaring his loyalty to the government, Plummer (like Ward before him, and like Holt, as we shall see below) sought to distance himself from the black majority in Jamaica. Nevertheless, he again outlined the merits of the proposal: 'Our main object is to get the people to plant cotton, and we would have had the means of the cotton supply association at our disposal. Then to establish model farms, industrial schools, savings banks throughout the island; but our scheme was looked on as too gigantic to be good.'¹⁵² Samuel Holt, speaking at a BMS meeting in Hertford, expressed the 'attachment' of the African Jamaicans to the queen, deplored the outbreak at Morant Bay (in which 'so many valuable lives were destroyed'), and declared himself to be 'one of the fruits of missionary labour': 'He was there before them [the BMS] to show them what the unpolished material was, and when they calculated the effects of the polishing they might form an estimate of what might be made of the negroes.'¹⁵³ As a sign of their commitment to the cause of 'polishing' the Jamaican people through their cooperative labours, Brydson and Plummer donated 10s each to the freedmen's aid movement; Holt donated 5s.¹⁵⁴

Holt's role was clearly subsidiary in other ways too. He did not accompany Plummer and Brydson when they appeared before the Birmingham Chamber of Commerce on 13 September 1866 to advertise the merits of their scheme. Perhaps the better educated 'coloured' men were thought to be more appropriate spokespeople for the fledgling cooperative association than the self-taught black preacher who 'never went to school' and felt, at the BMS meeting in Hertford, 'he was in danger of being brought up at the bar of grammar and tried for the murder of the Queen's English'. (The *Herts Advertiser* reporter who covered the meeting commented benevolently on Holt's 'very intelligent, appropriate, and modest address' that evening, delivered in 'very fair English'.¹⁵⁵) In Birmingham there were signs that the JCA was beginning to attract serious interest from the upper echelons of the antislavery and philanthropic movements in Britain: Plummer and Brydson were introduced by William Morgan, a veteran leader of the abolitionist cause, and by John Horne Payne, the inquisitor of Samuel Ringgold Ward at the JRC hearings, who had both recently returned from Jamaica.¹⁵⁶ Although it was perfectly understandable that the representatives of the Black River organisation would seek out the people in Britain from whom they could expect the friendliest reception – just as Ward had sought and obtained introductions into the same dissenting and abolitionist circles when he arrived in Britain in 1853 – the prospectus for the

JCA that emerged from these meetings suggests that it had been coopted almost immediately by the same 'friends of the negro'[157] whose investment in condescension had turned Ward into a 'coloured impostor' within two years of his arrival. The directors of the JCA, which began running full-page advertisements on the back page of *The Freed-Man*, included Lord Alfred Churchill, Thomas Hughes, John Estcourt (all prominent in abolitionist circles), and Edward Underhill, secretary of the BMS. Although at least four shipments of produce (mostly coffee and ginger) were sent from Jamaica to Britain in 1867 and 1868, the company quickly collapsed, leaving many small settlers facing substantial losses.[158] In what is perhaps a fitting historical irony, *The Freed-Man* itself was apparently put out of business in 1868 by the failure of the JCA to pay for the very same advertisements that had helped to bring the cause of the Jamaican smallholders to the attention of British philanthropy in the first place.[159]

The JCA, then, despite its grand plans for islandwide cooperation among the smallholders of the colony, succumbed in the way that many in Jamaica had predicted it would. The *Falmouth Post*, for instance, on first hearing of the Black River association, forecast that black Jamaicans would not benefit from the endeavour: 'There will be an immense amount of bamboozling and cheating by the Colonial Managers of each Association, and by the Agents whom they will employ in England.'[160] Seeing the whole episode as an example of grand extortion, the paper, edited by John Castello, himself part of the rising coloured class in the island, argued that 'There are but few, very few of them ['negroes of St. Elizabeth'] who believe that they will be treated fairly and honestly by Agents either white or coloured.'[161] Two years later, the paper happily reprinted a piece from the *Jamaica Guardian* sarcastically announcing that 'the bubble has burst' on 'this great institution, by which the small settler was to become the independent exporter of his own produce... The negroes at Montego Bay calling themselves shareholders have demanded a settlement of their account either by goods or money'. (The fact that the JCA had extended its activities from its Black River base all the way to the northwestern port and regional centre of Montego Bay, however, gives some indication of its scope and rapid growth, as indeed does the number of hostile articles like this one appearing in the Jamaican press.) Showing the unanimity of the island's newspapers against such ventures, the *Guardian* said,

We have no faith in these Companies – we never had, and we have all along been impressed with the conviction that those who *suffer from them* are those who put faith in their disinterestedness and feelings of philanthropy, and those who *benefit from them* are generally those who are the agents or servants of the institutions which hold out inducements to the ignorant or embarrassed.[162]

The Jamaican papers, then, continued throughout this experiment to hold more or less the same opinion as many of the leading white Baptist missionaries in the island, who responded to Governor Eyre's request for information about the state of the island in 1865 by claiming that the peasantry were too suspicious of each other and of the merchants to form cooperative societies in the island. From Falmouth, Thomas Lea reported that 'the people at present do not have sufficient confidence in each other or in their advisers for the formation of Joint Stock Companies for raising and exporting produce'; from Montego Bay, John Henderson said, 'I do not think they would form co-operative societies, as they have so little confidence in each other'; from St Ann's Bay, Benjamin Millard could not say 'whether the people will be willing to form co-operative and industrial societies. The want of mutual confidence, of persistent industry, and of energy, and also of education, will prove serious obstacles', although he hoped that 'with patient teaching, [these] may be modified'. From Savanna-la-Mar, the closest town to the Black River association, Rev. G. Clarke was even more emphatic: 'They are not prepared to form co-operative and industrial associations. They have no confidence in each other, nor in merchants. Confidence has been sorely shaken, and is now destroyed.' From Black River itself, James Barrett, the black missionary there, did not respond to the JBU circular.[163]

This must have come as something of a disappointment to Edward Underhill, who earnestly pushed the idea of cooperative trading societies to David East in early 1865, saying that all the Jamaican smallholders needed was 'combination, like that which Barrett has brought about at Black River', which would allow even small shippers to reach European markets: 'This mail, e.g., brings me a Bill of Lading from Mr. Barrett for 144 bags of Pimento; 15 barrels of Coffee; four barrels of Sarsaparilla; & one barrel of [illegible]. Why should not others do the same?'[164] Underhill seemed to fear resistance from his longtime correspondent in Jamaica, however, apologising for 'saying so much about this', and then again later on the same page: 'But I have said enough. I have no doubt you [the JBU 'brethren'] will all talk about it when you get together.'[165] Was Barrett's 'combination' a separate scheme from the one set up by Brydson, Plummer, and Holt later that same year? It is impossible to tell at this historical distance. But what is clear is that there was a stark division, based on race, on the question of the fitness of the Jamaican small settlers and peasantry for cooperative arrangements.

Despite the eventual failure of the JCA, however, it is clear, as the formation of Barrett's 'combination' shows, that the black smallholders *were* organising themselves, with or without agents and middlemen they trusted.

Strikingly, many of the 'native pastors' who responded to the JBU circular came to the opposite conclusion from the white leadership. From Bethlehem, J. J. Porter answered, 'As far as I have been able to ascertain, the people are willing to sustain Co-operative Societies'; from Boston, James Service replied, 'If aided and instructed they would make the trial of co-operative associations'; from Moneague and Mount Nebo, Joseph Gordon replied that 'They are prepared to form co-operative societies'; from Belle Castle and Stokes Hall, the only JBU stations in St Thomas-in-the-East at the time, Henry Bartholomew Harris declared that 'I believe they will be too happy to form co-operative and industrial societies.'[166] But the positive outlook of the 'native' pastors in the JBU – to say nothing of the many independent Baptist ministers spread throughout the island – on the question of peasant and smallholder 'combination' was no match for the much more powerful combination of ruling-class hostility and the scepticism of the white leadership of the 'friends of the negro' about the capacity for African Jamaicans for self-organisation. Confirming Underhill's suspicions about his opposition to such schemes, David East responded to the JBU circular by saying that 'They [the peasantry] would gladly unite in an industrial society for the exhibition of produce, but I question whether they would be prepared to form co-operative associations.'[167] The JBU's cautious endorsement of such associations was undercut by the following incautious observation in the letter they sent to the governor: 'It will be painfully evident to your Excellency, from our Returns, that a large measure of the poverty and distress is attributable to indolence.'[168]

Could cooperative societies possibly thrive in a place where such attitudes, on the part of those who endeavoured most directly to serve the interests of the black majority, combined so effortlessly with those of the economic and political elite? John Salmon, the custos (chief magistrate) of St Elizabeth (and a personal enemy of Charles Plummer), wrote to Governor Eyre during the period of martial law imposed after the October 1865 uprising, noting that 'meetings . . . have been called at several places by a Mr. Plummer, a Mr. Brydson (a magistrate), and a man Gilling' to tell 'the growers of produce [that they] are imposed upon and cheated'. Worrying that the proposed association 'will materially injure general society', he asked the governor, 'Is the Association at such a time as the present, and the meetings, legal?' The attorney-general of Jamaica, Alexander Heslop, gave his legal opinion that there was 'nothing illegal in the proposed Association. Trade is free and ought to be so.' Nevertheless, he went on, 'It is very certain . . . that a dead loss will accrue to all the shareholders.' Still, they should be allowed to fail: 'As by foolish or wicked counsels the small producers seem to have lost confidence in the mercantile capitalists, I know no better way of enabling them to find out their own blunders than that they should try their experiment.'[169] The leading pro-planter newspaper declared in the months leading up to the Morant Bay rising that the island's economy and society would collapse unless the sugar plantation remained at the centre of Jamaican life:

Above all, let the people understand that without the produce of the large properties we should have scarcely any export trade, and consequently no contact with the outside world sufficient to keep us in the march of civilization and improvement: and that without the existence of an upper class giving tone to society by its manners and example, they would soon revert to a state of barbarism.[170]

Such dismissive thinking had been around for a long time, of course, although here it might well indicate a certain worry about the increasingly important role of the small settlers in the island economy, a concern that Ward was right the following month when he declared to the St David Underhill meeting that 30,000 small farmers combining would make a difference 'in any part of the British empire'.

In the end, this sketch of the attenuated history of the Jamaica Commercial Agency – representing, here, both the possibility of black economic self-fashioning and the myriad forces arrayed against such relative autonomy – must return to the figures who inspired the JCA, and inspired the greatest hostility, Samuel Ward and Samuel Holt. The latter, as the most prominent black Jamaican associated with the JCA, generated the most opprobrium in the Jamaican press. Previously, in the period immediately after the Morant Bay rising, the authorities had questioned Holt, when they found out that George W. Gordon had given him a Bible some years earlier.[171] Now, the *Falmouth Post*, hearing of Holt's involvement in the JCA in July 1866, reminded him of who his benefactors were:

It was to the white people to whom he is indebted for employment that enabled him to purchase a freehold . . . it was upon the white people that he depended for the remunerative sale of his cultivated products, and it is the money of the white people with which he has made from time to time successful progress as an Agriculturalist.[172]

The paper had picked up its information about Holt's part in the scheme from an earlier report in *The Gleaner*, who had heard that 'Mr. Holt . . . addressed a large meeting of the peasantry of Manchester, on his way to Kingston, advising them to grow no more provisions or coffee for the white people; that if the white people wanted to grow these, they must do the labour themselves.'[173] When the success of Holt's deputation to Britain became clear, *The Gleaner* briefly turned conciliatory, reprinting the company's initial prospectus from *Lyon's Paper* in London, and reporting that, 'We have much pleasure in stating that the efforts of Mr. Holt [in England] have proven eminently successful.'[174] There seemed to be a brief window of opportunity for the JCA to take its place, at least as far as the merchant-oriented *Gleaner* was concerned, alongside that paper's endorsement of Samuel Oughton's departing manifesto for the island, the creation of 'artificial wants' in the black majority by encouraging and educating them to buy the commodities that to the Baptist minister meant 'civilisation'.[175] Soon after Holt's return from England, however, the paper relaunched its attack on him, after he had spoken in November at East Queen Street Baptist Church, almost immediately after Oughton's final departure from Jamaica.

The church was once again in a state of limbo, without an official pastor, and Holt – who had told the JRC shortly before his trip to England that he was affiliated with the 'English Baptists' but not formally a member of the JBU[176] – was at least symbolically filling Oughton's shoes. *The Gleaner* professed both shock and amusement that Holt, playing the stereotypical role of ignorant social climber, had called on his listeners to dress respectably as they strove to claim the status of citizens of Jamaica and the empire. The paper interpreted what was perhaps an attempt to foster upward mobility within the codes of British respectability as a buffoonish call for a patently 'ludicrous' crossing of the one sexual, racial, and class boundary that remained the most impervious in Jamaican society, that between black men and white women:

[Holt] informed his hearers that in the course of his visits in England, he had been interrogated by the White Ladies there as to whether any Black men in Jamaica had married White women. He was 'ashamed', he said, to be compelled to reply in the negative, and he recommended his people *to dress* in such a manner as to make them acceptable to the White Ladies of Jamaica as husbands!! The story is considered ludicrous enough, and has provoked many a smile in this Island.[177]

Ludicrous or not, the evidence collected by the JRC suggests that clothes were in fact an important status symbol and mark of respectability for the mass of the population in Jamaica, perhaps especially those churchgoers who wanted to claim their share of imperial citizenship. Several clergymen reported that the widespread poverty in Jamaica in 1865 led to a lack of suitable clothing for church attendance on the part of the people. James Hildebrand, for example, the Anglican curate of St David's church in

Manchester, Jamaica, noted that he knew there was 'distress' among the population because 'they frequently alleged want of clothes as a reason for not coming to church'.[178] Jane Wilson, a black woman interviewed by the commission because during martial law in October British soldiers had burned down her house outside Manchioneal, killing her two children inside, said that when a soldier pulled her and her late husband's clothes out of the house as the fire subsided, 'the soldier say, "A black person have all these; they must be the white clothes;" and I said, "No, massa, they my own clothes."'[179] Mimi Sheller argues, in an important article on black women's political organising in mid-nineteenth-century Jamaica, that black women 'exploited a "discourse of domesticity" ... to protect their household autonomy ... [and] promoted black power within the dissenting churches'.[180] The evidence of Jane Wilson bears out Sheller's argument, in her and her family's accumulation of 'white' clothing inside their modest, 'black' home, but also suggests the power of the Jamaican regime brutally to stamp out such fledgling self-organisation, with the power of the military when necessary.

Moreover, as Sheller also shows, the post-rebellion public discourse in the island served to reinforce this message. The news of Holt's lecture at East Queen Street was followed in *The Gleaner* by a parody letter from an imaginary black woman, 'Quasheba', under the heading 'Colour fe Colour' ('the erstwhile slogan of the defeated rebellion', as Sheller points out). The letter starts as an attack on Holt's deference to, and desire for, white women, and turns into a full-scale attack on black men in general: 'Dem niggar man is de real good for nutin nega, dem tump and trash we all time, dem cuss we wotless, dem make we labour for dem all time.' The newspaper, appealing to its elite readership by deploying a parodic version of black vernacular speech, stages an all too rare appearance of a black woman's voice solely in order to defend the status quo, in terms of class, racial, and gender divisions: 'Quasheba', balking at the prospect of black men marrying white women, exclaims, 'No massa Edita, me hope me will nebber see dat day.'[181] A few days later, *The Gleaner* returned to the attack, in even more personal terms, ridiculing Holt's family for their poverty: 'Me memba me see one Gal da Black Ribba, dem say da Holt daughta. Me good Massa, de Gal cum da de markit wid baskit pon him hed – no hab shoos; an me po tranga yerry sa him wife bin go na grung wid him son, an bring ninyam pon dem hed fo go da markit' ('I remember seeing a girl in Black River, and they say she is Holt's daughter. My good master, the girl came to the market with a basket on her head, and she had no shoes on. And this poor stranger [i.e., 'Quasheba' herself] heard them say his wife went to the fields with his son, and they brought yams on their heads to take to the market').[182] Recalling the slogan of the Morant Bay rebellion once more, Quasheba says, 'Massa, dem sa colar fe colar – den da fe turro Holt say Bukra Lady fe marry black man? Neba see dat day, me good Massa' ('Master, they say "colour for colour" – then why does Holt turn it around and say that white women should marry black men? That day will never come, my good master'). And Samuel Holt's involvement in the cooperative scheme, perhaps inevitably, also incites the Jamaican ruling class's longstanding distrust of Baptists by exploiting the very ambiguities in the relationship between official and 'native' Baptists that I analysed above, questioning Holt's credentials in this, as in every other area: 'Me beg you to tell me da warra part of de Highland ['which part of the island'] da man Holt bin mek Parsin?'[183]

Showing that Samuel Ringgold Ward retained a certain celebrity, or perhaps notoriety, in the island, despite his near obliteration from the Jamaican historical record, the two Quasheba letters in *The Gleaner* explicitly link Holt and Ward, two turbulent priests who hit a nerve in mid-nineteenth-century Jamaica. In Quasheba's telling of the story, the East Queen Street Baptist church, after Oughton's departure, was renamed to reflect its reversion to non-official, suspicious status: she hears of Holt's speech when her husband returns 'fram de Meeting a Ward's Chapel las week'. In the second letter she repeats the association: 'Holt preech da Ward Chapel da Tung [Town: i.e., Kingston].'[184] Now that both Ward and Holt were connected to transatlantic networks, *The Gleaner* reasserted the primacy of Holt's modest Jamaican roots, and tried to keep him in his place as a trained performer for the creole ruling class, rather than its critic: 'Him go da Englan; an him talk big big wud', but 'him is a false imprance black man, an me Quashie memba him lang lang time, when him da ride race da Panish Tung' ('He went to England, and he spoke a lot of big words'; 'he is a false, impertinent [?] black man, and my husband Quashie remembers him from long ago when he rode in horse races in Spanish Town').[185] In the context of 'Ward's chapel', Holt's 'big big wud' are literally unbelievable: 'Him tell plenty me yerry, but me can't bleeb him' ('He said a lot, I hear, but I can't believe him'). Holt's 'plenty' is reduced to nothing, made to fit the oldest and crudest stereotypes about black primitivism and heterodoxy.

Can we reconstruct the lineaments of Holt's message, and of Holt's and Ward's vision of black economic empowerment from the travesties that constitute the colonial archive? Is the use of the term 'Ward's Chapel' a backhanded way of acknowledging that this term was still in popular use – and positive use? Inez Knibb Sibley (descendant of William Knibb, one of the earliest and most radical of the British Baptist missionaries in Jamaica) notes in her history of Jamaican Baptism that the Hanover Street Baptist church in Kingston was popularly known as 'Palmer's Church', after its pastor of forty years, Edwin Palmer.[186] (Likewise, the public meetings called in response to Edward Underhill's letter to the colonial secretary on the state of Jamaica were popularly known as 'Underhill meetings', as we have seen, a term that has become part of latterday historians' vocabulary of 1860s Jamaica.) 'Ward's Chapel' fits this Jamaican pattern, but Ward still did not fit in Jamaica, and we have to conduct a risky rescue mission of our own to retrieve his eccentric points of view from the imperial archive.

Even in the midst of his egregious failure to support the goals of the Morant Bay rebels, blaming the authorities for 'lax discipline' and a 'want of vigilance' in relation to 'the visits of strolling demagogues, and the influence of a ribald press' in fomenting the rebellion, Ward felt compelled to remind his likely audience that 'the superior classes are dependant upon the negro class for the performance of the most necessary work of all kinds'.[187] On the one hand, Ward wrote after Morant Bay that 'The employers may have the satisfaction of knowing that the employed are loyal and true, as a rule, and that none other than a loyal and orderly example will be set by those of their own race mediately and immediately above them.'[188] On the other hand, he wrote self-deprecatingly that he could not speak 'positively, or with authority' about the rebellion because 'I know, too, very well that the opinion of a poor working man, is esteemed as of no value.'[189] In the end, despite the fact that Ward was telling the authorities, in Kingston as in London, what they wanted to hear, it is his not being able to speak with authority that really counts. How did Samuel Ward react to Samuel Holt's attempts to follow through on his grand vision of working men and women's self-empowerment? Was he cheering the JCA from the sidelines? We may never know, since he made no public statements one way or the other. Isolated, to the very end, from the main currents of Jamaican and imperial politics and culture, from the emerging brown creole political and economic leadership, from the official-if-dissenting Christian organisations, and from the upper reaches of the colonial and metropolitan governments, Ward allows us to set all of these in relief, to wrench them out of the narratives of modern history that each of them has helped to legitimate and thereby control.

All scholarship on Ward claims that he died in 1866, right after his endorsement of Governor Eyre and his appearance before the JRC.[190] But on 25 May 1867, *The Gleaner* printed a list of recent appointments made by the new governor of Jamaica, Sir John Peter Grant, who was dismantling the centuries-old system of planter-dominated self-government in the island after the 1865 uprising, in the name of modernisation, rationalisation, and imperial security. As head of a new Crown Colony, governed directly from London for the first time, Grant had done away with the Jamaican House of Assembly, and had also abolished the local elected assemblies of each parish, the vestries. Responsibility for parish affairs was turned over to non-elected bodies: municipal boards and road commissions for each district, appointed by the governor. The final name on the list of Parochial Road Commissioners appointed for the new parish of St Thomas (created by joining St David parish to St Thomas-in-the-East) is 'Rev. Samuel Ringgold Ward'.[191] Although his name is set down in *The Gleaner* with a lack of commentary commensurate with a newspaper item under the heading 'Government Notices', a remarkable and complex narrative lies behind Ward's appearance on this unremarkable list of minor imperial functionaries in one of the lesser corners of the British empire, as we have seen.

The idiosyncrasies and contradictions of the extraordinary life of this black Atlantic figure are smoothed out in the face of this historical fact – a minor sinecure in the new machinery of the modern British empire – preserved in the aspic of the archive. Three years later, Ward disappeared from view again. While the 1869 Jamaican almanac *Who's Who and What's What*, issued by *The Gleaner's* publisher, lists Ward as a member of the St Thomas roads commission, his name is missing from the list of municipal officials in the island that was published in the government newspaper, the *Jamaica Gazette*, in early 1870.[192] Ward's residence is listed in the almanac as 'Yallahs', so presumably he had moved after the uprising from his smallholding at Vickersfield to Yallahs, the principal town of St David. But in spite of this move towards the official centre, he still escaped conventional categories from his position on the margins: despite being identified as 'Revd. S. R. Ward', he does not appear in the almanac's list of 'dissenting clergy' for St Thomas. His independent pastorship remained unacknowledged, and Ward continued to be a misfit.

Predicated as it has been on the twin figures of the liberal subject and the modern nation-state, history has been unkind to Samuel Ringgold Ward. Too itinerant for inclusion in national histories, too deferential to the empire to be included in anticolonial and black histories, too militant to be included in imperial histories, Ward's life is a challenge to all of these ways of understanding the nineteenth-century Atlantic world. If my focus on his strange career constitutes a rescue mission of sorts, predicated on the romantic appeal of the figure of the eccentric individual, I hope also to have carried out a kind of patient history that seeks in Ward not a neglected hero but a representative 'somebody', precisely a typical rather than a marginal figure. Ward accepted the basic premise of historicism, that people in the present can only be understood as the result of historical forces and patterns in the past, but he noted the decisive importance of the historian who, in narrating those historical forces, gives them shape and finds their patterns. In his essay on the 'modern negro' for Frederick Douglass's newspaper, Ward writes:

We must do it [vindicate the 'modern negro'], or who will? Where is the history of the Negro? Alas! the history of our unhappy people consists of a single term and its cognate – slavery – slave trade – there is negro history, and what is more, some of the darkest and diabolical pages and chapters of *other* history as well; and while this has been our lot, and that of our fathers, how were we to raise up historians? That is done but by people in far different circumstances.[193]

Samuel Ringgold Ward strove to vindicate the modern negro while at the same time trying to ingratiate himself with those people in far different circumstances; avoiding romantic historicism led inexorably for Ward to an accommodation with the diffuse contemporary power of the British empire.

CHAPTER 4

Jamaica, genealogy, George Eliot: inheriting the empire after Morant Bay

In this chapter I keep the focus on the 1865 Morant Bay rebellion, but turn away from the situation on the ground in Jamaica, and shift the emphasis to Britain, analysing some of the debates in British intellectual and literary history of the 1850s and 1860s on questions of race, empire, and literary form. I hope that the discussion of Samuel Ringgold Ward and the black Atlantic world of the mid-nineteenth century will illuminate the discussion that follows, as I seek to put the Caribbean in general, and the question of the 'negro' in particular, back in the middle of an understanding of the transition after Morant Bay to new ideas of 'united empire', and of the disintegration of the inheritance plot as the preeminent feature of the English novel in this period. In a sense, the structure of my argument here is that the discussion of Jamaica and emerging forms of black internationalism ought logically and chronologically to come before an account of mid-Victorian British responses to what came to be known as the 'Governor Eyre case'. (In this respect, I follow the formal structure of Catherine Hall's *Civilising Subjects*, in which her history of Baptist missions in Jamaica in the period between emancipation and Morant Bay comes before and informs her discussion of reform and municipal politics and culture in Birmingham during the same period.[1]) I conclude this chapter with an analysis of the reconstruction of the 'British Empire' as an imaginary unit soldered together by modern humanitarianism, and the centrality of Jamaica in this new version of imperialism.

Looking back at the nineteenth century from our present vantage point, the mid-1860s do not immediately spring to mind as a period of great crisis in British domestic and imperial affairs. The mobilisation that led up to the Second Reform Bill lacks the revolutionary drama of the first round of Reform agitation and the great Chartist movement earlier in the century; and the 1865 Jamaican uprising was hardly on the same scale as the Sepoy Rebellion in India in 1857 or the later Anglo-Boer War that brought the Victorian age to an end. Nevertheless, British social commentators and cultural critics of the 1860s believed themselves to be living through a period of major upheaval. And although some anticipated a positive outcome from the winds of change they sensed blowing through musty old Britain, others saw only threats and possible catastrophe. Thomas Carlyle, for instance, blustery as ever in his old age, fired off a letter in August 1866 promising support for the Eyre Testimonial and Defence Fund, set up to defend the governor of Jamaica against criticism of his methods in suppressing the Morant Bay rebellion:

> The clamour raised against Governor Eyre appears to me to be disgraceful to the good sense of England; and if it rested on any depth of conviction...I should consider it of evil omen to the country, and to its highest interests, in these times...The English nation never loved anarchy; nor was wont to spend its sympathy on miserable mad seditions, especially of this inhuman and half-brutish type; but always loved order, and the prompt suppression of seditions.[2]

The shift to the past tense in the second of Carlyle's sentences here nicely conveys the sense that anarchy may actually be the new order of the day, and the disturbing fact that the opposition to Eyre not only rested on strongly held convictions but also had mass appeal. This second sentence also recalls (anachronistically, as it turns out) that most famous statement of the troubles of the 1860s, Matthew Arnold's *Culture and Anarchy*, first published as a series of magazine essays in 1867–8 and printed in book form in 1869.

In the conclusion to that work, writing about the disorder in Hyde Park in 1866 during a rally for parliamentary Reform, but writing also in the context of the mass mobilisation of public opinion for and against Governor Eyre and his counterinsurgency methods, Arnold likewise demonstrates his firm conviction that seditions of any kind – miserable, mad, or otherwise – must be forcefully put down: 'For us the framework of society, that theatre on which this august drama has to unroll itself, is sacred; and whoever administers it...we steadily and with undivided heart support them in repressing anarchy and disorder; because without order there can be no society, and without society there can be no human perfection.'[3] In the original magazine version of this essay, and in the first edition of *Culture and Anarchy*, this passage is followed by these notorious lines:

> With me, indeed, this rule of conduct is hereditary. I remember my father, in one of his unpublished letters, written more than forty years ago, when the political and social state of the country was gloomy and troubled and there were riots in many places, goes on, after strongly insisting on the badness and foolishness of the

government, and on the harm and dangerousness of our feudal and aristocratical constitution of society, and ends thus: 'As for rioting, the old Roman way of dealing with that is always the right one; flog the rank and file, and fling the ringleaders from the Tarpeian Rock!'[4]

In later editions of the book, Arnold deleted this passage, for reasons that have never been entirely clear.[5] Perhaps the country seemed less gloomy and troubled by the time of the second edition (1875), and thus less in need of Thomas Arnold's lawgiving. Or perhaps Matthew revised his text in response to the answer, now lost, that his mother gave to this letter that he sent to her on 25 July 1868:

In the passage quoted from Papa, [Arthur Penrhyn] Stanley's impression is that Papa's words were 'Crucify the slaves' instead of 'Flog the rank & file' – but as the latter expression is the milder, and I have certainly got it in my memory as what he said, I have retained it. Do you remember which the words were, and in what letter they occur?[6]

Buried deep within Arnold's text, we find a possible connection between contemporary debates over race and slavery animated by the Jamaica rebellion and the US Civil War – 'Crucify the slaves' – and the sometimes unruly agitation for working-class enfranchisement and parliamentary reform in Britain – 'Flog the rank and file.'[7] It was this conjunction that gave the Morant Bay uprising such a disproportionate significance in Britain at the time, and which forms the subject of this chapter. And it is, I argue, after Morant Bay that the modern notion of the British empire as a single conceptual, territorial, and political unit re-emerges, recalling an earlier invocation of a united empire in the wake of the American Revolution and the struggles over slavery in the Caribbean in the early nineteenth century.

Jamaica in the 1860s had been in serious economic decline for half a century; the days when ownership of a Jamaican sugar plantation was virtually a licence to print money were a distant memory. In keeping with this loss of economic clout, until the 1865 rebellion, Jamaica had largely drifted away from the centre of political discourse in Britain, so that Edward Underhill, secretary of the Baptist Missionary Society (BMS), could write to his friend David East in Jamaica in 1862,

I am afraid the cause of the negro is losing ground in England – not that antislavery sentiments are less cherished; but now that the negro is free & the field is open for him, he is to be left to his own exertions to complete his elevation. He must now fight his own battles like other people. This I fancy is the truth of the case, notwithstanding that 'The Times' continues to talk of the negro as only fitted for menial & servile labour.[8]

As Underhill's letter suggests, antislavery and missionary organisations in Britain found themselves caught between, on the one hand, promoting the cause of 'the negro' as an object of philanthropy, and, on the other hand, describing people of African descent as self-elevating agents in their own development. But the reference to *The Times* in Underhill's letter to East highlights a new element in this longstanding equation: despite the fact that the newspaper's derogation of 'the negro' had a long history, it now began to be articulated within a new discourse of race and racism in Britain, one that threatened to overturn the hegemony of philanthropic views of 'the negro' in particular. When Jamaica reappeared on centre stage of British public life in late 1865, it also found itself at the centre of a new set of political and cultural beliefs.

The response to the Jamaica events in England was predictable at first: the governor was generally praised for saving the island from destruction, as Samuel Ringgold Ward and the Jamaican ruling class had done unmediately after the rebellion was crushed (see chapter 3). It seemed unlikely that much controversy would ensue; Morant Bay promised to be just another in a long line of colonial rebellions put down with brutal force and then conveniently forgotten – except by their victims. But as more details began to emerge, opposition from liberals in England began to grow against Eyre's handling of the crisis, and by early 1866 the 'Governor Eyre Case' had become the hottest topic of national debate. A coalition of antislavery activists and radical politicians and lawyers formed the Jamaica Committee, chaired by John Stuart Mill; public pressure led the government to send a royal commission of inquiry to Jamaica to gather evidence on the uprising and its suppression. The Jamaica Royal Commission (JRC) delivered its report in April 1866, and while it broadly exonerated Eyre, it concluded that British and Jamaican troops had often used excessive force. The controversy raged throughout 1866, coinciding precisely, and sometimes intersecting, with the intense debates over parliamentary reform and the enfranchisement of the working classes in England.[9]

I argue in this chapter, as I have throughout this study, that the relationship among national, imperial, and Atlantic histories needs to be rethought. When Britain – or, still worse, England – is no longer the unexamined organising principle of cultural and historical studies, events in the Caribbean have a relevance beyond their traditional marginal locations (in the discrete field of imperial history and at those rare moments in national history when they happen to illuminate English questions). Thus, reversing the usual polarity of such comparisons, I suggest here that debate over the Second Reform Bill was so intense in Britain in the mid-1860s because it represented the entrance, however surreptitiously, of a new discourse of racial formation into the social fabric of the country. The 1860s were a time when constructions of race and class were undergoing substantial changes. A new scientific interest in race and descent combined with renewed political emphasis on equality of birth and the 'rights of man' to produce a highly contradictory and unstable situation. An older, romantic discourse of blood and breeding, associated with the 'feudal and aristocratical constitution of society', as Arnold put it, was being replaced by a newer rhetoric of citizenship and rights, which seemed more amenable to the mode of realist narration – although it remained a rhetoric that, nevertheless, incorporated elements of the older discourse in its emphasis on the natural disposition of particular groups, especially those that could be marked as racially other.

Thus, by a circuitous route, 'blood' made its reappearance in the new science of anthropology at precisely the moment it appeared to have lost its explanatory value in descriptions of English society. To quote Arnold again, 'Science has now made visible to everybody the great and pregnant elements of difference which lie in race.'[10] The career of novelist George Eliot exemplifies this movement, I might suggest: from the early novels' engagement with the traditional domestic inheritance plot to the emphasis in her last novel, *Daniel Deronda*, on international and racial questions in which, paradoxically, individual destiny is more a question of blood and breeding than it ever was in a novel like *Silas Marner*. In the penultimate section of this chapter I analyse her 1866 novel, *Felix Holt*, published in the midst of the Jamaica controversy, as enacting this transition from one literary and intellectual mode to the other.

MORANT BAY AND THE EMERGENCE OF 'HEREDITARIAN RACIALISM'

The revolt of October 1865 in and around the town of Morant Bay, on the southeastern coast of Jamaica, has been receiving increasing attention from cultural critics and historians in recent years. Belatedly, critics have begun to move away from earlier polemics that hinged on the actions and character of the governor, Edward Eyre, in the suppression of the revolt. Philip Curtin, Bernard Semmel, and, more recently, Catherine Hall and Gad Heuman have laid the groundwork for a more careful analysis of the events in Jamaica and their aftermath that situates them in the context of contemporary debates over race, slavery, labour, and empire – debates in which Eyre himself appears more as symptom than as cause. Such analyses, while avoiding the histrionics of earlier readings of 'the Governor Eyre controversy', tend to agree that Morant Bay was an extremely significant event in British imperial history, despite being relatively minor in terms of numbers of casualties. Although the Sepoy Rebellion (the so-called Indian Mutiny) of 1857 and the New Zealand Land Wars (once called the Maori Wars) of the mid-1860s were far bloodier, it was Morant Bay that crystallised debate in Britain about the imperial mission itself.[11]

Postcolonial scholars are coming belatedly to accept, therefore, that Morant Bay was as important as people believed it to be at the time. The journalist and historian Justin McCarthy remembered in the 1870s that back in 1866, 'for some weeks there was hardly anything talked of, we might almost say hardly anything thought of, in England, but the story of the rebellion that had taken place in the island of Jamaica, and the manner in which it had been suppressed and punished'.[12] A reading of the newspapers and magazines of the time will reveal, of course, that many other important and not-so important questions were also generating heat and light. Nevertheless, it is remarkable the extent to which a local rebellion in a British colony that had long ceased to be of the highest economic significance galvanised most of the major public figures of the day to take a stand on one side or the other. Defending the governor's methods on the executive committee of the Eyre Testimonial and Defence Fund were Ruskin and Carlyle, with Dickens also offering support.[13] On the other side, the chairman of the Jamaica Committee, set up to condemn the slaughter by British and Jamaican troops that followed the initial rebellion, was John Stuart Mill, who spent much of the next two years trying unsuccessfully to bring Eyre to trial on murder charges for the execution under martial law of the Jamaican politician George William Gordon. Supporting Mill were Thomas Huxley, Charles Darwin, Frederic Harrison, and Goldwin Smith, among others.[14]

The events in Jamaica generated such an intense response, I would suggest, because they connected a longstanding concern in English middle-class society over the consequences of the abolition of slavery with newer debates around working-class enfranchisement and citizenship. Of course, these issues had never been entirely separable, as the ubiquity of the rhetoric of slavery and freedom in Chartist texts of the 1840s amply demonstrates.[15] This connection was sharpened by English responses to the US Civil War, which was all too easily coded as a struggle between a modern, industrialised

North and an antiquated, paternalistic South, in which the abolition of chattel slavery came to represent the triumph of all the forces of Progress, that imaginary Victorian behemoth.

But beyond this historical link between abolition and liberal progress, what was new in the conjuncture of the mid-1860s was a widespread interest in questions of race, heredity, and breeding, which were now, after the publication of Darwin's *On the Origin of Species* in 1859, being transformed into scientific questions. However, this is a moment of transition, and these scientific concerns continued to be marked by their former place in the realm of the literary romance, their realisation in the tropes of inheritance, bloodlines, and genealogy. And it could even be argued that these new theories were doubly literary, because, as Gillian Beer argues in her magisterial analysis of the Darwinian revolution:

> Most major scientific theories rebuff common sense. They call on evidence beyond the reach of our senses and overturn the observable world. They disturb assumed relationships and shift what has been substantial into metaphor . . . When it is first advanced, theory is at its most fictive. The awkwardness of fit between the natural world as it is currently perceived and as it is hypothetically imagined holds the theory itself for a time within a provisional scope akin to that of fiction.[16]

It is this instability in meaning that allows us to locate and analyse these discourses of descent – of species, races, nations, families, and individuals – in a whole range of mid-Victorian texts, from novels and cultural criticism to popular journalism and scientific articles.

Morant Bay occurred at a moment when what we might call the romantic and the scientific (or realist) understandings of blood, race, and inheritance still overlapped. At their point of intersection in the mid-1860s stood the figure of 'the negro'. Africans and their descendants in the Americas occupied a particular place in the emergence at this moment of what George Stocking has aptly called 'hereditarian racialism':[17] that is, the notion that human difference is hereditary (and therefore more or less fixed) and that the name for that difference is 'race'. In 1863, a group of scientists led by James Hunt founded the Anthropological Society of London (ASL), bringing into the open a split within the older Ethnological Society of London – a division explicitly based on the status of 'the negro', in particular, and on the importance of 'race' in general. Hunt's inaugural address to the new body was at pains to stress the scientificity of the new discipline of anthropology, its adherence to a Gradgrindian positivism that sought only the facts and resisted the charms of non-scientific prejudices. Hunt's speech staked a claim for a huge field of inquiry: 'Anthropology is . . . the science of the whole nature of Man', he declared.[18] But within this field, the position of 'the negro' is closed off before the inquiry has even begun:

Whatever may be the conclusion to which our scientific inquiries may lead us, we should always remember, that by whatever means the Negro, for instance, acquired his present physical, mental, and moral character, whether he has risen from an ape or descended from a perfect man, we still know that the races of Europe have now much in their mental and moral nature which the races of Africa have not got.[19]

As Hunt continued his address, he made it clear that when it came to 'negroes' his fellow scientists were at liberty to disregard the conclusions to which their scientific inquiries might lead them – in particular, he wanted to avoid the 'vulgar error that the Negro only differs from the European in the colour of his skin and peculiar hair'.[20] Quickly, the disingenuousness of that 'for instance' – as in 'the Negro, for instance' – becomes clear. The 'negro' (and, as we shall see, the Jamaican 'negro' in particular) was not merely one example among many in this new science; 'he' became the very foundation of the science itself, in his exclusion from the project of 'civilisation'.[21]

The political goals of the ASL were thus explicit from the start: the society claimed the mantle of science in an overt rejection of an older discipline linked to the antislavery movement. The Ethnological Society from which Hunt and his followers felt compelled to distance themselves had been founded back in the 1840s as an offshoot of the Aborigines Protection Society, one of the abolitionist and philanthropic organisations that formed the backbone of middle-class dissenting culture from the late eighteenth century onwards. The motto of the Aborigines Protection Society was *ab uno sanguine* (of one blood), a reference to the biblical emphasis on the essential unity of humankind. There is obviously much common ground between this sentiment and the better known slogan of the abolitionist movement in Britain: 'Am I not a man and a brother?' (inscribed beneath an image of an African man kneeling in chains). But by the time of Morant Bay in the mid-1860s a new idea of race had arrived to disrupt the Victorian antislavery consensus; the founding of the ASL was one example of this cultural shift. Homilies on the oneness of the human race were out of fashion. The *Morning Herald*, finding the time for analysis of the events in Jamaica as early as November 1865, discovered that a great change had taken place in English attitudes, because 'the world-renowned question, once thought so convincing, of "Am I not a man and brother?"

would nowadays be answered with some hesitation by many – with a flat negative to its latter half by those who regard the blacks as an inferior race'.[22]

Delivering his annual presidential address to the ASL shortly after the outbreak at Morant Bay, James Hunt declared that

We anthropologists have looked on, with intense admiration, at the conduct of Governor Eyre . . . The merest novice in the study of race-characteristics ought to know that we English can only successfully rule either Jamaica, New Zealand, the Cape, China, or India, by such men as Governor Eyre.

Such revolutions will occur wherever the Negro is placed in unnatural relations with Europeans. Statesmen have yet to be taught the true practical value of race-distinctions, and the absolute impossibility of applying the civilisation and laws of one race to another race of man essentially distinct. Statesmen may ignore the existence of race-antagonism; but it exists nevertheless.[23]

This period witnessed the re-emergence of the long discredited theory of polygenism, which held that the various races of humankind had separate origins, and had developed as separate species which, all evidence to the contrary notwithstanding, were not fertile with one another. The ASL expended a great deal of intellectual energy on proving that races – especially the black and white races – were 'essentially distinct'. The irony, however, was that the hereditarian racialism peddled as modern and scientific by the likes of Hunt relied heavily on an older, romantic concept of blood.[24]

So analysis of the Jamaica events often had more in common with the inheritance plot of the romance than with the science of anthropology. Thus *The Times* declared on 18 November 1865 that 'though a fleabite compared with the Indian mutiny, it [Morant Bay] touches our pride more and is more in the nature of a disappointment . . . Jamaica is our pet institution, and its inhabitants are our spoilt children'.[25] A fortnight earlier, on 4 November, as the first sketchy reports of the events in Jamaica were arriving in Britain, *The Times* recoiled at the ingratitude of the 'negro':

He, who has come in as the favoured heir of a civilization in which he had no previous share – he, petted by philanthropists and statesmen and preachers into the precocious enjoyment of rights and immunities which other races have been too glad to acquire by centuries of struggles, of repulses, and of endurance – he, dandled into legislative and official grandeur by the commiseration of England, – that he should have chosen . . . to revolt . . . this is a thing so incredible that we will not venture to believe it now.[26]

A great deal is condensed in this quotation. First, since Carlyle's now notorious 'Occasional Discourse on the Nigger Question' (1849) had popularised the figure of 'Quashee' eating pumpkins and refusing to work, the myth of the lazy freedman had rapidly gained ground in Britain, the incredible notion that black people in the Caribbean had been 'favoured' by emancipation. Included in this potent myth was the false perception that blacks had been given the vote in large numbers in those Caribbean islands, such as Jamaica, where some form of representative government was in operation ('dandled into legislative and official grandeur').[27] This motif of favouritism also refers to the idea that British abolitionism and philanthropy had concerned themselves with the poor and dispossessed overseas while ignoring British poverty 'at home' (the ridiculous figure of Mrs Jellyby in Dickens's *Bleak House* being the epitome of this). Here the whole question of Caribbean wage labour in the post-emancipation period is displaced on to the discourse of family inheritance, with black Jamaicans as the 'favoured heirs' of British middle-class culture who fail to recognise their privilege. Their 'precocious' access to the 'rights and immunities' of civilisation is explicitly contrasted with the hard labour ('struggles . . . repulses . . . endurance') of other races. Here the language of filiation and inheritance sits uneasily with the language of citizenship and rights; the romantic novel vies with the science of political economy.

Thus we can begin to see how complicated is the relationship between the discourses of racial difference and working-class enfranchisement. The debate over the decline of the Jamaican economy, which was engaged once again after Morant Bay, concerned itself fundamentally with questions of capital and labour: after emancipation, did sugar plantations continue to fail because African Jamaicans were unused to the discipline of wage labour, or because the planters failed to pay wages regularly and failed to invest capital in modernising agricultural and industrial practices? When the black population withdrew its labour from the estates, were they working against their own economic interests or were they establishing themselves as an independent peasantry by saving money to buy small parcels of land and growing their own crops to sell in the Jamaican internal market (or even abroad, as in the JCA cooperative discussed above in chapter 3)?

However, these economic questions were constantly being supplemented by questions of race – did the African-Jamaican 'character' disprove the fundamental tenet of political economy, that men would work to further their economic self-interest?[28] For example, Governor Eyre's response to Underhill's letter to the colonial secretary, Edward Cardwell, on the state of the island converged with the new, harsher ideas of racial 'character' that had been brewing in Britain, borrowed partly from the discourse on slavery in the United States, exacerbated by the impact of the US Civil War, which was closely followed and debated in Britain.[29] Eyre wrote to Cardwell, in May 1865, arguing that the disaffection and agitation of 'a portion of the population... owes its origin in a great measure to the habits and character of the people, induced by the genial nature of the climate, the facility of supplying their wants in ordinary seasons at comparatively little exertion and their natural disposition to indolence and inactivity'.[30] Although Eyre's explanation of black 'character' is here couched as much in an older language of environmental influence ('induced by . . . the climate') as in the idea of 'natural disposition', it is easy to see how he could be readily claimed as a hero in the emergence of the dogmatic physical anthropology of writers like James Hunt, for whom the 'character' of 'the negro' could now be scientifically explained as a question of unmodifiable racial inheritance – Stocking's 'hereditarian racialism'. Such theories left 'the negro' doomed by bloodlines to remain at the bottom of a static taxonomy of racial types.

It is important to recognise that such a taxonomy implies the racialisation of the white English also, and that the intersection of Reform and Jamaica only makes sense when viewed in this light. Thus Edward Beesly, a prominent figure both on the Jamaica Committee and in the labour movement (and a close associate of Marx's in the First International), wrote to the labour newspaper *The Bee-Hive* in November 1865 the following response to the uprising in Morant Bay:

> I protest I am no negro-worshipper. I don't consider a black man a beautiful object, and I daresay he sings psalms more than is good for him. Some negroes may be men of ability and elevated character, but there can be no doubt that they belong to a lower type of the human race than we do, and I should not really like to live in a country where they formed a considerable part of the population. But there is no reason why the negro should work cheaper for us because he is ugly. If the white labourer has a right to put a price on his labour, so has the black labourer.[31]

The identity of the white and black labourers – the fact that capital treats them both as labour power from which value can be extracted – is riven by the assumption that black labourers 'work for us', where 'we' includes the white labourers whom Beesly claimed to represent. Thus Beesly can consider himself fortunate that he lives in a country where white labourers form a considerable part of the population. The subjection of Jamaican workers, who are of a lower racial type, ensures the stability of the frontier of the country of England (from which blacks are imagined as absent). And inside these racial and national frontiers there then opens up the possibility of citizenship for 'white labourers'.

GENEALOGY, ANTHROPOLOGY, AND HYBRIDITY

Ten years after Edward Beesly's comments in *The Bee-Hive*, George Eliot published *Daniel Deronda*, in which the following passage occurs:

The talk turned on the rinderpest and Jamaica . . . Grandcourt held that the Jamaican negro was a beastly sort of baptist Caliban; Deronda said he had always felt a little with Caliban, who naturally had his own point of view and could sing a good song; Mrs Davilow observed that her father had an estate in Barbadoes, but that she herself had never been in the West Indies; Mrs Torrington was sure she should never sleep in her bed if she lived among blacks; her husband corrected her by saying that the blacks would be manageable enough if it were not for the half-breeds; and Deronda remarked that the whites had to thank themselves for the half-breeds.[32]

Many of the issues addressed in this chapter are contained within this intellectually allusive piece of narrative. It is especially important here to trace the discourse of the inheritance of the 'estate' in the debates over Jamaica, since this connects with my earlier claim that this older language of a caste privileged by blood returns in descriptions of racial formation in the 1860s. I think this language can be glimpsed in Beesly's patrician assumption that black Jamaicans should be working 'for us'. And in George Eliot's passing reference to Morant Bay in *Daniel Deronda* we can clearly see how the polite chatter at Grandcourt's estate connects plantation life in the West Indies with the world of the English aristocracy (and lesser gentry), in which the question of breeding and pedigree intersects with the question of miscegenation ('the whites had to thank themselves for the half-breeds').[33] We should note that this passage also provides striking evidence of the prominence of the debate over Morant Bay at the time: ten years after the controversy had died down, George Eliot could be reasonably sure that a brief allusion to Jamaica would allow her readers to date the conversation at Grandcourt's estate as late 1865 or early 1866, the last time that Jamaica had taken centre stage in British culture.

This passage from *Daniel Deronda* bears striking witness to the mid-Victorian fascination with hybridity, in all its forms. In his book *Colonial Desire*, Robert Young shows how, across a wide range of discourses, from the biological sciences to Victorian poetry, the spectre of the 'hybrid' haunted the mid-nineteenth-century imagination in Britain. Young is careful to demonstrate that hybridity by no means always signified monstrosity for the Victorians – he cites many sources for the idea that progress could follow from the grafting together of different forms. For instance, the commonplace notion that the British were a hybrid people, derived from

Teutonic, Norman, and Celtic 'stock', led to claims such as that made by the *London Review* in 1861 that, 'We Englishmen may be proud of the results to which a mongrel breed and a hybrid race have led us.'[34] And Matthew Arnold's *On the Study of Celtic Literature* (1867) devotes more than a hundred pages to an analysis of the mixed nature of the English, and to his hope that in the future the mixture will yield benefits rather than strife: 'Then we may have the good of our German part, the good of our Latin part, the good of our Celtic part.'[35]

For some Englishmen, at least, the potential benefits of hybridity extended to the Caribbean also. In Anthony Trollope's travelogue *The West Indies and the Spanish Main*, the novelist reflected on his encounters with the emerging class of multiracial West Indians:

The coloureds [as Jamaicans of mixed descent were known] . . . have forced them-selves forward, and must be recognized as being in the van. Individuals decry them – will not have them within their doors – affect to despise them. But in effect the coloured men of Jamaica cannot be despised much longer . . . If the coloured people in the West Indies can overtop contempt, it is because they are acquiring education, civilization, and power. In Jamaica, they are, I hope, in a way to do this.

My theory . . . is this: that Providence has sent white men and black men to these regions in order that from them may spring a race fitted by intellect for civilization; and fitted also by physical organization for tropical labour . . .

When civilization, commerce, and education shall have been spread; when sufficient of our blood shall have been infused into the veins of those children of the sun; then, I think, we may be ready, without stain to our patriotism, to take off our hats and bid farewell to the West Indies.[36]

Trollope's position was certainly a minority one – the moral outrage in respectable circles over interracial relationships in the Caribbean was matched only by the continued prevalence of white men keeping black women as 'concubines', as Simon Taylor had almost a century earlier. Nevertheless, I think the confusion entailed in his argument is symptomatic. Trollope carried with him a middle-class sensibility that ruled out the pos-sibility of contempt for the emerging professional and managerial class in Jamaica, the majority of whom were 'coloureds'. And thus he is led to a position that celebrates miscegenation (infusing 'our blood into the veins of those children of the sun') while at the same time maintaining that it is commerce, education, and civilisation (or 'power', as he puts it) rather than race or blood that are putting multiracial Jamaicans 'in the van'. He appears hopelessly caught, in other words, between an analysis of the Caribbean based on the antinomies of race – 'the West Indian negro . . . has made no approach to the civilisation of his white fellow-creatures, whom he imitates as a monkey does a man'[37] – and one based on a model imported from the English class system, in which the 'coloureds' play the heroic role of a rising bourgeoisie vanquishing the feudal plantocracy.

Demonstrating the same fascination with racial hybridity, but drawing completely opposite conclusions from Trollope's celebration of the coloured class, the new scientific racism dwelt at length on the troubling figure of the 'mulatto'. Paul Broca's influential work on human hybridity laboured mightily to show that the offspring of unions between Europeans and Africans were infertile with each other, although they were said to be fertile with either 'parent race'.[38] This was a variant on the popular theory that hybrid human forms 'reverted' to pure races after two or three generations, a theory invoked in an attempt to prove the permanence of racial types, or, in extreme versions of this argument, to prove that different human races were in fact different species (the theory of polygenism). James Hunt, who modelled the ASL on Broca's Société anthropologique de Paris, argued torturously that it was not yet proven that 'the offspring of all the mixtures of the so-called races of man are prolific . . . At present it is only proved that the descendants of some of the different races of man are temporarily prolific; but there is the best evidence to believe that the offspring of the Negro and European are not indefinitely prolific.'[39] For Hunt, however, this need to deny the very existence of 'mulattoes' clashed with his belief in the improving powers of European blood: he explained the intelligence of African Americans in the United States (which he 'fully admit[ted]') as 'owing to the mixture of European and Negro blood' rather than being explicable by environmental factors.[40] Thus Hunt ended up endorsing a position not too far removed from that of Trollope.[41]

Trollope's position may have appeared idiosyncratic, but in fact it was essentially the same as the Jamaica policy followed by the Colonial Office in the period after emancipation was completed in 1838. Tired of the West Indian lobby's power in Parliament, and of the constant clashes between the Jamaican planters (who dominated the local House of Assembly) and the governor over who should have day-to-day control of the island's affairs, the Colonial Office tried to promote the interests of the merchant and professional class on the island as a counterweight to the anachronistic power of the white planters. This involved a delicate balancing act, since extending the franchise, for instance, to include more coloureds also risked empowering those elements in Jamaican society more sympathetic to the interests of the black peasantry. Thus there developed the anomalous situation that while the property qualifications for voting rights were gradually reduced (although the percentage of the population eligible to vote in Assembly elections remained minuscule at the time of Morant Bay), the restrictions on who could stand as candidates remained as onerous as ever, so that the number of black and multiracial Jamaicans holding Assembly seats never rose above fifteen out of forty-five. At the time of the 1865 rebellion, that number had been reduced still further, to twelve.[42]

The controversy surrounding the events in Jamaica in October 1865 hinged on the execution of George William Gordon, a wealthy merchant and landowner renowned in Jamaica for his outspoken support for the black masses, who was the representative in the House of Assembly of the district in St Thomas-in-the-East where the uprising took place, an ardent and vocal opponent of the governor, Edward Eyre, and, significantly enough, a 'coloured'. After the governor had declared martial law in effect in the east of the island on hearing of the uprising, he had Gordon arrested in Kingston (where martial law was not in place) and transported by boat to Morant Bay where he stood trial before a court martial, with the flimsiest of evidence against him, was sentenced to hang, and then duly executed on Eyre's personal orders.[43] It was Eyre's scant regard for legal niceties, the perception that he had taken advantage of a chaotic situation to rid himself of a turbulent adversary, that outraged liberals and radicals in England and Jamaica. Thus the debate tended to focus on the character, and especially the family history, of George William Gordon, son of a planter father and an enslaved mother, who had been cast out of his father's house, had pulled himself up by his bootstraps and made his fortune at an early age, and then rescued his father from ruin when the latter's sugar estate fell into bankruptcy. The uprising, about which Gordon apparently knew nothing in advance, was characterised crudely as a kind of personal feud between the governor and the radical politician.[44] The real story of the rebellion remained all but untold: the severe drought that had brought St Thomas-in-the-East to the brink of famine; local dissatisfaction with the magistrates, who all represented planter interests, and punished petty crimes like crop theft severely (crimes that had increased as poverty grew); the desire of poor smallholders to maintain their tenuous hold on land to which they often held no legal title, versus wealthy landowners' attempts to extract rent from them.

All of this was lost in Britain in the polemics over Gordon's execution. His final letter to his wife (a highly respectable white woman) was a major propaganda coup for Eyre's critics in England; in it he declared his allegiance to the queen, demonstrated Christian forgiveness for his persecutors, and generally behaved himself like a gentleman. The Baptist minister Wriothesley Noel felt 'compelled to conclude that the hatred which hunted him [Gordon] to death was like that which crucified the Lord of glory as a blasphemer and a traitor.'[45] In only marginally more prosaic terms, Noel quotes Gordon's mother-in-law: 'The late Mr. Gordon was bold as a lion in the cause of truth, but in domestic life, few, if any, could surpass him in urbanity of manner and kindness of disposition.'[46] Rev. David King cites a fellow Presbyterian minister, Rev. H. Renton, as saying 'I never knew a man who seemed to me actuated by more honourable and unselfish and purer motives. He had an enthusiastic admiration of the British Constitution, and an exalted estimate of the dignity, rights, and privileges of British citizenship.'[47] (King is himself quoted by Noel as saying that 'nothing but a total transformation of disposition, or unsettlement of reason, could involve such a man as he [Gordon] was in seditious schemes or bloody adventures').[48] Men such as these had no doubt, as an anonymous member of the Jamaican Assembly put it in a letter to the *Daily News* on 5 February 1866, that 'Jamaica had a worthy and faithful son in him.'[49]

The language of filiation and inheritance seemed inescapable in the furor over Gordon's death. In particular, opinion was sharply divided over Gordon's relationship with his father. On the one hand, there were accounts of Gordon's filial devotion, despite his father's alleged hostility to his non-white children. David King claimed that 'Through the reverses of the colony the father, from being very rich, came to lose all; and the coloured son bought his estate: not, however, to deprive him of it, but to leave him in occupancy, surrounded by the comforts he had been accustomed to enjoy. He always spoke to me with deferential regard for his father.'[50] Such a narrative works as a kind of allegory of the parental model of British imperialism, in which the colonies figure as children who will be guided slowly towards maturity (i.e., self-government and capitalism) while retaining their sense of responsibility towards their British fathers (for more on this particular trope, see the final section of this chapter below). On the other hand, in an anonymous letter to *The Times*, 'one who knew him for 21 years' claimed that

Mr. G. W. Gordon was a singular compound of opposites, a great pretender in religion, but one who altogether ignored the claims of truth and honesty. One who could expatiate eloquently on the sins of the people, and at the same time beat his own father and defraud all those who were so unfortunate as to place confidence in him.[51]

And, as if to demonstrate that Gordon's dubious lineage had its corollary in his willingness to disinherit a child, Governor Eyre included among the 170 pages of documents vilifying Gordon that he gave to the Royal Commissioners a copy of an anonymous letter to the *Colonial Standard and Jamaica Despatch*, claiming that Gordon had purchased half of 'a thrown-up sugar estate', the other half of which was being held in trust 'on behalf of an infant'. The letter claimed that Gordon had proceeded to dismantle the sugar works and everything else 'that was convertible into money' without even informing the trustees of his actions. The letter writer narrated this story to 'expose what is really known of this *said-to-be martyr*'. He concluded: 'All feelings of delicacy towards Gordon's family must subside.'[52]

This letter, showing by negation at least that the Gordon family romance was a story in the public domain, was published in Kingston on 13 January 1866. Three days later, on 16 January, the gentlemen of the ASL held their monthly meeting. (Women were not allowed to become members of the ASL; in fact, the proposal that the Ethnological Society permit women to join had been one of the reasons for the split that had produced the ASL in 1863.) There President Hunt informed the gathering that ASL stalwart William Pritchard 'had been appointed special commissioner from the Anthropological Society of London, to inquire into the causes of the recent negro insurrection in . . . Jamaica'.[53] Reassured their views on the rebellion would be made known in official circles, therefore, the members sat back to listen to a scholarly paper entitled 'Remarks on Genealogy in Connexion with Anthropology', by George Marshall. In his paper, later published in the *Memoirs* of the society, Marshall claimed that 'Genealogy, or the tracing of descent of individuals, and through them of nations, from some common progenitor, is a subject of vital importance to a society which includes among its various objects that of investigating the laws of man's origins and progress.'[54] It is no coincidence, I would maintain, that the public fascination with George William Gordon's family narrative is mirrored in this exactly contemporaneous debate on the uses of genealogy, as mid-Victorians attempted to work through the connection between the 'descent of individuals' and the descent of races and nations.

Marshall claimed that 'The genealogist is, in fact, the architect who builds up the structure of the science of man, stone upon stone, and story upon story. He is the author who compiles the history of man, of which the ethnologist, like a reviewer, presents to the public a general sketch of the contents.'[55] The genealogical 'author' is in search of lost origins, like the writer of romance, and these stories are the building blocks of anthropological science. Unsurprisingly, the discussion that followed Marshall's paper was unable to avoid the conflation of the history of noble families – the inheritance plot of the upper classes that was so central to the English novel – with the make-up of human groups or races. Augustus Goldsmid pointed out

one fact deserving of notice ... the thickness of the lip of the members of the House of Hapsburg ... observable in almost every branch of the family. Another instance was that of a gentleman belonging to a great aristocratic family, who had one white lock of hair, though his hair was generally dark, which peculiarity had been transmitted to him from a distant ancestor.[56]

Goldsmid's suggestions were immediately taken up by William Pritchard (who had just been appointed to take charge of the ASL's special mission to examine the causes of the Morant Bay rebellion, of course), who executed an apparently seamless transition from aristocratic families to 'natives':

Mr. Pritchard stated that among the natives of the Pacific he had met with individuals who had a white lock amongst the surrounding dark hair, which was said to be hereditary. With respect to the question of consanguinity, he stated that there are many of the small or *atoll* islands in the Pacific where the natives trace back their origin through three or four hundred years to the few persons who, drifting from their homes, originally landed there.[57]

Those present at the meeting found no difficulty in marrying their brand of physical anthropology (based largely on questions of blood and breeding) to the protocols of genealogical research. The meeting then adjourned, with President Hunt calling the members' attention to a special meeting of the ASL, 'at which Captain Bedford Pim would read a paper on the causes of the Negro insurrection in Jamaica'.[58] Demand for tickets was so great that a larger room would have to be obtained for the meeting, Hunt proudly declared.[59]

This intersection of genealogy, anthropology, and responses to the Morant Bay rebellion, I am suggesting, rests on more than a temporal coincidence. The flood of pamphlets, letters, and speeches about Jamaica in late 1865 and throughout 1866 occurred in the context of existing debates about the relation between the descent of individuals and races/nations. As William Pritchard suggested, the 'question of consanguinity' became critical at this moment, where inheritance through blood was perceived to explain human culture in all its variety. Here Charles Darwin's influence was extremely important, although never straightforward. *On the Origin of Species* (1859) emphasised the importance of descent from common ancestors; in the chapter on classification, Darwin suggests that this is the key to understanding the affinities of organic beings: 'Propinquity of descent, – the only known cause of the similarity of organic beings, – is the bond, hidden as it is by various degrees of modification, which is partially revealed to us by our classifications.'[60] Darwin proceeds to insist on the distinction between 'true affinities', those based on common descent, and 'adaptive or analogical characters', which, although they may be much more striking to the biologist, are of secondary importance when it comes to the correct classification of species. Darwin concludes

that the natural system is founded on descent with modification; that the characters which naturalists consider as showing true affinity between any two or more species, are those which have been inherited from a common parent, and, in so far, all true classification is genealogical; that community of descent is the hidden bond which naturalists have been unconsciously seeking, and not some unknown plan of creation, or the enunciation of general propositions.[61]

In other words, the theory of natural selection gave renewed life to the old figure of the family tree, and suggested (although human beings are almost entirely absent from the reasoning of the *Origin*) that the principle of genealogical classification would also hold good for the human sciences.

Therefore, as Gillian Beer puts it, Darwin's project 'seemed to accord with the surface ideals of his society and its literature. He sought the restoration of familial ties, the discovery of a lost inheritance, the restitution of pious memory, a genealogical enterprise.'[62] Here Beer quotes the passage from the *Origin* that demonstrates most clearly the affinity of the theory of natural selection with the genealogical enterprise of the hereditary aristocracy:

As it is difficult to show the blood-relationship between the numerous kindred of any ancient and noble family, even by the aid of a genealogical tree, and almost impossible to do this without this aid, we can understand the extraordinary difficulty which naturalists have experienced in describing, without the aid of a diagram, the various affinities which they perceive between the many living and extinct members of the same great natural class.[63]

It would seem to have been impossible to think evolutionary theory without this analogy, and this is where we can say that Darwin and William Marshall, despite their obvious differences, are operating in the same field, with similar intellectual inheritances. But where Marshall is falling back on familiar patterns of thought, Darwin is struggling to leave them behind. As Beer points out, the metaphor of the noble pedigree in Darwin's account becomes stretched to the limit:

In Darwinian myth, the history of man is of a difficult and extensive family network which takes in barnacles as well as bears, an extended family which will never permit the aspiring climber – man – quite to forget his lowly origins. One of the most disquieting aspects of Darwinian theory was that it muddied descent, and brought into question the privileged 'purity' of the 'great family'.[64]

After the theory of natural selection, the meaning of consanguinity could rapidly shift. The *Origin* opened up the possibility of 'an uncouth progenitor hard to acknowledge as kin', and it 'aroused many of the same dreads as fairy-tale in its insistence on the obligations of kinship, and the interdependence between beauty and beast. Many Victorian rejections of evolutionary ideas register a physical shudder.'[65] As the Darwinian revolution took hold in the 1860s, it spread in two directions. On the one hand, it adopted the dispassionate mode of scientific realism that created a web of lateral relations potentially extending the notion of consanguinity to join all life on the planet, and which sought in particular to find the 'missing link' between humans and other animals.[66] On the other hand, the new interest in genealogy found itself linked to the literary forms of the gothic and the romance in its emphasis on the exotic, the uncouth, beauty and the beast. And if the gothic and romance were in the air, could the Caribbean be far behind?

READING *FELIX HOLT* AFTER MORANT BAY

By turning now to George Eliot's novel *Felix Holt, the Radical,* first published in June 1866, at the height of the controversy over the suppression of the Morant Bay rebellion, I hope to shed light on some of these entangled problems of race, genealogy, and descent; I hope also to show that Eliot's complex tale of British Reform intersects in more than fleeting ways with the questions raised by the events in Jamaica, despite the fact that the Caribbean never appears in the novel. Thus this chapter will return to the relationship between slaves and the rank and file with which it began.

Critics, if they have paid attention to *Felix Holt* at all, have tended to see it as a flawed, transitional novel of George Eliot's, the subsidiary term in contrast with the better novels that come before and after it: thus the discovery that Esther is the true heir to the Transome estate, despite her humble station as Rev. Lyon's adopted child, could be read as a recapitulation of Eppie's story in *Silas Marner;* Eliot's attempt to capture the web of relations in the provincial town of Treby Magna in the period of the First Reform Bill might be seen as a precursor to the magnificence of *Middlemarch*. And it is true that the unimaginably convoluted inheritance plot on which the novel turns presents a major obstacle to reading (in the Penguin Classics edition of *Felix Holt* there is a ten-page appendix explaining the finer details of the law of entail). However, for my purposes, it is precisely this transitional, almost incoherent texture of the novel that makes it so important. Just as the likes of James Hunt were struggling to produce a new scientific theory of race that could never quite escape the doctrine of blood and breeding it claimed to supersede, *Felix Holt* represents the most striking example (because the most confused) in George Eliot's work of what Gillian Beer calls her 'two concepts of kinship': 'Kinship as descent within a patriarchal order in which property and authority move through the male line, and kinship as lateral connection: a newer concept of kin which had recently been immensely reinforced by Darwin's insistence on the "infinite web" of connections between all living forms.'[67] The central problem of *Felix Holt* is that the former concept of kinship is no longer acceptable but cannot yet be discarded because the latter form of kinship carries with it the risk of a culture and a nation dominated by the majority imagined to be living mean and savage existences. This conundrum takes George Eliot's novel of working-class enfranchisement right into the firestorm of debate about race and rights sparked by the Jamaica uprising.

Raymond Williams expresses well the dissatisfaction most modern critics have felt in reading *Felix Holt*. He says that the novel 'is made to turn on the inheritance of an estate, and this is a crucial surrender to that typical interest which preoccupied the nineteenth-century middle-class imagination'.[68] But for Williams this 'surrender' is not the same as the easy, casual way that Trollope, for instance, handles the traditional settlements of the romance genre in his novels; rather it deforms the structure of the novel, which is caught between aristocratic romance and modernist *Bildungsroman*:

George Eliot, by contrast [with Trollope], questioning in a profoundly moral way the real and assumed relations between property and human quality, accepts the emphasis of inheritance as the central action, and then has to make it external, contradictory, and finally irrelevant, as her real interest transfers to the separated and exposed individual, who becomes sadly resigned or must go away.[69]

Although I would question Williams's conclusion about the 'exposed individual', his insight into the narrative contradictions entailed in Eliot's use of the inheritance plot provides the best place to begin an analysis of *Felix Holt*.

The basic point here is that it is the very complexity of the inheritance plot that reveals its failure, in the 1860s, as the symbol of the transmission of the national heritage. In Disraeli's *Sybil, or the Two Nations*, to which *Felix Holt* is often compared, the hidden aristocratic lineage of Sybil must lead to the restitution of the estate to her: blood eventually 'tells'. In Eliot's novel, the relationship between property and virtue has been irrevocably severed, and the whole edifice of patrilineal inheritance appears to be crumbling:

not only does Esther ultimately reject her inheritance of the Transome estate, preferring the virtuous existence of an artisan's wife, but she is not even 'really' a Transome, her legal claim stemming from her descent from the Bycliffe family, whose relationship with the original Transomes is too complicated to be outlined here. As Catherine Gallagher writes, in the best modern reading of the novel:

Indeed, Frederic Harrison, who advised Eliot on the legal intricacies of the plot, implored her to make Esther a real Transome so that her claim would carry the weight of nature as well as that of legality, but Eliot insisted on grounding Esther's claim also in legal conventions. Thus, although *Felix Holt* resembles *Sybil* in that a young woman is discovered, in the aftermath of a popular uprising, to be the heir to an estate, it reverses *Sybil* by making that young woman no more the natural heir to the estate than is the family she has the power to dispossess.[70]

Disraeli needed to bind the naturally virtuous status of Sybil and her Chartist father, Gerard, to the institutional structures of the hereditary aristocracy; twenty years later, by contrast, George Eliot felt no compunction in poking fun at the claims of good breeding.[71] The last surviving real Transome, poor, mad Tommy Trounsem, claims that "'I allays felt it inside me as I was somebody, and I could see other chaps thought it on me too'", but this is patently false in the logic of the novel: although a certain pathos clings to Tommy, his fundamental role is to be trampled to death in the election-day riot so that Esther's non-natural right to the estate can be established.[72]

Thus Eliot disregarded the advice of Frederic Harrison, the young barrister whom she met while working on the novel, and who helped her with the details of the law of entail (that branch of inheritance law on which the plot of *Felix Holt* depends), advising her to make Esther both the lineal and the symbolic heir to the Transome estate. The extended correspondence between Eliot and Harrison is well known: not only does it provide rare insights into Eliot's thoughts during the composition of a novel, it also engages some key intellectual concerns of both Eliot's and Harrison's, especially the question of Comtism.[73] But critics have paid less attention to the fact that at exactly the same time as Harrison was providing legal counsel to George Eliot, he was also serving on the executive of the Jamaica Committee, the body led by John Stuart Mill to protest the suppression of the Morant Bay uprising. Soon after *Felix Holt* was published, Harrison began his series of essays on martial law – a key question in the Jamaica events – later published as number 5 in the Jamaica Papers series: *Martial Law: Six Letters to 'The Daily News'* (1867).[74] Harrison sent George Eliot the pamphlet: he wrote to her on 5 February 1867, saying, 'I sent you as you asked the letters on Martial law. The Prosecution commences at once.'[75] This connection is strengthened when we recall George Eliot's use of the Jamaica rebellion in her final novel, *Daniel Deronda*: the questions of inheritance, miscegenation, and unrest that are addressed via the Morant Bay uprising in that novel are also at the centre of *Felix Holt*.

In particular, we need to tease out the relationships between the fear of the mob that runs through *Felix Holt* and the question of miscegenation in the Transome family. If the country house can no longer represent the national heritage, as I have been arguing, then this is symbolised by the fact that the presumptive heir to the Transome estate is three-year-old Harry, son of Harold Transome and his now deceased 'Greek' wife. Harry's innate savagery, I will suggest, forms a complement to the anarchic violence of the working poor who must also, George Eliot's novel emphasises, not be allowed to inherit England. We see this juxtaposition in the 'Author's Introduction' to the novel, an imaginary stagecoach ride through the England of 'five-and-thirty years ago' (FH 75) – that is, 1831 – when 'there were pocket boroughs, a Birmingham unrepresented in Parliament and compelled to make strong representations out of it, unrepealed corn laws, three-and-sixpenny letters, a brawny and many-breeding pauperism, and other departed evils' (FH 75). Eliot's stagecoach criss-crosses the heartland of the country and deftly suspends the reader between a nostalgia for an easier, bygone age – when 'there were trim cheerful villages' where you could hear 'the pleasant tinkle of the blacksmith's anvil' and see 'small Britons dawdling' to the 'free school' carrying 'their marbles in the pockets of unpatched corduroys adorned with brass buttons' (FH 77–8) – and a recognition that that era, like the 1860s, by implication, was also haunted by violence and disorder. The pastoral scene in the cheerful village is only possible, Eliot makes clear, because 'the rick-burners had not found their way hither' (FH 78); the coach passes through 'the breath of the manufacturing town, which . . . diffused itself over all the surrounding country, filling the air with eager unrest . . . the scene of riots and trades-union meetings' (FH 79); for 'rural Englishmen', 'Reform was a confused combination of rick-burners, trades-unions, Nottingham riots, and in general whatever required the calling-out of the yeomanry' (FH 80). Finally, the coach passes through the town of Treby Magna, up the hill of the village of Little Treby, and thence to a sight of 'the neglected-looking lodges which interrupted the screen of trees' and 'the river winding through a finely-timbered park' (FH 82):

How many times in the year . . . had the coachman answered the same questions, or told the same things without being questioned! That? – oh, that was Transome Court, a place there had been a fine sight of lawsuits about. Generations back, the heir of the Transome name had somehow bargained away the estate, and it fell to the Durfeys, very distant connections, who only called themselves Transomes because they had got the estate. But the Durfeys' claim had been disputed over and over again; and the coachman, if he had been asked, would have said, though he might have to fall down dead the next minute, that property didn't always get into the right hands. (FH 82)

The disorder of what Matthew Arnold was about to call the 'populace' is matched by the disorder in the affairs of the Durfey-Transomes, and the status of the heir to the estate – ultimately, little Harry – is called into question before the novel proper even begins.[76]

The best hope for avoiding this disorder, George Eliot's novel suggests, is the cultural – but not political – enfranchisement of the civic-minded artisan represented by Felix Holt. As Catherine Gallagher points out, Felix is a version of Matthew Arnold's 'best self', the man of culture. However, Felix does not fulfil his mission by becoming the declassé 'alien' of *Culture and Anarchy*, as Gallagher argues; instead, his virtue lies in his determination to remain an artisan: "'I mean to stick to the class I belong to'" (FH 144).[77] In one of his first appearances in the novel, Felix explains to Rev. Lyon why he resisted his father's desire for him to become a doctor: "'Why should I want to get into the middle class because I have some learning? . . . That's how the working men are left to foolish devices and keep worsening themselves: the best heads among them forsake their born comrades, and go in for a house with a high door-step and a brass knocker'" (FH 145). As the political centre of the novel, Felix expresses the typical middle-class concern with the 'levelling' effects of extending the franchise (analogously, as I argued in chapter 2, the noble slave Hamel had predicted disaster if slavery should ever be abolished). Although he is a committed Radical, Felix lectures the crowd in Treby Magna on the dangers of premature democracy, saying that education and virtue are more important than the vote, which is a mere 'engine' (FH 400). As he says to Esther, "'I want to be a demagogue of a new sort; an honest one, if possible, who will tell the people they are blind and foolish, and neither flatter them nor fatten on them'" (FH 366).

However, just as in *Culture and Anarchy*, this political programme for the working classes cannot be thought outside of the discourse of race and descent. There is a clue to this in Felix's reference to his 'born comrades' in his refusal of the lure of upward mobility: at the moment when class boundaries appear more fluid – when, precisely, 'caste' becomes 'class' – Felix finds himself caught between the discourse of hereditary filiation, in which the lower orders are born into a station in life to which they are fitted, and the discourse of horizontal affiliation, in which alliances and kinship are more a question of choice and action than of breeding. And, as I hope the evidence presented in this chapter demonstrates, by the 1860s questions of breeding and blood were always questions of race, in its modern sense as well as in its romantic meaning.[78] So that when Felix continues his speech to Esther about wanting to be a new type of demagogue by saying '"I have my heritage – an order I belong to. I have the blood of a line of handicraftsmen in my veins"' (FH 366), we know that this is an anachronistic sentiment, a trace of nostalgia for a vanishing segment of the population; but it is also a statement transposed from the new hereditarian discourses of race that I analysed above, in line with Arnold's attempt the following year to classify England into quasi-racial categories (populace, philistines, barbarians).

This new discourse on race allows 'blood' to resurface as a meaningful concept, even, as here, reflecting back on to those class distinctions it would seem unable to explain now that 'family' and 'breeding' are no longer self-evidently positive. Thus the narrator comments on Esther's anticipation of the problems she will encounter in talking to Harold Transome about Felix:

She had a native capability for discerning that the sense of ranks and degrees has its repulsions corresponding to the repulsions dependent on differences of race and colour; and she remembered her own impressions too well not to foresee that it would come on Harold Transome as a shock, if he suspected that there had been any love-passages between her and this young man, who to him was of course no more than any other intelligent member of the working class. (FH 522–3)

The relationship between Harold Transome, who represents the English gentry's inability to adjust to the changes associated with Reform, and Felix, the new symbol of honest, hard-working Englishness, corresponds to 'differences of race and colour' – and these differences, the narrator implies, are not open to question. This is the equivalent of Matthew Arnold's statement that 'science has now made visible to everybody the great and pregnant differences which lie in race'. Since Esther has managed to counter her own 'first impressions' and overcome the natural 'repulsion' between herself and Felix, this statement also raises the possibility of racial (and class) crossing and hybridity; and this possibility will return us to the troubling figure of Harry.

The novel opens with Mrs Transome nervously awaiting the return from 'the East' of her son Harold to take over the running of the Transome estate, now that her wild older son Durfey has finally died and Harold is the heir apparent. Her anxiety is magnified because Harold has only recently informed her 'that he had been married, that his Greek wife was no longer living, but that he should bring home a little boy, the finest and most desirable of heirs and grandsons' (FH 100) – his mother's response to Harold's revelation of this long-kept secret was to tear up the letter 'in a rage' (FH 100). Mrs Transome's anger at this suppression of the place of women in questions of descent is in fact bitterly appropriate, since the reader eventually discovers that the arriviste lawyer Jermyn is Harold's biological father, and thus Harold's (and Harry's) descent and inheritance is entirely dependent on Mrs Transome.[79] Thus right at the outset the novel undermines the traditional claims of patrilineal inheritance – Harold's belief that his mother was 'a good elderly lady, who would necessarily be delighted with the possession on any terms of a healthy grandchild' (FH 100). The return of the prodigal son to take over the estate and save the nation is made possible by the relegation of Mrs Transome – who has been managing the estate up to this point – to the role of domestic ornament: Harold says to his mother, "'Ah, you've had to worry yourself about things that don't properly belong to a woman . . . We'll set all that right. You shall have nothing to do now but to be grandmamma on satin cushions'" (FH 95). Lying behind this suppression lies the silent (and convenient) death of Harold's Greek wife.[80]

Harold returns from the East darker, wealthier, with a taste for spicy food, and with new ideas about politics and the role of women. These threads are all entangled in George Eliot's Orientalism: Harold's decision to become a Radical shocks his Tory mother 'as if her son had said that he had been converted to Mahometanism at Smyrna, and had four wives, instead of one son' (FH 92). Similarly, Harold's corruptibility, the fact that his Radicalism (unlike Felix's, of course) is a veneer rather than a deeply held commitment, is signalled by his seduction by the delights of 'Oriental' women: 'Western women were not to his taste . . . Harold preferred a slow-witted, large-eyed woman, silent and affectionate, with a load of black hair, weighing much more heavily than her brains. He had seen no such woman in England, except one whom he had brought with him from the East' (FH 454–5). The narrator makes this observation at the moment when the possibility arises of Harold and Esther getting married, which would resolve the problem of the inheritance plot with a union straight out of the romance genre. But George Eliot refuses the easy way out: Harold's

Orientalism is utterly incompatible with Esther's independence of spirit. She is tempted, 'but it was a fact that Harold's previous married life had entered strongly into her impressions about him. The presence of Harry made it inevitable' (FH 540).[81] Harold tries to woo her: "'You don't suppose, I hope, that any other woman has ever held the place that you could hold in my life?'", and as proof of this sentiment he delivers the revelation that opens up *Felix Holt* to the debates over Morant Bay: "'Harry's mother had been a slave – was bought, in fact'" (FH 541). This is the decisive moment in the novel. While Harold thinks that this statement demonstrates that Harry's mother is of a different type altogether from an Englishwoman, for Esther it shows that Harold can never be the right choice for her. The reader, of course, agrees, and the nagging suspicion that Harold has brought a mistress with him from Turkey – 'one whom he had brought with him from the East' – confirms his unsuitability, and aligns him with the imperial adventurers and Caribbean creoles whose defining feature from the British point of view was cross-cultural and interracial sex. The figure of the 'native' woman hidden in the country house would also make *Felix Holt* an explicit reworking of *Jane Eyre*, and strengthen the claims made here for the connections between George Eliot's novel and Jamaica.[82]

Thus Harold is aligned with the slaveholding planters of the Caribbean who kept black mistresses but eventually married respectable white women of their own class. In this too Harold is contrasted unfavourably with Felix, who cheers the Chartist speaker in Treby Magna denouncing the 'slave's share' the workers have at present and calls for a 'freeman's share' of the nation's wealth (FH 396). And although slavery is displaced from the Caribbean to Turkey in George Eliot's novel, it is clear that the trouble with Harry is that he is a mulatto. If he is still too young to be a political rebel, as George William Gordon was, his wild nature is already apparent. We see him first through the eyes of the Debarrys, sole representatives of the old aristocracy in *Felix Holt*; Lady Debarry initially mistakes him for "'a charming little fellow . . . [a] round-cheeked cherub'" (FH 178). But she is soon disabused, as Harry sinks his teeth into Mrs Transome's arm: "'What a little savage!'", Lady Debarry quickly corrects herself; and then, when she has had time to reflect a little: "'That savage boy – he doesn't look like a lady's child'" (FH 178–9).

Lady Debarry is right the second time around. It may no longer be possible, in the age of Reform and industrialisation, to be sure what a lady's child looks like; we cannot rely on genealogy to tell the truth about good breeding when a 'brawny and many-breeding pauperism' (FH 75) threatens the land. But there can be no doubt, in the age of anthropology, what the characteristics of the savage are. The problem this poses for the novel, however, is insuperable. Although Harry's paternity is almost the only line of descent in the book that is not in doubt, there is such uneasiness about Harry that he and his father almost never appear together. When Harold first arrives back at Transome Court and his mother asks him about his son, Harold replies casually, "'O, I left him behind in town . . . My man Dominic will bring him, with the rest of the luggage'" (FH 92). In this narrative distancing, I think we can read the trace of George William Gordon's expulsion from his father's house.

Nevertheless, Harry will eventually inherit Transome Court, despite everything – although the text cannot bring itself to acknowledge the fact. We are told that the Transomes are allowed to keep the estate, and the fact that 'Mrs Transome died there . . . and throughout that neighbourhood there was silence about the past' (FH 605). As the novel closes with Felix and Esther's long promised union and, as hope for the future, the birth of 'a young Felix' (FH 606), it tries unsuccessfully to ensure silence about the fractured lines of descent from Mrs Transome to Harold to Harry that have sustained the reader's interest, when this very incoherence is the condition of possibility of Felix and Esther's inheriting the national culture. The new, respectable male working-class citizen (Felix) and his dependent family are made possible by the suppression of the uncouth, racially marked other (Harry) who, nevertheless, remains inside the boundaries of the nation that has attempted to expel him.

CONCLUSION: INHERITING THE EMPIRE

The third quarter of the nineteenth century used to be characterised by historians as the period of 'anti-imperialism', when prominent intellectual figures like John Bright and Goldwin Smith publicly called for the independence of 'the Colonies', which were seen as a financial and military drain on the resources of Britain. This notion of anti-imperialism has more recently given way to an understanding of the continuities in British imperial policies, the fact that the empire expanded throughout the nineteenth century (in both its formal and informal incarnations), and a recognition that those who advocated the independence of the white settler colonies never even considered the possibility that British dependencies peopled predominately by non-whites ought to govern themselves. However, without wanting to endorse the idea of mid-Victorian anti-imperialism, I would suggest that this period needs to be rethought once more in the light of the Jamaica events and the responses to them. In short, it is my argument here that when the possibility emerges of the end of British rule over the declining colony of Jamaica, the spectre of the end of imperial hegemony arises. And the response to this threat is to reconceive the empire as a whole, no longer insisting on the distinctions among the Colonial Empire, the Indian Empire, Crown Colonies, and other dependencies.

In the mid-1860s, Victorian writers began once again to talk of the British empire in the sense that seems so familiar to us now, reviving a popular use of 'empire' that had been dormant since the period of imperial reconstruction after the American Revolution. Richard Koebner, in his meticulous study of the changing significance of the word 'imperialism', notes that during the first thirty years of Queen Victoria's reign the term 'British Empire', if it was used at all, 'was governed by the interpretation which related the name to the United Kingdom of the British Isles and to England in particular'.[83] The common phrase 'Imperial Parliament' referred primarily to England's hegemony over Scotland, Wales, and, more particularly, Ireland, which after the Act of Union of 1800 sent representatives to sit in the House of Commons in London. Thus, in a way that seems distinctly counterintuitive to those of us at the other end of the British empire, 'the Colonies and the Indian Empire were regarded as dependent on the British Empire rather than being parts of it'.[84] In 1865, Jamaica was in the anomalous position of being a colony not generally included in the phrase 'the Colonies', which tended to encompass only the white settler territories (although administratively it was part of the domain of the Colonial Office). Paradoxically, therefore, the fact that Jamaica was unassimilable to the standard contemporary discourses of imperialism enabled it to become the locus of the construction of the empire. The Morant Bay uprising, far more than the Sepoy Rebellion of 1857 to which it was often compared, crystallised concern on questions of governance, citizenship, and rights, both domestic and imperial, and in so doing inaugurated the new era of 'the Empire'.

Perhaps we can read this awkward transition in the letter from Carlyle I alluded to in the opening paragraph of this chapter. After opining that 'penalty and clamour are not the thing this Governor merits from any of us, but honour and thanks, and wise *imitation* (I will farther say), should similar emergencies arise, on the great scale or on the small, in whatever *we* are governing!',[85] Carlyle goes on to pledge his active support for the campaign of support for Eyre so that, by wise effort and persistence, a blind and disgraceful act of public injustice may be prevented [i.e., the prosecution of Eyre brought by the Jamaica Committee]; and an egregious folly as well, – not to say, for none can say or compute, what a vital detriment throughout the British empire, in such an example set to all the colonies and governors the British Empire has.[86]

Here, as Carlyle piles clause upon clause with his characteristic rhetorical abandon, we can detect the instability of meaning between the lower-case 'empire' – which seems to approximate to the more modern concept – and the capitalised 'Empire' – which 'has' colonies and governors that, nevertheless, do not seem to be a part of it.

The solution that Carlyle proposes to this crisis of British imperialism is a throwback to the romance inheritance plot that George Eliot struggled to leave behind in *Felix Holt*. In *Shooting Niagara: And After?* (1867), his tirade against democratic government and the 'knot of rabid Nigger-Philanthropists' who made up the Jamaica Committee, Carlyle devotes several pages to the island of Dominica.[87] ('Jamaica', he claims implausibly, 'is an angry subject, and I am shy to speak of it.'[88]) He elaborates a fantasy scenario, in which

the Queen 'in Council' . . . [will] pick out some gallant-minded, stout, well-gifted Cadet, – younger son of a Duke, of an Earl, of a Queen herself . . . and say to him . . . , 'See, I have scores on scores of "Colonies", all ungoverned, and nine-tenths of them full of jungles, boa-constrictors, rattlesnakes, Parliamentary Eloquences, and Emancipated Niggers ripening towards nothing but destruction: one of these *you* shall have, you as Vice-King; on rational conditions, and *ad vitam aut culpam* it shall be yours (and perhaps your posterity's if worthy).'[89]

Carlyle suggests a model of governance based on the protocols of inheritance rooted in the structural power of the hereditary aristocracy in England; I have argued in this chapter that this residual conception of society fuelled the emergent discourses of anthropology and racial science. By contrast, Joseph Howe, in a pamphlet called *The Organization of the Empire* (1866), signals the end of the inheritance plot as a trope for empire, one that assimilates the relationship between 'mother' country and colony to a family affair. Some people, he says, argue that colonies 'grow up' and should therefore receive independence:

The parental relationship is assumed to sanction this policy. Young men grow, and, when they are of age, marry and set up for themselves, and why should not colonies do the same. But the analogy is not perfect. One house would not hold all the married members of a large family, nor one estate maintain them. They scatter that they may live. They are kept in friendship by the domestic affections, and personal ties, which in respect of distant communities, do not exist, and at the death of the founder of the family there is an estate to divide.

Not so with Colonies. Their life begins at a distance from the homestead. There are few personal attachments. There is no estate to divide, and no security that when they separate they may not drift into antagonism to each other, and to the parent colony.[90]

The old metaphors are worn out, Howe is arguing. The inheritance of an estate, be it Transome Court, an 'ungoverned colony' like Jamaica, or the estate of 'the Empire', can no longer signify the mode of British power after the 1860s.

Instead, the practice of imperialism, in its late Victorian manifestation of a mission to educate and civilise 'backward peoples', emerges, paradoxically enough, in the writings of those mid-Victorian liberals who advocated equal rights for whites and blacks and the extension of the franchise and citizenship to the working classes in England. Frederic Harrison, for instance, George Eliot's adviser on *Felix Holt*, can be heard bringing this new empire into being in his treatise on martial law written to protest the suppression of the Jamaica revolt:

> In the name of the people, of the great family of citizens of the British empire, it again becomes vital to crush the pretensions of the executive abroad; it again becomes necessary to vindicate beyond the seas the first principles of civil liberty... This is why an association of Englishmen has undertaken to bring this cause to an issue [i.e., by prosecuting Eyre] ... simply to hear from the lips of an English judge what is the right to civil justice of English citizens, what are the safeguards of life throughout the breadth of our vast empire.[91]

The repetition of Englishness here (Englishmen, English judge, English citizens) appears to be in opposition to the principle of formal equality that Harrison is celebrating. The 'people', the 'family of citizens' – the genealogical term persists as a link to the discourses Harrison was ostensibly refuting – for whom these 'Englishmen' speak are marked as subjects as well as citizens in this unstable equation. Defended against the unlawful force of the executive power, they become subject to a new kind of discipline, one formed through education, church missions, public health policies, and the apparatus of civil law: 'The precise issue we raise is this – that throughout our empire the British rule shall be the rule of law; that every British citizen, white, brown, or black in skin, shall be subject to definite, and not to indefinite powers'.[92] Connecting this rule of law with the enfranchisement of the working classes 'at home', Harrison wrote in *The Bee-Hive* in December 1865,

The question is, whether *legality* is to be co-extensive with the Queen's rule, or whether our vast foreign dominions are to be governed by the irresponsible will of able, absolute, and iron-willed satraps. It is on this ground that it so peculiarly concerns the working-classes. They alone are as yet untainted by the reckless injustice with which our empire has been won and kept.[93]

In this strategy for managing what he calls 'our vast unresting empire', Harrison is taking up the definition of empire of his fellow executive committee member of the Jamaica Committee, Goldwin Smith.[94] In 1863, Smith had written in the foreword to a collection of his pieces from the *Daily News*, given the title *The Empire* for its book publication:

The term Empire is here taken in a wide sense, as including all that the nation holds beyond its own shores and waters by arms or in the way of dominion, as opposed to that natural influence which a great power, though confining itself to its own territories, always exercises in the world. In the case of our Empire this definition will embrace a motley mass of British Colonies, conquered Colonies of other European nations, conquered territories in India, military and maritime stations, and protectorates, including our practical protectorate of Turkey [where Harold Transome struck it rich, in fact], as well as our legal protectorate of the Ionian islands. These various dependencies stand in the most various relations to the Imperial country.[95]

Koebner and Schmidt comment on the novelty of this definition, arguing that 'by making the name of Empire the comprehensive headline of a critical survey of colonial, Indian, and certain external affairs, the author [Smith] was not so much referring to an established terminology as intending to create such usage on his own account'.[96] I would argue that the better known beginnings of the imperial federation movement in the late 1860s – for instance the founding of the Colonial Society in 1868, with its motto 'United Empire' – are made possible by the efforts of liberal thinkers such as Smith and Harrison; that the call for an integrated empire begins with the same invocation of formal equality before the (English) law that Samuel Ringgold Ward had thanked heaven for in his autobiography, as I discussed in chapter 3. This gesture may even be explicitly anti-imperialist – as when Goldwin Smith argued for the independence of Canada – but covertly the expansion of English law around the empire works to consolidate the very inequalities that British rule worked by, at the same time as it established a formal discourse of equality, rights, and citizenship.

That this new imperial apparatus of discipline and surveillance emerged in the aftermath of the controversy over Morant Bay can be seen clearly in the writing of Charles Roundell, who had acted as secretary to the Royal Commission of inquiry while it collected its hundreds of pages of evidence in Jamaica in 1866. Later that same year, he published a pamphlet of his own, *England and her Subject Races, with Special Reference to Jamaica*, in which he extrapolated from the Jamaica situation to provide a blueprint for the organisation of the empire as a whole. The rebellion of 1865, he concluded, showed the need for 'an impartial and trusted administration of justice' and a system of 'regulating native settlements':[97]

The principal agents for effecting these primary requirements will be an efficient police, the enactment of a bastardy law, a systematic registration of births and deaths, the establishment of hospitals, and a well-organized system of medical supervision, the construction of roads, the instruction of the people in improved methods of agriculture, and, above all, a system of industrial, compulsory, unsectarian education.[98]

The problem of descent, inheritance, and miscegenation will be handled by a bastardy law; the state will take over the genealogical enterprise of recording births and deaths; and the emphasis on compulsory state education is in line with the thinking of Matthew Arnold: here we can see the outlines of a theory of late Victorian high imperialism. From the minor rebellion at Morant Bay, via the agitation for parliamentary reform, there emerges this checklist for the reconstruction of a modern, humanitarian empire.

However, Roundell's checklist is remarkable for another reason too. In most of its particulars, it echoes the concerns about the future of Jamaica expressed by Samuel Ringgold Ward in his testimony before the Jamaica Royal Commission, testimony therefore that Roundell himself would have heard. In this case Ward's opinions on the problem of illegitimacy in Jamaica and on the need for compulsory education were by no means idiosyncratic, but were widely held by those who saw themselves as imperial modernisers. But, as I want to suggest in the epilogue that follows, we can usefully look at this new version of humanitarian empire as borrowing from black Atlantic writers such as Ward, rather than simply seeing him and others like him as complicit with the dominant power of imperialism. Here, in Roundell's insistence on the need for the 'construction of roads [and] the instruction of the people', we are returned to Ward's appointment to the St Thomas roads commission that I discussed at the end of the previous chapter, and to his and his daughter's little schoolhouse in eastern Jamaica. These, then, represent forgotten catalysts, rather than odd outposts, for the establishment of a new (but to us, familiar) figure: the citizen-subject of the modern British empire.

Epilogue: 'And the sword will come from America'

Shortly before the outbreak of the Morant Bay rebellion, a now famous placard was posted near the dock in Lucea, in the northwest of Jamaica, signed by 'A Son of Africa':

I heard a Voice speaking to me in the year 1864, saying, 'Tell the Sons and Daughters of Africa, that a great deliverance will take place for them from the hand of Oppression; for, said the Voice, they are oppressed by Government, by Magistrates, by Proprietors, and by Merchants.' And this voice also said 'tell them to call a solemn Assembly, and to sanctify themselves for the day of deliverance which will surely take place; but, if the People will not hearken, I will bring the Sword into the land to chastise them for their disobedience, and for the iniquities which they have committed. And the Sword will come from America. If the people depend upon their Arms, and upon our Queen, and forget Him who is our God, they will be greatly mistaken, and the mistake will lead to great distress.'[1]

What is interesting here is the way in which this prophetic voice calls on the 'sons and daughters of Africa' to look beyond the language of colonial loyalty – 'depend[ing] upon . . . our Queen' – and to hearken to 'America' as the origin of deliverance. At first glance, this strikes an odd note, since 'America' was often seen as a source of threat by ordinary Jamaicans in this period.

Deborah Thomas notes that the discourse of loyalty to the Crown in Jamaica in the later nineteenth century – the continuation of the language spoken so forcefully by Samuel Ringgold Ward – coexisted with the 'recognition that the position of blacks in Jamaica was part of a world-wide conception of blacks, Africa, and African civilization' in need of uplift, and that the merging of these two positions was prompted partly by local concerns about 'the planters' intermittent dalliances with the idea of annexation to the United States'.[2] Such fears were certainly current in the mid-nineteenth century, as a letter from 'A Negro' to the *Watchman*, George William Gordon's newspaper, made plain in 1859:

Our liberties and our lives are endangered by the way things are carried on in this island, and we fear that unless something is done to alter the present oppression that upwards of 300,000 of Her Majesty's subjects of this island will be starved or sold into slavery, and, no doubt, we may have the mortification of seeing the much dreaded and hated American stars and stripes flying over our head.[3]

Indeed, the planters and their allies in the island did regularly look for help from proslavery elements within the United States, and after Morant Bay and the end of the US Civil War, a prominent group of Jamaicans lobbied the new governor, John Peter Grant, for financial incentives to encourage Southern landowners to migrate to Jamaica in the hope that this would revitalise the plantation sector of the economy.[4] However, the Lucea placard, and the history of pan-American black migration, suggests that alternative, even emancipatory ideas of 'America' were also in circulation in the island during this period – just as they had been since at least the arrival of George Liele and Moses Baker as black Baptist missionaries from the early United States in the late eighteenth century.

Periodically, elite groups and individuals in Jamaica had tentatively endorsed free black emigration from the US as one way of addressing what was perceived to be a labour shortage on the sugar plantations after emancipation, when many freedpeople had withdrawn from the estates in order to work on their own smallholdings. While attempts to recruit indentured labourers from India and West Africa were much more persistent (although neither effort would lead to mass migration on the scale witnessed elsewhere in the anglophone Caribbean), occasional calls could be heard for African Americans to move to the island.[5] Sometimes, Jamaican governors adopted this point of view, as when Henry Barkly wrote to the colonial secretary, the duke of Newcastle, suggesting that amongst all possible immigrants, 'I should myself give the preference . . . to the Colored People of the United States, and should indeed deem [Jamaica's] regeneration certain if they could be induced to flock to it in considerable numbers' – although it is clear that geopolitical rivalries between Britain and the US were uppermost in Barkly's thoughts, since he imagined Jamaica after such emigration to be 'convert[ed] . . . into an enduring bulwark against the spread of slavery or the love of annexation'.[6] Even Edward Eyre himself, shortly after his arrival as lieutenant-governor in Jamaica in 1862, wrote to London reporting on a recent public meeting in Kingston calling for free black migration to Jamaica, and remarking that 'the people who would emigrate from the United States are of industrious habits, and superior as a class to the present peasantry of the West Indian Islands', such that 'the existing population would be improved and stimulated by the example of the immigrants'. Receiving no encouragement, however, from a British government anxious not to exacerbate tensions with the US during the Civil War, Eyre quickly changed his mind, and reassured his superiors, 'I do not apprehend . . . any further immediate agitation on the subject.'[7] Despite their ineffectiveness, perhaps we can read these high-level appeals as recognition of the ongoing set of relationships on the ground between Jamaicans and African Americans, in which 'America' could offer regeneration to Jamaica, just as Jamaica could offer freedom to such migrants as Joseph Anderson, the Maryland slave rescued at Savanna-la-Mar mentioned in chapter 3.

The central place of 'America' in a Jamaican imagined community of blacks worldwide can be seen, for instance, in the annual report of the Jamaica Baptist Union for 1862. After surveying the state of the local Baptist churches, the report ends by noting that, in addition to seeking blessings for themselves,

the churches have not failed to sympathise with and pray for those who are suffering in other parts of the world, either from the oppression of Slavery or the horrors of war. Earnest have been the petitions to the throne of grace on behalf of the enslaved in America, and fervently is it hoped that the fearful and fratricidal war on that continent will issue in the full realisation of civil liberty to every Slave. May the time soon come when all in Jamaica and every other part of the world shall be freemen of the Lord.[8]

A few years earlier, before his move from Kingston to rural St David, Samuel Ringgold Ward had tried to lobby Jamaican public opinion on behalf of free African-American migration to Jamaica, arguing that 'this island would be greatly benefited by the accession to the population of a portion of their American brethren', who would be able to obtain 'letters of naturalization obtained without cost, conferring the equal rights and privileges of British subjects', and who would find the move to Jamaica beneficial also because of 'the excellence of the climate, the rich and varied productions of the soil, the abundance of unoccupied land, and its [Jamaica's] social and political condition'.[9] Ward's plea, of course, fell on deaf ears, but provides further evidence that an imperial British identity (provided by 'letters of naturalization') and an incipient Jamaican national identity (Ward would later call himself 'your adopted countryman' in his letter to the St David Underhill meeting discussed in chapter 3) could easily coincide with a black internationalist identity of 'brethren', African, American, and West Indian alike.[10] Despite Ward's nod to British liberties – Jamaica 'opens to all equally every avenue to the attainment of a

Figure 5.1 John Willis Menard

comfortable and respectable position in life, under free institutions'[11] – his appeal is striking in the fact that it is addressed directly to African Americans themselves, rather than to the interests of the Jamaican ruling class, which once again become the medium, rather than the point, of Ward's proposal.

By the time Ward declared himself the 'adopted countryman' of the people of St David, another African American had also settled in the small parish just outside Kingston: John Willis Menard (see figure 5.1). Younger than Ward (he was born in 1838 in Illinois), Menard was just as politically ambitious. He had arrived, probably in 1864, after an 1863 trip to British Honduras (then a dependency of Jamaica; now independent Belize), where he had been sent by the US government to report on the possibilities of black emigration and settlement in the British colony, after his appointment as the first black clerk in the US Interior Department.[12] After his return to Washington, Menard apparently downplayed the possibilities of a black settlement in Belize. A correspondent of black Philadelphia-based newspaper the *Christian Recorder* reported that, 'He [Menard] expressed himself as being highly pleased with Honduras; but would not, he said, like to see a great influx of emigrants to that country, as they would necessarily suffer for the want of proper necessaries and facilities on their arrival.'[13] However, Menard quickly 'suggested the idea of calling a National Convention [of African Americans] for the purpose of petitioning Congress to grant the colored people the State of Florida as a home'.[14] His separatist campaigning came to nothing at this time, and by late 1864, Menard had moved to Jamaica, where he married a local woman, Elizabeth.

We do not know what made him settle in St David, where he worked on the Albion estate (which had years earlier been one of the many properties of Simon Taylor, the wealthy planter discussed in chapter 1), but for almost a year leading up to the Morant Bay rebellion he rapidly established a public profile for himself in the island, writing in the local newspapers and founding a literary society in the parish. When the rising broke out, he was arrested by the authorities, deemed 'able and likely to be very mischievous' by H. J. Kemble, clerk of the peace in St Andrew parish, and deported back to the United States.[15] Moving to New Orleans, he was elected to Congress to fill the unexpired term of a deceased Louisiana representative in 1868 – Menard was the first African American to be elected to the US Congress – but the House refused to seat him. In making his case for his right to sit in the national legislature, Menard also became the first African American to deliver a speech in Congress in February 1869. In the later 1860s and 1870s he edited newspapers in Louisiana and Florida, and became a prominent figure in state politics in the latter state. He published a volume of poetry, *Lays in Summer Lands*, in 1879.[16]

There has been increasing interest of late in his place in African-American history, as the republication of *Lays in Summer Lands* in 2002 demonstrates. From the Jamaican side, Menard is mentioned in Gad Heuman's history of the Morant Bay rebellion as one of the 'further dissidents' caught up in the post-uprising crackdown by the Jamaican government that also led to the deportation of several Haitian émigrés, and Clinton Hutton, in his fine account of Jamaican political thought in the period leading up to 1865, devotes some time to a valuable discussion of Menard's life and activities in Jamaica.[17] But accounts of Menard's life and career have thus far not been able to follow him back and forth in his pan-American movements, so that (just as with Ward) a full biography has not yet been written, and his role in the Jamaica events tends to be glossed over or ignored in writings on his later political life in the United States (just as his later public role in the United States plays no part in the account of Menard in the Morant Bay events). National and nationalist frames of reference for history writing are still evidently powerful, despite the fact that the Caribbean and Africa are prominent in Menard's poetry, both before and after his Jamaica sojourn.[18]

In 1868, when news of Menard's candidacy for the US House of Representatives reached Jamaica, the *Morning Journal*, one of the more radical Jamaican papers, celebrated the news, and reminded the reading public that Menard had been in Jamaica at the time of Morant Bay, 'when Mr. Eyre took it into his head to murder where he could every man holding liberal opinions, and to offend as much as he dared all dark skinned natives of other countries', so that Menard, despite the lack of evidence against him, had to be 'hurried out of the country at once'.[19] The *Morning Journal*, a newspaper that Menard had written for during 1865, 'wish[ed] Mr. Menard success in his candidature. All things considered Americans are not so bad after all . . . Had he remained here, although by dint of perseverance, he *might* have risen to the surface of society, yet what a fearful struggle it would have cost him.'[20] During Menard's time in Jamaica, he was clearly something of a political rival of Ward's in St David. Samuel Clarke, later executed for alleged sedition after Morant Bay, agitated 'to have all the schoolmasters [of the parish] turned out, and they asked me [Ward] to take one of the schools. I, of course, declined; then they said they must have a man of the name of Minard [sic], an American, put into one of the schools, and a person turned out for that purpose. I objected to that.'[21] Menard, unlike Ward, was present at the St David Underhill meeting, chaired by Clarke, in June 1865, and was listed as a member of the deputation sent by the meeting to lobby Governor Eyre, and of the 'communicating committee' established by the meeting at Ward's suggestion but later disavowed by him.[22] Menard and Clarke were obviously close allies. The custos of St David, William Georges, testified in the court martial that sentenced Clarke to death on 3 November 1865 that after Georges had posted the notorious 'Queen's Advice' in St David, 'I rode over to Easington, and on my arrival at the yard I saw Clarke and a man named Menard talking. He [Clarke] . . . in the presence of all, said, "That [the placard] is a lie, a damned red lie."'[23] When troops arrived to arrest Clarke in October, he was not at home (he had travelled to Kingston, stopping at Samuel Ward's house in Vickersfield on the way), but Menard was there, and the American was arrested and transported to Up Park Camp barracks in Kingston with the other 'political prisoners' before his deportation.[24] Menard was listed last (he was number 127) in a document of prisoners confined at Up Park Camp on 28 October, with the notation 'released, being deemed innocent; no evidence'; but on 3 November 'John Willis Mamoud [sic]' was among the group of 'aliens' ordered by Governor Eyre 'to quit Jamaica within fourteen days, and not return to it again'.[25] The minute of the Executive Committee ordering Menard's expulsion further suggested that 'he should be included in the warning to be given to the Governors of other Brit. W. I. Colonies, against the deported'.[26] The newly arrived US consul in Kingston, Aaron Gregg, tried to intercede on Menard's behalf with the governor, but to no avail, and in March 1866 Gregg reported to Washington that Menard 'is now in New Orleans, employed as a clerk... [and] his wife and infant (born since his banishment) are here in destitute circumstances. The wife is unable to labor on account of defective sight.'[27] Evidently the US government requested more information on Menard's deportation in late 1866, and the Colonial Office tried to put the matter to rest by forwarding to the US minister in London the account of Menard's papers given by H. J. Kemble, the clerk of the peace for St Andrew (the parish including Kingston), in which were found 'speeches and letters... printed in America... [in which] he speaks of his "deep hatred to the ruling class" of that country. "I am for Black Nationalities – the prosperity and happiness of our race and their posterity lay [sic] in a separation from the white race."'[28]

Clearly, Menard was a thorn in the side of the British authorities in Jamaica, but interestingly enough, the activity for which he was most feared – and the one that made him a minor casualty in the aftermath of Morant Bay – was his establishment in St David of a literary and philosophical debating society, and not necessarily his espousal of an early form of black separatism (useful as that may have been in keeping the US authorities quiet about the flagrant illegality of Menard's expulsion from Jamaica). Thomas Oughton, a Kingston lawyer (and the son of Samuel Oughton), who examined Menard's papers on behalf of Aaron Gregg, the US consul, found nothing incriminating in them, but remarked that, 'I may mention that in casual conversation [with Kemble, presumably] the main thing, which seemed objectionable was that Mr. Menard was the President of a debating society and that one subject of debate was the relative merits of a Monarchical or Republican form of Government.'[29] This local reading group, the Workingmen's Literary Society of St David, was another example of the myriad ways in which forms of black self-organisation were proliferating in Jamaica at this moment. It was described in a contemporary letter to *The Sentinel* (a short-lived progressive Jamaican newspaper of the mid-1860s):

Through the untiring efforts of our widely respected and talented new parishioner, J. W. Menard, Esqr., the above named society was started on the 18th of January last [1865], and now has a membership of sixteen. It meets once a week, and is growing in importance and interest. The last question debated was 'which is more powerful, the Pen or the Sword?'.

The Sentinel article was written by 'Samuel Wilson', perhaps a pseudonym of Samuel Clarke himself, who went on to say that 'Mr. Menard, the President and founder, is a very valuable acquisition to this parish, and too much credit cannot be bestowed upon him for setting on foot this much needed work among us. These societies form the only remaining hope for the redemption of this island from the power of ignorance.'[30]

This theme of education and uplift was taken up by Menard in his own writing for the Jamaican newspapers in 1865, just as it was the lasting preoccupation of Samuel Ward in his Jamaica years. At the end of Ward's pamphlet on the rebellion, he called on 'black people of all grades' to stop 'follow[ing] bad mulatto leadership, to disloyalty, to the gallows, and to perdition', and proposed that 'a good compulsory educational law [should be] imposed, which would dispel the gloomy prospect of ignorance which now darkens our horizon'.[31] Menard, writing in *The Sentinel*, published two articles on 'popular education', in which he claimed that the 'happiness and prosperity of a nation depends – not on its mineral wealth, [or] largeness of population, but mainly upon the intelligence of the great mass of its people', and that people are fooled into thinking of 'the fine arts and sciences as unattainable – great impossibilities! This belief forms another formidable barrier to the spread of education in this beautiful island.'[32] Like Ward, Menard too called for government regulation and promotion of education, since 'the greater portion of the parents of this rising generation are not sufficiently educated to lay the basis of this much needed reformation'. So although he was shortly to run afoul of the Jamaican government, Menard joined with Ward in his call for a humanitarian intervention on the part of the imperial authorities in creating 'civilisation' in Jamaica:

If Government does its duty in this great humane work, it will only help to strengthen its own life – building its foundation on a firmer and more lasting basis; for it is easier to rule a fully civilized man (comparatively speaking) than a barbarian. The English Government is and has been the wisest and most enduring Government on earth; and why? because its organization is built on [a] fully civilized and enlightened basis![33]

In the end, despite their obvious personal differences, and despite their different relationships to the emerging political movements in Jamaica in the mid-1860s, Ward and Menard both spoke the same languages of, on the one hand, black autonomy and self-organisation, and, on the other hand, imperial loyalty and the civilising mission.

Both also spoke in the language of an incipient Jamaican nation, which, I would argue, needs to be understood historically in its relation to an international black perspective at least as much as it depended on the register and discourse of British political life.[34] Ward hoped that in the aftermath of the rebellion, if blacks could avoid 'bad mulatto leadership', 'our beloved country will remain quiet, and loyal, and peaceable'; Menard worried that without British-led education reforms, 'the unexplored wealth which has so long been sleeping in the mountains of this island, waiting, apparently, for imported genius to be developed, will still rest undisturbed beneath the sweet, sad chorus of the weeping hills'.[35] Ironically, Menard, the alien, called on Jamaicans to organise themselves, and not to 'wait to be fed with manna from abroad', just as Ward praised the labouring classes of the island for being 'rooted to the soil' and not planning, as many planters did, 'to gather up all you will have made in Jamaica, and carry it beyond the seas, to invest and expend in other lands, to enrich them'.[36] And yet, it was perhaps precisely their 'alien' status, their access to streams of black internationalist thought from 'abroad', and principally from 'America', that enabled Menard and Ward to speak within and help to develop a creolised political discourse of Jamaicanness. We should not be surprised, therefore, to find that Paul Bogle himself, in his exhortations to the rebels in St Thomas-in-the-East, should, on the one hand, send off his petition to the governor pledging loyalty to the Crown, and, on the other hand, tell his followers that he and his patron, George William Gordon, 'would send people from foreign to come to Jamaica to have a war – to mix with Jamaica people and fight the war'.[37]

Bogle's hopes for a sword coming from 'foreign' in general, and 'America' in particular, were of course dashed in the suppression of the Morant Bay uprising. Menard was shipped off to New Orleans, and Ward was given his minor imperial sinecure as parochial roads commissioner for St Thomas. But of course Jamaican–US connections continued, as they always had: apart from anything else, the island was dependent on US trade for much of its food and textiles. News from the United States often pushed London events into second place in the international sections of Jamaican papers like *The Gleaner* and the *Falmouth Post*. A few years after Ward's imperial appointment, in 1871, the US steamer *Tennessee* arrived in Kingston harbour from Port-au-Prince, Haiti, carrying on board the visiting Santo Domingo Commissioners, who stopped off in Jamaica for a few days before their return to Washington, DC. *The Gleaner* reported their arrival on 13 March 1871, listing all the officers, crew, and passengers on board the vessel, commenting that 'the mission of the *Tennessee* is too well known to our readers, to need recapitulation'.[38] In nineteenth-century Jamaica the deliberations of the US government over the status of its Caribbean neighbour states were matters of daily concern, but we latterday historians of the

Atlantic world may need to be reminded that in 1871 the Grant adminis-tration in Washington was considering the annexation of the Dominican Republic: hence the 'Santo Domingo Commissioners'. Their arrival in Jamaica marked another, albeit minor, episode in the intra-American his-tory of the Caribbean that tends to get obscured when the region is viewed through the lens of European empire. 'Among the Commissioners from San Domingo', remarked *The Gleaner*, 'is Mr. Frederick Douglass, the col-ored orator and political agitator'. (Douglass was in fact the secretary to the commissioners, one of whom, in a nice historical irony, was Samuel Howe, the educator of Laura Bridgman, whose donation to Irish Famine victims in the 1840s Samuel Ringgold Ward had used to attack Thomas Carlyle's anti-Americanism, as I discussed in chapter 3.) Frederick Douglass's arrival in Jamaica, perhaps merely a footnote to a minor historical episode, is nevertheless a significant epilogue to the story that I have told in this book.

The symbolic convergence of Douglass and Ward on Jamaican soil is interesting. They had been rivals and allies in the antislavery movement in New York and Massachusetts in the 1840s, correspondents and contribu-tors to each other's newspapers into the 1850s, both had visited and toured Britain on the antislavery circuit to great success, and now both had been engaged in dubious alliances with the governments of the global powers in trying to influence their policies in favour of a particular, and increas-ingly international, vision of black uplift. Ward had publicly praised the former governor of Jamaica, Edward Eyre, for his prompt and merciless military suppression of the uprising at Morant Bay, on the grounds that agitators there had been leading decent black folks away from the path to respectability and development; now Douglass was appointed secretary to the Santo Domingo Commission by President Grant because of his support of annexation for the eastern portion of the island of Hispaniola: 'To me it meant the alliance of a weak and defenseless people, having few or none of the attributes of a nation ... to a government which would give it peace, stability, prosperity, and civilization.'[39] While we may easily quarrel with Ward's and Douglass's positions, my argument in this book is that the circuitous routes they took to elaborate and gain support for these positions were to some considerable extent the same circuits that were later used by US and British imperial defenders and spokespeople. In other words, the roots of the newfound language of empire in the last quarter of the nineteenth century, right up to the 'white man's burden' that Kipling hoped might be shared by the USA and Britain alike, can be found in the transatlantic routes of peripatetic black figures like Ward and Douglass.

I do not want to overemphasise the similarities between Ward and Douglass here. For all of Ward's distaste for the 'lower orders' of black societies in the Americas, his decision to settle amongst the poor in Jamaica gave him a different perspective from the Washington-bound Douglass, who commented in a private letter to Samuel Howe, after this visit to the Dominican Republic and Haiti, that 'if this is all my poor colored fellowmen have been able to do in seventy years, God help the race'.[40] On the other hand, Douglass strongly deprecated Eyre's handling of the 1865 rebellion, 'when more than a thousand negroes were slaughtered by the murderous Governor Eyre, who has been rewarded for his butcheries by a testimonial of more than fifteen thousand pounds sterling'.[41] Douglass's position as a brief American visitor in Jamaica rather than a sometimes troublesome American settler like Ward perhaps accounts for *The Gleaner*'s glowing portrait of the former, in contrast to its virtual silence about the presence of Ward in the island for over a decade. Deference and distance produce the following encomium, comparing the secretary of the Santo Domingo Commission to the recently deceased 'coloured' (i.e., mixed race) Jamaican politician, Edward Jordon, who had been Governor Eyre's secretary at the time of the Morant Bay rebellion (and the mayor of Kingston at the time of the East Queen Street disturbances):

> Mr. Douglass, as our readers are well aware, bears the reputation of being the foremost colored politician of his time in America... The name of Frederick Douglass in America is like that of Edward Jordon, (of blessed memory) in Jamaica; both these men have lived to behold the triumph of Right over Might, and both have been recognized by their respective Governments as worthy of patronage. Frederick Douglass has special claims upon the 'people' of Jamaica; and we welcome him in the name of that people – embracing the vast intelligence and wealth of the island – on his arrival among us.[42]

A certain kind of black internationalism – perhaps even the kind that Ward and Douglass used to preach, when they celebrated West Indian emancipation in the US rather than American independence[43] – has here been defused and made saleable for a new imperialism, so that *The Gleaner* could even cheerfully report that Douglass 'paid a flying visit' to the exiled Haitian president, Fabre Nicolas Geffrard, while in Jamaica, along with a trip to the Mona sugar estate just outside Kingston that would later be the site of the University of the West Indies campus in Jamaica.[44] Perhaps Douglass also searched for his old comrade, Samuel Ringgold Ward, of whom he wrote in his autobiography, 'in depth of thought, fluency of speech, readiness of wit, logical exactness, and general intelligence, Samuel

R. Ward has left no successor among the colored men amongst us'.[45] But one final meeting of the two men was not to be, for Ward had almost certainly died a couple of years earlier, in 1869, as I showed at the end of chapter 3.

Douglass's eulogy for his old comrade and rival turns suddenly to reiterate the terms and borders of the US nation-state: 'It was a sad day for our cause when he was laid low in the soil of a foreign country.'[46] But Douglass's own trip to the Caribbean, not to mention the writings and peripatetic careers of Ward and Menard and all the other African-American travellers in the British empire during this period, shows that the border between 'domestic' and 'foreign' is not fixed, and that 'our cause' cannot easily be narrowed to the outlines of the United States. What is the relationship between Ward's complicity with British imperialism and Douglass's complicity with US expansionism in this conjuncture? Douglass's and Ward's struggles for justice for black people became grist to the mill for a militant humanitarianism that (in the words of *The Gleaner*'s gushing correspondent on Douglass cited above) proclaimed the virtues of Right over Might, while everywhere maintaining its definition of 'right' with mighty force. Ward did his bit for the modern empire, trying to improve the notorious state of Jamaica's roads. (Frederick Douglass, in implausible contrast to the frequent complaints in the Jamaican press about their appalling state, claimed that 'the roads of Jamaica are after the model of the roads in England, broad, solid, and smooth – a type of English civilization.'[47]) At the same time, Douglass did his bit for American expansion: he took the model of the Jamaican sugar plantations that he saw outside Kingston, 'under the highest cultivation', as a possible model for US annexation of the Dominican Republic: 'The same might be true of Santo Domingo if that country were to feel the freedom and stability of the American Government', he wrote in the last of a series of articles in his Washington newspaper, the *New National Era*, recounting his Caribbean trip.[48] And in a nice ironic twist, Douglass's visit to Jamaica on behalf of the US government temporarily upstaged a public lecture on the possibilities of West Indian federation within the British empire. *The Gleaner* had reported on the day that the *Tennessee* arrived that a certain S. Powell Thompson would lecture at Wolmer's school in Kingston 'on the Confederation Scheme of Sir Benjamin Pine, by which the whole of the West Indian Islands are proposed to be Confederated'.[49] But when Thompson arrived at the venue, 'the audience, including some of the most intelligent people of Kingston, requested Mr. Thompson to postpone the lecture and to invite Mr. Frederick

Douglass, the great American orator, to take the chair', which he did to popular acclaim.[50]

What is it that allows Douglass to be simply 'American' here, without also being 'coloured' or 'negro'? The dream of imperial federation, either in the regional sense (as in Pine's West Indian scheme), or in the broader imperial register must recognise the power of the United States to intervene and disrupt all such matrices. When news of proposals in Britain for colonial representation in Parliament reached Jamaica in the late 1860s, they were seized on as a possible means of reviving the island's fortunes, not least because of the ever-present threat that US power represented in the region. The *Falmouth Post*, responding enthusiastically to such proposals, noted that,

The principle of Colonial Representation . . . is a right that should no longer be withheld from Canada and Nova Scotia, in consequence of their contiguity to the United States of America, where, the Government, notwithstanding its professions of peace and good will to the sovereignty of Great Britain, is anxious, and ready if a favourable opportunity should occur, to carry out its policy of annexation, especially in cases where annexation would be prejudicial to British interests in every point of view.

Clearly, for this newspaper, this 'policy of annexation' could extend to the British West Indies themselves: the possible American annexation of Cuba meant that there was a 'necessity of making provision for keeping our "Isle of Springs" free from the acquisitive propensity of the President and other functionaries of the great Modern Republic'.[51] However, when he arrived in 1871, Douglass was not simply the representative of US military, diplomatic, and political power, a 'functionary of the great Modern Republic', despite his enthusiasm for annexation in the Caribbean. He was also, like Ward, a black traveller and (to return to David Scott's formulation), a 'conscript of modernity', who sought to articulate a version of black emancipation to the workings of an expansionist US state, however imperfectly, just as Ward found himself defending British imperial authority to the end of his life in his quest for a self-reliant black collective.

After the 1860s, the people of Jamaica and the rest of the anglophone Caribbean were increasingly forced to look north, towards the United States, rather than east, towards Britain. I hope to have shown, however, that this does not mean that the Caribbean territories were transferred like small objects from one great power to another. Instead, I have tried to show that the local, regional, international, and imperial networks that linked the plantations and churches of St Thomas-in-the-East and St David to the rest of Jamaica and the Caribbean, to the east and Gulf coasts of North America, and to the port cities and regional towns of Britain were articulated together in ways that consistently put the ordinary people of the Caribbean at the centre of nineteenth-century history. This process begins with a move that might be seen as romantic, the demand to see people from the cultural and historical margins as 'in some sense our contemporaries', as Dipesh Chakrabarty puts it in *Provincializing Europe*.[52] However, the final result ought to be a complicated, multilayered story, one that can only be told according to the capacious protocols of realism, adept as it is at yoking disparate elements together, whether in history writing, in fiction, or in cultural critique.

Notes

INTRODUCTION: REALISM AND ROMANCE IN THE NINETEENTH-CENTURY CARIBBEAN

1. 'Current Literature', *Illustrated London News*, vol. 43, 5 December 1863, 575.
2. 'Current Literature', 575.
3. 'The War in America: Confederate Sharpshooters Firing on a Federal Supply Train on the Tennessee River', *Illustrated London News*, vol. 43, 5 December 1863. The illustration was by Frank Vizetelly, an English artist who openly sympathised with the South; three more of his drawings are in this same number of the *News*.
4. 'Slaves at Worship on a Plantation in South Carolina', *Illustrated London News*, vol. 43, 5 December 1863, 574.
5. The artist is unknown, but is not Frank Vizetelly, since the editorial note on the illustration says that it is 'from another source [and] of an entirely different aspect' from the four drawings depicting war scenes. 'Slaves at Worship on a Plantation in South Carolina', 574. Eileen Southern and Josephine Wright attribute 'Family Worship' to the political cartoonist Thomas Nast, who did indeed do work for the *Illustrated London News* in his early career, but they do not give evidence for this attribution, and I have not been able to find corroborating information for this intriguing possibility. See Eileen Southern and Josephine Wright (comps.), *African-American Traditions in Song, Sermon, Tale, and Dance, 1600s–1920: An Annotated Bibliography of Literature, Collections, and Artworks* (Westport, Conn.: Greenwood, 1990), 180.
6. Winston James, *Holding Aloft the Banner of Ethiopia: Caribbean Radicalism in Early Twentieth-Century America* (London: Verso, 1998), 9–11.
7. 'Slaves at Worship on a Plantation in South Carolina', 574.
8. Willie Lee Rose, *Rehearsal for Reconstruction: The Port Royal Experiment* (London: Oxford University Press, 1964).
9. John Lang, *Outposts of Empire* (London: T. C. and E. C. Jack, [1908]), vii.
10. Qtd in Catherine Hall, 'What Is a West Indian?', in *West Indian Intellectuals in Britain*, ed. Bill Schwartz (Manchester: Manchester University Press, 2003), 31–50, quotation on 32. The quotation is from Naipaul's *The Middle Passage* (1961).

11. James Anthony Froude, *The English in the West Indies, or, The Bow of Ulysses* (New York: Scribner, 1888), 347.
12. 'Current Literature', 575.
13. On empire and another famous nineteenth-century history of England, see Catherine Hall, 'At Home with History: Macaulay and the *History of England*', in *At Home with the Empire: Metropolitan Culture and the Imperial World*, ed. Hall and Sonya O. Rose (Cambridge: Cambridge University Press, 2006), 32–52. On imperial romance fiction, see Laura Chrisman, *Rereading the Imperial Romance: British Imperialism and South African Resistance in Haggard, Schreiner, and Plaatje* (Oxford: Oxford University Press, 2000).
14. For example, Catherine Hall, *Civilising Subjects: Metropole and Colony in the English Imagination, 1830–1867* (Chicago: University of Chicago Press, 2002); David Lambert, *White Creole Culture, Politics and Identity during the Age of Abolition* (Cambridge: Cambridge University Press, 2005); Diana Paton, *No Bond but the Law: Punishment, Race, and Gender in Jamaican State Formation, 1780–1870* (Durham, N.C.: Duke University Press, 2004); Mimi Sheller, *Democracy after Slavery: Black Publics and Peasant Radicalism in Haiti and Jamaica* (Gainesville: University Press of Florida, 2000).
15. Lambert, *White Creole Culture,* 4 n. 15.
16. Dipesh Chakrabarty, *Provincializing Europe: Postcolonial Thought and Historical Difference* (Princeton: Princeton University Press, 2000), 90.
17. Benjamin Moseley, *A Treatise on Tropical Diseases; on Military Operations; and on the Climate of the West-Indies*, 4th edn (London: T. Cadell and W. Davies, 1803), and Moseley, *A Treatise on Sugar, with Miscellaneous Medical Observations*, 2nd edn (London: John Nichols, 1800). On Moseley and the story of Three-Fingered Jack, see Srinivas Aravamudan, 'Introduction', in *Obi; or, The History of Three-Fingered Jack*, by William Earle, ed. Aravamudan (Peterborough, Ont.: Broadview, 2005), 7–51.
18. Hall, *Civilising Subjects*, esp. 'Introduction', 1–22.
19. Sadly, provenance records of this volume were lost when the library converted its card catalogue to a digital database in the 1990s.
20. Gayatri Chakravorty Spivak, 'Three Women's Texts and a Critique of Imperialism', in *'Race,' Writing, and Difference*, ed. Henry Louis Gates, Jr (Chicago: University of Chicago Press, 1986), 262–80; and Edward W. Said, *Culture and Imperialism* (New York: Knopf, 1993), 80–97. On *Mansfield Park*, see also Tim Watson, 'Improvements and Reparations at Mansfield Park', in *Literature and Film: A Guide to the Theory and Practice of Film Adaptation*, ed. Robert Stam and Alessandra Raengo (Malden, Mass.: Blackwell, 2004), 53–70.
21. Srinivas Aravamudan, *Tropicopolitans: Colonialism and Agency, 1688–1804* (Durham, N.C.: Duke University Press, 1999); Moira Ferguson, *Colonialism and Gender Relations from Mary Wollstonecraft to Jamaica Kincaid: East Caribbean Connections* (New York: Columbia University Press, 1993); Thomas Krise (ed.), *Caribbeana: An Anthology of English Literature of the West Indies, 1657–1777* (Chicago: University of Chicago Press, 1999); Keith A. Sandiford, *The Cultural Politics of Sugar: Caribbean Slavery and Narratives of Colonialism* (Cambridge: Cambridge University Press, 2000); Jenny Sharpe, *Ghosts of*

Slavery: A Literary Archaeology of Black Women's Lives (Minneapolis: University of Minnesota Press, 2003); Sean X. Goudie, *Creole America: The West Indies and the Formation of Literature and Culture in the New Republic* (Philadelphia: University of Pennsylvania Press, 2006).

22. Daniel Defoe, *Robinson Crusoe*, ed. John Richetti (1719; London: Penguin, 2001), page numbers in parentheses.

23. Defoe, *Robinson Crusoe*, 160.

24. William Bosman, for example, in his description of local customs in the Gold Coast (modern-day Ghana), says, 'As soon as the Child is born and the Priest has consecrated it, if above the common Rank, it hath three Names bestowed on it (though always called by one;) the first is that of the Day of the Week on which it is born.' Bosman, *A New and Accurate Description of the Coast of Guinea, Divided into The Gold, The Slave, and The Ivory Coasts*, ed. John Ralph Willis et al. (1705; New York: Barnes and Noble, 1967), 209.

25. Defoe, *Robinson Crusoe*, 162.

26. Defoe, *Robinson Crusoe*, 76.

27. Defoe, *Robinson Crusoe*, 83.

28. Ian Baucom, *Specters of the Atlantic: Finance Capital, Slavery, and the Philosophy of History* (Durham, N.C.: Duke University Press, 2005), 42.

29. Baucom, *Specters of the Atlantic*, 231.

30. Baucom, *Specters of the Atlantic*, 232.

31. Paton, *No Bond but the Law*, 5.

32. See Sylvia R. Frey and Betty Wood, *Come Shouting to Zion: African American Protestantism in the American South and British Caribbean to 1830* (Chapel Hill: University of North Carolina Press, 1998), 131–2; and Shirley C. Gordon, *God Almighty Make Me Free: Christianity in Preemancipation Jamaica* (Bloomington: Indiana University Press, 1996), 5–6.

33. David Scott, *Conscripts of Modernity: The Tragedy of Colonial Enlightenment* (Durham, N.C.: Duke University Press, 2004).

34. Scott, *Conscripts of Modernity*.

35. 'Slaves at Worship on a Plantation in South Carolina', 574.

36. Elizabeth Ware Pearson (ed.), *Letters from Port Royal Written at the Time of the Civil War* (Boston, Mass.: W. B. Clarke, 1906), 26. I identify 'H. W.' as Harriet Ware based on the references to her role on Pine Grove plantation in William H. Pease, 'Three Years among the Freedmen: William C. Gannett and the Port Royal Experiment', *Journal of Negro History* 42.2 (April 1957), 98–117.

37. Pearson (ed.), *Letters from Port Royal*, 34.

1 CREOLE REALISM AND METROPOLITAN HUMANITARIANISM

1. John Venn to Thomas Sherlock, 15 June 1751, Fulham Papers, American Colonial Section, vol. 18, fos. 45, 47, Lambeth Palace Library (consulted on microfilm, reel 9).

2. Venn to Sherlock, 15 June 1751, Fulham Papers, vol. 18, fo. 47, reel 9.

3. On Inkle and Yarico, see Frank Felsenstein (ed.), *English Trader, Indian Maid: Representing Gender, Race, and Slavery in the New World: An Inkle and Yarico Reader* (Baltimore: Johns Hopkins University Press, 1999).

4. Lambert, *White Creole Culture*, 39, emphases in the original.

5. Venn to Sherlock, 15 June 1751, Fulham Papers, vol. 18, fo. 48, reel 9.

6. See Edward [Kamau] Brathwaite, *The Development of Creole Society in Jamaica, 1770–1820* (Oxford: Clarendon, 1971), esp. chapter 15, 'The "Folk" Culture of the Slaves', 212–42; and Maureen Warner-Lewis, 'The Character of African-Jamaican Culture', in *Jamaica in Slavery and Freedom: History, Heritage and Culture*, ed. Kathleen E. A. Monteith and Glen Richards (Mona, Jamaica: University of the West Indies Press, 2002), 89–114. On obeah, see Jerome Handler, 'Slave Medicine and Obeah in Barbados, circa 1650–1834', *New West Indian Guide / Nieuwe West-Indische Gids* 74.1–2 (2000), 57–90; Jerome Handler and Kenneth M. Bilby, 'On the Early Use and Origin of the Term "Obeah" in Barbados and the Anglophone Caribbean', *Slavery and Abolition* 22.2 (2001), 87–100; and Alan Richardson, 'Romantic Voodoo: Obeah and British Culture, 1797–1807', *Studies in Romanticism* 32 (1993), 3–28.

7. Venn to Sherlock, 15 June 1751, Fulham Papers, vol. 18, fo. 47, reel 9.

8. Baucom, *Specters of the Atlantic*, 42.

9. Baucom, *Specters of the Atlantic*, 40.

10. Baucom, *Specters of the Atlantic*, 40.

11. Baucom, *Specters of the Atlantic*, 279.

12. Bryan Edwards, *The History, Civil and Commercial, of the British Colonies in the West Indies*, 3rd edn, 3 vols. (London: John Stockdale, 1801); Edward Long, *The History of Jamaica, or, General Survey of the Antient and Modern State of That Island*, 3 vols. (London: T. Lowndes, 1774).

13. Long and Edwards both figure prominently, for example, in Gordon K. Lewis, *Main Currents in Caribbean Thought: The Historical Evolution of Caribbean Society in its Ideological Aspects, 1492–1900* (Baltimore: Johns Hopkins University Press, 1983), and to a lesser extent in B. W. Higman, *Writing West Indian Histories* (London: Macmillan, 1999), 49–50. On Long, see Elizabeth Bohls, 'The Gentleman Planter and the Metropole: Edward Long's *History of Jamaica* (1774)', in *The Country and the City Revisited: England and the Politics of Culture, 1550–1850*, ed. Gerald MacLean, Donna Landry, and Joseph Ward (Cambridge: Cambridge University Press, 1999), 180–96; on Long, Edwards, and the description of the Caribbean landscape, see John E. Crowley, 'Picturing the Caribbean in the Global British Landscape', *Studies in Eighteenth-Century Culture* 32 (2003), 323–46.

14. Brathwaite, *Development of Creole Society*, xvi.

15. The term 'contact zone' comes from Mary Louise Pratt, *Imperial Eyes: Travel Writing and Transculturation* (London: Routledge, 1992), 6: 'The space of colonial encounters, the space in which people geographically and historically separated come into contact with each other and establish ongoing relations, usually involving conditions of coercion, radical inequality, and intractable conflict.'

16. Lambert, *White Creole Culture*, 11.

17. Venn to Sherlock, 15 June 1751, Fulham Papers, vol. 18, fo. 45, reel 9. Biographical information from Frank Cundall, *Historic Jamaica* (London: West India Committee; Kingston: Institute of Jamaica, 1915), 94.

18. On Stedman's narrative in general, and on the role of Joanna in particular, see Sharpe, *Ghosts of Slavery*, chapter 2, '"An Incomparable Nurse": The Obi of Domesticity', 44–86. See also Tassie Gwilliam, '"Scenes of Horror", Scenes of Sensibility: Sentimentality and Slavery in John Gabriel Stedman's *Narrative of a Five Years Expedition against the Revolted Negroes of Surinam*', *ELH* 65 (1998), 653–73, and Pratt, *Imperial Eyes*, chapter 5, 'Eros and Abolition', 86–110. In this chapter, I do not discuss the voluminous literature on sentimental fiction and antislavery, but for a fine recent account, see Brycchan Carey, *British Abolitionism and the Rhetoric of Sensibility: Writing, Sentiment and Slavery, 1760–1807* (Basingstoke, UK: Palgrave Macmillan, 2005).

19. John Gabriel Stedman, *Stedman's Surinam: Life in an Eighteenth-Century Slave Society: An Abridged, Modernized Edition of* Narrative of a Five Years Expedition against the Revolted Negroes of Surinam *by John Gabriel Stedman*, ed. Richard Price and Sally Price (Baltimore: Johns Hopkins University Press, 1992), 300. For more on Quacy, known as Kwasímukámba amongst the Saramaka (descendants of Maroons) in Surinam, see Richard Price, 'Kwasímukámba's Gambit', in Price, *First-Time: The Historical Vision of an Afro-American People* (Baltimore: Johns Hopkins University Press, 1983), 151–69.

20. Stedman, *Stedman's Surinam*, 300–1.

21. Stedman, *Stedman's Surinam*, 301.

22. Stedman, *Stedman's Surinam*, 301.

23. Stedman, *Stedman's Surinam*, 301. Quacy was not the original discoverer of the root's medicinal properties, which were already well known to the native populations of Surinam. See Londa Schiebinger, *Plants and Empire: Colonial Bioprospecting in the Atlantic World* (Cambridge, Mass.: Harvard University Press, 2004), 211–14.

24. Stedman, *Stedman's Surinam*, 301. Dahlberg was said to be furious with Linnaeus for naming the root after Quacy and not him: see Schiebinger, *Plants and Empire*, 213.

25. See Tim Watson, 'Indian and Irish Unrest in Kipling's *Kim*', in *Postcolonial Theory and Criticism: Essays and Studies 1999*, ed. Laura Chrisman and Benita Parry (Cambridge: D. S. Brewer, 2000), 95–114.

26. Maria Edgeworth, *Belinda*, ed. Kathryn J. Kirkpatrick (Oxford: Oxford University Press, 1994), 75. Hereafter cited in the body of the text as B; all references are to this edition, a reprint of the second, 1802, edition of Edgeworth's novel.

27. Taylor's correspondence and other papers are collected in two main locations: the Vanneck-Arcedeckne Papers in the Cambridge University Library and the Taylor Family Papers at the Institute of Commonwealth Studies (ICS) in London. In 2005, both collections were published together on microfilm as *Plantation Life in the Caribbean: Part One: Jamaica, c. 1765–1848: The Taylor and Vanneck-Arcedeckne Papers from Cambridge University Library and the Institute of Commonwealth Studies, University of London* (Marlborough,

Wilts.: Adam Matthew, 2005). Hereafter abbreviated as PLC. I consulted the Taylor Family Papers in London in 2002; where I read, or re-read, material on microfilm, I have indicated that in the notes. I have retained Taylor's spelling, but sometimes added or amended punctuation where necessary. One portion of the Vanneck-Arcedeckne Papers has been published as 'The Letters of Simon Taylor of Jamaica to Chaloner Arcedekne, 1765–1775', ed. Betty Wood, in *Travel, Trade and Power in the Atlantic, 1765–1884: Camden Miscellany Vol. XXXV* (Cambridge: Cambridge University Press, 2002), 1–164. For a brief account of Taylor's life and world, see Richard Sheridan, 'Simon Taylor, Sugar Tycoon of Jamaica, 1740–1813', *Agricultural History* 45 (1971), 285–96.

28. Simon Taylor to Chaloner Arcedeckne, 12 March 1774, ARC/3A/1774/2, PLC, reel 1.

29. Taylor to David Reid, 10 March 1801, Taylor Family Papers, 1/D/53, ICS, London.

30. Taylor to Robert Taylor, 15 August 1807, Taylor Family Papers, 1/I/39, PLC reel 9.

31. Taylor to Chaloner Arcedeckne, 13 October 1799, ARC/3A/1799/21, PLC reel 4.

32. Taylor to Chaloner Arcedeckne, 10 January 1794, ARC/3A/1794/1, PLC reel 4.

33. Taylor to Chaloner Arcedeckne, 13 October 1799, ARC/3A/1799/21, PLC reel 4.

34. For example, in Taylor to Chaloner Arcedeckne, 6 June 1800, ARC/3 A/1800/11, PLC reel 4; also in Taylor to Robert Taylor, 20 May 1798, Taylor Family Papers, 1/B/22, ICS, London. Wilberforce is also the 'Imp of Darkness', in Taylor to Chaloner Arcedeckne, 2 May 1799, ARC/3A/1799/7, PLC reel 4.

35. On the importance of bills of exchange in transatlantic slavery, see Baucom, *Specters of the Atlantic*, 60–4.

36. All figures are from the 1799 accounts of Golden Grove, ARC/3A/1799/26, PLC reel 4.

37. 'List of the Negroes and Other Slaves on Golden Grove Estate and Batchelors Hall Pen belonging to Chaloner Arcedeckne, Esq., with their Increase & Decrease from the 31st of December 1791 to the 30th June 1792', ARC/3C/1792/5, PLC reel 7.

38. 'List of the Negroes and Other Slaves on Golden Grove', ARC/3C/1792/5, PLC reel 7.

39. Sharpe, *Ghosts of Slavery*, xvii–xviii. The most notorious documents of rape and concubinage in the Caribbean are the diaries of Thomas Thistlewood. Douglas Hall, *In Miserable Slavery: Thomas Thistlewood in Jamaica, 1750–1786* (Kingston: University of the West Indies Press, 1999).

40. Alexander Barclay, *A Practical View of the Present State of Slavery in the West Indies* (London: Smith, Elder, 1826), 100. Maria Nugent, *Lady Nugent's Journal of her Residence in Jamaica from 1801 to 1805*, ed. Philip Wright (Kingston: Institute of Jamaica, 1966), 68.

41. Taylor to Robert Taylor, 19 September 1811, Taylor Family Papers 1/J/48, PLC reel 9.

42. Taylor to Elizabeth Haughton Taylor, 12 May 1800, Taylor Family Papers, 1/D/11, ICS, London.
43. Taylor to Robert Taylor, 9 June 1810, Taylor Family Papers, 1/J/9, PLC reel 9.
44. See, for example, Susanne Seymour, Stephen Daniels, and Charles Watkins, 'Estate and Empire: Sir George Cornewall's Management of Moccas, Herefordshire and La Taste, Grenada, 1771–1819', *Journal of Historical Geography* 24.3 (1998), 313–51.
45. Taylor to Robert Taylor, 9 June 1810, Taylor Family Papers, 1/J/9, PLC reel 9.
46. Taylor to John Taylor, 27 January 1783, Taylor Family Papers, 11/B/36, PLC reel 9. This is a copy of the letter made by John Taylor, Simon Taylor's younger brother in London. The letter itself was also transcribed by Simon Taylor in his own letterbooks, but without the copy of the will itself: Taylor Family Papers, 1/I/27, PLC reel 8.
47. Taylor to John Taylor, 27 January 1783, Taylor Family Papers, 11/B/36, PLC reel 9.
48. Sharpe, *Ghosts of Slavery*, 51, 57.
49. John Cooper to Anna Susannah Taylor, 1 January 1835, Taylor Family Papers, vii/B/1, PLC reel 11.
50. A first-hand account of the problems with the apprenticeship system that followed the legal abolition of slavery in Jamaica is James Williams, *A Narrative of Events, since the First of August, 1834, by James Williams, an Apprenticed Labourer in Jamaica*, ed. Diana Paton (1837; Durham, N.C.: Duke University Press, 2001). See also R. R. Madden, *A Twelvemonth's Residence in the West Indies during the Transition from Slavery to Apprenticeship*, 2 vols. (1835; Westport, Conn.: Negro Universities Press, 1970), esp. ii: 165–215.
51. Taylor to Robert Taylor, 15 February 1800, Taylor Family Papers, 1/D/2, ICS, London.
52. Taylor to Robert Taylor, [?] October 1798, Taylor Family Papers, 1/B/27, ICS, London.
53. Taylor to Chaloner Arcedeckne, 10 July 1799, ARC/3A/1799/14, PLC reel 4.
54. Taylor to Robert Taylor, [?] November 1799, Taylor Family Papers, 1/B/31, ICS, London.
55. Taylor to Robert Taylor, [?] February 1800, Taylor Family Papers, 1/D/9, ICS, London.
56. An excellent account of North American/Caribbean links is Andrew Jackson O'Shaughnessy, *An Empire Divided: The American Revolution and the British Caribbean* (Philadelphia: University of Pennsylvania Press, 2000).
57. Taylor to George Hibbert, 22 January 1801, Taylor Family Papers, 1/D/45, ICS, London.
58. Taylor to Robert Taylor, 26 September 1799, Taylor Family Papers, 1/C/22, ICS, London.
59. Taylor to Chaloner Arcedeckne, 23 July 1798, ARC/3A/1798/22, PLC reel 4.
60. Taylor to George Hibbert, 22 January 1801, Taylor Family Papers, 1/D/45, ICS, London.

61. Taylor to Simon R. B. Taylor, 8 August 1807, Taylor Family Papers, 1/I/31, ICS, London.
62. George Hibbert to Simon Taylor, 5 September 1803, Taylor Family Papers, xvii/A/47, ICS, London.
63. Hibbert to Taylor, 5 September 1803, Taylor Family Papers, xvii/A/47, ICS, London.
64. Christopher L. Brown, 'Empire without Slaves: British Concepts of Emancipation in the Age of the American Revolution', *William and Mary Quarterly* 3rd series 56.2 (1999), 273–306, quotation on 275.
65. [James Stephen], *Reasons for Establishing a Registry of Slaves in the British Colonies* (London: n.p., 1814), 37.
66. Stephen, *Reasons for Establishing a Registry*, 35.
67. Stephen, *Reasons for Establishing a Registry*, 64.
68. James Stephen, *A Defence of the Bill for the Registration of Slaves, by James Stephen, Esq., in Letters to William Wilberforce, Esq., M.P.: Letter the Second* (London: J. Butterworth, 1816), 130.
69. As late as 1826, the journal of the Anti-Slavery Society in London was noting letters from prominent Jamaican planter James MacQueen and another white creole in the Jamaican *Royal Gazette* exhorting slave owners to keep 'secret' the knowledge they had of the enslaved people of Jamaica. See *Anti-Slavery Monthly Reporter* 15 (31 August 1826), 213–15.
70. Qtd in Stephen, *A Defence of the Bill for the Registration of Slaves*, 135–6; emphasis in original.
71. Taylor to George Hibbert, 13 December 1807, Taylor Family Papers, 1/I/48, PLC reel 8.
72. Hall, *Civilising Subjects*, 10.
73. Marcus Wood, *Slavery, Empathy, and Pornography* (Oxford: Oxford University Press, 2002), 403.
74. John Locke, *The Second Treatise of Government* (1689), in Locke, *Political Writings*, ed. David Wootton (New York: Mentor, 1993), 274. Also quoted in Jonathan Lamb, 'Modern Metamorphoses and Disgraceful Tales', *Critical Inquiry* 28 (2001), 133–66, quotation on 147.
75. On this case, see Simon Schama, *Rough Crossings: Britain, the Slaves, and the American Revolution* (New York: Ecco, 2006), 44–55.
76. On the connection between Pope's poem and Edgeworth's novel, see Susan C. Greenfield, '"Abroad and at Home": Sexual Ambiguity, Miscegenation, and Colonial Boundaries in Edgeworth's *Belinda*', *PMLA* 112.2 (1997), 214–28, reference on 216.
77. Lamb, 'Modern Metamorphoses', 158.
78. Lamb, 'Modern Metamorphoses', 166.
79. Lamb, 'Modern Metamorphoses', 166.
80. See Kathryn Kirkpatrick, 'Note on the Text', in *Belinda*, by Maria Edgeworth, ed. Kirkpatrick, xxx.
81. Kirkpatrick, 'Introduction', *Belinda*, by Maria Edgeworth, ed. Kirkpatrick, x.
82. Kirkpatrick, 'Introduction', xiv.

83. On the trope of reading in Edgeworth's novel, see Heather MacFadyen, 'Lady Delacour's Library: Maria Edgeworth's *Belinda* and Fashionable Reading', *Nineteenth-Century Literature* 48.4 (1994), 423–39.
84. Beth Kowaleski-Wallace, 'Home Economics: Domestic Ideology in Maria Edgeworth's *Belinda*', *Eighteenth Century* 29.3 (1988), 242–62, quotation on 242.
85. MacFadyen, 'Lady Delacour's Library', 424.
86. Qtd in Kathryn J. Kirkpatrick, '"Gentlemen Have Horrors upon the Subject": West Indian Suitors in Maria Edgeworth's *Belinda*', *Eighteenth-Century Fiction* 5.4 (1993), 331–48, quotation on 338. See also Edgeworth's letter to her Aunt Ruxton, 9 January 1810: 'I have done my best to warm her a *leetle* [sic] but the composition does not admit of it – and without making her over again she will never I fear be a girl after your own heart – or mine'. Qtd in Kirkpatrick, 'Note on the Text', xxvii.
87. Andrew McCann, 'Conjugal Love and the Enlightenment Subject: The Colonial Context of Non-Identity in Maria Edgeworth's *Belinda*', *Novel* 30.1 (1996), 56–77, quotation on 57.
88. Qtd in Kirkpatrick, 'Introduction', xi.
89. Hans Sloane, *A Voyage to the Islands Madera, Barbados, Nieves, S. Christophers and Jamaica, with the Natural History of the Herbs and Trees, Four-footed Beasts, Fishes, Birds, Insects, Reptiles, &c. of the Last of those Islands*, vol. 1 (London: B. M., 1707), cxiv.
90. Sloane, *Voyage to the Islands*, xc.
91. Sloane, *Voyage to the Islands*, liv, lvi, cxxiv.
92. Matthew Lewis, *Journal of a West India Proprietor: Kept during a Residence in the Island of Jamaica*, ed. Judith Terry (1834; Oxford: Oxford University Press, 1999), 91.
93. Moseley, *Treatise on Tropical Diseases*, 610–11.
94. Moseley, *Treatise on Tropical Diseases*, 570–1.
95. Moseley, *Treatise on Tropical Diseases*, 119.
96. Moseley, *Treatise on Tropical Diseases*, 646–7.
97. W. Stanford, rector of Westmoreland, Jamaica, to bishop of London, 22 July 1788. Fulham Papers, American Colonial Section, vol. 18, fo. 66, reel 9.
98. Biographical information on Bancroft comes from Ray Desmond, *Dictionary of British and Irish Botanists and Horticulturalists, Including Plant Collectors, Flower Painters and Garden Designers* (London: Taylor and Francis/Natural History Museum, 1994), 41, and Cundall, *Historic Jamaica*, 176–7. Bancroft's father, also Edward Bancroft, was the author of a standard English-language natural history of Surinam, *An Essay on the Natural History of Guiana, in South America* (1769), and a novel set partly in Surinam, *The History of Charles Wentworth, Esq.* (1770).
99. E[dward] N. Bancroft, 'An Account of the Tree which Produces the Hog-Gum of Jamaica, Read before the Jamaican Society for the Encouragement of Agriculture and Horticulture, on the 18th February, 1829', *Journal of Botany* n.s. 4 (1842), 136–47.

100. Bancroft, 'Account of the Tree', 137.
101. Bancroft, 'Account of the Tree', 136–7, editorial note.
102. Bancroft, 'Account of the Tree', 140–1.
103. Bancroft, 'Account of the Tree', 140, note.
104. Bancroft, 'Account of the Tree', 138.
105. 'Account of an Ascent to the Summit of the Blue Mountains of Jamaica', *Blackwood's Edinburgh Magazine* 4 (1818–19), 654–6. I take the idea of 'transperipheral' cultural circuits from Katie Trumpener, *Bardic Nationalism: The Romantic Novel and the British Empire* (Princeton: Princeton University Press, 1997), esp. xiii, 11–12.
106. 'Account of an Ascent', 654.
107. 'Account of an Ascent', 654.
108. 'Account of an Ascent', 654–5.
109. 'Account of an Ascent', 655–6.
110. 'Account of an Ascent', 655. For an excellent general account of nineteenth-century British writing about mountain climbing, see Elaine Freedgood, *Victorian Writing about Risk* (Cambridge: Cambridge University Press, 2000), chapter 4, 'The Uses of Pain: Cultural Masochism and the Colonization of the Future in Victorian Mountaineering Memoirs', 99–131.
111. 'Account of an Ascent', 655, 656.
112. 'Account of an Ascent', 654; Alan Eyre, *The Botanic Gardens of Jamaica* (London: André Deutsch, 1966), 20. This identification of Higson as the author seems probable, but not yet definitive. The author is not identified in Alan Lang Strout, *A Bibliography of Articles in* Blackwood's Magazine, *Volumes 1 through XVIII, 1817–1825* (Lubbock, Tex.: Texas Technological College Library, 1959). The piece is instead one of several that were grouped together under the heading 'Various' in the authorship log kept by William Blackwood during the period between summer 1818 and winter 1819 when the magazine was jointly owned by Blackwood and John Murray in London, suggesting that the piece came to Blackwood from Murray during this period. See Alan Lang Strout, 'The Authorship of Articles in *Blackwood's Magazine*, Numbers XVII–XXIV (August 1818–March 1819)', *The Library* 11 (1956), 187–201, reference on 187. Higson was born in 1773 and died in Kingston in 1836; biographical details are taken from Desmond, *Dictionary of British and Irish Botanists and Horticulturalists*, 341. See also Cundall, *Historic Jamaica*, 29, 175–6.
113. *The Jamaica Almanac for the Year 1816* (Kingston: Alexander Aikman, [1816]), 'Return of Proprietors and Properties, &c.', 30. Frank Cundall identifies Higson as a 'merchant of Kingston' (*Historic Jamaica*, 175), but clearly the dividing line between merchant and planter was hard to draw in the creole society of Jamaica.
114. Thomas Higson, 'The Guaco Plant', *Jamaica Physical Journal* 1 (1834), 234–6, quotation on 235.
115. James Hakewill, *A Picturesque Tour of the Island of Jamaica, from Drawings Made in the Years 1820 and 1821* (London: Hurst and Robinson, 1825), plate 3.

116. On the superimposition of European on to tropical and imperial landscapes, see Jill H. Casid, *Sowing Empire: Landscape and Colonization* (Minneapolis: University of Minnesota Press, 2005), esp. chapter 1, 'The Hybrid Production of Empire', 1–44.

117. Hakewill, *Picturesque Tour*, 4.

118. Barclay, *A Practical View of the Present State of Slavery*, 53–4.

119. Benjamin Greene, *Slavery as It Now Exists in the British West Indian Colonies: Discussed in a Series of Letters between Thomas Clarkson, Esq. and Benjamin Greene, Esq, of Bury St. Edmunds* (London: Hurst and Chance, 1829), 19. Greene's information was somewhat out of date: Taylor had died in 1813.

120. For a fascinating account of the various meanings of fire in the eastern Caribbean in the late nineteenth century and early twentieth century, see Bonham C. Richardson, *Igniting the Caribbean's Past: Fire in British West Indian History* (Chapel Hill: University of North Carolina Press, 2004).

121. 'List of the Negroes and Other Slaves on Golden Grove Estate and Batchelors Hall Pen belonging to Chaloner Arcedeckne, Esq., with their Increase & Decrease from the 31st of December 1791 to the 30th June 1792', ARC/3C/1792/5, PLC reel 7.

122. 'List of Purchased and Other Slaves on Bachelor's Hall Pen on the 1st Day of January 1820', ARC/3C/1820/1, PLC reel 7.

123. 'List of Purchased and Other Slaves on Bachelor's Hall Pen on the 1st Day of January 1820', ARC/3C/1820/1, PLC reel 7.

124. 'List of Slaves Belonging to Bachelors Hall Pen, 1st January 1823', ARC/3C/1823/1, PLC reel 7.

125. *Report of the Incorporated Society for the Conversion and Religious Instruction and Education of the Negro Slaves in the British West India Islands for the Year MDCCCXXVI [1826]* (London: R. Gilbert, 1827), 104.

126. A possible candidate for the man that Hakewill met is Scotland, baptised as Richard Lindsay, who had risen from the position of 'cattle boy' in 1792 to that of 'penkeeper' in 1820, the only slave listed as having this occupation in the 1820 and 1823 lists. See the lists of the enslaved in ARC/3C/1792/5, ARC/3C/1820/1, and ARC/3C/1823/1, PLC reel 7.

127. John M. Trew and John Stainsby to Rev. Dr Barrett, [?] February 1826, Papers of the Christian Faith Society, Lambeth Palace Library (consulted on microfilm), CFS/F/1, fo. 289, reel 7.

128. Barclay, *A Practical View of the Present State of Slavery*, 50–1.

129. *Report of the Incorporated Society . . . for the Year [1826]*, 90; Papers of the Christian Faith Society, CFS/E/12, reel 7. See also [Simon Houghton Clarke], *Notes in Defence of the Colonies: On the Increase and Decrease of the Slave Population of the British West Indies. By a West Indian* ([Kingston]: n.p., 1826), and James MacQueen, *The West India Colonies: The Calumnies and Misrepresentations Circulated against Them by the Edinburgh Review, Mr Clarkson, Mr Cropper, &c.* (London: Baldwin, Craddock and Joy, 1824).

130. Papers of the Christian Faith Society, CFS/E/12, reel 7; *Report of the Incorporated Society for the Conversion and Religious Instruction and Education of*

the Negroe Slaves in the British West India Islands, from July to December, MDCCCXXIII (London: R. Gilbert, 1824), 41–8. For a typical, and rather envious, Anglican complaint about dissenting success amongst the enslaved, see the letter written from St James, Jamaica, by Rev. H. Beams, 2 July 1824, Papers of the Christian Faith Society, CFS/F/1, fo. 94, reel 8.

131. J. R. Grosett, *Remarks on West India Affairs* (London: J. M. Richardson, 1824), 50–1, note. Grosett was himself a St Thomas-in-the-East landowner: his estate of Petersfield had 496 slaves in 1816: see *The Jamaica Almanac for the Year 1816*, 'Return of Proprietors, Properties, &c.', 35.

132. *The Jamaica Almanack for the Year 1827* (Kingston: Alexander Aikman, [1827]), 50–1.

133. *Report of the Incorporated Society. . . for the Year [1826]*, 8.

134. Papers of the Christian Faith Society, CFS/E/13, reel 7.

135. Papers of the Christian Faith Society, CFS/F/1, fos. 316, 317, reel 8.

136. *Report of the Incorporated Society. . . for the Year [1826]*, 44. Adult catechists were found attached to chapels rather than estates: there were 160 at Morant Bay church and 300 at Manchioneal chapel. The Taylor brothers' graves are described in Cundall, *Historic Jamaica*, 250–1. Simon Taylor's tomb, established by his nephew and heir Simon R. B. Taylor, tries to reclaim him for the empire as 'a Loyal Subject, a firm Friend, & an Honest man' (Cundall, *Historic Jamaica*, 251).

137. Lloyd is quoted in Cundall, *Historic Jamaica*, 252–3; Cundall's description of the chalice is on 253. In the 1833 accounts of Golden Grove, prepared by Thomas M'Cornock, the minister of the chapel is identified as Rev. R. Panton; he was paid £140 a year, the same sum as the Jamaican catechists of the St Thomas-in-the-East conversion society. See Vanneck–Arcedeckne Papers, ARC/3C/1833/1, PLC reel 7. The pleasing young man, Richard Panton, went on to have a long career in the church in Jamaica; he later became archdeacon of the county of Surrey, and died in the island in 1860: see *Gentleman's Magazine* n.s. 9 (1860), 438, and Cundall, *Historic Jamaica*, 207; see Hall, *Civilising Subjects*, 155–6, for Panton's complaints about Baptist heterodoxy in the island, and his allegations that 'deceit and lying are the great characteristics of the negro' (quoted in Hall, *Civilising Subjects*, 155); see also Gordon, *God Almighty Make Me Free*, 129–32.

2 CARIBBEAN ROMANCE AND SUBALTERN HISTORY

1. [Henry Nelson Coleridge], *Six Months in the West Indies, in 1825* (London: John Murray, 1826), 318–19. The author was the nephew of Samuel Taylor Coleridge.

2. Cynric R. Williams, *A Tour through the Island of Jamaica, from the Western to the Eastern End, in the Year 1823* (London: Hunt and Clarke, 1826), 65–6, 67–8. Hereafter abbreviated as T, with page numbers cited parenthetically in the text.

3. Christopher Lipscomb to Rev. Dr Barrett, 13 June 1828, Papers of the Christian Faith Society, CFS/F/1, fo. 438, reel 8. The first report of the St Thomas-in-the-East branch highlights the disparity between the lowland districts of the parish, like Manchioneal and Plantain Garden River, where the first stipendiary catechists were employed on many different estates, as described in the previous chapter, and the Blue Mountain district, where no catechist was named, only three estates were listed (Blue Mountain, Mount Lebanus, and Mount Pleasant), and on only one, Blue Mountain, had any children been catechised. Nevertheless, the report called the district 'a most promising field', perhaps based on the fact that Charles Scott, the vice president and treasurer of the society in St Thomas, had donated £20 on behalf of Christopher Nockells, absentee owner of Mount Pleasant. *Report of the Incorporated Society . . . for the Year [1826]*, 45, 103.

4. Lambert, *White Creole Culture*, 65–72.

5. *The Jamaica Almanack for the Year 1823* (Kingston: Alexander Aikman, [1823]), 'Returns of Proprietors, Properties, &c.', 76.

6. See, for example, *The New Jamaica Almanac and Register for the Year of Our Lord 1811* (Kingston: Smith and Kinnear, 1811), 71; *The New Jamaica Almanac and Register for the Year of Our Lord 1812* (Kingston: Smith and Kinnear, 1812), 72, 167; *Jamaica Almanac for the Year 1816*, 41.

7. 'Account of an Ascent', 654, 655.

8. 'Account of an Ascent', 655.

9. 'Account of an Ascent', 655.

10. 'Account of an Ascent', 655.

11. Geographical information taken from two official maps, 'Map of Jamaica, Prepared from the Best Authorities' (Kingston: Public Works Department, 1888; corrected 1926); and 'Jamaica 1/50,000', sheet N, 'Morant Bay' (Kingston: Survey Department, 1967). 'Duck Worth' still appears as a place-name on the 1967 map, although there appears to be no settlement there.

12. Williams is listed as a magistrate for the parish in the 1811, 1812, 1816, 1819, and 1820 Jamaica almanacs, for instance, but disappears from the list in 1822; however, he continued to own Duckworth until his death in 1832, when it passed to his son Charles White Williams, Jr, who had by that time emigrated from England to Canada. See *New Jamaica Almanac . . . for the Year of Our Lord 1811*, 71; *New Jamaica Almanac . . . for the Year of Our Lord 1812*, 72; *Jamaica Almanac for the Year 1816*, 41; *The Jamaica Almanack for the Year 1819* (Kingston: Alexander Aikman, 1819), 65; *The Jamaica Almanack for the Year 1820* (Kingston: Alexander Aikman, 1820), 44; *The Jamaica Almanack for the Year 1822* (Kingston: Alexander Aikman, 1822), 'Return of Proprietors, Properties, &c.', 78. I am extremely grateful to Terry Roberts for sharing with me much of his extensive genealogical research into the White Williams family.

13. 'Jamaica', *London Magazine* n.s. 4 (Apr. 1826), 553.

14. 'I found no great difficulty in arranging my little matters of business with the executors of my deceased relation' (T 233). Charles White Williams was added

to the standing committee of the West India Committee at a meeting held in London on 10 February 1824; the meeting was attended by J. R. Grosett, George Watson Taylor (heir to Simon Taylor's estates in eastern Jamaica), Simon Houghton Clarke, and George Hibbert, among many others. Minutes of the West India Committee, WIC/1/MIN, Institute of Commonwealth Studies, microfilm copy, reel 11, fos. 172–5; many thanks to Nadia Ellis for carrying out this microfilm research at ICS. On the literary committee of the WIC, see Douglas Hall, *A Brief History of the West India Committee* (St Lawrence, Barbados: Caribbean Universities Press, 1971), 10–12. On the subsidies WIC paid to the writers of proslavery books, pamphlets, and articles, see 'The West India Committee, and Its Mercenaries of the Press', *Anti-Slavery Monthly Reporter* 45 (February 1829), 427–9.

15. *Monthly Review* 3rd series 2 (1826), 307.
16. Papers of the Christian Faith Society, CFS/E/12, reel 7. Like Wilberforce, however, Williams declined to subscribe in future years, although whereas the antislavery campaigner received the note 'refused' against his name, the obscure absentee planter was given the annotation 'unknown'. See Papers of the Christian Faith Society, CFS/E/13, reel 7. Perhaps the organisation had the wrong address: in subsequent years, until his death in 1832, Williams's address was 55 Burton Crescent, London, the one given in the records of the West India Committee and appearing on his death certificate (see the list of WIC standing committee members as of 1831, Minutes of the West India Committee, WIC/1/MIN, reel 15: thanks to Nadia Ellis for this research); moreover, his wife Harriet, née Chubb, died in Orléans, France, in January 1828, so it is possible Williams and his family were living abroad in the mid- to late 1820s. (I am grateful to Terry Roberts for the information about Harriet's death and for Williams's address on his death certificate.) The 1826 report of the conversion society prints his name in the list of subscribers as 'C. N. Williams, Esq., Epsom, Surrey', but I think this is a mistranscription. See *Report of the Incorporated Society... for the Year [1826]*, 100.
17. Trumpener, *Bardic Nationalism*, 141.
18. Trumpener, *Bardic Nationalism*, 141.
19. Trumpener, *Bardic Nationalism*, 141.
20. Baucom, *Specters of the Atlantic*, 45.
21. Baucom, *Specters of the Atlantic*, 46.
22. Chakrabarty, *Provincializing Europe*, 98.
23. Chakrabarty, *Provincializing Europe*, 90.
24. Catherine Hall, 'Epilogue: Imperial Careering at Home; Harriet Martineau on Empire', in *Colonial Lives across the British Empire: Imperial Careering in the Long Nineteenth Century*, ed. David Lambert and Alan Lester (Cambridge: Cambridge University Press, 2006), 335–59, quotation on 344.
25. Hall, 'Imperial Careering', 353.
26. Harriet Martineau, 'Demerara', in *Harriet Martineau's Writing on the British Empire*, vol. 1, *The Empire Question*, ed. Deborah Logan (1833; London:

Pickering & Chatto, 2004), 81. Hereafter abbreviated as D, with page numbers in parentheses in the text.

27. On the 1816 Barbados revolt, see Lambert, *White Creole Culture*, chapter 4, 'Locating Blame for the 1816 Rebellion', 105–39.

28. Emilia Viotti da Costa, *Crowns of Glory, Tears of Blood: The Demerara Slave Rebellion of 1823* (New York: Oxford University Press, 1994), 291. These paragraphs summarising the Demerara revolt are indebted – as are all analyses now of the colony in the 1820s – to da Costa's important book.

29. For Smith as martyr, see Edwin Angel Wallbridge, *The Demerara Martyr: Memoirs of the Rev. John Smith, Missionary to Demerara* (1848; New York: Negro Universities Press, 1969). This view of the case has persisted well into the twentieth century: see, for example, Cecil Northcott, *Slavery's Martyr: John Smith of Demerara and the Emancipation Movement, 1817–24* (London: Epworth, 1976). It was not until da Costa's *Crowns of Glory, Tears of Blood* (1994) that a full-fledged history of the revolt appeared that was told primarily from the rebels' own point of view.

30. Gauri Viswanathan, *Outside the Fold: Conversion, Modernity, and Belief* (Princeton: Princeton University Press, 1998), 16.

31. William Wilberforce, *An Appeal to the Religion, Justice, and Humanity of the Inhabitants of the British Empire, in Behalf of the Negro Slaves in the West Indies* (London: J. Hatchard and Son, 1823).

32. Wilberforce, *Appeal*, 45, 30–1.

33. Wilberforce, *Appeal*, 54.

34. *An Authentic Copy of the Minutes of Evidence of the Trial of John Smith, a Missionary, in Demerara; Held at the Colony House, in George Town, Demerara, on Monday the 13th Day of October, 1823, and 27 Following Days* (London: Samuel Burton, 1824), 14. Hereafter cited as *Minutes of Evidence*.

35. *Minutes of Evidence*, 14, 16.

36. *Minutes of Evidence*, 14.

37. Great Britain, *Parliamentary Papers (House of Commons)*, 1824 (no. 333), vol. XXIII, 'Demerara. Further Papers. Copies or Extracts of Correspondence with the Governors of Colonies in the West Indies, respecting Insurrection of Slaves; for the 1st of January 1822 to the Present Time; with Minutes of Trials', 487. Hereafter cited as 'Demerara. Further Papers'.

38. *Minutes of Evidence*, 16.

39. *Minutes of Evidence*, 17–18.

40. *Minutes of Evidence*, 9.

41. *Minutes of Evidence*, 23.

42. *Minutes of Evidence*, 55–6. On the remarkable uses to which African-American communities in the early nineteenth-century United States put the Exodus myth, see Eddie S. Glaude, Jr, *Exodus! Religion, Race, and Nation in Early Nineteenth-Century Black America* (Chicago: University of Chicago Press, 2000).

43. *Minutes of Evidence*, 52.

44. 'Demerara. Further Papers', 508.

45. 'Demerara. Further Papers', 499.
46. *Minutes of Evidence*, 94.
47. *Minutes of Evidence*, 94.
48. *Minutes of Evidence*, 96.
49. Chakrabarty, *Provincializing Europe*, 112, 101.
50. Chakrabarty, *Provincializing Europe*, 109, 101.
51. Chakrabarty, *Provincializing Europe*, 96.
52. Chakrabarty, *Provincializing Europe*, 98.
53. Chakrabarty, *Provincializing Europe*, 104. See Ranajit Guha, 'The Prose of Counter-Insurgency', in *Selected Subaltern Studies*, ed. Guha and Gayatri Chakravorty Spivak (New York: Oxford University Press, 1988), 45–86.
54. Gladstone's confession is reproduced in full in Joshua Bryant, *Account of an Insurrection of the Negro Slaves in the Colony of Demerara, which Broke out on the 18ᵗʰ of August, 1823* (Georgetown, Guyana: A. Stevenson, 1824), 73–80, quotation on 79. Quamina and his son Jack were both enslaved on the plantation Success, owned by Henry Gladstone, father of the future British prime minister.
55. Bryant, *Account of an Insurrection*, 80.
56. Bryant, *Account of an Insurrection*, 80.
57. Bryant, *Account of an Insurrection*, 79.
58. Bryant, *Account of an Insurrection*, 61.
59. Bryant, *Account of an Insurrection*, 80.
60. Bryant, *Account of an Insurrection*, 73.
61. Murray to Bathurst, 24 August 1823, 'Demerara. Further Papers', 457.
62. Bryant, *Account of an Insurrection*, 5.
63. Smith's letter is reproduced in the preface to a book issued by the London Missionary Society as part of their defence of Smith's reputation in England. See *The Missionary Smith: Substance of the Debate in the House of Commons on Tuesday the 1ˢᵗ and on Friday the 11ᵗʰ of June, 1824, on a Motion of Henry Brougham, Esq., respecting the Trial and Condemnation to Death by a Court Martial of the Rev. John Smith, Late Missionary in the Colony of Demerara* (London: Ellerton and Henderson, 1824), xxxvii.
64. Da Costa, *Crowns of Glory*, 197–8.
65. *Minutes of Evidence*, 16.
66. Da Costa, *Crowns of Glory*, 194.
67. *The Missionary Smith: Substance of the Debate*, xxxvii.
68. Nevertheless, an emphasis on the benefits of literacy, and especially of writing, was also prevalent in West Africa before and during the period of the transatlantic slave trade, especially among Muslims – some of whom carefully preserved their skills against all the odds in the Americas. Abdallah, in Williams's *Tour*, is an example; another is the Muslim scholar Abon Becr Sadika, enslaved in Jamaica as Edward Donlan, whose remarkable testimony is reproduced in Madden, *A Twelvemonth's Residence in the West Indies*, II:108–47. See also Moustafa Bayoumi, 'Moving Beliefs: The Panama Manuscript of Sheikh Sana See and African Diasporic Islam', *Interventions*

5.1 (2003), 58–81, and Sylviane A. Diouf, *Servants of Allah: African Muslims Enslaved in the Americas* (New York: New York University Press, 1998).

69. 'Demerara. Further Papers', 532.

70. *Minutes of Evidence*, 23.

71. 'Demerara. Further Papers', 457.

72. Eugene D. Genovese, *Roll, Jordan, Roll: The World the Slaves Made* (New York: Vintage, 1976), 284.

73. Chakrabarty, *Provincializing Europe*, 90.

74. *Report of the Committee of the Society for the Mitigation and Gradual Abolition of Slavery throughout the British Dominions* (London: Richard Taylor, 1824), 60–1.

75. Paris's confession, 'Demerara. Further Papers', 485.

76. *Report of the Committee of the Society for the Mitigation and Gradual Abolition of Slavery*, 13.

77. The debate on the Haitian material is at http://www.webster.edu/~corbetre/haiti/history/revolution/caiman.htm; thanks to Kate Ramsey for this reference. The debate on the Denmark Vesey case was sparked by Michael P. Johnson, 'Denmark Vesey and his Co-Conspirators', *William and Mary Quarterly* 3rd series 58.4 (2001), 915–76; critical and supporting remarks were offered by Edward A. Pearson, Douglas R. Egerton, Philip D. Morgan, Winthrop D. Jordan, James Sidbury, and others, in the subsequent number of *William and Mary Quarterly*, 59.1 (2002), 137–202.

78. Walter Scott, *Waverley, or Sixty Years Since*, ed. Andrew Hook (1814; London: Penguin, 1972), 492–3.

79. Edward [Kamau] Brathwaite, 'Creative Literature of the British West Indies during the Period of Slavery', *Savacou* 1 (1970), 46–73.

80. New editions are in preparation from Macmillan Caribbean and from Broadview Press (Candace Ward and I are the editors of the Broadview edition). Two excellent recent articles on *Hamel*, which complement my argument here, are: Janina Nordius, 'Racism and Radicalism in Jamaican Gothic: Cynric R. Williams's *Hamel, the Obeah Man*', *ELH* 73.3 (2006), 673–93, and Candace Ward, '"What Time Has Proved": History, Rebellion, and Revolution in *Hamel, the Obeah Man*', *ARIEL: A Review of International English Literature* 38.1 (2007), 49–74. Barbara Lalla gives a fine account of the novel; she notes, as I discuss below, that the part of the text that focuses on Hamel himself disrupts the anti-missionary thrust of the novel, although she argues in the end that Hamel 'supplies the imperial need for a Caliban in the wilderness'. See Barbara Lalla, *Defining Jamaican Fiction: Marronage and the Discourse of Survival* (Tuscaloosa: University of Alabama Press, 1996), 44–52, quotation on 52. Other analyses of *Hamel* can be found in Henrice Altink, 'Deviant and Dangerous: Pro-Slavery Representations of Jamaican Slave Women's Sexuality, c. 1780–1834', *Slavery and Abolition* 26.2 (2005), 271–88, and Lizabeth Paravisini-Gebert, 'Colonial and Postcolonial Gothic: The Caribbean', in *The Cambridge Companion to Gothic Fiction*, ed. Jerrold E. Hogle (Cambridge: Cambridge University Press, 2002), 229–57.

81. Two contemporary reviews of *Hamel*, in the *London Magazine* and in the *Westminster Review*, both attribute the novel to the author of *A Tour through the Island of Jamaica*. See *London Magazine* n.s. 8 (June 1827), 182–7, esp. 182; and *Westminster Review* 7, 14 (April 1827), 444–64, esp. 445. I owe the reference to the *Westminster Review* attribution to Altink's essay, 'Deviant and Dangerous'; see her footnote 30. Janina Nordius's essay has further confirmed this identification: Nordius, 'Racism and Radicalism in Jamaican Gothic'. Hunt and Clarke were Henry Leigh Hunt, the poet Leigh Hunt's nephew, and Charles Cowden Clarke, close friend of John Keats.

82. George Wilson Bridges, *A Voice from Jamaica; in Reply to William Wilberforce, Esq. M.P.* (London: Longman, Hurst, Rees, Orme, Brown, and Green, 1823), 5.

83. See Mary Turner, *Slaves and Missionaries: The Disintegration of Jamaican Slave Society, 1787–1834* (Urbana: University of Illinois Press, 1982), 148–78, and Hall, *Civilising Subjects*, 106.

84. *Hamel, the Obeah Man*, 2 vols. (London: Hunt and Clarke, 1827), 1:176. Hereafter abbreviated as H, with page numbers in parentheses in the text.

85. Bridges, *Voice from Jamaica*, 46.

86. Aravamudan, *Tropicopolitans*, 4. Emphases in the original.

87. On the place of the Haitian Revolution, and of the figure of Toussaint in particular, in French and British culture at the turn of the nineteenth century, see Aravamudan, *Tropicopolitans*, 289–325.

88. Brathwaite, 'Creative Literature of the British West Indies', 71.

89. Lalla, *Defining Jamaican Fiction*, 48.

90. Lalla, *Defining Jamaican Fiction*, 48.

91. Brathwaite, 'Creative Literature of the West Indies', 72.

92. See Paul Hamilton, '*Waverley*: Scott's Romantic Narrative and Revolutionary Historiography', *Studies in Romanticism* 33 (1994), 611–34.

93. Ina Ferris, *The Achievement of Literary Authority: Gender, History, and the Waverley Novels* (Ithaca: Cornell University Press, 1991), 205.

94. Chakrabarty, *Provincializing Europe*, 96.

95. Chakrabarty, *Provincializing Europe*, 108, 109.

3 'THIS FRUITFUL MATRIX OF CURSES': THE INTERESTING NARRATIVE OF THE LIFE OF SAMUEL RINGGOLD WARD

1. The best account of Morant Bay is Gad Heuman, '*The Killing Time': The Morant Bay Rebellion in Jamaica* (Knoxville: University of Tennessee Press, 1994), from which this quick sketch of the uprising is drawn. For the sparing of the house at Golden Grove, see Heuman, '*The Killing Time*', 22. See also Thomas C. Holt, *The Problem of Freedom: Race, Labor, and Politics in Jamaica and Britain, 1832–1938* (Baltimore: Johns Hopkins University Press, 1992); Philip D. Curtin, *Two Jamaicas: The Role of Ideas in a Tropical Colony*,

1830–1865 (1955; New York: Atheneum, 1970); and Abigail B. Bakan, *Ideology and Class Conflict in Jamaica: The Politics of Rebellion* (Montreal: McGill-Queen's University Press, 1990). A fictional version of the events at Morant Bay forms the heart of Jamaican writer V. S. Reid's 1949 novel *New Day* (London: Heinemann, 1973).

2. To date, the only book that focuses principally on Ward is Ronald K. Burke, *Samuel Ringgold Ward: Christian Abolitionist* (New York: Garland, 1995).

3. Samuel Ringgold Ward, 'The Modern Negro, no. 1', 'The Modern Negro, no. 2', and 'The Modern Negro, no. 3', *Frederick Douglass' Paper*, 23 February, 13 April, and 20 April 1855. The first two articles are also reproduced in C. Peter Ripley (ed.), *The Black Abolitionist Papers*, vol. 1, *The British Isles, 1830–1865* (Chapel Hill: University of North Carolina Press, 1985), 412–22.

4. Scott, *Conscripts of Modernity*, 81.

5. Ward, 'The Modern Negro, no. 3'.

6. Ward, 'The Modern Negro, no. 1'.

7. Ward, 'The Modern Negro, no. 1', emphasis in original.

8. Brent Hayes Edwards, *The Practice of Diaspora: Literature, Translation, and the Rise of Black Internationalism* (Cambridge, Mass.: Harvard University Press, 2003), 11, emphasis in original.

9. Edwards, *Practice of Diaspora*, 12. Stuart Hall's influential essay on articulation hinges precisely on the question of slavery in the development of capitalism. It is the complex relationship between West Indian chattel slavery and the emergence of modern capitalism that breaks open, for Hall, the inadequate teleological narratives of capital handed down by classical Marxism and liberal political economy. See Stuart Hall, 'Race, Articulation, and Societies Structured in Dominance', in *Black British Cultural Studies: A Reader*, ed. Houston A. Baker, Jr, Manthia Diawara, and Ruth H. Lindeborg (Chicago: University of Chicago Press, 1996), 16–60, esp. 32–9. Another fine recent theorisation of articulation in an analysis of the relationship among race, slavery, and capital in the Americas is David Kazanjian, *The Colonizing Trick: National Culture and Imperial Citizenship in Early America* (Minneapolis: University of Minnesota Press, 2003), 'Introduction: Articulation, Graft, Flashpoint', 1–34.

10. Edwards, *Practice of Diaspora*, 12, 13.

11. Scott, *Conscripts of Modernity*, 81.

12. Ward, 'The Modern Negro, no. 1'.

13. Ward, 'The Modern Negro, no. 1', emphases in original.

14. *British Banner*, 20 July 1853.

15. Frederick Douglass, *Life and Times of Frederick Douglass* (1885; New York: Gramercy, 1993), 266.

16. *British Banner*, 20 July 1853. Rev. Thomas Binney introduced Ward to the annual meeting of the Colonial Missionary Society in this way: 'Here you know (pointing to Mr. Ward, who was on the platform), we have something very like "Uncle Tom" himself. (Cheers.) . . . You will find him [Ward] a noble specimen of humanity, though a black. (Applause.)'. 'Colonial Missionary

Society', *British Banner*, 11 May 1853, supplement. More generally, on the reception of *Uncle Tom's Cabin* in Britain in the 1850s, see Audrey A. Fisch, *American Slaves in Victorian England: Abolitionist Politics in Popular Literature and Culture* (Cambridge: Cambridge University Press, 2000), 12–14.

17. Samuel Ringgold Ward, *Autobiography of a Fugitive Negro: His Anti-Slavery Labours in the United States, Canada, and England* (1855; Eugene, Oreg.: Wipf and Stock, 2000), 248.

18. Scott, *Conscripts of Modernity*, 19, emphasis in original.

19. Scott, *Conscripts of Modernity*, 6, 8, 7, emphasis in original.

20. Samuel R[inggold] Ward, *Reflections upon the Gordon Rebellion* (n.p. [Jamaica]: n.p., 1866), 6, emphases in original.

21. 'Mr. Ward to Governor Eyre', in Great Britain, *Parliamentary Papers (House of Commons)*, 1866 (no. 3682), vol. xxx, 'Jamaica: Papers Laid before the Royal Commission of Inquiry by Governor Eyre', 258, emphasis in original (hereafter cited as 'JRC Papers'). Eyre requested information meant to support his handling of the rebellion from many prominent Jamaicans.

22. 'Speech of Governor Eyre on the Opening of the Legislative Session', enclosure 1 in Edward Eyre to Edward Cardwell, no. 30, 8 November 1865, in CO 884/2/2, 'Papers relating to the Insurrection in Jamaica (Confidential)', National Archives, Kew.

23. On Menard, see my discussion in the epilogue below. On the Haitian exiles and émigrés, see Sheller, *Democracy after Slavery*, 227–38.

24. Ward's discussion of his connections with Clarke and Gordon can be found in his testimony before the Jamaica Royal Commission, in Great Britain, *Parliamentary Papers (House of Commons)*, 1866 (no. 3683-1), vol. xxxi, 'Report of the Jamaica Royal Commission (1866), Part II, Minutes of Evidence and Appendix' (hereafter cited as 'JRC Minutes of Evidence'). 'I was exceedingly pained to see that an old acquaintance of mine, Mr. George William Gordon, to whom I was introduced in England in 1854, was going about the country holding meetings . . . to unsettle the peasantry,' 'JRC Minutes of Evidence', 555. 'Sam Clarke, with whom I was quite intimate, said to me that he wanted to go to England to lay *our* case before the English people', 'JRC Minutes of Evidence', 556, emphasis mine. On the meeting between Clarke and Ward, see 'JRC Minutes of Evidence', 558, and 'JRC Papers', 259.

25. 'JRC Minutes of Evidence', 555. The Underhill meetings were held around the island in 1865, so called because their initial spur was a public letter from the secretary of the Baptist Missionary Society in London, Edward Underhill, to the colonial secretary, Edward Cardwell, in January 1865, complaining of the parlous condition of the island's economy and people. See Edward Bean Underhill et al., *Dr. Underhill's Letter: A Letter Addressed to the Rt. Honourable E. Cardwell, with Illustrative Documents on the Condition of Jamaica and an Explanatory Statement* (London: Arthur Miall, n.d. [1865]), 11–17, for the text of Underhill's original letter. On the Underhill meetings, see Heuman, '*The Killing Time*', 48–60, and Sheller, *Democracy after Slavery*, 188–95.

26. On the denial of the courthouse to Gordon's meeting, see Heuman, '*The Killing Time*', 58. Ward's account of the counter-meeting is in 'JRC Minutes of Evidence', 555. See also 'JRC Papers', 34.
27. 'JRC Minutes of Evidence', 556. George McIntosh's name is listed in 'JRC Minutes of Evidence', appendix IIIA, 'Return of Persons Put to Death in Course of the Suppression of the Insurrection [etc.]', 1135.
28. *The Gleaner*, 6 August 1866.
29. Jamaica, *Addresses to his Excellency Edward John Eyre, Esquire, &c, &c., 1865, 1866* ([Kingston]: M. DeCordova, 1866), 57.
30. Jamaica, *Addresses to his Excellency*, 133–66. Emily Ward's name appears on 136. In a 19 December 1840 number of Ward's Syracuse newspaper, the *Impartial Citizen*, a small item records Emily Ward's thanks for a quilt that has been given to her by the 'Anti-Slavery ladies of Cortlandville, Homer, Scott, and Preble', and she signs the thank-you card 'Emily E. R. Ward'.
31. Jamaica, *Addresses to his Excellency*, 63.
32. Eyre to Cardwell, January 1866, enclosure 1 in Storks to Cardwell, no. 28, 19 February 1866, 'JRC Papers', 1–19, with statements by Ward appearing on 10 and 14 (both referring to Samuel Clarke's purported role in the rebellion).
33. 'Acknowledgment', *Falmouth Post*, 23 March 1866: 'We have to acknowledge the receipt of a pamphlet entitled "Reflections upon the Gordon Rebellion" by the Reverend Samuel R. Ward. We shall refer to it at a future time.'
34. The principal planter paper was the *Colonial Standard and Jamaica Despatch*, but all of the daily and weekly papers, with the exception of the *Watchman and Jamaica Free Press*, which had been George William Gordon's paper, supported Eyre in his handling of the rebellion. Other papers, besides the *Falmouth Post*, were *The Gleaner*, *Jamaica Guardian*, *Morning Journal*, and the *County Union*: the latter two were more sympathetic to the rising 'coloured' political and economic class in the island, and the editor of the *County Union*, Sydney Levien, was even briefly imprisoned for sedition after Morant Bay. For a list of nineteenth-century Jamaican newspapers, see Sheller, *Democracy after Slavery*, 62, and Frank Cundall, *Bibliographia Jamaicensis: A List of Jamaica Books and Pamphlets, Magazine Articles, Newspapers, and Maps [etc.]* (Kingston: Institute of Jamaica, n.d. [1902]), 62–4. An interesting account of the Jamaican papers' coverage of the Morant Bay uprising, although it overstates criticism of Eyre, I think, is Cheryl Marguerite Cassidy, 'Islands and Empire: A Rhetorical Analysis of the Governor Eyre Controversy 1865–1867', Ph.D. dissertation, University of Michigan, 1988, esp. chapter 3.
35. 'Truth Compared with Sensation', *The Gleaner*, 13 March 1866. On John Gorrie, see Bridget Brereton, *Law, Justice, and Empire: The Colonial Career of John Gorrie, 1829–1892* (Mona, Jamaica: University of the West Indies Press, 1997).
36. *The Gleaner*, 12 January 1866.
37. *The Gleaner*, 5 March 1866. David Panton was the son of Richard Panton, who was sent to minister to the enslaved Jamaicans of Simon Taylor's Golden Grove estate in the 1830s, as I discussed at the end of chapter 1.

38. *The Gleaner*, 19 March 1866, and 23 April 1866. Oughton's authorship of this screed can be established by looking at the 23 April advertisement for the book: "'Who's to Blame?" / Being a review of thirty years residence in the Agricultural Districts of Jamaica, and embracing two Chapters entitled "The Problem" and "Jeopardy of Jamaica["], / By the Revd. Samuel Oughton, / Minister of the Baptist Church in Kingston'.

39. *The Gleaner*, 23 April 1866.

40. 'Paul Bogle', *The Gleaner*, 27 October 1866: 'This Arch-Traitor's Hymn Book!! taken from his pocket [after his hanging, presumably] by our Special Correspondent, is to be seen at the Stationery Establishment of Messrs. M. DeCordova, McDougall & Co., 62, Harbour Street'; 'Hymns Selected and Marked by Paul Bogle', *The Gleaner*, 3 November 1866. For a very interesting discussion of the hymns and psalms marked by Bogle, see Clinton Alexander Hutton, '"Colour for Colour; Skin for Skin": The Ideological Foundations of Post-Slavery Society, 1838–1865: The Jamaican Case', Ph.D. dissertation, University of the West Indies, Mona, 1992, 231–3.

41. *The Gleaner*, 26 March 1866. John Walton, a magistrate in St Thomas-in-the-East, was killed by the crowd during the first day of the rebellion; Augustus Hire, a local attorney, was killed during an attack on Amity Hall estate on 12 October. Heuman, *'The Killing Time'*, 9, 22–3.

42. Ward, *Reflections*, 4.

43. See 'Mr. Ward to Governor Eyre', 'JRC Papers', 258–60.

44. Ward, *Reflections*, 6.

45. Ward, *Reflections*, 6, 7.

46. Edwards, *Practice of Diaspora*, 38.

47. 'Coloured Impostors', *Anti-Slavery Reporter*, 2 May 1864, 111–12. This was the official journal of BFASS. On the figure of the black 'impostor' in antislavery politics, see Fisch, *American Slaves in Victorian England*, epilogue, '"How Cautious and Calculating": English Audiences and the Impostor, Reuben Nixon', 91–100.

48. 'JRC Minutes of Evidence', 558.

49. 'JRC Minutes of Evidence', 557.

50. Ward, *Autobiography*, 125.

51. Enclosed in US Consul Robert Monroe Harrison to Secretary of State William Marcy, no. 434, 21 June 1855, in Despatches from United States Consuls in Kingston, Jamaica, 1796–1906, National Archives, Washington, DC, consulted on microfilm, reel 16.

52. Ward, *Reflections*, 1.

53. The most detailed account of the incident is in Heuman, *'The Killing Time'*, 4–5. Ward's summary account in his *Reflections upon the Gordon Rebellion* is incorrect in its details. According to Heuman, Geoghegan was not convicted of trespass; instead, he was ordered arrested by the magistrates for interrupting proceedings when he shouted that a boy convicted of assault should not pay the court costs imposed on him, and when police tried to take him into custody outside the courthouse, dozens of people, including Paul Bogle, intervened

to rescue him. This was on 7 October 1865. The rebellion itself began on 11 October. Two people named 'James Geoghegan' are on the list of those executed after the rebellion: see 'JRC Minutes of Evidence', 1136, 1138.

54. Diana Paton's recent book provides an excellent account of the nineteenth-century Jamaican legal system. Paton, *No Bond but the Law*.

55. Great Britain, *Parliamentary Papers (House of Commons)*, 1866 (no. 3683) vol. xxx, 'Report of the Jamaica Royal Commission (1866)', 40.

56. Thomas Harvey and William Brewin, *Jamaica in 1866: A Narrative of a Tour through the Island, with Remarks on its Social, Educational and Industrial Condition* (London: A. W. Bennett, 1867), 22.

57. 'JRC Minutes of Evidence', 'Appendix 11: Returns and Documents relative to the Administration of Justice', 1099–101. Diana Paton, however, makes a powerful case for a more wide-ranging view of the Jamaican courts in the post-emancipation period, one that emphasises the fact that non-elite Jamaicans did have recourse to, and sometimes even found justice through, the legal system in the island. Paton, *No Bond but the Law*, chapter 5, 'Justice and the Jamaican People', 156–90.

58. 'JRC Minutes of Evidence', 1082–98. For more recent accounts of the importance of the justice system in the lead-up to Morant Bay, see Heuman, *'The Killing Time'*, 69–70, and Noelle Chutkan, 'The Administration of Justice in Jamaica as a Contributing Factor in the Morant Bay Rebellion of 1865', *Savacou* 11/12 (1975), 78–85.

59. 'JRC Papers', 426–7. Full emancipation had been achieved in 1838 (after the abolition of the quasi-slavery of the 'apprenticeship' system imposed in 1833): hence the petition's reference to twenty-seven years of post-emancipation oppression.

60. Qtd in Heuman, *'The Killing Time'*, 5.

61. For a persuasive and judicious recent account of the alternative court system set up by the small settlers in St Thomas-in-the-East in the 1860s, see Paton, *No Bond but the Law*, 178–82. Harvey and Brewin, in noting the Bogle petition, present a different set of alternatives for its interpretation: 'Paul Bogle and his friends . . . sent the following letter, which was delivered at the King's House [i.e., to the governor] on the morning of the 11th by special messenger. It may be read either as a last and *bona fide* appeal against oppression, or as a sort of declaration of war. The Royal Commissioners put the latter construction upon it: we think the other the just inference.' Harvey and Brewin, *Jamaica in 1866*, 24, footnote.

62. Evidence of Robert Francis Thomas, 20 June 1855, Savanna-la-Mar courthouse, encl. in Harrison to Marcy, no. 442, 17 July 1855, Despatches from US Consuls in Kingston, reel 17.

63. See *OED*, 'Stalwart', main heading, for the derivation from Scott, and noun, 2a.: 'The epithet "Stalwart" as applied to a class of politicians was first used by Mr. [James G.] Blaine in 1877 to designate those Republicans who were unwilling to give up hostility and distrust of the South as a political motive.' Quotation from *The Nation* (1881).

64. Peter Linebaugh and Marcus Rediker, _The Many-Headed Hydra: Sailors, Slaves, Commoners, and the Hidden History of the Revolutionary Atlantic_ (Boston, Mass.: Beacon, 2000).

65. Ward, _Autobiography_, 120. A good recent account of the Jerry case is Monique Patenaude Roach, 'The Rescue of William "Jerry" Henry: Antislavery and Racism in the Burned-over District', _New York History_ 82.2 (2001), 135–54. An older version of the story is in Eber M. Pettit, _Sketches in the History of the Underground Railroad_ (1879; Freeport, N.Y.: Books for Libraries Press, 1971), 50–5. Neither Pettit nor Roach mention Ward at all in connection with the rescue, despite Ward's assertion in his memoir that he had 'helped to file off' Jerry's chains (which were 'packed in a neat mahogany box, and sent to President Fillmore'). See Ward, _Autobiography_, 128. A more contemporary account does point the finger at Ward specifically: _Frederick Douglass' Paper_ reprinted a piece from the _Utica Gazette_ (itself citing the _Syracuse Star_), sympathising with a policeman, Mr Fitch, 'who was brutally beaten by the ruffians whom the Rev. Samuel R. Ward, and other eminent "Christians" incited to the attack on the Police office, on Wednesday evening'. _Frederick Douglass' Paper_, 9 October 1851.

66. Ward, _Reflections_, 1.

67. Ward, _Autobiography_, 135, emphasis in original.

68. Ward, _Autobiography_, 122.

69. On US 1 August celebrations, see Benjamin Quarles, _Black Abolitionists_ (New York: Oxford University Press, 1969), 118–29, and R. J. M. Blackett, _Building an Antislavery Wall: Black Americans in the Atlantic Abolitionist Movement, 1830–1860_ (Baton Rouge: Louisiana State University Press, 1983), 7–8

70. _Impartial Citizen_, 22 May 1850, emphases in original. 'At last she had finished a beautiful piece of embroidery, which was sold to the merchants, and the money that was paid for it procured a "barrel of flour," and the barrel of flour was sent to the starving Irish, as Laura Bridgman's offering to their poverty and woe.' Unattributed quotation, probably from one of Bridgman's teachers, in Samuel Howe's annual reports on her education, in Maud Howe and Florence Howe Hall, _Laura Bridgman: Dr. Howe's Famous Pupil and What He Taught Her_ (Boston, Mass.: Little, Brown, 1904), 235.

71. Thomas Carlyle to Samuel Howe, 23 October 1842, qtd in Elisabeth Gitter, _The Imprisoned Guest: Samuel Howe and Laura Bridgman, the Original Deaf-Blind Girl_ (New York: Farrar, Straus and Giroux, 2001), 102.

72. Thomas Carlyle, letter to Hamilton Hume, 23 August 1866, in Gillian Workman, 'Thomas Carlyle and the Governor Eyre Controversy: An Account with Some New Material', _Victorian Studies_ 18.1 (1974), 77–102, quotations on 91, 92. The work of this committee, later renamed the Eyre Defence and Aid Fund, was well publicised in Jamaica; other prominent supporters of Eyre in England included Charles Dickens and John Ruskin. _The Gleaner_ reprinted an early letter from Ruskin to the _Daily Telegraph_ on the Jamaica events, deploring 'this fatuous outcry against Governor Eyre'. See 'Mr Ruskin on the Jamaica Insurrection', _The Gleaner_, 29 January 1866. I discuss the events in

Britain that followed the Jamaica rebellion in much more detail in chapter 4 below.

73. Carlyle to Hume, in Workman, 'Carlyle and the Governor Eyre Controversy', 92.
74. Ward, *Autobiography*, 149.
75. Elisa Tamarkin, 'Black Anglophilia; or, The Sociability of Antislavery', *American Literary History* 14.3 (2002), 444–78, quotation on 451.
76. Ward, *Autobiography*, iii.
77. Ward, *Autobiography*, iii.
78. Ward, *Autobiography*, iv.
79. Ward, *Autobiography*, iv.
80. Tamarkin, 'Black Anglophilia', 458, 463.
81. S[amuel] R[inggold] W[ard], 'Letters from Jamaica: Number One', *Franklin Visitor*, 8 June 1859.
82. 'The Despising of the Poor', *Impartial Citizen*, 28 February 1849, emphasis in original .
83. 'Working Man's Column', *Impartial Citizen*, 11 July 1849.
84. 'Correspondence: Hear a Working Man', *Impartial Citizen*, 17 October 1849.
85. 'Attitude of Black Men', *Impartial Citizen*, 21 November 1849.
86. 'Correspondence: Hear a Working Man', *Impartial Citizen*, 17 October 1849. Luther had written that 'On the voters of this nation rests the responsibility of all laws, statutes, and acts of the nation, and amongst them all the diabolism of the Mexican war'. *Impartial Citizen*, 17 October 1849.
87. See Quarles, *Black Abolitionists*, 185.
88. 'Additional Accounts of the Trinidad Riot', *Impartial Citizen*, 31 October 1849.
89. 'Minutes of the Liberty Party Convention', *Impartial Citizen*, 11 July 1849; 'State Convention', *Impartial Citizen*, 11 July 1849, emphases in original.
90. 'Self-Elevation', *Impartial Citizen*, 14 March 1849, emphasis in original.
91. *Impartial Citizen*, 7 December 1850, emphasis in original.
92. 'Colonial Missionary Society', *British Banner*, supplement, 11 May 1853.
93. Ward, *Autobiography*, 253.
94. Ward, *Autobiography*, 253.
95. John Scoble to the Committee of BFASS, 7 April 1853, Papers of the British and Foreign Anti-Slavery Society, Rhodes House Library, Oxford, MS Brit. Emp. s.18 C23/61, consulted on microfilm, *The Rhodes House Library, Oxford, Anti-Slavery Collection, 1795–1880*, reel 13. Hereafter cited as BFASS Papers.
96. Thomas Henning to Louis Chamerovzow, 10 December 1855, BFASS Papers, c32/38a, reel 17.
97. Henning to Chamerovzow, 10 December 1855, BFASS Papers, c32/38a, reel 17. The story must remain obscure, of course, without fuller documentation. Henning's claim that Ward had represented himself as worth £5,000 comes second-hand; Ward himself made many public statements throughout his career complaining of his poverty. Nonetheless, it is unclear for whom Ward was raising money, or indeed how he kept himself financially, in the year that

he spent in England after winding up his collection activities on behalf of the Canadian Anti-Slavery Society some time in the winter of 1854–5. We do know that he declared bankruptcy in Jamaica. See [Samuel Oughton], *Jamaica: Who Is to Blame? By a Thirty Years' Resident* (London: Effingham Wilson, n.d. [1866]), 69, note. For more on Oughton and Ward, see below. The fullest account of the financial scandal surrounding Ward at the end of his British sojourn is in Alexander Murray, 'Canada and the Anglo-American Anti-Slavery Movement: A Study in International Philanthropy', Ph.D. dissertation, University of Pennsylvania, 1960, 274–7. See also Robin W. Winks, *The Blacks in Canada: A History*, 2nd edn (Montreal: McGill-Queen's University Press, 1997), 265–6.

98. Henning to Chamerovzow, 17 January 1856, BFASS Papers, c32/39, reel 17. By April 1856, Henning sounded less sure about Baynham's accusation against Ward, asking Chamerovzow, 'Could you find me out particularly the character of Mr. Baynham and his wife[?] . . . We shall use the information so communicated as strictly confidential.' Henning to Chamerovzow, 19 April 1856, BFASS Papers, C32/41, reel 17.

99. Ward is listed as a corresponding member from Jamaica at the start of the 1856 volume (3rd series, vol. 4) of the *Anti-Slavery Reporter*, but by the time a supplement attached to the June 1856 number was issued, Ward's name had been removed from the list. See *Anti-Slavery Reporter*, 2 June 1856, supplement, 142.

100. Ward, letter to the *Anti-Slavery Standard*, 2 July 1840, qtd in Quarles, *Black Abolitionists*, 47.

101. Samuel R. Ward, 'Letter', *Frederick Douglass' Paper*, 21 January 1853. On the Refugee Home Society, see Winks, *Blacks in Canada*, 204–8.

102. Ward, *Autobiography*, 406.

103. Ward, *Autobiography*, 405–6; Burke, *Samuel Ringgold Ward*, 57–8. There is, however, no evidence that Ward ever settled on the donated land. He lived in Kingston from 1855 to 1860, and moved subsequently to the district of St David, a few miles east of Kingston.

104. 'Colonial Missionary Society', *British Banner*, 11 May 1853.

105. Ward, *Autobiography*, 411, note, emphasis in original.

106. Qtd in Blackett, *Building an Antislavery Wall*, 150.

107. Ward, *Autobiography*, 406.

108. Ward, *Autobiography*, 379.

109. *Anti-Slavery Reporter*, 1 June 1854, 138. See also Blackett, *Building an Anti-slavery Wall*, 204.

110. *Anti-Slavery Reporter*, 1 June 1854, 138, 139.

111. *British Banner*, 24 May 1854. These audience reactions were not transcribed in the *Anti-Slavery Reporter*'s account of Ward's speech.

112. *Anti-Slavery Reporter*, 1 June 1854, 139. In the *British Banner* report, this statement is followed by 'loud applause'.

113. John Clark, *A Brief Account of the Settlements of the Emancipated Peasantry in the Neighbourhood of Brown's Town, Jamaica; in a Letter from John Clark,*

Baptist Missionary, to Joseph Sturge, of Birmingham (Birmingham: John Whitehouse Showell, 1852), 8.

114. Clark, *A Brief Account of the Settlements*, 9, 11. On the Jamaica 'free villages', see Hall, *Civilising Subjects*, 120–39.

115. On the rise of the smallholding and peasant classes in Jamaica after emancipation, see Holt, *The Problem of Freedom*, 143–68.

116. See Douglas Hall, *Free Jamaica, 1838–1865: An Economic History* (New Haven: Yale University Press, 1959), esp. chapter 6, 'The Small Farmers', and chapter 8, 'Crisis and Assessment'.

117. Clark, *A Brief Account of the Settlements*, 9–10.

118. S[amuel] R[inggold] W[ard], *Provincial Freeman*, 10 June 1854.

119. 'Negro Emancipation', *Provincial Freeman*, 15 July 1854. Ward's description of the post-emancipation economy in Jamaica, if rough and ready, is accurate enough. It also describes the analogous situation in the British colony of Kenya in the early twentieth century, where large, inefficient white settler farms were undercut by peasant and smallholder agricultural skills until the white elites and the Colonial Office reorganised the economy to force most Kenyans into wage labour on the large estates. The parallels between the nineteenth-century Caribbean and twentieth-century Kenya are striking, and to my knowledge unstudied. See Caroline Elkins, *Imperial Reckoning: The Untold Story of Britain's Gulag in Kenya* (New York: Henry Holt, 2005), chapter 1, 'Pax Britannica', esp. 11–18.

120. The history of the Baptist mission in Jamaica is part of the subject of Catherine Hall's remarkable book, *Civilising Subjects*, to which the following section of my chapter is indebted. See also Horace O. Russell, *Foundations and Anticipations: The Jamaica Baptist Story, 1783–1892* (Columbus, Ga.: Brentwood Christian Press, 1993). On Liele and other black American Baptist preachers in Jamaica, see Gordon, *God Almighty Make Me Free*, chapter 3, 'Black Preachers', 41–55, and Frey and Wood, *Come Shouting to Zion*, 131–2. Frey and Wood also give an account of Liele's earlier career as an itinerant preacher in Georgia, 115–17.

121. Burke, *Samuel Ringgold Ward*, 58.

122. Governor Sir Henry Barkly to Colonial Secretary Sidney Herbert, no. 24, 12 March 1855, CO 137/326, National Archives, Kew. On the dispute over East Queen Street, see Hall, *Civilising Subjects*, 246–8.

123. Richard A. Leake (Kingston police inspector) to Henry Barkly, 6 March 1855, enclosed in Barkly to Herbert, 12 March 1855, CO 137/326, National Archives, Kew.

124. 'Foreign Letters Received', *Baptist Magazine*, August 1858, 590.

125. 'Colour fe Colour', *The Gleaner*, 16 November 1866.

126. Russell, *Foundations and Anticipations*, 95. Russell was himself pastor of East Queen Street Baptist Church between 1976 and 1989: Horace Russell, conversation with the author, September 2004.

127. 'Report of the Deputation to Jamaica to the Committee of the Baptist Missionary Society' (1860), table 2, p. 5, in Baptist Missionary Society Archives,

1792–1900 (consulted on microfilm), reel 18, Western Committee, 1850–1914: vol. 2, 'West Indies and Africa Sub-Committee Report Book, Sep. 1850–July 1866'. Hereafter cited as BMS Archives. Edward Underhill, visiting Jamaica as the leader of a BMS deputation to the island in November 1859, reported that Oughton's congregation was 'about 300 – rather less than more'. Edward Underhill to David East, 10 November 1859, BMS Archives, reel 27, BMS Home Correspondence, vol. 9, 'Correspondence between D. J. East and Underhill, 1852–1895'.

128. [Oughton], *Jamaica: Who Is to Blame?*, 69, note. On Oughton's life and career in Jamaica, see Hall, *Civilising Subjects*, 160–1, 246–64.

129. Oughton claimed that Ward 'was convicted by a jury (to which he had ventured to appeal by an action for the vindication of his character) of being guilty of the gross and polluting crimes that had been attributed to him, and is now an object of contempt and disgust'. [Oughton], *Jamaica: Who Is to Blame?*, 69–70, note.

130. Hall, *Civilising Subjects*, 154–5.

131. 'Minutes', 3 December 1867, BMS Archives, reel 18, Western Committee, 1850–1914: vol. 2a, 'Africa and West Indies Sub-Committee, June 1861–Feb. 1872'. The report that effectively blocked Wood's nomination for the position was passed on to the BMS in London by two of Oughton's fellow veteran missionaries, D. J. East and J. M. Phillippo. Eventually, BMS decided to move the Baptist training college, Calabar, of which East was director, to the East Queen Street site, and appointed East pastor of the church also. 'Minutes', 4 July 1868, BMS Archives, reel 18, Western Committee, 1850–1914: vol. 2a, 'Africa and West Indies Sub-Committee, June 1861–Feb. 1872'.

132. John Clarke, *Memorials of Baptist Missionaries in Jamaica, Including a Sketch of the Labours of Early Religious Instructors in Jamaica* (London: Yates and Alexander, 1869), 221.

133. Qtd in Hall, *Civilising Subjects*, 238.

134. Clarke, *Memorials of Baptist Missionaries*, 224.

135. Clarke, *Memorials of Baptist Missionaries*, 222. John Clarke (not to be confused with John Clark, also a Baptist missionary in Jamaica, who wrote the pamphlet on the free villages in post-emancipation Jamaica referred to above) would certainly have been aware of Ward's role in Kingston Baptist affairs in the 1850s, since he took it upon himself after Oughton's resignation in 1866 to send 'a brief outline of the history of [East] Queen St Chapel and Mr. Oughton's connexion with it' to the BMS in London, 'expressing his views as to the future pastorate' of the church. I have been unable, however, to locate Clarke's letter. See 'Minutes', 28 August 1866, BMS Archives, reel 18, Western Committee, 1850–1914: vol. 2a, 'Africa and West Indies Sub-Committee, June 1861–Feb. 1872'.

136. Even William Wemyss Anderson, a longstanding abolitionist and philanthropic figure in Jamaica, correspondent of BFASS, and the lawyer who arranged the transfer of John Candler's land to Ward in 1855, donated the

sizeable sum of £10 to the Eyre testimonial fund. See 'Eyre Testimonial', *The Gleaner*, 25 July 1866.

137. 'JRC Minutes of Evidence', 555. Ward put the number of pupils in his school as 'some forty between myself and my daughter'. Harvey and Brewin, during their visit to St David in 1866, commented on the poor quality of education generally in the district. The free, parochial school 'had but fourteen or sixteen pupils . . . The teaching and its results were of a humble order. According to the report of the school inspector this parish is the lowest in the island in point of education, both in regard to the number and quality of its schools; and it would seem the proportion of its population at school is but one in twenty-five.' Harvey and Brewin, *Jamaica in 1866*, 10.

138. 'JRC Minutes of Evidence', 555, 558.

139. 'JRC Minutes of Evidence', 555.

140. For Holt's passage to England, see 'Passengers Sailed', *The Gleaner*, 26 June 1866. Little has been written on the JCA, but there is a brief account of it in Sheller, *Democracy after Slavery*, 205–6; see also Hall, *Free Jamaica*, 200–2 (although Hall claims that the association never got beyond the planning stage).

141. Samuel Ringgold Ward, 'To the Meeting of the Inhabitants of St. David', in 'Printed Copy of Resolutions Passed at Meeting in St. David's', encl. 3 in Eyre to Cardwell, 12 July 1865, no. 47, in Great Britain, *Parliamentary Papers (House of Commons)*, 1866 (no. 3595), vol. LI, 'Papers relative to the Affairs of Jamaica', 230–1. Hereafter cited as Ward, 'To the Inhabitants of St David'.

142. Ward, 'To the Inhabitants of St David', 231.

143. 'JRC Minutes of Evidence', 559. On the political career of Samuel Clarke, see the careful and persuasive historical study by Swithin Wilmot, 'The Politics of Samuel Clarke: Black Political Martyr in Jamaica, 1851–1865', *Jamaican Historical Review* 19 (1996), 17–30; see also Wilmot, 'From Bondage to Political Office: Blacks and Vestry Politics in Two Jamaican Parishes, Kingston and St David, 1831–1865', in *Jamaica in Slavery and Freedom: History, Heritage and Culture*, ed. Kathleen E. A. Monteith and Glen Richards (Mona, Jamaica: University of the West Indies Press, 2002), 307–23.

144. 'Printed Copy of Resolutions Passed at Meeting in St. David's', encl. 3 in Eyre to Cardwell, 12 July 1865, no. 47, in Great Britain, *Parliamentary Papers (House of Commons)*, 1866 (no. 3595), vol. LI, 'Papers relative to the Affairs of Jamaica', 232. The 'Communicating Committee', in addition to Ward and Clarke, also included Edwin Palmer, the JBU minister at Yallahs, and John Willis Menard, another African-American resident in Jamaica, whom I discuss in the epilogue below. It is possible that Ward did indeed visit Governor Eyre with this deputation, led by Samuel Clarke: Ward told the JRC that he 'very much regretted' the deputation's visit, and 'I regretted the sort of interview they had with the Governor, and the remarks men made I thought bad'. 'JRC Minutes of Evidence', 559.

145. 'St. David's Small Settlers', encl. 2 in Eyre to Cardwell, no. 234, 6 August 1864, in CO 884/2/11, 'Reports of a Tour through Jamaica Made by Governor

Eyre, in 1864. Confidential', 18–19, National Archives, Kew. Eyre promised to send 'another copy of the address, with the names attached' in the 'next mail', but I have been unable to locate this item.

146. 'Reply', encl. 2 in Eyre to Cardwell, no. 234, 6 August 1864, in CO 884/2/11, 19, National Archives, Kew.

147. Qtd in Heuman, *'The Killing Time'*, 54–5, emphasis added.

148. Christine Bolt, *The Anti-Slavery Movement and Reconstruction: A Study in Anglo-American Cooperation, 1833–77* (London: Oxford University Press, 1969), esp. chapter 2, 'The Civil War, Jamaica, and the Abolitionists'.

149. On the split within the freedmen's aid movement, see Bolt, *Anti-Slavery Movement and Reconstruction*, 46–53.

150. 'Deputation from Jamaica', *The Freed-Man*, 1 August 1866, 7.

151. Charles Plummer, 'Jamaica', *The Freed-Man*, 1 September 1866, 15, 14.

152. The letter is reprinted in the anonymous pamphlet *Jamaica: Its State and Prospects; with an Exposure of the Proceedings of the Freed-Man's Aid Society, and the Baptist Mission Society* (London: William Macintosh, 1867), 12–13. This pamphlet is a blistering attack on the JCA, on the Baptists, and on the freedmen's aid movement in England. On John Salmon, see below.

153. 'Rev. S. W. Holt', *The Freed-Man*, 1 September 1866, 27.

154. 'Receipts for July & August', *The Freed-Man*, 1 September 1866, 28.

155. 'Rev. S. W. Holt', *The Freed-Man*, 1 September 1866, 27.

156. 'Negro Enterprize in Jamaica', *The Freed-Man*, 1 October 1866; 'The Jamaica Commercial Agency Company, Limited', *Falmouth Post*, 12 October 1866. On William Morgan, see Hall, *Civilising Subjects*, 325–6, 411–18. Morgan had travelled to Jamaica in 1866 with Harvey and Brewin, acting as a 'special correspondent' for BFASS. Catherine Hall mentions Morgan's discovery of 'an association at Black River, established to collect and ship produce'. See Hall, *Civilising Subjects*, 411–12, 416.

157. Hall, *Civilising Subjects*, 416.

158. See, for example, 'The Jamaica Commercial Agency Company, (Limited)', *The Gleaner*, 20 April 1867, for the details of one shipment. In 1869 Benjamin Millard, secretary of the JBU, sent several letters to Frederick Newton, the Jamaica-based financial manager of the JCA, and to Samuel Hole, the official liquidator of the company, attempting in vain to obtain payment for shipments sent to England in October and December 1867 and April 1868. Millard had obviously coordinated shipments from several smallholders: he commented to Newton angrily, 'I felt so disgraced by being mixed up with a transaction which did not reflect any credit that I promised one of the parties something out of my own pocket till I heard how matters stood'. Benjamin Millard to F[rederick] W. Newton, 9 July 1869, in BFASS Papers, E3/1/59, reel 51. See also Millard to Newton, 27 April 1869, BFASS Papers E3/1/26–7, reel 51; Millard to Samuel Hole, 6 May 1869, BFASS Papers, E3/1/31, reel 51.

159. Pledging to keep *The Freed-Man* going in 1867, its editor, John Waddington, printed a letter from Frederick Tomkins, secretary of the London Freedmen's Aid Society, saying that although the magazine was substantially in debt,

'a considerable sum is due from the Jamaica Commercial Agency Company, for advertisements in the F R E E D-M A N, which, I hope, will more than counterbalance [the] deficiencies'. [John Waddington], 'Personal Explanation', *The Freed-Man*, 1 October 1867, 285. The magazine folded after the May 1868 issue.

160. 'The New Movement for Protecting Native Industry', *Falmouth Post*, 6 July 1866.

161. 'The Jamaica Commercial Agency Company, Limited', *Falmouth Post*, 12 October 1866.

162. 'The Jamaica Commercial Trading Company', *Falmouth Post*, 8 December 1868, emphases in original.

163. 'Letter of the Ministers of the Jamaican Baptist Union to His Excellency Edward John Eyre, Esq.', Schedule G, 'Agricultural Occupations, Etc., of the Peasantry Apart from the Estates, Rented Lands, Productions, Exports, Etc.', in Underhill et al., *Dr. Underhill's Letter*, 77, 78, 81, 79.

164. Underhill to East, 30 January 1865, BMS Archives, reel 27, Home Correspondence, vol. 9, 'Correspondence between D. J. East and Underhill, 1852–1895'.

165. Underhill to East, 30 January 1865, BMS Archives, reel 27, Home Correspondence, vol. 9: 'Correspondence between D. J. East and Underhill, 1852–1895'.

166. 'Letter of the Ministers of the JBU to Edward Eyre', in Underhill et al., *Dr. Underhill's Letter*, 80, 81. 'Native' pastors can be identified by looking at the brief biographies in John Clarke's *Memorials of Baptist Missionaries in Jamaica*.

167. 'Letter of the Ministers of the JBU to Edward Eyre', Underhill et al., *Dr. Underhill's Letter*, 78.

168. 'Letter of the Ministers of the JBU to Edward Eyre', Underhill et al., *Dr. Underhill's Letter*, 28.

169. John Salmon to Eyre, 31 October 1865, and 'Attorney-General's Opinion', 2 November 1865, encls. 32 and 33 in Eyre to Cardwell, no. 21, 7 November 1865, in CO 884/2/2, 'Papers relating to the Insurrection in Jamaica. Confidential', 119–21, National Archives, Kew. During martial law in October 1865, Salmon had ordered Plummer's house searched for incriminating documents, but had found nothing. See 'Endowed Schools in Jamaica', *The Freed-Man*, 1 May 1867, 145.

170. *Colonial Standard and Jamaica Despatch*, 16 May 1865, quoted in Curtin, *Two Jamaicas*, 118.

171. 'Rev. S. W. Holt', *The Freed-Man*, 1 September 1866, 27.

172. 'The New Movement for Protecting Native Industry', *Falmouth Post*, 6 July 1866.

173. 'Mr. Holt, the Black Proprietor', *The Gleaner*, 29 June 1866.

174. 'The Jamaica Commercial Agency Company', *The Gleaner*, 5 October 1866; 'The Black Man's Mission to English Capitalists', *The Gleaner*, 4 October 1866.

175. See, for example, 'Jamaica: Why It Is Poor, and How It May Become Rich', a report on one of Oughton's Kingston lectures with this title, *The Gleaner*, 30 June 1866. Oughton's lectures on 'Artificial Wants' were also announced in the 17 April and 24 April numbers of *The Gleaner* in the same year. See [Samuel Oughton], *Jamaica: Why It Is Poor, and How It May Become Rich* (Kingston: M. DeCordova, McDougall & Co., 1866). See Hall, *Civilising Subjects*, 250–1.

176. 'JRC Minutes of Evidence', 1044.

177. 'Mr. Samuel Holt', *The Gleaner* (packet edition), 24 November 1866, emphasis in original.

178. 'JRC Minutes of Evidence', 550.

179. 'JRC Minutes of Evidence', 146. Wilson's husband 'was a clerk in the church and a schoolmaster'.

180. Mimi Sheller, 'Quasheba, Mother, Queen: Black Women's Public Leadership and Political Protest in Post-Emancipation Jamaica, 1834–1865', *Slavery and Abolition* 19 (1998), 90–117, quotations on 112–13.

181. 'Colour fe Colour', *The Gleaner* (packet edition), 24 November 1866. This was a weekend edition of the paper, sent out to England, which reprinted the letter (with some minor spelling variations) that had originally appeared on 16 November under the same heading. Sheller cites a portion of the 16 November version of the letter, and notes the use of the rebellion's slogan as its title, on p. 112 of her article 'Quasheba, Mother, Queen'.

182. '"Parson" Holt', *The Gleaner*, 26 November 1866. For help with the translation of this letter, many thanks to Nadia Ellis and Stephen Russell.

183. '"Parson" Holt', *The Gleaner*, 26 November 1866.

184. 'Colour fe Colour', *The Gleaner*, 24 November 1866; '"Parson" Holt', *The Gleaner*, 26 November 1866.

185. '"Parson" Holt', *The Gleaner*, 26 November 1866. John Clarke, in his brief sketch of Holt, says that 'in early life he was a trainer of race horses'. Clarke, *Sketches of Baptist Missionaries*, 218.

186. Inez Knibb Sibley, *The Baptists of Jamaica* (Kingston: JBU, 1965), 39. Ward, however, has no place in Sibley's history.

187. Ward, *Reflections*, 7.

188. Ward, *Reflections*, 7.

189. Ward, *Reflections*, 5.

190. See, for example, F[red] L[andau], 'Samuel Ringgold Ward', *Dictionary of American Biography*, vol. XIX (New York: Scribner's, 1936), 440; Robin W. Winks, 'Samuel Ringgold Ward', *Dictionary of Canadian Biography*, vol. IX (Toronto: University of Toronto Press, 1976), 820–1.

191. 'Government Notices', *The Gleaner*, 25 May 1867.

192. *Who's Who and What's What, In Which Is Incorporated DeCordova's Almanack and Jamaica Pocket Book for 1869* (Kingston: M. DeCordova, McDougall, [1869]), 115; *Jamaica Gazette*, 6 January 1870.

193. Ward, 'The Modern Negro, no. 1', *Frederick Douglass' Paper*, 23 February 1855, emphasis in original.

4 JAMAICA, GENEALOGY, GEORGE ELIOT: INHERITING THE EMPIRE AFTER MORANT BAY

1. Hall, *Civilising Subjects*. See also Hall, 'Rethinking Imperial Histories: The Reform Act of 1867', *New Left Review* 208 (Nov.–Dec. 1994), 3–29, and Hall, 'The Economy of Intellectual Prestige: Thomas Carlyle, John Stuart Mill, and the Case of Governor Eyre', *Cultural Critique* 12 (1989), 167–96.
2. Workman, 'Thomas Carlyle and the Governor Eyre Controversy', 91–2.
3. Matthew Arnold, *Culture and Anarchy: An Essay in Political and Social Criticism*, in Arnold, *'Culture and Anarchy' and Other Writings*, ed. Stefan Collini (1869; Cambridge: Cambridge University Press, 1993), 180–1.
4. Matthew Arnold, *The Complete Prose Works*, ed. R. H. Super, vol. v (Ann Arbor: University of Michigan Press, 1965), 526.
5. This act of textual suppression was singularly unsuccessful, because J. Dover Wilson restored the excised lines in the edition of *Culture and Anarchy* that has remained the most popular since its publication in 1931.
6. Qtd in Arnold, *Complete Prose Works*, vol. v, 455. Arthur Penrhyn Stanley was Thomas Arnold's biographer. The letter in question does not appear in Stanley's *Life and Correspondence of Thomas Arnold, D.D.*, 2 vols. (London: John Murray, 1887).
7. Robert Young, in his analysis of Matthew Arnold, also hears the trace of rebellion in Jamaica in these lines: 'Though Arnold refused to take sides in the bitter controversy about Governor Eyre's conduct, his comments in *Culture and Anarchy* about the correct way to deal with rioting ("flog the rank and file, and fling the ring-leaders from the Tarpeian Rock!") more or less describes what happened to those in Jamaica after the Morant Bay uprising four years previously.' See Robert J. C. Young, *Colonial Desire: Hybridity in Theory, Culture and Race* (London: Routledge, 1995), 87. The connection between Jamaica and Reform is reinforced by the passage in *Culture and Anarchy* immediately following the deleted lines, in which Arnold declares that 'monster-processions in the streets and forcible irruptions into the parks . . . ought to be unflinchingly forbidden and repressed', even when they are in support of 'undoubtedly precious' causes 'such as the abolition of the slave-trade'. Arnold, *Culture and Anarchy*, 181.
8. Edward Underhill to David East, 13 August 1862, BMS Archives, reel 27, BMS Home Correspondence, vol. 9, 'Correspondence between D. J. East and Underhill, 1852–1895'.
9. The standard account of the Eyre case in England, although it now appears rather dated, is Bernard Semmel, *The Governor Eyre Controversy* (London: MacGibbon & Kee, 1962). The best historiographical work on this intersection of Jamaican and British affairs in the 1860s is the writing of Catherine Hall, as exemplified in her *Civilising Subjects*. Hall also provides a compelling account of Eyre's career in Australia, New Zealand, and the Caribbean. Hall, *Civilising Subjects*, 'Prologue: The Making of an Imperial Man', 23–65.
10. Arnold, *Culture and Anarchy*, 135.

11. Other important recent analyses of the British response to Morant Bay include Ian Baucom, *Out of Place: Englishness, Empire, and the Locations of Identity* (Princeton: Princeton University Press, 1999), 41–7, and Simon Gikandi, *Maps of Englishness: Writing Identity in the Culture of Colonialism* (New York: Columbia University Press, 1996), 51–6.

12. Qtd in Semmel, *Governor Eyre Controversy*, 13.

13. The committee was later renamed the Eyre Defence and Aid Fund. Although accounts often assume that Carlyle was the driving force behind the group, in fact he left much of the day-to-day running of affairs to others, especially Ruskin and Hamilton Hume, Eyre's first biographer. See Workman, 'Thomas Carlyle and the Governor Eyre Controversy', and Hall, 'The Economy of Intellectual Prestige'. Dickens wrote in a letter on 13 November 1865, 'The Jamaica insurrection is another hopeful piece of business. That platform sympathy with the black, or the native, or the devil – afar off, and that platform indifference to our own countrymen at enormous odds in the midst of bloodshed and savagery, makes me stark wild'. Qtd in George H. Ford, 'The Governor Eyre Case in England', *University of Toronto Quarterly* 18.3 (1948), 219–33, quotation on 228.

14. On Mill's involvement see Hall, 'Economy of Intellectual Prestige', and Semmel, *Governor Eyre Controversy*.

15. On connections between working-class and black emancipation, see Catherine Gallagher, *The Industrial Reformation of English Fiction: Social Discourse and Narrative Form, 1832–1867* (Chicago: University of Chicago Press, 1985), 3–35. On abolitionism in Europe, see Robin Blackburn, *The Overthrow of Colonial Slavery, 1776–1848* (London: Verso, 1988).

16. Gillian Beer, *Darwin's Plots: Evolutionary Narrative in Darwin, George Eliot and Nineteenth-Century Fiction* (London: Ark-Routledge, 1985), 3.

17. George W. Stocking, Jr, *Victorian Anthropology* (New York: Free Press, 1987), 142.

18. James Hunt, 'Introductory Address on the Study of Anthropology', *Anthropological Review* 1 (1863), 1–20, quotation on 2.

19. Hunt, 'Introductory Address', 3.

20. Hunt, 'Introductory Address', 3, note.

21. Good historical accounts of the Anthropological Society of London can be found in George W. Stocking, Jr, 'What's in a Name? The Origins of the Royal Anthropological Institute (1837–71)', *Man* 6 (1971), 369–90; Ronald Rainger, 'Race, Politics, and Science: The Anthropological Society of London in the 1860s', *Victorian Studies* 22 (1978), 51–70; and Young, *Colonial Desire*.

22. Qtd in Douglas A. Lorimer, *Colour, Class and the Victorians: English Attitudes to the Negro in the Mid-Nineteenth Century* (Leicester: Leicester University Press, 1978), 198–9.

23. James Hunt, 'Presidential Address', *Journal of the Anthropological Society* 4 (1866), lix–lxxxi, quotation on lxxviii.

24. Robert Young develops a similar argument in his analysis of Gobineau, whose *Essay on the Inequality of Human Races* (1853–5) was just becoming known to

English audiences at this time. Gobineau's book, Young suggests, 'rests on a clever fusion of the implications of the older and newer uses of the word "race": the traditional meaning involves bloodlines, the "lineage" of an ancient family, with an aristocratic pedigree like a thoroughbred horse. The line of such a family is distinguished by its breeding, by the blood that flows through its veins through the act of procreation from father to son. Gobineau adapts this aristocratic notion of race as ancient stock to the modern notion, derived from linguistic families, of families of races, and assumes that however large they too are distinguished by their "breeding", by a particular blood that flows through their veins, passed on through the act of reproduction from generation to generation'. Young, *Colonial Desire*, 105.

25. Qtd in Christine Bolt, *Victorian Attitudes to Race* (London: Routledge; Toronto: University of Toronto Press, 1971), 77.

26. Qtd in Bolt, *Victorian Attitudes to Race*, 87.

27. One of the consequences of the Jamaica rebellion was the abolition of the Jamaican House of Assembly and the imposition of direct rule from London (Jamaica became a Crown Colony after 1866), thus ending even the pretence of self-government in the British West Indies.

28. 'The old pre-emancipation claim that the Jamaican worker would not follow his own economic interest – would not behave like the "economic man" – was brought out again. It was held that the Jamaican had such limited desires, that he would work only for a bare subsistence. When he had earned it he would stop. If this was generally true, it would reverse the traditional supply curve for labor – the higher the wages, the less labor would be offered.' Curtin, *Two Jamaicas*, 142.

29. On the response to the Civil War in Britain, see R. J. M. Blackett, *Divided Hearts: Britain and the American Civil War* (Baton Rouge: Louisiana State University Press, 2001), and Bolt, *The Anti-Slavery Movement and Reconstruction*.

30. Qtd in Heuman, 'The Killing Time', 54.

31. Qtd in Lorimer, *Colour, Class and the Victorians*, 191.

32. George Eliot, *Daniel Deronda* (1876; Harmondsworth: Penguin, 1986), 376.

33. Space precludes a detailed reading of *Daniel Deronda* here, although it should be noted that this reported conversation carries the weight of wider debates in the novel: for instance, we could trace the connection between Deronda's identification with the downtrodden Calibans of the world and his eventual discovery that he is Jewish and racially 'pure'. For a good reading of the novel, see Gillian Beer's analysis in her *George Eliot* (Brighton: Harvester, 1986).

34. Qtd in Young, *Colonial Desire*, 17.

35. Matthew Arnold, *On the Study of Celtic Literature and Other Essays* (London: Dent; New York: Dutton, 1910), 132.

36. Anthony Trollope, *The West Indies and the Spanish Main*, 2nd edn (London: Chapman & Hall, 1860), 74–5, 84. Young cites the second and third of these paragraphs: see Young, *Colonial Desire*, 142.

37. Trollope, *West Indies and the Spanish Main*, 56.

38. Paul Broca, *On the Phenomena of Hybridity in the Genus Homo*, ed. [and trans.?] C. Carter Blake (London: Longman, Green, 1864), 28–39.
39. James Hunt, *On the Negro's Place in Nature* (London: Trübner, 1863), 24–5.
40. Hunt, *On the Negro's Place*, 33.
41. On the importance of fertility in discussions of racial 'crossing', see Young, *Colonial Desire*, 6–16, and chapter 4, 'Sex and Inequality', 90–117.
42. These figures on political representation in the Assembly are taken from Holt, *Problem of Freedom*, 226–7, table 7.1.
43. On Gordon's arrest and execution, see Heuman, '*The Killing Time*', 146–51.
44. For a powerful analysis of the ways in which this debate turned on competing versions of middle-class masculinity, see Hall, 'Economy of Intellectual Prestige'. The real leader of the rebellion, Paul Bogle (who was a kind of political agent for Gordon in the district around Morant Bay), remained all but invisible in contemporary accounts of the uprising and its suppression. The status of Morant Bay as a founding event in the nationalist history of Jamaica has ensured that Bogle's role is now more fully acknowledged: see especially Heuman, '*The Killing Time*'.
45. Baptist Wriothesley Noel, *The Case of George William Gordon, Esq. of Jamaica* (London: James Nisbet, 1866), 8–9.
46. Noel, *Case of George William Gordon*, 7–8.
47. Qtd in David King, *A Sketch of the Late Mr. G. W. Gordon, Jamaica* (Edinburgh: William Oliphant, 1866), 8.
48. Qtd in Noel, *Case of George William Gordon*, 4.
49. Qtd in Noel, *Case of George William Gordon*, 6.
50. Qtd in Noel, *Case of George William Gordon*, 3–4.
51. 'JRC Papers', 245.
52. 'JRC Papers', 174.
53. 'Minutes of the Meeting of January 16, 1866', *Journal of the Anthropological Society* 4 (1866), lxxxii–lxxxix, quotation on lxxxii.
54. George W. Marshall, 'Remarks on Genealogy in Connexion with Anthropology', in *Memoirs Read before the Anthropological Society of London, 1865–6* (London: Trübner, 1866), 68–73, quotation on 68.
55. Marshall, 'Remarks on Genealogy', 69.
56. 'Minutes of the Meeting', lxxxviii.
57. 'Minutes of the Meeting', lxxxviii.
58. 'Minutes of the Meeting', lxxxix.
59. The meeting was held at St James's Hall on 1 February 1866. Pim's paper was later published in the ASL's short-lived *Popular Magazine of Anthropology* and as a separate pamphlet, *The Negro and Jamaica*. Pim, a major landowner in the Caribbean and Central America, in amongst his scientific analysis of the unchanging degraded character of 'the negro' since antiquity, found space to make a connection to the Reform debates: 'I make bold to say that 50 million of blacks have not been placed on this magnificent globe of ours for no purpose; it is therefore our duty, by wise legislation, to utilize this large mass of human beings. They must be dealt with from no sentimental standpoint, but from a

knowledge of their nature and characteristics, discarding at once the theory of equality. We do not admit equality even amongst our own race, as is proved by the state of the franchise at this hour in England! and to suppose that two alien races can compose a political unity is simply ridiculous.' Bedford Pim, *The Negro and Jamaica. Read before the Anthropological Society of London, February 1, 1866* (London: Trübner, 1866), 35.

60. Charles Darwin, *On the Origin of Species by Means of Natural Selection, or The Preservation of Favoured Races in the Struggle for Life*, ed. J. W. Burrow (1859; Harmondsworth: Penguin, 1968), 399.

61. Darwin, *Origin of Species*, 404.

62. Beer, *Darwin's Plots*, 62.

63. Darwin, *Origin of Species*, 413; qtd in Beer, *Darwin's Plots*, 63.

64. Beer, *Darwin's Plots*, 63.

65. Beer, *Darwin's Plots*, 9.

66. See Gillian Beer, *Forging the Missing Link: Interdisciplinary Stories* (Cambridge: Cambridge University Press, 1991).

67. Beer, *George Eliot*, 116–17.

68. Raymond Williams, *The Country and the City* (New York: Oxford University Press, 1973), 174.

69. Williams, *Country and the City*, 175.

70. Gallagher, *Industrial Reformation of English Fiction*, 262.

71. Gillian Beer also makes the comparison between *Felix Holt* and *Sybil*. Beer, *George Eliot*, 141.

72. George Eliot, *Felix Holt, the Radical* (1866; Harmondsworth: Penguin, 1987), 378. Hereafter abbreviated as FH, with page numbers cited parenthetically in the text.

73. The correspondence between the two is conveniently collected in George Eliot, *Selected Essays, Poems and Other Writings*, ed. A. S. Byatt and Nicholas Warren (Harmondsworth: Penguin, 1990). It was Harrison whose response to Matthew Arnold's 'Culture and Its Enemies' so provoked Arnold that he took the writer to task in the next of the essays that eventually became *Culture and Anarchy*. See Frederic Harrison, 'Culture: A Dialogue', in Harrison, *'The Choice of Books' and Other Literary Pieces* (London: Macmillan, 1886), and Arnold, *Culture and Anarchy*, 55–7, 78.

74. This series of pamphlets was published by the Jamaica Committee in an attempt to influence public opinion in Britain over Morant Bay.

75. Gordon S. Haight (ed.), *The George Eliot Letters*, 9 vols. (New Haven: Yale University Press, 1954–78), IV:343. The prosecution Harrison was referring to was the private case brought by the Jamaica Committee against Col. Alexander Nelson and Lt. Herbert Brand, the presiding officers at George William Gordon's trial, on charges of wilful murder. Although the lord chief justice, Sir Alexander Cockburn, delivered a famous address to the grand jury virtually instructing them to proceed with the trial, the grand jury refused to indict Nelson and Brand. In 1866, the Committee began the first of its two unsuccessful attempts to secure a conviction of Edward Eyre, the first time

on murder charges, the second time for 'high crimes and misdemeanours' (see Semmel, *The Governor Eyre Controversy*, 142–70). The Jamaica Committee's lead attorney was Sir James Fitzjames Stephen, son of James Stephen, the abolitionist and Colonial Office civil servant whom I discuss in chapter 1.

76. Characteristically, this information is conveyed through an unnamed, minor character. Bruce Robbins's book *The Servant's Hand*, which analyses the centrality of these apparently marginal figures in English fiction, contains a good reading of *Felix Holt*: 'Throughout the novel, the news that "property doesn't always get into the right hands", as the coachman of the introduction puts it, is specifically and almost obsessively placed in the hands of propertyless servants.' Bruce Robbins, *The Servant's Hand: English Fiction from Below* (Durham, N.C.: Duke University Press, 1993), 211.

77. 'He [Felix] is the embodiment of the best self, the self absolutely unconditioned by mere social facts. In short, he is Arnold's "alien", and hence there is not, nor can there be, any social explanation for his development, for any such explanation would make the best self the mere product of the very conditions that shape and constrain the ordinary self.' Catherine Gallagher, 'The Politics of Culture and the Debate over Representation', *Representations* 5 (1984), 115–47, quotation on 128.

78. The distinction between 'filiation' and 'affiliation' comes from Edward Said's essay 'Secular Criticism', and his periodisation of the shift from one mode to the other – associated with Matthew Arnold, among others – is compatible with the argument I make here. See Edward W. Said, 'Introduction: Secular Criticism', in Said, *The World, the Text, and the Critic* (Cambridge, Mass.: Harvard University Press, 1983), 1–30.

79. Of course, this does not prevent Mrs Transome herself clinging to the very notion of breeding that the novel in general, and her own life in particular, renders obsolete: 'Poor Mrs Transome, with her secret bitterness and dread, still found a flavour in this sort of pride [of family and blood]; none the less because certain deeds of her own life had been in fatal inconsistency with it. Besides, genealogies entered into her stock of ideas, and her talk on such subjects was as necessary as the notes of the linnet or the blackbird. She had no ultimate analysis of things that went beyond blood and family – the Herons of Fenshore or the Badgers of Hillbury' (FH 494).

80. Gillian Beer comments: 'The book opens with the suppression of a woman's [Mrs Transome's] independence, a suppression which has been previously put at her [George Eliot's] works' conclusion, and therefore out of reach of question.' Beer, *George Eliot*, 136.

81. Interestingly, Esther and Harry (the two heirs to Transome Court) have a spontaneous attraction to each other: 'Between her and little Harry there was an extraordinary fascination' (FH 491).

82. For an excellent analysis of *Jane Eyre*, however, that emphasises the role of American, rather than Caribbean, slavery in the novel, see Julia Sun–Joo Lee, 'The (Slave) Narrative of Jane Eyre', *Victorian Literature and Culture*, forthcoming.

83. Richard Koebner and Helmut Dan Schmidt, *Imperialism: The Story and Significance of a Political Word, 1840–1960* (Cambridge: Cambridge University Press, 1964), 45.
84. Koebner and Schmidt, *Imperialism*, 37.
85. Workman, 'Thomas Carlyle and the Governor Eyre Controversy', 91–2, emphases in original.
86. Workman, 'Thomas Carlyle and the Governor Eyre Controversy', 92.
87. Thomas Carlyle, *Shooting Niagara: And After?* (London: Chapman and Hall, 1867), 14.
88. Carlyle, *Shooting Niagara*, 19.
89. Carlyle, *Shooting Niagara*, 18–19, emphasis in original.
90. Joseph Howe, *The Organization of the Empire* (London: Edward Stanford, 1866), 4.
91. Frederic Harrison, *Martial Law: Six Letters to 'The Daily News'* (London: Jamaica Committee, 1867), 3.
92. Harrison, *Martial Law*, 4.
93. Qtd in Bolt, *Victorian Attitudes to Race*, 84, emphasis in original.
94. Harrison, *Martial Law*, 4.
95. Goldwin Smith, *The Empire: A Series of Letters Published in 'The Daily News'* (Oxford: Parker, 1863), viii.
96. Koebner and Schmidt, *Imperialism*, 32.
97. Charles Savile Roundell, *England and her Subject Races, with Special Reference to Jamaica* (London: Macmillan, 1866), 31, 32.
98. Roundell, *England and her Subject Races*, 32–3.

EPILOGUE: 'AND THE SWORD WILL COME FROM AMERICA'

1. *Falmouth Post*, 16 June 1865, qtd in Monica Schuler, *'Alas, Alas, Kongo': A Social History of Indentured African Immigration into Jamaica, 1841–1865* (Baltimore: Johns Hopkins University Press, 1980), 105. The placard was also quoted, with one or two minor differences, in the evidence of Joseph Williams, advocate-general of Jamaica, during the JRC hearings: 'JRC Minutes of Evidence', 849. See also Heuman, *'The Killing Time'*, 86–7, and Robert J. Stewart, *Religion and Society in Post-Emancipation Jamaica* (Knoxville: University of Tennessee Press, 1992), 121–2.
2. Deborah A. Thomas, 'Modern Blackness: "What We Are and What We Hope to Be"', *Small Axe* 12 (2002), 25–48, quotation on 34.
3. *Falmouth Post*, 24 May 1859, qtd in Hutton, '"Colour for Colour; Skin for Skin"', 64.
4. See, for example, 'New Hints for Emigration to Jamaica', *Falmouth Post*, 1 October 1867, and 'Immigration from the Southern States of America', *The Gleaner*, 24 July 1867.
5. See, for example, [Alexander Barclay], *Remarks on Emigration to Jamaica: Addressed to the Coloured Class of the United States* (New York: James Van

Norden, 1840). Barclay was the New York-based 'Commissioner of Emigration for Jamaica', and his pamphlet described the benefits of migration for free blacks, although he felt the need to warn his potential audience that 'idle, improvident, and intemperate habits will lead to destitution in Jamaica as well as elsewhere'. [Barclay], *Remarks on Emigration*, 16. In the same period immediately after emancipation, William Wemyss Anderson also hoped for American emigration to Jamaica, although he appealed to white businessmen and agriculturalists to settle there. See William Wemyss Anderson, *Jamaica and the Americans* (New York: Stanford and Swords, 1851). On indentured Africans in Jamaica, see Schuler, *'Alas, Alas, Kongo'*.

6. Barkly to Newcastle, 9 February 1854, no. 19, CO 137/322, National Archives, Kew.

7. Eyre to Newcastle, 5 July 1862 and 1 January 1863, 'Despatches from the Governor of Jamaica', in 'Correspondence respecting the Emigration of Free Negroes from the United States to the West Indies. Confidential', CO 884/2/15, National Archives, Kew.

8. 'The Annual Report of the Jamaica Baptist Union for the Year Ending Dec. 31, 1862', handwritten copy, in BMS Archives, reel 18, Western Committee, 1850–1914: vol. 2, 'West Indies and Africa Sub-Committee Report Book, Sept. 1850–July 1866'.

9. *Falmouth Post*, 4 May 1858, quoted in Burke, *Samuel Ringgold Ward*, 59.

10. Ward signed his letter to the St David meeting 'Your adopted countryman, / Samuel Ringgold Ward'. Ward, 'To the Inhabitants of St David', 231.

11. *Falmouth Post*, 4 May 1858, quoted in Burke, *Samuel Ringgold Ward*, 59.

12. Larry Eugene Rivers and Canter Brown, Jr, 'John Willis Menard and *Lays in Summer Lands*', in John Willis Menard, *Lays in Summer Lands*, ed. Rivers, Richard Mathews, and Brown (Tampa, Fla.: University of Tampa Press, 2002), 104, and Richard Mathews, 'The Poetry of J. Willis Menard: Rediscovering an American Voice and Vision', in Menard, *Lays in Summer Lands*, 127–8.

13. G. L. C., letter to the editor, *Christian Recorder*, 26 September 1863.

14. 'Uncle Sam', letter to the editor, *Christian Recorder*, 25 April 1863.

15. H. J. Kemble to N. R. Myers, 2 November 1865, extract, encl. 1 in John Peter Grant to Duke of Buckingham, 23 May 1867, no. 97, CO 137/424, National Archives, Kew.

16. Some of these details of Menard's post-Jamaica life are taken from Rivers and Brown, 'John Willis Menard', Mathews, 'Poetry of J. Willis Menard', and Edith Menard, 'John Willis Menard: First Negro Elected to Congress', *Negro History Bulletin* 28 (1964), 53–4.

17. Heuman, *'The Killing Time'*, 157–8; Hutton, '"Colour for Colour; Skin for Skin"', 202–14. In what follows, I am much indebted to the work of Hutton in uncovering Menard's Jamaican writings and placing them in the political milieu of pre-Morant Bay Jamaica.

18. See, for example, his poems 'Liberia', *Christian Recorder*, 7 March 1863, and 'To E. M. T., of Jamaica', 'Stanzas on Cuba', 'Just over the Sea', 'To My Wife', and 'Free Cuba', in *Lays in Summer Lands*, 7, 9, 10, 20–1, and 49.

19. 'Mr. J. W. Menard', *Morning Journal*, reprinted in *Falmouth Post*, 17 November 1868.
20. *Falmouth Post*, 17 November 1868, emphasis in original. On Menard's writing for the *Morning Journal*, see Thomas Oughton to Aaron Gregg, 3 February 1866, encl. in Gregg to William Seward, 1 March 1866, no. 18, Despatches from US Consuls in Kingston, reel 22.
21. Evidence of Samuel R. Ward, 'JRC Minutes of Evidence', 556.
22. 'Printed Copy of Resolutions Passed at Meeting in St. David's', in *Parliamentary Papers*, 1866 (no. 3595), vol. LI, 230–2.
23. 'JRC Minutes of Evidence', appendix IV, 'Official Proceedings of Courts-Martial in the Cases of William Grant, George McIntosh, [and] Samuel Clarke', 1149. See also evidence of W. P. Georges, 'JRC Minutes of Evidence', 892 (question 41,797).
24. See Hutton, '"Colour for Colour; Skin for Skin"', 215. See also, 'J. W. Menard', *The Gleaner*, 28 October 1865: 'A person of this name was yesterday captured, and taken to Up-Park Camp for safe custody.'
25. 'Statement of Civil Prisoners Confined at Up-Park Camp, Jamaica, from October 14, to October 28, 1865', encl. 7, and Eyre to Major-General O'Connor, 3 November 1865, encl. 16, both in Eyre to Cardwell, 8 November 1865, no. 24, CO 884/2/2, 'Papers relating to the Insurrection in Jamaica. Confidential', 150–2, 155, National Archives, Kew. See also 'JRC Papers', 303.
26. Minute of the Executive Committee, 2 November 1865, encl. 2 in Grant to Buckingham, 23 May 1867, no. 97, CO 137/424, National Archives, Kew.
27. Aaron Gregg to William Seward, 1 March 1866, no. 18, in Despatches from US Consuls in Kingston, reel 22. See also Gregg to Seward, 6 December 1865, no. 9, Despatches of US Consuls in Kingston, reel 22.
28. Kemble to N. R. Myers, 2 November 1865, encl. 1 in Grant to Buckingham, 23 May 1867, no. 97, CO 137/424, National Archives, Kew.
29. Oughton to Gregg, 3 February 1866, encl. in Gregg to Seward, 1 March 1866, Despatches of US Consuls in Kingston, reel 22. See also 'JRC Papers', 36.
30. *The Sentinel*, 25 February 1865, qtd in Hutton, '"Colour for Colour; Skin for Skin"', 96. Hutton suggests that 'Wilson' was a pen-name of Clarke's: see Hutton, '"Colour for Colour"', 96, note 161.
31. Ward, *Reflections*, 8. (Despite Menard's identification with blacks, and his call for black separatism, he would have been classed as 'coloured' in Jamaica.) On education, see also Ward's testimony to the JRC in 'JRC Minutes of Evidence', 555, 557, 558, and his letter 'To the Inhabitants of St David', 231: 'You have some important duties to perform as free men. Among them is the education of your children, and the training of yourselves to an improved moral status.'
32. *The Sentinel*, 16 January and 30 January 1865, quoted in Hutton, '"Colour for Colour; Skin for Skin"', 205, 206.
33. *The Sentinel*, 30 January 1865, quoted in Hutton, '"Colour for Colour; Skin for Skin"', 208.
34. The importance of internationalist strains of thought in Jamaican nationalism is compellingly explored in Anthony Bogues, 'Nationalism and Jamaican

Political Thought', in *Jamaica in Slavery and Freedom: History, Heritage and Culture*, ed. Kathleen E. A. Monteith and Glen Richards (Mona, Jamaica: University of the West Indies Press, 2002), 363–87.

35. Ward, *Reflections*, 8; Menard, *The Sentinel*, 30 January 1865, qtd in Hutton, "'Colour for Colour; Skin for Skin'", 210.

36. Menard, *The Sentinel*, 20 January 1865, quoted in Hutton, "'Colour for Colour; Skin for Skin'", 210; Ward, 'To the Inhabitants of St David', 231.

37. Evidence of George Lake, 'JRC Minutes of Evidence', 1036. The inclusion of Gordon in this statement must be treated sceptically, since there is no evidence that Gordon knew about the rebellion in advance, despite Lake's report that Bogle had said that 'Mr. George William Gordon was at the back' of the rebellion. 'JRC Minutes of Evidence', 1036.

38. 'Arrival of the Tennessee', *The Gleaner*, 13 March 1871.

39. Douglass, *Life and Times*, 401.

40. Qtd in Benjamin Quarles, *Frederick Douglass* (1948; New York: Da Capo Press, 1997), 256. Towards the end of his life, of course, Douglass was to become the US minister and consul-general in Haiti (1889–91), and he developed a much more sympathetic and complex analysis of Haitian and Caribbean culture at that time.

41. 'Santo Domingo, No. 8', *New National Era*, 15 June 1871.

42. *The Gleaner*, 13 March 1871.

43. See Frederick Douglass, 'What to the Slave is the Fourth of July?' (1852), in *The Oxford Frederick Douglass Reader*, ed. William L. Andrews (New York: Oxford University Press, 1996), 108–30, and Douglass, 'Speech on West Indies Emancipation' (1880), appendix II, in Douglass, *Life and Times*, 491–504.

44. *The Gleaner*, 14 March 1871.

45. Douglass, *Life and Times*, 266.

46. Douglass, *Life and Times*, 266. Carter Woodson cites Douglass, unfortunately with no bibliographical details, praising Ward, and mourning his early death 'in the midst of his years'. Carter G. Woodson, *The History of the Negro Church* (Washington, DC: Associated Publishers, 1921), 183.

47. 'Santo Domingo, No. 8', *New National Era*, 15 June 1871.

48. 'Santo Domingo, No. 8', *New National Era*, 15 June 1871.

49. *The Gleaner*, 13 March 1871.

50. *The Gleaner*, 15 March 1871.

51. 'Representation for the Colonies', *Falmouth Post*, 5 October 1869.

52. Chakrabarty, *Provincializing Europe*, 109.

Bibliography

ARCHIVAL SOURCES

National Archives, Kew, England

CO 137, 'Original Correspondence of Jamaica Governors'.
CO 884/2/2, 'Papers relating to the Insurrection in Jamaica. Confidential'.
CO 884/2/11, 'Reports of a Tour through Jamaica Made by Governor Eyre, in 1864. Confidential'.
CO 884/2/15, 'Correspondence respecting the Emigration of Free Negroes from the United States to the West Indies. Confidential'.

Institute of Commonwealth Studies, London

Simon Taylor Papers.

ARCHIVAL MATERIAL CONSULTED ON MICROFILM

Baptist Missionary Society, London. Archives, 1792–1900.
    reel 18, Western Committee, 1850–1914
        vol. 2, 'West Indies and Africa Sub-Committee Report Book, Sep. 1850–July 1866'
        vol. 2a, 'Africa and West Indies Sub-Committee, June 1861–Feb. 1872'
    reel 27, BMS Home Correspondence
        vol. 9, 'Correspondence between Rev. D. J. East and Underhill, 1852–1895'
Cambridge University Library/Institute of Commonwealth Studies. *Plantation Life in the Caribbean: Part One: Jamaica, c. 1765–1848: The Taylor and Vanneck-Arcedeckne Papers from Cambridge University Library and the Institute of Commonwealth Studies, University of London.* Marlborough, Wilts.: Adam Matthew, 2005.
Lambeth Palace Library. Fulham Papers, American Colonial Section.
Lambeth Palace Library. Papers of the Christian Faith Society.
Rhodes House Library, Oxford. Papers of the British and Foreign Anti-Slavery Society. *The Rhodes House Library, Oxford, Anti-Slavery Collection, 1795–1880.*
United States Department of State. Despatches from United States Consuls in Kingston, Jamaica, 1796–1906.

West India Committee. Minutes. Consulted at the Institute of Commonwealth Studies, London.

OFFICIAL PUBLICATIONS

GREAT BRITAIN

Parliamentary Papers (House of Commons), 1824 (no. 333), vol. XXIII, 'Demerara. Further Papers. Copies or Extracts of Correspondence with the Governors of Colonies in the West Indies, respecting Insurrection of Slaves; for the 1st of January 1822 to the Present Time; with Minutes of Trials'.

Parliamentary Papers (House of Commons), 1866 (no. 3682), vol. XXX, 'Jamaica: Papers Laid before the Royal Commission of Inquiry by Governor Eyre'.

Parliamentary Papers (House of Commons), 1866 (no. 3683), vol. XXX, 'Report of the Jamaica Royal Commission (1866)'.

Parliamentary Papers (House of Commons), 1866 (no. 3683-1), vol. XXXI, 'Report of the Jamaica Royal Commission (1866), Part II, Minutes of Evidence and Appendix'.

Parliamentary Papers (House of Commons), 1866 (no. 3595), vol. LI, 'Papers relative to the Affairs of Jamaica'.

JAMAICA

The New Jamaica Almanac and Register for the Year of Our Lord 1811. Kingston: Smith and Kinnear, 1811.

The New Jamaica Almanac and Register for the Year of Our Lord 1812. Kingston: Smith and Kinnear, 1812.

The Jamaica Almanac for the Year 1816. Kingston: Alexander Aikman, [1816].

The Jamaica Almanack for the Year 1819. Kingston: Alexander Aikman, 1819.

The Jamaica Almanack for the Year 1820. Kingston: Alexander Aikman, 1820.

The Jamaica Almanack for the Year 1822. Kingston: Alexander Aikman, 1822.

The Jamaica Almanack for the Year 1823. Kingston: Alexander Aikman, [1823].

The Jamaica Almanack for the Year 1827. Kingston: Alexander Aikman, [1827].

Addresses to his Excellency Edward John Eyre, Esquire, &c, &c., 1865, 1866. [Kingston]: M. DeCordova, 1866.

Who's Who and What's What, In Which Is Incorporated DeCordova's Almanack and Jamaica Pocket Book for 1869. Kingston: M. DeCordova, McDougall, [1869].

NEWSPAPERS AND MAGAZINES

JAMAICA

Falmouth Post
The Gleaner
Jamaica Gazette

GREAT BRITAIN

Anti-Slavery Monthly Reporter
Anti-Slavery Reporter
Baptist Magazine
British Banner
Evangelical Magazine
The Freed-Man
Illustrated London News

UNITED STATES

Christian Recorder
Franklin Visitor
Frederick Douglass' Paper
Impartial Citizen
New National Era

CANADA

Provincial Freeman

UNPUBLISHED DISSERTATIONS

Cassidy, Cheryl Marguerite. 'Islands and Empire: A Rhetorical Analysis of the Governor Eyre Controversy 1865–1867'. Ph.D. dissertation, University of Michigan, 1988.

Hutton, Clinton Alexander. '"Colour for Colour; Skin for Skin": The Ideological Foundations of Post-Slavery Society, 1838–1865: The Jamaican Case'. Ph.D. dissertation, University of the West Indies, Mona, Jamaica, 1992.

Murray, Alexander Lovell. 'Canada and the Anglo-American Anti-Slavery Movement: A Study in International Philanthropy'. Ph.D. dissertation, University of Pennsylvania, 1960.

BOOKS AND ARTICLES

'Account of an Ascent to the Summit of the Blue Mountains of Jamaica'. *Blackwood's Edinburgh Magazine* 4 (1818–19), 654–6.

Altink, Henrice. 'Deviant and Dangerous: Pro-Slavery Representations of Jamaican Slave Women's Sexuality, c. 1780–1834'. *Slavery and Abolition* 26.2 (2005), 271–88.

Anderson, William Wemyss. *Jamaica and the Americans*. New York: Stanford and Swords, 1851.

Aravamudan, Srinivas. 'Introduction'. In *Obi; or, The History of Three-Fingered Jack*. By William Earle. Ed. Aravamudan. Peterborough, Ont.: Broadview, 2005.

Tropicopolitans: Colonialism and Agency, 1688–1804. Durham, N.C.: Duke University Press, 1999.

Arnold, Matthew. *The Complete Prose Works.* Ed. R. H. Super. Vol. v. Ann Arbor: University of Michigan Press, 1965.

Culture and Anarchy: An Essay in Political and Social Criticism. In Arnold, *'Culture and Anarchy' and Other Writings.* Ed. Stefan Collini. Cambridge: Cambridge University Press, (1869) 1993.

On the Study of Celtic Literature and Other Essays. London: Dent; New York: Dutton, (1867) 1910.

An Authentic Copy of the Minutes of Evidence of the Trial of John Smith, a Missionary, in Demerara; Held at the Colony House, in George Town, Demerara, on Monday the 13th Day of October, 1823, and 27 Following Days; on a Charge of Exciting the Negroes to Rebellion; Copied Verbatim, From a Report as Ordered to be Printed, by the House of Commons, 22d of March, 1824. With an Appendix, including the Affidavit of Mrs. Jane Smith, the Petition Presented to the House of Commons, from the Directors of the London Missionary Society, Letters of Mr. John Smith, and Other Interesting Documents. London: Samuel Burton, 1824.

Bakan, Abigail B. *Ideology and Class Conflict in Jamaica: The Politics of Rebellion.* Montreal: McGill-Queen's University Press, 1990.

Bancroft, E[dward] N. 'An Account of the Tree which Produces the Hog-Gum of Jamaica, Read before the Jamaican Society for the Encouragement of Agriculture and Horticulture, on the 18th February, 1829'. *Journal of Botany* n.s. 4 (1842), 136–47.

Barclay, Alexander. *A Practical View of the Present State of Slavery in the West Indies.* London: Smith, Elder, 1826.

[Barclay, Alexander]. *Remarks on Emigration to Jamaica: Addressed to the Coloured Class of the United States.* New York: James Van Norden, 1840.

Baucom, Ian. *Out of Place: Englishness, Empire, and the Locations of Identity.* Princeton: Princeton University Press, 1999.

Specters of the Atlantic: Finance Capital, Slavery, and the Philosophy of History. Durham, N.C.: Duke University Press, 2005.

Bayoumi, Moustafa. 'Moving Beliefs: The Panama Manuscript of Sheikh Sana See and African Diasporic Islam'. *Interventions* 5.1 (2003), 58–81.

Beer, Gillian. *Darwin's Plots: Evolutionary Narrative in Darwin, George Eliot and Nineteenth-Century Fiction.* London: Ark-Routledge, 1985.

Forging the Missing Link: Interdisciplinary Stories. Cambridge: Cambridge University Press, 1991.

George Eliot. Brighton: Harvester, 1986.

Blackburn, Robin. *The Overthrow of Colonial Slavery, 1776–1848.* London: Verso, 1988.

Blackett, R. J. M. *Building an Antislavery Wall: Black Americans in the Atlantic Abolitionist Movement, 1830–1860.* Baton Rouge: Louisiana State University Press, 1983.

Divided Hearts: Britain and the American Civil War. Baton Rouge: Louisiana State University Press, 2001.

Bogues, Anthony. 'Nationalism and Jamaican Political Thought'. In *Jamaica in Slavery and Freedom: History, Heritage and Culture*. Ed. Kathleen E. A. Monteith and Glen Richards. Mona, Jamaica: University of the West Indies Press, 2002, 363–87.

Bohls, Elizabeth. 'The Gentleman Planter and the Metropole: Edward Long's *History of Jamaica* (1774)'. In *The Country and the City Revisited: England and the Politics of Culture, 1550–1850*. Ed. Gerald MacLean, Donna Landry, and Joseph Ward. Cambridge: Cambridge University Press, 1999, 180–96.

Bolt, Christine. *The Anti-Slavery Movement and Reconstruction: A Study in Anglo-American Cooperation, 1833–77*. London: Oxford University Press, 1969.

  Victorian Attitudes to Race. London: Routledge; Toronto: University of Toronto Press, 1971.

Bosman, William. *A New and Accurate Description of the Coast of Guinea, Divided into The Gold, The Slave, and The Ivory Coasts*. Ed. John Ralph Willis et al. New York: Barnes and Noble, (1705) 1967.

Brathwaite, Edward [Kamau]. 'Creative Literature of the British West Indies during the Period of Slavery'. *Savacou* 1 (1970), 46–73.

  The Development of Creole Society in Jamaica, 1770–1820. Oxford: Clarendon, 1971.

Brereton, Bridget. *Law, Justice, and Empire: The Colonial Career of John Gorrie, 1829–1892*. Mona, Jamaica: University of the West Indies Press, 1997.

Bridges, George Wilson. *A Voice from Jamaica; in Reply to William Wilberforce, Esq. M.P.* London: Longman, Hurst, Rees, Orme, Brown, and Green, 1823.

Broca, Paul. *On the Phenomena of Hybridity in the Genus Homo*. Ed. [and trans.?] C. Carter Blake. London: Longman, Green, 1864.

Brown, Christopher L. 'Empire without Slaves: British Concepts of Emancipation in the Age of the American Revolution'. *William and Mary Quarterly* 3rd series 56.2 (1999), 273–306.

Bryant, Joshua. *Account of an Insurrection of the Negro Slaves in the Colony of Demerara, which Broke out on the 18th of August, 1823*. Georgetown, Guyana: A. Stevenson, 1824.

Burke, Ronald K. *Samuel Ringgold Ward: Christian Abolitionist*. New York: Garland, 1995.

Carey, Brycchan. *British Abolitionism and the Rhetoric of Sensibility: Writing, Sentiment and Slavery, 1760–1807*. Basingstoke, UK: Palgrave Macmillan, 2005.

Carlyle, Thomas. *Shooting Niagara: And After?* London: Chapman and Hall, 1867.

Casid, Jill H. *Sowing Empire: Landscape and Colonization*. Minneapolis: University of Minnesota Press, 2005.

Chakrabarty, Dipesh. *Provincializing Europe: Postcolonial Thought and Historical Difference*. Princeton: Princeton University Press, 2000.

Chrisman, Laura. *Rereading the Imperial Romance: British Imperialism and South African Resistance in Haggard, Schreiner, and Plaatje*. Oxford: Oxford University Press, 2000.

Chutkan, Noelle. 'The Administration of Justice in Jamaica as a Contributing Factor in the Morant Bay Rebellion of 1865'. *Savacou* 11/12 (1975), 78–85.

Clark, John. *A Brief Account of the Settlements of the Emancipated Peasantry in the Neighbourhood of Brown's Town, Jamaica; in a Letter from John Clark, Baptist Missionary, to Joseph Sturge, of Birmingham*. Birmingham: John Whitehouse Showell, 1852.

Clarke, John. *Memorials of Baptist Missionaries in Jamaica, Including a Sketch of the Labours of Early Religious Instructors in Jamaica*. London: Yates and Alexander, 1869.

[Clarke, Simon Houghton]. *Notes in Defence of the Colonies: On the Increase and Decrease of the Slave Population of the British West Indies. By a West Indian*. [Kingston]: n.p., 1826.

[Coleridge, Henry Nelson]. *Six Months in the West Indies, in 1825*. London: John Murray, 1826.

Crowley, John E. 'Picturing the Caribbean in the Global British Landscape'. *Studies in Eighteenth-Century Culture* 32 (2003), 323–46.

Cundall, Frank. *Bibliographia Jamaicensis: A List of Jamaica Books and Pamphlets, Magazine Articles, Newspapers, and Maps [etc.]*. Kingston: Institute of Jamaica, n.d. [1902].

Historic Jamaica. London: West India Committee; Kingston: Institute of Jamaica, 1915.

Curtin, Philip D. *Two Jamaicas: The Role of Ideas in a Tropical Colony, 1830–1865*. New York: Atheneum, (1955) 1970.

da Costa, Emilia Viotti. *Crowns of Glory, Tears of Blood: The Demerara Slave Rebellion of 1823*. New York: Oxford University Press, 1994.

Darwin, Charles. *On the Origin of Species by Means of Natural Selection, or The Preservation of Favoured Races in the Struggle for Life*. Ed. J. W. Burrow. Harmondsworth: Penguin, (1859) 1968.

Defoe, Daniel. *Robinson Crusoe*. Ed. John Richetti. London: Penguin, (1719) 2001.

Desmond, Ray. *Dictionary of British and Irish Botanists and Horticulturalists, Including Plant Collectors, Flower Painters and Garden Designers*. London: Taylor and Francis/Natural History Museum, 1994.

Diouf, Sylviane A. *Servants of Allah: African Muslims Enslaved in the Americas*. New York: New York University Press, 1998.

Douglass, Frederick. *Life and Times of Frederick Douglass*. New York: Gramercy, (1885) 1993.

'What to the Slave Is the Fourth of July?' (1852). In *The Oxford Frederick Douglass Reader*. Ed. William L. Andrews. New York: Oxford University Press, 1996, 108–30.

Edgeworth, Maria. *Belinda*. Ed. Kathryn J. Kirkpatrick. Oxford: Oxford University Press, (1801) 1994.

Edwards, Brent Hayes. *The Practice of Diaspora: Literature, Translation, and the Rise of Black Internationalism*. Cambridge, Mass.: Harvard University Press, 2003.

Edwards, Bryan. *The History, Civil and Commercial, of the British Colonies in the West Indies*. 3 vols. 3rd edn. London: John Stockdale, 1801.

Eliot, George. *Daniel Deronda*. Harmondsworth: Penguin, (1876) 1986.

Felix Holt, the Radical. Harmondsworth: Penguin, (1866) 1987.

Selected Essays, Poems and Other Writings. Ed. A. S. Byatt and Nicholas Warren. Harmondsworth: Penguin, 1990.

Elkins, Caroline. *Imperial Reckoning: The Untold Story of Britain's Gulag in Kenya*. New York: Henry Holt, 2005.

Eyre, Alan. *The Botanic Gardens of Jamaica*. London: André Deutsch, 1966.

Felsenstein, Frank, ed. *English Trader, Indian Maid: Representing Gender, Race, and Slavery in the New World: An Inkle and Yarico Reader*. Baltimore: Johns Hopkins University Press, 1999.

Ferguson, Moira. *Colonialism and Gender Relations from Mary Wollstonecraft to Jamaica Kincaid: East Caribbean Connections*. New York: Columbia University Press, 1993.

Ferris, Ina. *The Achievement of Literary Authority: Gender, History, and the Waverley Novels*. Ithaca: Cornell University Press, 1991.

Fisch, Audrey A. *American Slaves in Victorian England: Abolitionist Politics in Popular Literature and Culture*. Cambridge: Cambridge University Press, 2000.

Ford, George H. 'The Governor Eyre Case in England'. *University of Toronto Quarterly* 18.3 (1948), 219–33.

Freedgood, Elaine. *Victorian Writing about Risk*. Cambridge: Cambridge University Press, 2000.

Frey, Sylvia R. and Betty Wood. *Come Shouting to Zion: African American Protestantism in the American South and British Caribbean to 1830*. Chapel Hill: University of North Carolina Press, 1998.

Froude, James Anthony. *The English in the West Indies, or, The Bow of Ulysses*. New York: Scribner, 1888.

Gallagher, Catherine. *The Industrial Reformation of English Fiction: Social Discourse and Narrative Form, 1832–1867*. Chicago: University of Chicago Press, 1985.

'The Politics of Culture and the Debate over Representation'. *Representations* 5 (1984), 115–47.

Genovese, Eugene D. *Roll, Jordan, Roll: The World the Slaves Made*. New York: Vintage, 1976.

Gikandi, Simon. *Maps of Englishness: Writing Identity in the Culture of Colonialism*. New York: Columbia University Press, 1996.

Gitter, Elisabeth. *The Imprisoned Guest: Samuel Howe and Laura Bridgman, the Original Deaf-Blind Girl*. New York: Farrar, Straus and Giroux, 2001.

Glaude, Jr, Eddie S. *Exodus! Religion, Race, and Nation in Early Nineteenth-Century Black America*. Chicago: University of Chicago Press, 2000.

Gordon, Shirley C. *God Almighty Make Me Free: Christianity in Preemancipation Jamaica*. Bloomington: University of Indiana Press, 1996.

Goudie, Sean X. *Creole America: The West Indies and the Formation of Literature and Culture in the New Republic*. Philadelphia: University of Pennsylvania Press, 2006.

Greene, Benjamin. *Slavery as It Now Exists in the British West Indian Colonies: Discussed in a Series of Letters between Thomas Clarkson, Esq. and Benjamin Greene, Esq, of Bury St. Edmunds*. London: Hurst and Chance, 1829.

Greenfield, Susan C. '"Abroad and at Home": Sexual Ambiguity, Miscegenation, and Colonial Boundaries in Edgeworth's *Belinda*'. *PMLA* 112.2 (1997), 214–28.

Grosett, J. R. *Remarks on West India Affairs*. London: J. M. Richardson, 1824.

Guha, Ranajit. 'The Prose of Counter-Insurgency'. In *Selected Subaltern Studies*. Ed. Guha and Gayatri Chakravorty Spivak. New York: Oxford University Press, 1988, 45–86.

Gwilliam, Tassie. '"Scenes of Horror," Scenes of Sensibility: Sentimentality and Slavery in John Gabriel Stedman's *Narrative of a Five Years Expedition against the Revolted Negroes of Surinam*'. *ELH* 65 (1998), 653–73.

Haight, Gordon S., ed. *The George Eliot Letters.* 9 vols. New Haven, Conn.: Yale University Press, 1954–78.

Hakewill, James. *A Picturesque Tour of the Island of Jamaica, from Drawings Made in the Years 1820 and 1821*. London: Hurst and Robinson, 1825.

Hall, Catherine. *Civilising Subjects: Metropole and Colony in the English Imagination, 1830–1867*. Chicago: University of Chicago Press, 2002.

 'The Economy of Intellectual Prestige: Thomas Carlyle, John Stuart Mill, and the Case of Governor Eyre'. *Cultural Critique* 12 (1989), 167–96.

 'Epilogue: Imperial Careering at Home; Harriet Martineau on Empire'. In *Colonial Lives across the British Empire: Imperial Careering in the Long Nineteenth Century*. Ed. David Lambert and Alan Lester. Cambridge: Cambridge University Press, 2006, 335–59.

 'At Home with History: Macaulay and the *History of England*'. In *At Home with the Empire: Metropolitan Culture and the Imperial World*. Ed. Hall and Sonya O. Rose. Cambridge: Cambridge University Press, 2006, 32–52.

 'Rethinking Imperial Histories: The Reform Act of 1867'. *New Left Review* 208 (Nov.–Dec. 1994), 3–29.

 'What Is a West Indian?'. In *West Indian Intellectuals in Britain*. Ed. Bill Schwartz. Manchester: Manchester University Press, 2003, 31–50.

Hall, Douglas. *A Brief History of the West India Committee*. St Lawrence, Barbados: Caribbean Universities Press, 1971.

 Free Jamaica, 1838–1865: An Economic History. New Haven: Yale University Press, 1959.

 In Miserable Slavery: Thomas Thistlewood in Jamaica, 1750–1786. Kingston: University of the West Indies Press, 1999.

Hall, Stuart. 'Race, Articulation, and Societies Structured in Dominance'. In *Black British Cultural Studies: A Reader*. Ed. Houston A. Baker, Jr, Manthia Diawara, and Ruth H. Lindeborg. Chicago: University of Chicago Press, 1996, 16–60.

Hamel, the Obeah Man. 2 vols. London: Hunt and Clarke, 1827.

Hamilton, Paul. '*Waverley*: Scott's Romantic Narrative and Revolutionary Historiography'. *Studies in Romanticism* 33 (1994), 611–34.

Handler, Jerome. 'Slave Medicine and Obeah in Barbados, circa 1650–1834'. *New West Indian Guide / Nieuwe West-Indische Gids* 74.1–2 (2000), 57–90.

Handler, Jerome and Kenneth M. Bilby. 'On the Early Use and Origin of the Term "Obeah" in Barbados and the Anglophone Caribbean'. *Slavery and Abolition* 22.2 (2001), 87–100.

Harrison, Frederic. *'The Choice of Books' and Other Literary Pieces*. London: Macmillan, 1886.

Martial Law: Six Letters to 'The Daily News'. London: Jamaica Committee, 1867.

Harvey, Thomas and William Brewin. *Jamaica in 1866: A Narrative of a Tour through the Island, with Remarks on its Social, Educational and Industrial Condition*. London: A. W. Bennett, 1867.

Heuman, Gad. *'The Killing Time': The Morant Bay Rebellion in Jamaica*. Knoxville: University of Tennessee Press, 1994.

Higman, B. W. *Writing West Indian Histories*. London: Macmillan, 1999.

Higson, Thomas. 'The Guaco Plant'. *Jamaica Physical Journal* 1 (1834), 234–6.

Holt, Thomas C. *The Problem of Freedom: Race, Labor, and Politics in Jamaica and Britain, 1832–1938*. Baltimore: Johns Hopkins University Press, 1992.

Howe, Joseph. *The Organization of the Empire*. London: Edward Stanford, 1866.

Howe, Maud and Florence Howe Hall. *Laura Bridgman: Dr. Howe's Famous Pupil and What He Taught Her*. Boston, Mass.: Little, Brown, 1904.

Hunt, James. 'Introductory Address on the Study of Anthropology'. *Anthropological Review* 1 (1863), 1–20.

On the Negro's Place in Nature. London: Trübner, 1863.

'Presidential Address'. *Journal of the Anthropological Society* 4 (1866), lix–lxxxi.

'Jamaica'. [Rev. of Cynric R. Williams, *Tour through the Island of Jamaica*.] *London Magazine* n.s. 4 (Apr. 1826), 543–53.

Jamaica: Its State and Prospects; with an Exposure of the Proceedings of the Freed-Man's Aid Society, and the Baptist Mission Society. London: William Macintosh, 1867.

James, Winston. *Holding Aloft the Banner of Ethiopia: Caribbean Radicalism in Early Twentieth-Century America*. London: Verso, 1998.

Johnson, Michael P. 'Denmark Vesey and his Co-Conspirators'. *William and Mary Quarterly* 3rd series 58.4 (2001), 915–76.

Kazanjian, David. *The Colonizing Trick: National Culture and Imperial Citizenship in Early America*. Minneapolis: University of Minnesota Press, 2003.

King, David. *A Sketch of the Late Mr. G. W. Gordon, Jamaica*. Edinburgh: William Oliphant, 1866.

Kirkpatrick, Kathryn J. '"Gentlemen Have Horrors upon the Subject": West Indian Suitors in Maria Edgeworth's *Belinda*'. *Eighteenth-Century Fiction* 5.4 (1993), 331–48.

Koebner, Richard and Helmut Dan Schmidt. *Imperialism: The Story and Significance of a Political Word, 1840–1960*. Cambridge: Cambridge University Press, 1964.

Kowaleski-Wallace, Beth. 'Home Economics: Domestic Ideology in Maria Edgeworth's *Belinda*'. *Eighteenth Century* 29.3 (1988), 242–62.

Krise, Thomas, ed. *Caribbeana: An Anthology of English Literature of the West Indies, 1657–1777*. Chicago: University of Chicago Press, 1999.

Lalla, Barbara. *Defining Jamaican Fiction: Marronage and the Discourse of Survival.* Tuscaloosa: University of Alabama Press, 1996.

Lamb, Jonathan. 'Modern Metamorphoses and Disgraceful Tales'. *Critical Inquiry* 28 (2001), 133–66.

Lambert, David. *White Creole Culture, Politics and Identity during the Age of Abolition.* Cambridge: Cambridge University Press, 2005.

L[andau], F[red]. 'Samuel Ringgold Ward'. *Dictionary of American Biography.* Vol. XIX. New York: Scribner's, 1936, 440.

Lang, John. *Outposts of Empire.* London: T. C. and E. C. Jack, [1908].

Lee, Julia Sun-Joo. 'The (Slave) Narrative of Jane Eyre'. *Victorian Literature and Culture.* Forthcoming.

Lewis, Gordon K. *Main Currents in Caribbean Thought: The Historical Evolution of Caribbean Society in its Ideological Aspects, 1492–1900.* Baltimore: Johns Hopkins University Press, 1983.

Lewis, Matthew. *Journal of a West India Proprietor: Kept during a Residence in the Island of Jamaica.* Ed. Judith Terry. Oxford: Oxford University Press, (1834) 1999.

Linebaugh, Peter and Marcus Rediker. *The Many-Headed Hydra: Sailors, Slaves, Commoners, and the Hidden History of the Revolutionary Atlantic.* Boston, Mass.: Beacon, 2000.

Locke, John. *The Second Treatise of Government* (1689), in Locke, *Political Writings.* Ed. David Wootton. New York: Mentor, 1993.

Long, Edward. *The History of Jamaica, or, General Survey of the Antient and Modern State of That Island.* 3 vols. London: T. Lowndes, 1774.

Lorimer, Douglas A. *Colour, Class and the Victorians: English Attitudes to the Negro in the Mid-Nineteenth Century.* Leicester: Leicester University Press, 1978.

McCann, Andrew. 'Conjugal Love and the Enlightenment Subject: The Colonial Context of Non-Identity in Maria Edgeworth's *Belinda*'. *Novel* 30.1 (1996), 57–77.

MacFadyen, Heather. 'Lady Delacour's Library: Maria Edgeworth's *Belinda* and Fashionable Reading'. *Nineteenth-Century Literature* 48.4 (1994), 423–39.

MacQueen, James. *The West India Colonies: The Calumnies and Misrepresentations Circulated against Them by the Edinburgh Review, Mr Clarkson, Mr Cropper, &c.* London: Baldwin, Craddock and Joy, 1824.

Madden, R. R. *A Twelvemonth's Residence in the West Indies during the Transition from Slavery to Apprenticeship.* 2 vols. Westport, Conn.: Negro Universities Press, (1835) 1970.

Marshall, George W. 'Remarks on Genealogy in Connexion with Anthropology'. In *Memoirs Read before the Anthropological Society of London, 1865–6.* London: Trübner, 1866, 68–73.

Martineau, Harriet. 'Demerara' (1833). In *Harriet Martineau's Writing on the British Empire.* Vol. 1. *The Empire Question.* Ed. Deborah Logan. London: Pickering & Chatto, 2004, 65–141.

Menard, Edith. 'John Willis Menard: First Negro Elected to Congress'. *Negro History Bulletin* 28 (1964), 53–4.

Menard, John Willis. *Lays in Summer Lands*. Ed. Larry Eugene Rivers, Richard Mathews, and Canter Brown, Jr. Tampa, Fla.: University of Tampa Press, 2002.

'Minutes of the Meeting of January 16, 1866'. *Journal of the Anthropological Society* 4 (1866), lxxxii–lxxxix.

The Missionary Smith: Substance of the Debate in the House of Commons on Tuesday the 1ˢᵗ and on Friday the 11ᵗʰ of June, 1824, on a Motion of Henry Brougham, Esq., respecting the Trial and Condemnation to Death by a Court Martial of the Rev. John Smith, Late Missionary in the Colony of Demerara. London: Ellerton and Henderson, 1824.

Moseley, Benjamin. *A Treatise on Sugar, with Miscellaneous Medical Observations*. 2nd edn. London: John Nichols, 1800.

A Treatise on Tropical Diseases; on Military Operations; and on the Climate of the West-Indies. 4th edn. London: T. Cadell and W. Davies, 1803.

Noel, Baptist Wriothesley. *The Case of George William Gordon, Esq. of Jamaica*. London: James Nisbet, 1866.

Nordius, Janina. 'Racism and Radicalism in Jamaican Gothic: Cynric R. Williams's *Hamel, the Obeah Man*'. *ELH* 73.3 (2006), 673–93.

Northcott, Cecil. *Slavery's Martyr: John Smith of Demerara and the Emancipation Movement, 1817–24*. London: Epworth, 1976.

Nugent, Maria. *Lady Nugent's Journal of her Residence in Jamaica from 1801 to 1805*. Ed. Philip Wright. Kingston: Institute of Jamaica, 1966.

O'Shaughnessy, Andrew Jackson. *An Empire Divided: The American Revolution and the British Caribbean*. Philadelphia: University of Pennsylvania Press, 2000.

[Oughton, Samuel]. *Jamaica: Who Is to Blame? By a Thirty Years' Resident*. London: Effingham Wilson, n.d. [1866].

Jamaica: Why It Is Poor, and How It May Become Rich. Kingston: M. DeCordova, McDougall & Co., 1866.

Paravisini-Gebert, Lizabeth. 'Colonial and Postcolonial Gothic: The Caribbean'. In *The Cambridge Companion to Gothic Fiction*. Ed. Jerrold E. Hogle. Cambridge: Cambridge University Press, 2002, 229–57.

Paton, Diana. *No Bond but the Law: Punishment, Race, and Gender in Jamaican State Formation, 1780–1870*. Durham, N.C.: Duke University Press, 2004.

Pearson, Elizabeth Ware, ed. *Letters from Port Royal Written at the Time of the Civil War*. Boston, Mass.: W. B. Clarke, 1906.

Pease, William H. 'Three Years among the Freedmen: William C. Gannett and the Port Royal Experiment'. *Journal of Negro History* 42.2 (April 1957), 98–117.

Pettit, Eber M. *Sketches in the History of the Underground Railroad*. Freeport, N.Y.: Books for Libraries Press, (1879) 1971.

Pim, Bedford. *The Negro and Jamaica. Read before the Anthropological Society of London, February 1, 1866*. London: Trübner, 1866.

Pratt, Mary Louise. *Imperial Eyes: Travel Writing and Transculturation*. London: Routledge, 1992.

Price, Richard. *First-Time: The Historical Vision of an Afro-American People.* Baltimore: Johns Hopkins University Press, 1983.

Quarles, Benjamin. *Black Abolitionists.* New York: Oxford University Press, 1969. *Frederick Douglass.* New York: Da Capo Press, (1948) 1997.

Rainger, Ronald. 'Race, Politics, and Science: The Anthropological Society of London in the 1860s'. *Victorian Studies* 22 (1978), 51–70.

Reid, V. S. *New Day.* London: Heinemann, (1949) 1973.

Report of the Committee of the Society for the Mitigation and Gradual Abolition of Slavery throughout the British Dominions. London: Richard Taylor, 1824.

Report of the Incorporated Society for the Conversion and Religious Instruction and Education of the Negroe Slaves in the British West India Islands, from July to December, MDCCCXXIII [1823]. London: R. Gilbert, 1824.

Report of the Incorporated Society for the Conversion and Religious Instruction and Education of the Negro Slaves in the British West India Islands for the Year MDCCCXXVI [1826]. London: R. Gilbert, 1827.

Rev. of Cynric R. Williams, *Tour through the Island of Jamaica.* In *Monthly Review* 3rd series 2 (1826), 307–14.

Rev. of *Hamel, the Obeah Man.* In *London Magazine* n.s. 8 (June 1827), 182–7.

Rev. of *Hamel, the Obeah Man.* In *Westminster Review* 7, 14 (April 1827), 444–64.

Richardson, Alan. 'Romantic Voodoo: Obeah and British Culture, 1797–1807'. *Studies in Romanticism* 32 (1993), 3–28.

Richardson, Bonham C. *Igniting the Caribbean's Past: Fire in British West Indian History.* Chapel Hill: University of North Carolina Press, 2004.

Ripley, C. Peter, ed. *The Black Abolitionist Papers.* Vol. 1. *The British Isles, 1830–1865.* Chapel Hill: University of North Carolina Press, 1985.

Roach, Monique Patenaude. 'The Rescue of William "Jerry" Henry: Antislavery and Racism in the Burned-over District'. *New York History* 82.2(2001), 135–54.

Robbins, Bruce. *The Servant's Hand: English Fiction from Below.* Durham, N.C.: Duke University Press, 1993.

Rose, Willie Lee. *Rehearsal for Reconstruction: The Port Royal Experiment.* London: Oxford University Press, 1964.

Roundell, Charles Savile. *England and her Subject Races, with Special Reference to Jamaica.* London: Macmillan, 1866.

Russell, Horace O. *Foundations and Anticipations: The Jamaica Baptist Story, 1783–1892.* Columbus, Ga.: Brentwood Christian Press, 1993.

Said, Edward W. *Culture and Imperialism.* New York: Knopf, 1993. *The World, the Text, and the Critic.* Cambridge, Mass.: Harvard University Press, 1983.

Sandiford, Keith A. *The Cultural Politics of Sugar: Caribbean Slavery and Narratives of Colonialism.* Cambridge: Cambridge University Press, 2000.

Schama, Simon. *Rough Crossings: Britain, the Slaves, and the American Revolution.* New York: Ecco, 2006.

Schiebinger, Londa. *Plants and Empire: Colonial Bioprospecting in the Atlantic World.* Cambridge, Mass.: Harvard University Press, 2004.

Schuler, Monica. *'Alas, Alas, Kongo': A Social History of Indentured African Immigration into Jamaica, 1841–1865.* Baltimore: Johns Hopkins University Press, 1980.

Scott, David. *Conscripts of Modernity: The Tragedy of Colonial Enlightenment.* Durham, N.C.: Duke University Press, 2004.

Scott, Walter. *Waverley, or Sixty Years Since.* Ed. Andrew Hook. London: Penguin, (1814) 1972.

Semmel, Bernard. *The Governor Eyre Controversy.* London: MacGibbon & Kee, 1962.

Seymour, Susanne, Stephen Daniels, and Charles Watkins. 'Estate and Empire: Sir George Cornewall's Management of Moccas, Herefordshire and La Taste, Grenada, 1771–1819'. *Journal of Historical Geography* 24.3 (1998), 313–51.

Sharpe, Jenny. *Ghosts of Slavery: A Literary Archaeology of Black Women's Lives.* Minneapolis: University of Minnesota Press, 2003.

Sheller, Mimi. *Democracy after Slavery: Black Publics and Peasant Radicalism in Haiti and Jamaica.* Gainesville: University Press of Florida, 2000.

'Quasheba, Mother, Queen: Black Women's Public Leadership and Political Protest in Post-Emancipation Jamaica, 1834–1865'. *Slavery and Abolition* 19 (1998), 90–117.

Sheridan, Richard. 'Simon Taylor, Sugar Tycoon of Jamaica, 1740–1813'. *Agricultural History* 45 (1971), 285–96.

Sibley, Inez Knibb. *The Baptists of Jamaica.* Kingston: JBU, 1965.

Sloane, Hans. *A Voyage to the Islands Madera, Barbados, Nieves, S. Christophers and Jamaica, with the Natural History of the Herbs and Trees, Four-footed Beasts, Fishes, Birds, Insects, Reptiles, &c. of the Last of those Islands.* Vol. 1. London: B.M., 1707.

Smith, Goldwin. *The Empire: A Series of Letters Published in 'The Daily News'.* Oxford: Parker, 1863.

Southern, Eileen and Josephine Wright, comps. *African-American Traditions in Song, Sermon, Tale, and Dance, 1600s–1920: An Annotated Bibliography of Literature, Collections, and Artworks.* Westport, Conn.: Greenwood, 1990.

Spivak, Gayatri Chakravorty. 'Three Women's Texts and a Critique of Imperialism'. In *'Race,' Writing, and Difference.* Ed. Henry Louis Gates, Jr. Chicago: University of Chicago Press, 1986, 262–80.

Stanley, Arthur Penrhyn. *Life and Correspondence of Thomas Arnold, D.D.* 2 vols. London: John Murray, 1887.

Stedman, John Gabriel. *Stedman's Surinam: Life in an Eighteenth-Century Slave Society: An Abridged, Modernized Edition of* Narrative of a Five Years Expedition against the Revolted Negroes of Surinam *by John Gabriel Stedman.* Ed. Richard Price and Sally Price. Baltimore: Johns Hopkins University Press, 1992.

Stephen, James. *A Defence of the Bill for the Registration of Slaves, by James Stephen, Esq., in Letters to William Wilberforce, Esq., M.P.: Letter the Second.* London: J. Butterworth, 1816.

[Stephen, James]. *Reasons for Establishing a Registry of Slaves in the British Colonies.* London: n.p., 1814.

Stewart, Robert J. *Religion and Society in Post-Emancipation Jamaica.* Knoxville: University of Tennessee Press, 1992.

Stocking, Jr, George W. *Victorian Anthropology.* New York: Free Press, 1987.

'What's in a Name? The Origins of the Royal Anthropological Institute (1837–71)'. *Man* 6 (1971), 369–90.

Strout, Alan Lang. 'The Authorship of Articles in *Blackwood's Magazine*, Numbers XVII–XXIV (August 1818–March 1819)'. *The Library* 11 (1956), 187–201.

A Bibliography of Articles in Blackwood's Magazine, *Volumes 1 through XVIII, 1817–1825.* Lubbock, Tex.: Texas Technological College Library, 1959.

Tamarkin, Elisa. 'Black Anglophilia; or, The Sociability of Antislavery'. *American Literary History* 14.3 (2002), 444–78.

Thomas, Deborah A. 'Modern Blackness: "What We Are and What We Hope to Be"'. *Small Axe* 12 (2002), 25–48.

Trollope, Anthony. *The West Indies and the Spanish Main.* 2nd edn. London: Chapman & Hall, 1860.

Trumpener, Katie. *Bardic Nationalism: The Romantic Novel and the British Empire.* Princeton: Princeton University Press, 1997.

Turner, Mary. *Slaves and Missionaries: The Disintegration of Jamaican Slave Society, 1787–1834.* Urbana: University of Illinois Press, 1982.

Underhill, Edward Bean et al. *Dr. Underhill's Letter: A Letter Addressed to the Rt. Honourable E. Cardwell, with Illustrative Documents on the Condition of Jamaica and an Explanatory Statement.* London: Arthur Miall, n.d. [1865].

Viswanathan, Gauri. *Outside the Fold: Conversion, Modernity, and Belief.* Princeton: Princeton University Press, 1998.

Wallbridge, Edwin Angel. *The Demerara Martyr: Memoirs of the Rev. John Smith, Missionary to Demerara.* New York: Negro Universities Press, (1848) 1969.

Ward, Candace. '"What Time Has Proved": History, Rebellion, and Revolution in *Hamel, the Obeah Man*'. *ARIEL: A Review of International English Literature* 38.1 (2007), 49–74.

Ward, Samuel Ringgold. *Autobiography of a Fugitive Negro: His Anti-Slavery Labours in the United States, Canada, and England.* Eugene, Oreg.: Wipf and Stock, (1855) 2000.

Reflections upon the Gordon Rebellion. n.p. [Jamaica]: n.p., 1866.

Warner-Lewis, Maureen. 'The Character of African-Jamaican Culture'. In *Jamaica in Slavery and Freedom: History, Heritage and Culture.* Ed. Kathleen E. A. Monteith and Glen Richards. Mona, Jamaica: University of the West Indies Press, 2002, 89–114.

Watson, Tim. 'Improvements and Reparations at Mansfield Park'. In *Literature and Film: A Guide to the Theory and Practice of Film Adaptation.* Ed. Robert Stam and Alessandra Raengo. Malden, Mass.: Blackwell, 2004, 53–70.

'Indian and Irish Unrest in Kipling's *Kim*'. In *Postcolonial Theory and Criticism: Essays and Studies 1999.* Ed. Laura Chrisman and Benita Parry. Cambridge: D. S. Brewer, 2000, 95–114.

Wilberforce, William. *An Appeal to the Religion, Justice, and Humanity of the Inhabitants of the British Empire, in Behalf of the Negro Slaves in the West Indies*. London: J. Hatchard and Son, 1823.

Williams, Cynric R. *A Tour through the Island of Jamaica, from the Western to the Eastern End, in the Year 1823*. London: Hunt and Clarke, 1826.

Williams, James. *A Narrative of Events, since the First of August, 1834, by James Williams, an Apprenticed Labourer in Jamaica*. Ed. Diana Paton. Durham, N.C.: Duke University Press, (1837) 2001.

Williams, Raymond. *The Country and the City*. New York: Oxford University Press, 1973.

Wilmot, Swithin. 'From Bondage to Political Office: Blacks and Vestry Politics in Two Jamaican Parishes, Kingston and St David, 1831–1865'. In *Jamaica in Slavery and Freedom: History, Heritage and Culture*. Ed. Kathleen E. A. Monteith and Glen Richards. Mona, Jamaica: University of the West Indies Press, 2002, 307–23.

'The Politics of Samuel Clarke: Black Political Martyr in Jamaica, 1851–1865'. *Jamaican Historical Review* 19 (1996), 17–30.

Winks, Robin W. *The Blacks in Canada: A History*. 2nd edn. Montreal: McGill-Queen's University Press, 1997.

'Samuel Ringgold Ward'. *Dictionary of Canadian Biography*. Vol. IX. Toronto: University of Toronto Press, 1976, 820–1.

Wood, Betty, ed. 'The Letters of Simon Taylor of Jamaica to Chaloner Arcedekne, 1765–1775'. In *Travel, Trade and Power in the Atlantic, 1765–1884: Camden Miscellany Vol. XXXV*. Cambridge: Cambridge University Press, 2002.

Wood, Marcus. *Slavery, Empathy, and Pornography*. Oxford: Oxford University Press, 2002.

Woodson, Carter G. *The History of the Negro Church*. Washington, DC: Associated Publishers, 1921.

Workman, Gillian. 'Thomas Carlyle and the Governor Eyre Controversy: An Account with Some New Material'. *Victorian Studies* 18.1 (1974), 77–102.

Young, Robert J. C. *Colonial Desire: Hybridity in Theory, Culture and Race*. London: Routledge, 1995.

Index

CAMBRIDGE STUDIES IN NINETEENTH-CENTURY
LITERATURE AND CULTURE

General editor
Gillian Beer, *University of Cambridge*

Titles published